Bud Moore's Right Hand Man

Bud Moore's Right Hand Man

A NASCAR Team Manager's Career at Full Throttle

GREG MOORE
with PERRY ALLEN WOOD
Foreword by Leonard Wood

McFarland & Company, Inc., Publishers
Jefferson, North Carolina, and London

ALSO OF INTEREST

Declarations of Stock Car Independents: Interviews with Twelve Racers of the 1950s, 1960s and 1970s, by Perry Wood (McFarland, 2010)

Silent Speedways of the Carolinas: The Grand National Histories of 29 Former Tracks, by Perry Wood (McFarland, 2007)

LIBRARY OF CONGRESS CATALOGUING-IN-PUBLICATION DATA

Moore, Greg, 1957–
Bud Moore's right hand man : a NASCAR team manager's career at full throttle / Greg Moore with Perry Allen Wood ; foreword by Leonard Wood.
pages cm
Includes bibliographical references and index.

ISBN 978-0-7864-7288-8
softcover : acid free paper ∞

1. Moore, Greg, 1957– 2. Moore, Bud, 1925–
3. Automobile racing managers—United States—Biography.
4. Stock car racing—United States—History.
5. NASCAR (Association)—History.
I. Wood, Perry Allen, 1952– II. Title.
GV1032.M539A3 2013   796.720922—dc23   [B]   2013030863

BRITISH LIBRARY CATALOGUING DATA ARE AVAILABLE

© 2013 Greg Moore and Perry Allen Wood. All rights reserved

No part of this book may be reproduced or transmitted in any form or by any means, electronic or mechanical, including photocopying or recording, or by any information storage and retrieval system, without permission in writing from the publisher.

Front cover: Greg Moore sports his trademark look for over two decades in the NASCAR garage area (Bud Moore Engineering Archives); Bobby Allison, driving the "Junkyard" Cougar, won the 1980 Firecracker 400 at Daytona (Perry Wood Racing Collection)

Manufactured in the United States of America

McFarland & Company, Inc., Publishers
Box 611, Jefferson, North Carolina 28640
www.mcfarlandpub.com

This book is lovingly dedicated to my mother, Betty Clark Moore. She was the glue that held our family together as my father was often away from home, traveling around the country to provide for her, my two brothers, and me. My mother always gave her total support to my father and was one of the pioneering women in NASCAR. Our family endured the very emotional depths of tragedies and the incredible highs of victories and championships. Through it all she never doubted her faith in God and in our family's goals, abilities, and ideals. As "the Baby," I stayed around home longer than my brothers and had her support and encouragement in deciding what path to take in life. She has since passed away, but I still feel her presence every day in the confidence she gave me to take on things that seemed impossible to overcome. With my father in the Hall of Fame, and with the help of a childhood friend, it is time for this story to be told. It is the story of an incredible journey through my eyes, from my point of view. It was a journey that my mother guided me through with her wisdom, understanding, and love. It is a debt to my mother I can never repay, but I will honor her memory with this dedication.

— Greg Moore

Table of Contents

Foreword by Leonard Wood — 1
Preface by Perry Allen Wood — 3
Introduction by Perry Allen Wood — 7

One • The Baby — 11
Two • Becoming Gregory — 19
Three • "Stella, There's Been a Wreck" — 29
Four • Fernwood Farms — 33
Five • Good Times Return — 37
Six • That First Taste of Racing — 48
Seven • Back in NASCAR and Seriously Involved — 57
Eight • The Pulpit or the Pits — 70
Nine • Changes — 83
Ten • Earnhardt — 88
Eleven • The Roosters — 104
Twelve • Cooking with Crisco — 116
Thirteen • Skating Back to the Front — 127
Fourteen • The Yankee Speedster — 139
Fifteen • Quality Care and the Factory Farewell — 156
Sixteen • Wally's World and Beyond — 171
Seventeen • Looking for a Savior — 181
Eighteen • Going Once, Going Twice, *Sold* — 192
Nineteen • Moving On — 201
Twenty • Closure — 207

Bibliography — 219
Index — 221

Foreword by Leonard Wood

Greg Moore is one of my best friends and among the most likeable persons I've ever met. I very much enjoyed talking to him at every race because he has such an interesting personality. People enjoyed talking to him. I was always highly focused in getting the car ready, and I remember when he first started coming around, people were kidding him about his long hair a little bit. I thought he was kind of cool. Greg would come over to the car, checking us out, and would always have something nice to say. He could find out a lot of the things that the other competitors were doing and carry it back to their shop and put it to use. Greg had a way of doing it that didn't tick anybody off.

He did a lot of research and development work helpful to his brother Daryl building the motors. He had a great attitude and was one of the finest guys in the garage. He could get the inside information on what people were doing and what they were using—like camshafts, manifolds, and whatever—just in conversation. I remember one time I made a set of 180-degree headers, and the problem was, all the people that were making them were having to make them too long. So I came up with the idea of how to make them shorter, and they sounded so pretty. They sounded like an Indy car. I think we sat on the pole at Darlington with them. Greg loved them and said, "I told Daddy even if it didn't run as good, I'd rather have it for the sound of it."

He was always complimenting the Wood Brothers and myself. He worked hard and did a lot of work in the engine room as well. Greg is a wonderful guy and was very helpful to Bud with all the research he would dig up on what people were doing. A guy like Bud Moore would come around and you're not going to tell him much, but Greg could get all that information easier than Bud could.

I want to stress that he worked hard at what he was doing. Greg Moore took it seriously, dug in there, and it paid off. He is a very intelligent person. He and Daryl could still do well. Greg has the ability to do the research and development parts that need to be done. He was and still is so complimentary to the Wood Brothers and has been a great friend to us for all these years. I know when we won the Daytona 500 in 2011, Greg was about as excited as we were. That just shows that he is still our friend—that he was so excited about us winning the race. Greg Moore is a true friend, and I just think the world of him.

Leonard Wood is the younger of the famous Wood Brothers of Stuart, Virginia, one of the premier auto racing organizations for over 60 years. A crew chief, engine builder, and innovator, he choreographed the modern pit stop in the 1960s and was voted into the 2013 class of the NASCAR Hall of Fame.

Preface by Perry Allen Wood

I am not sure when Greg Moore and I first met. We moved to the Spartanburg suburb of Fernwood Farms, off East Main Street, on my ninth birthday, January 28, 1961. The suburb got its name from the rolling hills covered with barns and apple trees bisected by historic Lawson's Fork Creek. The barns and trees vanished — slowly at first, then rapidly — as hundreds of family homes sprang up.

About half a mile from my house was that of Greg Moore, who was five years younger than me. Another Moore boy, Brent, was two years older than me, and it was Brent whom I first got to know, playing for the Fernwood Tigers youth football team. We became friends and spent a lot of time together. More often than not, we would hit the back door running to go out and play before little Greg knew we were gone. But Greg would always get wise and come running after us, yelling, "Momma said I could play!" Sure enough, Betty Moore would walk out the back door into the carport and shout, "Y'all have to let the baby play!" And so we did. It was clear that Greg was "the Baby." In fact, he was called "the Baby" as much as he was "Greg" at his house. Frequently, the Baby was with Brent and me and absorbed whatever came along.

One of the major sports we participated in was bicycle racing, and the neighborhood kids would be out in full force at the two major venues we had. The first was at the corner of Pineville Road and Overland Drive, a vacant lot where bricks were stored in big stacks by the home builders in this fast-growing neighborhood. It was called The Brickyard. On the dirt there, we raced and crashed and bled and knocked out each other's spokes. Brent even used to tow a wood and tin downhill racer Bill Shoolbred and I built around that track behind his brother Daryl's Honda 50 motorbike. That car was painted up like Billy Wade's 1964 Bud Moore Mercury number 1.

We raced bikes on that lot all day until dark. Then the lot went dark for good when a house went up there, and we moved to another location. It was at the corner of Greengate and Applewood lanes and actually had a banked first turn. It was here that probably the nastiest crash in Fernwood bike racing history took place — but Greg can tell it better later.

As our bike races probably make obvious, the Moore boys and I shared an interest in fast-moving machines. Brent and Greg were the sons of Bud Moore, the pioneering builder of powerful stock cars whose contribution to racing would one day put him in the NASCAR Hall of Fame. As for me, I am the son of a Spartanburg City Police Officer, Jesse L. "Smoky" Wood, and he knew practically everybody in town, especially those who raced for a living. He and I visited those great shops regularly where the racers built by Bud Moore, Cotton Owens, Louis and Crawford Clements, Jack Smith, Buck Baker, Mario Rossi, David Pearson, Elmo Henderson, Tommy Irwin, G. C. Spencer, James Hylton, and others put their voluminous lists of drivers or themselves on the track and into Victory Lane. From a small boy to teenager, I got as close to that action as I could.

Brent and I hung out for a couple of years, and our families even vacationed together a couple of times. Truth be told, though, it was the Woods who were vacationing; the Moores were just going to the races like they did every week. One notable trip was in June of 1964 when we stayed at the Atlanta Motel on Highway 41 and 19 between Atlanta and the Atlanta International Raceway. There I was introduced to the Jarrett boys. We also stayed next door to the Moores at the Castaway Motel on Daytona Beach for the week of the 1965 Firecracker 400. That was a dream vacation for me, with all the drivers and crews staying there, along with the *ABC Wide World of Sports* team including Jim McKay, Jackie Stewart, and Chris Economacki. My highlight was getting to know A. J. Foyt, who was coming off his near fatal crash at Riverside six months earlier. We all played a lot of shuffleboard and swam. A. J. won that 400 for the second straight year and said I was his good luck charm. My brothers, the Moore boys, and I had a ball.

In later years Brent and I drifted apart. Greg and I stayed pals, but because of the difference in our ages we weren't really close. When I went off to the University of South Carolina, Greg was still at Evans Junior High. But even though he was younger, he got ahead of me in at least one way. When I graduated from college in May of 1974 and came back to Spartanburg to work various lousy jobs, Greg was living my dream of going racing. He was fortunate to be doing it with his dad and his brother Daryl, who was the team's engine builder.

In the late 1970s I began to run into Greg regularly on the street and especially in the bars. One watering hole in particular was the Nu-Way Lounge on St. John Street — the oldest bar in Spartanburg. More often than not, the conversation in that bar centered on auto racing of all types, but especially the stockers. This went on night after night, week after week, for years! After The Nu-Way closed on a Friday or Saturday night the crowd would usually move over to someone's house for more late-night entertainment. It was during this wonderful period that Greg and I reconnected.

In December of 1976, I established credit for the first time in my life as my father co-signed with me for the purchase of a Panasonic Beta VCR. It cost $1,000 and took both of us to carry it from the electronics department at Sears to the trunk of my Toyota Celica. It was then that I started taping everything I could about racing. (Of course, I now have a splendid video tape library in storage because I have no Beta VCR any longer.) When that gang of revelers would relocate from the Nu-Way to my pad, we would watch racing videos, or at least have them on for a backdrop. As Greg worked the pits on race day at Bud Moore Engineering, it was not unusual for CBS' Ned Jarrett or ESPN's Larry Nuber to stick a microphone in Greg's bearded face and ask him how the car was running. We'd all cheer as Greg — who by then was often sitting in our presence, watching himself on tape — would give his off-the-cuff reply. What a time we had.

In those days, that gang, or some combination of it, went to most of the races at Darlington, Charlotte, Atlanta, Talladega, and Rockingham. Naturally, Greg went to them all in a working capacity. We would load up our cars and pickup trucks and head for the infield and spend the weekend immersed in racing, love and friendship, and the wildest times of my life. I was very proud of my photography in those days. I still am. We sat in carefully selected spots at those tracks and I was able to capture many dramatic, action-filled moments on and off the speedway. I have used dozens of these photos in my other books and this one will be no different.

At the tracks, I had not one, but two aces in the hole: Greg Moore and Danny Fowler.

Danny was the jack man for Bud Moore for over two decades and a friend of mine as well. Every single time I asked to "borrow" a pit pass, one or the other of them came through. The pass would be secreted to me through the garage area fence, concealed in a dirty red shop rag. Sometimes I'd have to give it back when I got in and hope I would not get caught. I never did. Once on Bill Drake's Spartanburg morning radio show, I explained my pit access system while sitting right beside Bud Moore himself, and Bud said that he knew what was going on all along — but I wonder.

I always returned before the start of the race to be with my fellow infield companions. The only times I watched the whole race from the pits was when I was going it alone, which was usually at Talladega. The photographic records of those races are something that I am still very proud of, and the shots Greg and Danny allowed me access to take are the icing on the cake.

Many, many thanks to Bud Moore as well, if indeed he did know, for that access and for all he put up with from me through those years. All those times I sat in his race cars at the shop, I never once saw him frown in my direction. If he ever had, I would have probably left scared and never gone back. For those and more reasons than I can count, when Bud Moore Engineering loaded up after the race and went back to 400 North Fairview Avenue in Spartanburg for the last time, stock car racing was never the same for me. I still watch on TV, but it is not even close to being the same.

The year 1982 brought some significant changes to my life. What I sadly remember most is my father slowly fading away that spring from colon cancer. I still went to the races, but I remember praying that Daddy would not die while I was gone. On April 4, the yellow and blue number 15 took the checkers by a whisker over Cale Yarborough, and I made it home to joyfully tell my father that his old pal Bud had won Darlington, again. I never got to tell him about another Bud Moore win. He passed away on May 14, and the man who took his little boy all over Spartanburg to meet the drivers and mechanics and sit in the racers was gone. My father's funeral included a big yellow and blue wreath from Bud Moore Engineering.

Greg and Danny continued to come through with the credentials, but when the 1982 season ended for me at Atlanta I laid that precious privilege aside. On Christmas Day 1982, I loaded up everything I could cram into a 1979 Honda Prelude and left for Chicago and a job in the United States Secret Service.

Except for very infrequent visits to Bud Moore Engineering during trips home for the holidays, I did not see or communicate with Greg for over 25 years. I followed his team, of course, and saw him on television with a microphone in his face, still being asked how the car was running. Some things never changed. By the time I returned to Spartanburg in 2006, I had a beautiful wife, Yaneth, and a couple of great kids, Jake and Hannah. With my mom in a nursing home, we moved right back into the house in which I grew up.

When I wrote *Silent Speedways of the Carolinas*, I felt it an honor to give copies to Bud and Greg Moore, who had long ago turned off the lights and locked the doors for the last time at their famous race car factory on 400 North Fairview Avenue. Then one day, out of the blue, Greg called to tell me of a radio show he was co-hosting with Dale Wilkerson called *Droppin' the Hammer* which aired on Saturday mornings from eleven until noon on WSPG-AM, otherwise known as ESPN1400 Spartanburg. He advised me to stop by and watch them do the show at a basement bar called the Cellar. After the kids' soccer games the next Saturday morning, we all went, had delicious burgers and beverages, and watched the radio show that just happened to have Greg's dad as a guest. Daryl, his family, and many others were on hand, and it was wonderful to see them all again.

Greg introduced me to Dale and to station manager Mark Hauser, who also happened to be the Voice of the Wofford Terriers. The next thing I knew, I was at a meeting with the radio people, and shortly thereafter I became part of the show with a weekly feature called "Silent Speedways of America." It runs about a minute in length. First, a professional announcer (called "Mr. Big Voice"—I honestly do not know his name) introduces the spot and me. I tell the tale of some long lost silent speedway like the Piedmont Interstate Fairgrounds in Spartanburg or Lakewood Speedway in Atlanta over a background of some melancholy bluegrass. I love doing it, and the listeners seem to enjoy the spots. Regularly Dale, Greg, and technical engineer and co-host Ronnie Black have me on as a guest. Ronnie makes the show go on both sides of the glass.

Thanks to good ratings and Mark Hauser, *Droppin' the Hammer* recently expanded to two hours to enable the boys to cover more completely the local scene and the national racing news, and to expand the legends segment where we speak with the greats of auto racing: Mike Helton, Bud Moore, David Pearson, Bobby Allison, Mario Andretti, Dan Gurney, Ned Jarrett, Dr. Jerry Punch, Buz McKim, Edsel Ford, and so on. Greg knows them all, and if a great racer hasn't been on yet, stand by, because he's on the way. They have also done remotes from all over Spartanburg, Darlington, Rockingham, the Memory Lane Museum in Mooresville, N.C., and the NASCAR Hall of Fame in Charlotte. The added hour also gave me the opportunity to go to about two and half minutes for my new feature, "The Declarations of Stock Car Independents." It is based on my second book, and I am able to honor the guys who, in my opinion, really made the sport go: Brave men like James Hylton, Joe Frasson, Elmo Henderson, Wendell Scott, Gene Hobby, Captain America Raymond Williams, and dozens of others.

Just like a wheel or a speedway or life itself, what goes around comes around. I am back in Spartanburg talking racing with my pals. It is all in large part due to a friendship born in the neighborhood I lived in as a child. Fernwood Farms on the Cowpens side of Spartanburg is where Greg and I met and where half a century later we are still at it, a little grayer, but no less enthusiastic.

This is Greg Moore's story of growing up with greatness and living with it every day since. In writing this, Greg sometime refers to me or something we did, but I have tried not to include myself in his statements. My contributions to the story is shown in *italics* but the book is about Gregory Clyde Moore, not me.

Some names Greg mentions throughout are Brent (or Brenty) and Daryl, his brothers; Roberta, Greg's wife; Big Smoke or Smoke, Sr., my father; Smoke, Jr., or Little Smoke, my older brother; and Anne, Little Smoke's wife. There are lots of other neighborhood friends mentioned. Some are still around and some are not.

I was fortunate enough to have crossed Greg's path and been included in the periphery of this remarkable life. Greg is willing to relive it for us, but there is an understandable caveat. Greg told me right off the bat, "What happened on the road, stays on the road." Greg has built up an amazing inventory of personal experiences with the famous and the infamous, and he wants to tell it like it was. But alas, he cannot tell all. We must respect that. I watched Greg during our interviews wrestle with himself as to whether or not to tell me a story. He never related a yarn and then retracted it. He either told it for all of us to enjoy or left it out. Greg's strength and integrity on this point was both admirable and steadfast.

Following a scene-setting Introduction, here are his honest recollections, which add up to one fascinating story.

Introduction by Perry Allen Wood

Fifty years ago, there was no place in the universe of NASCAR Grand National racing with more clout than Spartanburg, South Carolina. The most teams and drivers by far called it home in the late fifties and sixties. Perhaps one reason is that Spartanburg's roots as a center of progress and mechanical innovation run deep. The first steam engine rumbled into town on November 25, 1859, which led directly to the city's nickname, "the Hub City." Allegedly, the moniker was first applied in 1890 from the top of the 178 foot smokestack at the brand new, steam-powered Spartan Mill. The newspaper, *The Carolina Spartan*, reported that mill owner Captain John H. Montgomery served a "sumptuous turkey dinner" atop that airy perch, "the tallest structure in the south," for local dignitaries. He supposedly noted that the rail lines radiated from town in every direction like the spokes of a wheel. The truth of this story cannot be confirmed, but regardless of who first spoke the name "Hub City," there's no doubt that Spartanburg was a hub for transportation. Historic photos show passenger trains smoking and steaming away at Magnolia Street's Union Station every day for decades, taking its citizens north to New York, south to New Orleans, to Charleston on the coast, and over the mountains to Cincinnati. Wheels and tracks and Spartanburg as the hub: It was the birth of a relationship between a city and its fast machines.

Moving forward about thirty years to the roaring twenties finds Spartanburg hosting a pair of famous national tours. Perhaps the most renowned personality in the world flew his racer, the *Spirit of St. Louis*, into South Carolina's first and only commercial airport in downtown Spartanburg on October 12, 1927. Colonel Charles H. Lindbergh went on a whirlwind tour of the United States after winning the Ortieg Prize in May of 1927. That deadly race was for the first aviators, or solo pilot, to fly non-stop across the Atlantic Ocean between New York and Paris—it did not matter which direction. Colonel Lindbergh did it alone, west to east, and his only tour visit in the Palmetto State was to Spartanburg. Lucky Lindy did not just do a touch-and-go, either. After a parade from Morgan Square downtown, he gave a speech to an overflow crowd at the new baseball stadium in Duncan Park and proceeded that evening to Converse College for a formal reception and another public address. Colonel Lindbergh spent the night in the luxurious Cleveland Hotel on Morgan Square before disappearing into the clouds over Spartanburg the next day in his silver *Spirit*.

The twenties also ushered into Spartanburg the most exclusive auto racing circuit in the world as the Automobile Association of America, the AAA, came to town. Local historians Cotton Eubanks and Ronnie Nodine documented events at the Piedmont Interstate Fairgrounds as early as November 2, 1928, the last "meet of the season" for the open-wheel daredevils. Many stars who ran the Indianapolis 500, such as Billy Winn, Bob Sall, and Doc MacKenzie, scorched the clay there for years with leather helmets, open cockpits, and no seat belts in Millers and Dusenbergs. On Armistice Day 1939, stockcars apparently first ran the ruby-red dirt of the Fairgrounds, setting off a new era of speed exhibitions and excitement. This breed of stock-bodied race cars was much better suited to the local clientele spawning builders and racers of the pre–World War II years. Blazing around the oval here was the Father of Spartanburg Auto Racing, Joe Littlejohn, along with Bill France, Sr., Red Byron, Gober Sosebee, Lloyd Seay, Bob and Fonty Flock, and scores of others.

When World War II ended and the boys came marching home, auto racing got real. Brave, fearless men who had seen death firsthand built and climbed into high-powered bombs and raced! Locals Cotton Owens, Hugh Lanford, and Joe Eubanks raced and won more often than not. In particular, Eubanks buddied up with a long, lanky, local war hero named Walter "Bud" Moore, and they won and won and won in the modifieds. That is, except when Cotton Owens won so often he became known as "the King of the Modifieds." Spartanburg, Greenville-Pickens, Columbia, Charlotte Fairgrounds, Shelby — it did not matter. The hardware and the green were more than likely going back to the Hub City with Cotton or Bud and Joe. With stockcar sanctioning officiated by various fly-by-night outfits, Big Bill France, who raced in Spartanburg, brought law and order to the stockcar racing frontier with the forming of NASCAR in 1948 at the Streamline Hotel on Daytona Beach. Joe Littlejohn and Alvin Hawkins represented the Hub City at those proceedings.

The Strictly Stock Division of NASCAR hit the dirt for the first time in Charlotte on June 19, 1949, and although no Spartanburg cars or drivers were in the field, they were on site watching. The next race on the sands of Daytona Beach less than a month later found Joe Littlejohn starting and finishing fourth in Frank Christian's Olds. With the renaming of the premier stock car racing circuit as the *Grand National Division* in 1950, Spartanburg became a player. The city intensified its involvement to multiple champions and scores of wins through that decade and into the sixties and seventies before Spartanburg racing gradually slowed during the eighties, nineties, and all but died in the twenty-first century. However, it flared again with a spectacular upset Sprint Cup victory for Phoenix Racing and Brad Keselowski's number 09 Miccosukee Indian Gaming Chevrolet at Talladega on April 26, 2009. It was the first time the winner's trophy had come back to Spartanburg from a Cup race since Bud Moore's number 15 Motorcraft Thunderbird driven by Geoff Bodine won at Sonoma, California, on May 16, 1993. The Hub City was still alive as a winner in the top tier of stock car racing. It still had what it takes.

Probably the beginning of Spartanburg's reign as the Hub City of Stock Car Racing was in 1960. Rex White won the Grand National Championship in Louis Clements' Chevy. That was a Spartanburg driver in a Spartanburg car. David Pearson was Rookie of the Year — another Spartanburg driver in an ex–Jack Smith Chevy number 67 Spartanburg car. Bud Moore, 1957 champion crew chief for Buck Baker, tuned Jack Smith's big burgundy Bonneville number 47 and won the Firecracker 250 at Daytona and then the Southern 500 with Buck Baker driving. You guessed it: Spartanburg drivers in a Spartanburg car! Bobby Johns won the first Atlanta 500 driving Cotton Owens' number 5 Pontiac and finished third in the standings. Cotton even sat on the pole and won in Spartanburg in number 6. It goes on and on and gets better through 1969, with Spartanburg car builders winning championships. Bud Moore won in 1962 and '63, and Cotton Owens won in 1966. David Pearson won the championship in 1966 for Cotton and in '68 and '69 for Holman-Moody. Rookie of the Year honors went to Spartanburg driver Billy Wade in Cotton's number 5 in 1963. James Hylton did it driving ex–Cotton Owens Dodge number 48 for himself in 1966, and Dick Brooks likewise in an ex–Mario Rossi Plymouth number 32 in 1969. Additionally, many other races big and small were won in the '60s by Spartanburg residents Buck Baker, Jack Smith, David Pearson, and Cotton Owens, not to mention local sportsman drivers Elmo Henderson and Floyd Powell taking track championships and scores of victories. The entire list is impressive. I think you get the point.

One man with a very close and personal perspective on this great history of racing is Gregory Clyde Moore, the youngest son of car builder Bud Moore. Starting out performing the most menial of tasks which usually involved a long wooden handle, Greg worked his way up the ladder at the shop at 400 North Fairview Avenue — and you can rest assured that Bud Moore did not make that ladder easy to climb. Eventually, Greg Moore was negotiating multi-million dollar contracts with Ford and dozens of other companies, as well as with race-winning drivers of the 1980s and 90s. He saw victory and tragedy; he saw great success and unspeakable loss. He has lived it all, and without question he helped his father achieve the zenith of recognition in his field with Bud Moore's election into the NASCAR Hall of Fame.

In the work that follows, text in *italics*, sprinkled throughout, is by Perry Allen Wood. All the rest is Greg Moore.

Chapter One

The Baby

Not many 55-year-old men would appreciate being called "The Baby" or just plain "Baby." However, there is one who not only doesn't mind, but volunteers the name from time to time. Gregory Clyde Moore was born into a family just a little different from most people. With two older brothers, a beautiful loving mother, and a battle-decorated father who was gaining racing fame at an alarming rate, being the baby of the house wasn't such a bad gig.

From the time I was born, Daddy was a pretty big name in NASCAR. I was born on March 22, 1957, six months before we moved to Fernwood. We had lived on St. John Street where Daddy had moved us over from Johnson Street, which was on the mill hill. That's over by Spartan Mills where my brothers Daryl and Brenty grew up.

I was the baby by a bunch. Brenty was seven years older than me, Perry Wood was five years older than me, and Daryl and Perry's brother Smoke were 11 years older than me. They had just started Fernwood, and Fernwood Drive was a tar and gravel road with big ditches on each side. We all were baby boomers born between 1946 and 1960. I was at the tail end, Perry and Brenty were in the middle, and Smoke and Daryl were at the very beginning. All our daddies were in the war. I knew that Perry's daddy and my daddy were buddies, and everybody already knew each other when I was born.

My momma's momma, Ethel Gregory Clark, was where I got my name. They took Gregory from her maiden name. It's a family name. The name Greg, Daddy will tell you, "That's racing stuff." I was Gregory and never had a problem with it. Somewhere along the line in the racing deal, maybe the first time I signed an autograph or something, I put "Greg" Moore. If my real name had been Gregg Clyde Moore I would have spelled it with two Gs at the end. But I was Gregory and spelled it with one G at the end. I was always Gregory or Baby. The name Clyde was from my mother's only full brother, who passed away in 1962 from a brain aneurysm. Uncle Clyde Clark went to the races some and worked at the downtown airport. Daddy and he were the same age, born in '25. Momma, Betty Clark, was born in '27. That's where brother Brent got Brent Clark Moore. It was after I was probably 20 years old that Daddy would refer to me as Greg. But I was always Gregory, or Baby, and never took offense to it. I never did.

What was so cool was that I don't ever remember Perry or Brenty or that bunch ever being anything but nice to let me hang around. When I started walking around by myself, I can't remember a time when there wasn't Perry and Smoke, the Dickersons, and that crowd. They were always there. I was pretty much an infant when we moved over to Fernwood.

Baby's racing recollections are very dim, but come into focus with age.

Daryl and the Baby poolside at Daytona Beach in 1958 (Moore Family Collection).

I kind of got confused back then because we had those red race cars. Jack Smith's was red, and he left after 1960. Weatherly's was red when he came in '61. I barely remember Smith driving the car, but I was sitting on it over at Greenville-Pickens or somewhere and I would only have been about two years old. He was always good to me because I was The Baby.

In 1960 I was in Daytona at the Dunes Motel on the beach strip on the north side. Smith was driving, and we ran pretty well in the 500 and the lugs broke or something. Momma took a picture of me and I'm only about three years old. But I don't really start remembering things well until Weatherly came to drive in 1961 and I was four. We got a Pontiac deal that year, and back then, if you had a factory deal, well, that was the best. You didn't just have a sponsor. Daddy had worked for Carl Kiekhaefer in the mid–1950s and didn't work for him long because Kiekhaefer fired him. So Daddy was part owner in Smith's car and started Bud Moore's Garage on St. John Street in Spartanburg.

Too old for some kids and too young for the others in the neighborhood, Baby had a tough time for a while finding a place to fit in around Fernwood.

I was a little kid at that time. The closest kid in age to me was David Murr, Bob Murr's younger brother, and he was three years older. I didn't really have anyone my age to play with except Perry Poole, and he got run over on Dupre Drive right in front of Spartan High. We were the same age and played together. When he got hit it was awful. I knew his brothers Steve and Randy and loved those people to death. My next door neighbor was John Wilson and living across Monroe Road were the Phifers. Peggy Phifer grew up to be a beautiful girl. Across Fernwood Drive was Gary Baker and next door to him was E. W. Taylor, who was a chiropractor. He founded the Sherman Chiropractic College.

Gregory in uniform and racing down the hallway at 500 Fernwood Drive with a co-driver (Moore Family Collection).

I wore a back brace for a while and they were talking about doing some experimental fusions on it. And what did I end up doing? Fooling with those heavy cylinder heads, taking them on and off the flow bench.

Back then we rode our bicycles all over the place. When I was six years old, our parents didn't worry so much about us. Fernwood Drive was a busy two-lane road and I'd ride my bike up to Hillcrest Shopping Center which was a good mile or more away. There were about three stores, Smith-Outz Drugs, Community Cash, and Lambert's five and dime. We'd ride our bicycles all over the place. There were two Sinclair stations up there. How in the world they ever did that I don't know.

I remember one time I rode to Perry's house by myself and I shouldn't have been that far away from home all alone. Perry's momma called my momma and told her where I was, and I rode back home. But it was no big deal. We walked a lot and I was always following Perry and Brenty. I was The Baby, and Brenty and Daryl always looked after me.

When we were growing up, Daddy told Momma, "Bud Moore's Garage is my corporation. I run that deal. This house here, the kids, the babies, what goes on here is your deal." So Momma handled the family situations and Daddy handled the racing. Back then, Momma would go to the races and we'd tag along when we weren't in school.

At home, we always ate together as a family unless Daddy was gone. We ate breakfast, lunch, and dinner right there at the kitchen table. At night, we'd sit there and watch TV in that little tiny den. I think the whole house was 1,701 square feet.

Daddy never disciplined any of us as far as telling us what we needed to do or not to do. He never laid a hand on any of us, but Momma would get a switch. Now, it wasn't a beating, but by today's standards it probably would have been.

Everything was smooth. It was a really smooth upbringing. I had things better than Daryl and Brenty because they grew up on Spartan Mill hill. That's all they knew, and they talk fondly of all that stuff. We were all charter members of Green Street Baptist Church. But when we moved to Fernwood, that was pretty high end for the late 1950s and early '60s. To get off the mill hill and St. John's Street and move over to Fernwood Farms was cooler than heck. There just weren't that many kids to play with until later on. Remember my nickname was "Baby."

So I was hanging around with Perry and John Wilson, both five years older, and Gary Baker, also five years older, and David Murr and on and on and on. They were all I had to play with, and that was really cool. It was fun to hang out with the big guys.

I went to Houston Elementary and got to know all the guys from Drayton, another mill neighborhood. Then they built Jesse Boyd Elementary School for the kids in Hillbrook, Pierce Acres, and Fernwood, and I was in the inaugural class that moved over there in the middle of the third grade. Over there were Steve Fuller, the Mahaffey boys, and others.

One of the pivotal events in the neighborhood was when Daryl got his Honda. It was a big event for us kids to get Daryl to take us for a ride on it.

In about 1963 at Daytona, they wanted Daryl to be the escort to Miss Teen America, and he took her all over. These Japanese guys were invited over by Bill France, Sr., and they brought this Honda motor scooter as a demonstrator. Nobody knew what a Honda was. It was red with gray fins until I broke them off. They were going to leave it because it was going to cost them too much to ship the son-of-a-gun back. So Daddy asked them what they were going to do with it and said he'd give them $500 for it. It would have cost them more to ship it back to Japan. So they loaded it on the truck and brought it back to the shop with Weatherly's race car and stuff. That bike never had a license plate on it, and Daryl never got a ticket. Perry's daddy, Big Smoke—Lt. Smoky Wood, Spartanburg City Police—probably had a lot to do with that.

The Honda was like a moped. Lenny Carroll had a moped with pedals on it, but there were only a few. I remember the homemade go-kart Perry and Shoolbred built that was painted up red and black just like Billy Wade's Mercury. That thing was cool!

Greg shared his house with a famous guest and acquired himself a nickname at the shop.

Fireball would spend the night with us over there in Fernwood. He was going to drive one of the convertibles or something. Smokey Yunick wouldn't cut the top of his car off, so Fireball would drive one of Daddy's convertibles for the Rebel 300. I always got along with Fireball really well.

Daryl chauffeured and escorted Miss Teenage America in Daytona (Moore Family Collection).

They called me "Stomper" at the old Bud Moore Garage because they'd all throw cigarette butts on the floor and I'd go over there and stomp them out. Big Jim DeLoach named me Stomper. "Here comes Stomper!" Anyway, Perry and I both got babysat at Bud Moore's Garage while our mommas got their hair done over at Keller's Styling Salon, which was in the adjacent building. An amazing thing is that a big part of that floor of the garage where they built all those great race cars was dirt. It was oil-soaked and almost like concrete, but it was dirt. It had an oil-changing pit in it that was concrete, and the rest was dirt.

The back room at Bud Moore's Garage didn't just store racing parts, tools, and paint. There was a real sporty side to the shop, and although a neighbor might have taken offense, the city officials saw nothing.

At Bud Moore's Garage on St. John's Street during the Weatherly time, nobody drank during the day unless Pop Eargle would sneak back there for a drink. But there were lots of folks hanging around. You had Charlie Guy from Wakefield Buick, who painted the cars. Bill "Fat Willie" Nash did the lettering and cooking. He worked for *The Spartanburg Herald-Journal*, too. There was Bunny Brockman, who was a city policeman; the mayor, whoever he was at that time; Pop Eargle, Joe Littlejohn, Sr., and Daddy. They'd play cards.

We were also bad about betting on the Coke bottle, too. It used to be, you'd get one out of the Coke machine with the name of the town where it was bottled on the bottom. On the wall we had a map of the United States with a string on it so we could measure the distance from Spartanburg. We'd put up a dollar each and see whose bottle came from the furthest away. Columbia, South Carolina, wasn't very good, but Yuma, Arizona, was a damn good one. If you pulled that, you knew you had $5.00.

Now, little Daryl was working the roulette wheel. That was the bench grinder that had a buffing wheel or a wire brush on one side and a stone on the other. We kept that thing when we moved to the new shop. We had numbers on the stone side and to make it neutral, Daryl would flip the switch, just up and down, and it would take the damn thing two minutes to stop. So Daryl was running the roulette wheel when he was down there. There was just playful drinking. It wasn't like a Moon's Tavern–type gambling casino. It was just friends.

One time, the guy across the street got a case of the ass over a gutter Daddy made him fix to keep from washing our tools out the back door. The guy had a dry cleaning business, and I don't think he was much of a race fan. We used Buster Bell for our dry cleaning anyway. So one night all these people were in there gambling and this guy had ratted on them. Maybe he was mad because he wasn't invited, since this had been going on for two or three years. Finally the police showed up like a raid and got to looking around, and there's Joe Littlejohn, Sr.; Bunny Brockman, a policeman; the mayor; and other prominent people. The cops said, "Damn!" This was a bunch of police officers the gamblers had never seen. Then Joe Littlejohn, Sr., got on that black telephone in Daddy's little office and called somebody: Perry's daddy, Lt. Smoky Wood. He got him at home, probably, and Big Smoke wanted to talk to the officer. Joe Littlejohn, Sr., said, "Somebody wants to talk to you," and gave the cop the phone. The cop on the shop phone said, "Yes sir? Uh huh. That so. Yeah. That right? Uh huh. Right. Yes sir!" He hung up the phone and said, "Come on, ya'll. Let's get out of this man's business" and out the door they went. Lt. Wood wasn't anybody to mess with. Big Smoke was the boss.

Gregory actually boasted triple identities during this period of childhood. To most of the world—for example, at school and church—he was Gregory. When he was around his house or with family, he was usually "Baby." But when he was hanging out at the shop, or on those occasions when he was on the road for a race, he was "Stomper" to many. It was this persona that often became the minion of the stars.

We were down at Daytona in '61 or '62 for the Firecracker 250, staying at the Castaway, which was brand new and the nicest place on the beach. I remember this comedy act called *Houston and Dorsey* that seemed like it played downstairs in the lounge forever. There was always a big sign in the lobby for them. This was a really fancy hotel, with bellhops and everything.

Joe Weatherly was known as "The Clown Prince of Racing" and was always joking around—I mean always. He had lots of props. He had this wooden box with a spring-loaded foxtail in it, and he would get people to look down into it so they could see his "Texas Bloodsucker." When you looked down in there real close, Weatherly would trip the

Fireball Roberts (left) and Joe Weatherly were sometimes pranksters and teammates in Bud Moore Pontiacs and simply the best (Moore Family Collection).

switch and the foxtail would come flying out in your face and it was terrifying. Of course, Weatherly would be over there laughing his ass off. Anyway, he had this really big, real-looking rubber snake he bought, and he and Fireball Roberts saw me running around the hotel. Weatherly said, "Stomper, come here. Go throw this snake on that bellboy over there." Being raised to respect and obey my elders, I took the snake and when he wasn't looking, I threw it on the bellboy. He went nuts! He jumped around trying to get it off of him and when it landed on the floor, he still jumped all over it, and it bounced back up at him because it was made of rubber. Meanwhile, Fireball and Weatherly were over there watching, laughing like crazy. I mean they were in hysterics! I don't remember what happened after that, but it was all good. Stuff like that was normal with Weatherly and lots of the drivers and racing people. I wish I could remember them all.

> *What a fabulous childhood: growing up with your heroes and being part of their lives, too! Most people who hung out in the race shops of Spartanburg experienced the* Texas Bloodsucker *at one time or another.*
>
> *In mid–1963, the white concrete block building that housed Bud Moore's Garage and Keller's Styling Salon at 482 East St. John Street in Spartanburg gave way to a spacious, state of the art facility at 400 North Fairview Avenue that would produce top-notch race cars for the next 37 years.*

Dolph Vermont and Daddy got together and built the new shop. Daddy bought that property in early '63 next to the railroad tracks for about $2,800 for the 2.9 acres of land.

At first the building was just one section, and they wanted it to be super neat because we had the Lincoln-Mercury deal coming. We had just won the 1962 Grand National Championship in a Pontiac and wanted the new shop to be first class for Mercury. One of the biggest deals was that it had an eight-inch concrete floor with the coloring in it. We were the ones that started the deal with the real clean floors. Up until about the early '90s, ours was a palace. Everybody was impressed with it. The Wood Brothers were working out of a converted gas station. Holman-Moody was a big place, but it was a dump.

Away from stock car racing, one of the many sports played in the Wood family's Fernwood backyard was golf on a rather well-groomed, one-holed par three course. But there were hidden hazards not normally associated with that sport.

I remember we had a lot of energy back then, and it was so much fun coming up to Perry's house and playing that one par-three hole. We played in the same direction and rehashed the previous shots walking back up to the tee box to play the same hole again. We had a scoreboard, a carpet with a hole cut in it for a green, and real golf clubs. We were pretty serious about it. It was fun as all get out because I loved to be with my brother Brenty, Perry, John Wilson, Shoolbred, Cleve Brown, Dickerson, Sam Forry, David Ball, all those guys. And we had real golfer names. I was Miller Barber. Perry was Jack Nicklaus. Sam was Sam Snead. Dickerson was Gary Player. The little sissy on the corner was Betsy Rawls.

It was so cool. There was a row of pine trees you had to go over, and you had to clobber a nine iron to do it. Or get lucky and go between them with any club. I liked Miller Barber because he'd just walk up to it and hit it. Sort of like me hiring race drivers years later. "You want to drive a race car?" "Yeah, OK." But it was a pretty tough par three. We had a water bottle and Mrs. Wood would bring out refreshments.

It was even tougher because of Duke. I never knew what a Welsh Corgi was until I met Duke. He was a great dog. Mrs. Wood would throw out dinner scraps and Duke would bury the biscuits all over the yard. Then you would be walking around out there looking for your golf ball and out of nowhere Duke would run up and bite you on the ass. If you got near where he had a biscuit buried, he'd think you were after his biscuit. It was like a minefield out there. He never bit me. I guess he knew I was Baby and showed some mercy on me. He was cool. That was the coolest dog, Duke.

There is no telling how many rounds of golf I played out there. I always told people that I never was worth a damn at golf, but I could always play the short game. And the reason I could play the short game was because of that par three. I could play chip and putt and me and Joe Littlejohn, Sr., could play the same game.

Greg speaks fondly as he remembers growing up in Fernwood in the 1960s and realizes now just how many good friends he had. He was The Baby then, but that baby could hang with the big boys. In some roundabout way that might have helped him become the respected racer he is and always will be.

CHAPTER TWO

Becoming Gregory

A family dream vacation to California with sunshine, no school, Hollywood stars, movie studios, Disneyland, and road course racing excitement was much anticipated by the Moores. However, the innocence of being almost seven years old was about to come crashing down. Baby would receive an unexpected jolt of reality and would be a baby no more. Spending a couple of weeks of the normally cold, bitter winter in warm Southern California was confusing enough without the devastation he and his family were to experience there. Things would never be the same. This was the beginning of a 13-month period that not only changed Baby to Gregory, not only changed the lives of all the Moores, but changed the face of auto racing forever. It was January 1964.

My first trip to Riverside was when Momma, Daddy, and I got on an airplane at Greenville-Spartanburg International Airport and went there anticipating running real good and having a great vacation. Weatherly ran good with the Pontiac and later the Mercury and won three races on the way to the 1963 Grand National Championship. It was our second in a row, and we had won in October at Hillsborough and finished up good with a seventh at Riverside to end the season. We were pretty close to Weatherly, and when we got out there to Riverside, Dick McCann with Lincoln-Mercury had set up some really neat things with Joe's fiancée, JoAnne. We called her "Short Track." Weatherly had been living with her for years. We got to go to Paramount Studios and on the set of *Bonanza*. We met Hoss [Dan Blocker] and Adam Cartwright [Pernell Roberts]. We went to the original Disneyland. It was just a fairy book–type deal. I got a picture from Jerry Lewis that says, "Best Wishes, Gregory," when he was at his height of popularity. We went to see the filming of a space movie. Momma, JoAnne, and I went out to the racetrack the day before the race and walked across the Champion Bridge over the backstretch. Weatherly came roaring underneath there during practice and he recognized us. He could tell Stomper and JoAnne were there and waved when he spotted us as he went under the bridge.

Bill Stroppe was Mercury's west coast man as Bud Moore was for the east coast. Stroppe had come out with some new brakes, and Daddy had sent the car out two weeks early to get them put on. Stroppe had been running road courses out there on the west coast, and it was some good stuff for the drum brakes. Parnelli Jones was Stroppe's main driver and actually drove our car a couple of laps, and it ran well. That was something they did back then. Drivers would swap around. Anyway, Weatherly had the new brakes on it for the race.

So we went out to the track the next day for the race. They had a family grandstand set up for the women and children on the front straightaway that was pretty nice. Weatherly started 16th and had only run about 13 laps when the transmission went out. It was going to take a lot of laps to put a new transmission in it, so Daddy said, "Let's park it. Put it on the truck."

Weatherly didn't want to do that because he was running for the point championship. He was in a quest for a third straight Grand National Championship with Bud Moore and had been in all four previous races in the 1964 season, which actually started in November of 1963. He had a second in the Moore Pontiac at Concord, and then fourth, fourteenth, and tenth place finishes driving for other people. Joe Weatherly was leading the point standings again and wanted to race.

About that time they red-flagged the race for a real bad crash involving Clem Proctor. Daddy and the crew were about to load up the car when Weatherly came running over yelling, "They've red-flagged the race. Put a transmission in it! Put a transmission in it!" Back then you could work on the car during a red flag. So Daddy and the crew rolled the car back off the truck, they threw a transmission in it, and sure enough they didn't lose that many laps.

Everything was cool, and Weatherly went back out there and ran. Daddy had put on fresh tires and Joe was getting around there pretty good. He was killing that son-of-a-gun. He was a so-so road racer, but he was a fantastic race driver. He was moving up, gaining spots.

Well, those new brakes had a self-adjuster in them. The problem was that if they adjusted all the way out, the bolts would fall loose, which had never happened, and you wouldn't have any brake pressure. You would not have any brakes at all.

So when Weatherly started into right-hand turn five, the brakes had worn slap out because he was running so hard to get caught up. The brakes had adjusted all the way out, and when he went into turn five, he tried to get it whoa'd down. He hit the tires lining the inside edge of the track, jumped on the brakes, and he didn't have any. He wasn't wearing a shoulder harness and his head was hanging out there and BOOM! He hit the wall on the driver's side and took a big lick. No shoulder harness, no window net, nothing.

Momma, JoAnne, and I didn't know it had killed him for probably 15 minutes or so, but we knew something was wrong. We knew he had crashed. We couldn't see it, but we heard about it. People had their little AM transistor radios, and we knew he was hurt and was put on a stretcher. Seems like Momma, JoAnne, and I ran down there and the guy let us across the track. Daddy stopped JoAnne and had to break the news to her.

That happened on January 19, 1964, and that night we were staying at the Caravan Inn, which was a nice motel in Riverside. Back then, of course, there were no cell phones and everything was charged to the room. Many years later, we remembered that night when we found our old motel bill and it showed all the calls JoAnne had made back home to tell family people what had happened. Back then, you just didn't make long distance phone calls, especially from the west coast. So today, if you look at the bill for January 19th, Caravan Inn, you can tell something happened just from the number of phone calls.

We found all that when we sold the shop and cleaned out the records years later. We wound up staying out there three or four days longer. Because of the death we missed our flight. We couldn't get on an airplane and fly straight back. They had to reschedule our flight, and we were flying Eastern, and they didn't have a flight every day.

After NASCAR looked the car over, they carried it over to Stroppe's shop. I was a kid and went over there to see it sitting in the back of his shop. They pulled the wheel off and found out exactly what had happened to it. We found the nuts that had adjusted out down in the wheel. Later they welded a little stop on there so it couldn't happen again. The car

The end came for Joe Weatherly at Riverside, California, on January 19, 1964, during Gregory's dream vacation (Moore Family Collection).

was unfixable. Daddy left it out there, and somebody later claimed that Stroppe sold it two years later for junk for $2,000 to somebody. That's the story I was told.

They had a funeral up in Virginia for Weatherly, but I did not go. I was in school at the time and couldn't go. We stayed in touch with JoAnne for a while. Weatherly didn't have any kids and we didn't know any of his relatives or anything. Daddy thought seriously about quitting, just saying, "The hell with it." But we had a contract with Mercury and they wanted to continue on. That's when Billy Wade showed up at the shop.

A postscript to the story of that California trip reveals a very special friend Gregory made out there and their personal relationship.

Judy Judge was Fireball's girlfriend and was out at Riverside when we were there. She had black hair, was real nice looking, and was the aunt of Smokey Yunick's daughter, Trish. She was real good friends with JoAnne, Weatherly's girlfriend. Fireball was in the process of divorcing his wife, Doris.

Judy was a schoolteacher and a very sweet person. She worked with me on my ABCs and noticed that I have a lazy eye. I always thought I was just messed up because I'm left-handed anyway. The only other person in the whole family on either side that is a true lefty was Daddy's daddy, Dick Moore. Back in his day, when he was born in 1898 and was in school in 1910, they wouldn't let you write with your left hand. They *made* you write with your right hand. He did everything left-handed but write. It was not politically correct to be a lefty. Lefties were screwed up!

The lazy eye is still a problem. If I'm concentrating, I keep my eyes straight. If I'm not concentrating, then my left eye will drift. It affects me more now because I fight double vision with it. But Judy picked up on that early, at Riverside, and helped me.

Ford Motor Company's Lincoln-Mercury Division wanted Bud Moore to hire two drivers and get their two new Mercury Marauders ready for Speedweeks 1964 in Daytona. They had only a matter of days to get this done, which did not leave a lot of time for grieving and reflection on the tragedy just passed. Incredibly, Mercurys numbers 01 and 1 were at Daytona on time and well-prepared with new drivers hired to win. This accomplishment showed that Bud Moore and his family are racers of amazing fortitude!

Billy Wade had just won Rookie of the Year in 1963 for Cotton Owens and wanted to drive our car. He said, "I know you got this deal with Lincoln-Mercury, and I don't want to be second driver to Pearson at Cotton Owens. I'll tell you what; I'll run ten percent cheaper and thirty percent deeper into the corner if you'll put me in that car." Daddy knew that Wade had moved from Houston, Texas, to Spartanburg and that he had run good in Cotton's car. Daddy said, "Yeah, you got the ride." I think Daddy talked to Cotton about it. Pearson was his number one driver and Cotton was still driving a race car himself a little bit. There really wasn't much discussion about it. In fact, Daryl said that Wade had a pickup truck and helped them move stuff over to the new shop in 1963.

Billy Wade was friendly as could be, and he had good-looking daughters. He and his family had moved to Spartanburg. We used to go all over the place together. We'd go to the Wagon Wheel Fish Camp in Cowpens to eat. They came over to the house and we played with the daughters. We were real close with them.

February 1964 found two brand new, identically prepared Mercury Marauders for Billy Wade in number 1 and Texan Johnny Rutherford in number 01. The cars had Bud Moore red sides and were black on the hood, roof, and deck lid. They had white script lettering with "Bud Moore Engineering" on the front fenders, the drivers' names on the tops above their heads, and "Bristol Lincoln-Mercury, Bristol, Va." on the rear quarter panels. The cars were beautiful and fast. They were the first cars to leave the fantastic new digs at 400 North Fairview Avenue in Spartanburg and head to Speedweeks in Daytona Beach.

We got to Daytona, and by that time Richard Petty was running real good in the hemi. We had trouble running against the hemis with Petty, Ray Fox, Ray Nichels, and Cotton. And they all had a couple of cars each and real good drivers. The 427 high-riser had also come out at Ford. The cars were faster. There was a big jump in speed from 1962 to 1964 and there was no big jump in safety at all.

We were staying at the Castaway with drivers Wade and Rutherford. Lincoln-Mercury wanted Rutherford in the 01 car. I remember he was from Texas and had himself some big old boots.

In the race, Jarrett's Bondy Long Ford teammate, a French grand prix driver named Joe Schlesser, put Rutherford on his roof. He slid down the backstretch upside down and about wore the roll bars slap through, and it didn't even hurt him. Wade finished a decent sixth place.

As was his battle-tested trademark, Bud Moore stood by his convictions and would not waver. Such was the case before the start on April 26, 1964, in Martinsville, Virginia.

We were up there with Wade and had everybody covered like snow. Wade flew around short tracks. He sat on the pole, I think, or was second. They were out there on the line and were talking about the brake duct openings. Junior or somebody had protested illegal brake ducts on the front of our car. They were raising Cain, saying this wasn't right or that wasn't right. But everybody else had theirs fixed the same way. Daddy finally grabbed France Sr., and said, "Look, that's the same thing they got on theirs." France said, "Yeah, but nobody's protesting their car, they're protesting your car." Daddy said, "I'll tell you what we'll do. We'll load the son-of-a-gun up and carry it home." He took it off the line and loaded up over the brake ducts.

Drivers crashed every week and did not die. They usually didn't even get hurt. Things were returning to normalcy. Just when the healing was beginning to take hold, auto racing was shocked to its very roots and Gregory had a front row seat. It was Sunday, May 24, 1964.

I knew that racing was dangerous. Everybody still had Weatherly on their minds. His getting killed, and how dangerous it was, seemed to always be in the background. When it really got to us was up there at Charlotte at the World 600. We were sitting in our family Mercury with the doors open and the radio going in the paddock behind the pits, and they hadn't run but a few laps of the race. Junior Johnson's girlfriend, Flossie, was with us. (Later she and Junior would get married.) Momma and Flossie were pretty good friends. When Flossie would go to the races, Junior would spin out and she would start crying. She was a real sensitive woman. Anyway, I remember I was sitting on Flossie's lap. It was just another race.

All of a sudden we heard a KERWHOOM! I remember that explosion like it was yesterday. Back then you could hear a tire blow and it sounded like a shotgun blast. BOOM! But this was like a loud WHOOM! You *felt* it. We knew it had to be a race car, but we couldn't see what was going on because there were so many people and we were at ground level. We heard something on the radio about Fireball and Ned. There was this big billow of black smoke and everyone started screaming. I'm just a seven-year-old kid thinking, "What in the world is going on?"

Momma got out of the car, the black smoke came up, and everybody screamed because they knew somebody was burning up or had been killed. All the ambulances they had headed out that way, and Flossie started crying. She had heard that Junior was moving up and was involved in the crash with Ned and Fireball. It broke Fireball's gas tank, Junior said later, and the fuel ran in the roof of the car and ignited. Fireball was upside down hanging in the belts, and he hollered, "Oh God, Ned. Help me! I'm on fire! Get me out!" Ned burned his arms pulling Fireball out of his car.

We didn't run to the wreck, but I remember the ambulance went by with the doors open and I was looking through the fence. You could see Fireball, and they had an oxygen mask on him and his arms were black. They didn't have real good safety equipment back then.

Everybody was in shock. Weatherly had just got killed, and I'm still trying to comprehend that as a seven-year-old. It was like, this is *really* dangerous! It finally sank in that this wasn't just us racing bicycles around a dirt track or something. This was serious. And the next Saturday, Eddie Sachs and Dave McDonald got killed at Indy.

> *Ironically, that horrible day at Charlotte was statistically a good day for Bud Moore Engineering. Spartanburg's Rex White had replaced Johnny Rutherford after the Daytona 500 in the new Mercury number 4 car. He and Billy Wade started side by side in the seventh row. In the 600 they finished an excellent third with White and fifth with Wade. The Pettys had taken first and second with Jim Paschal and Richard Petty and Lorenzen was fourth in Holman-Moody's Ford.*
>
> *But the uneasy peace that had been returning to auto racing after Weatherly's death four months earlier was shattered. The infernos at Charlotte and Indianapolis the last week of May 1964 brought on the untimely deaths of three huge auto racing stars: Eddie Sachs, Dave McDonald, and Fireball Roberts. The year did not get much better; tragedy carried over all the way through 1965.*
>
> *However, the next race after Charlotte was the Dixie 400 at Atlanta International Raceway on June 7. This was the first time Bud Moore ever arranged for the Wood family to come along, and it was unforgettable on a couple of different fronts. Greg recalls it well.*

Man, that was a blast! That was the first time the Moore and Wood families ever stayed at the same place for a race. We were at the Atlanta Motel on Highway 41/19. We always stayed there, and so did as many drivers and teams as they could cram in the joint. I remember that both our cars ran good and Rex White was the fastest qualifier, but it was on the second day so he started 11th.

That Saturday before the race we swam all day long with Smoke, Brent, Daryl, Perry, me, and the two Jarrett boys, Dale and Glenn. Smoke and Daryl were in high school and they weren't around too much. I recall that we all started matching pennies for a long time that evening, and Perry wore Dale out for 76 cents. The crazy thing was, Mrs. Wood made Perry give it back.

That was also the night that Big Smoke snored so loud Dale and Glenn said that Ned couldn't sleep over in the next room. He was still burnt up a little from pulling Fireball out of his car two weeks earlier at Charlotte. Maybe that's why he couldn't sleep.

It must not have bothered him too much because he won the race the next day. I remember Rex had

Lounging by the Atlanta Motel pool in June of 1964 were Betty Moore (left), Naomi, and Big Smoke Wood (Moore Family Collection).

that race won with about 25 laps to go and the motor stalled on the last pit stop and he wound up fifth. What was real weird was that he up and retired from Grand Nationals after that and only messed with some sportsman cars from then on. Wade was eighth, I think.

You know, a lot of references say that Bobby Johns drove one of our cars in that race, but that's not true. Hell, Daddy never ran three cars in the same race. Johns took over for Fireball in Holman-Moody's Fords. That trip was a blast!

> *The union of the Moore boys, the Jarrett boys, and the Wood boys had a grand finale on the red clay at Spartanburg on June 26, 1964. A bunch of top drivers and mechanics destined for the NASCAR Hall of Fame were there, such as Richard Petty, David Pearson, Ned Jarrett, Buck Baker, Cale Yarborough, and those in the pits like Bud Moore, Cotton, Owens, Dale Inman, and Lee Petty. Billy Wade, Buddy Baker, LeeRoy Yarbrough, Wendell Scott, and others were competing that dusty night. It was a perfect storm. Bud Moore Engineering used an open flatbed hauler to carry the race car on to the track, and it made a quite spacious viewing platform. On that hot, spectacular summer night, it was the vantage point for Greg, Brent, Smoke, Dale Jarrett, Glenn Jarrett, Donnie Allen, Sam Forry, and maybe some others. It was the best race many people ever saw.*

That was a great race. The Fairgrounds were packed and all the good dirt track drivers were there. Pearson was on the pole and Petty was second, Wade was third and Ned was fourth, and Buck was fifth and LeeRoy Yarbrough was sixth. What a great lineup that was.

From left to right on the morning of the 1964 Dixie 400 are Gregory Moore, Perry Allen Wood, Brent Moore, and Little Smoke (Moore Family Collection).

I remember there were a bunch of wrecks and it came down to Wade and Jarrett. They were swapping the lead and we were all going crazy up on Daddy's truck. Then Wade passed Ned pretty close to the end and Jarrett spun him. Well, half the people on Daddy's truck were happy and the other half weren't. My half weren't.

Wade lost a couple of laps and after a caution with about 15 laps to go, Wade drove right straight through Jarrett going into turn one. Wade hadn't backed off of it yet! Both cars flipped and both were trying to get restarted. We all jumped off the truck and ran to the wreck. People were going nuts, yelling at Wade to get back in the car, and he did. Half the infield pushed him off, and I think they both drove to the pits. Everybody expected a big fight between Ned and Billy, but nothing happened. That's just the way you raced back then. It was a tougher time, and nobody is tougher than that bunch.

What a great night! That was the seed of a match race there a couple of months later. As for Bud Moore Engineering and Billy Wade, the long, hot summer saw them perform extremely well, accomplishing an historical first in NASCAR stock car racing. But first there was an added surprise.

We went to Daytona for the Firecracker 400 with a new driver to replace Rex White. Rex drove five races for us and did a real good job. He never ran the Grand Nationals again. Darel Dieringer came over to us from Bill Stroppe, and the first thing he did was win the pole for the July 4 race at Daytona. Both our cars were running as well as the Fords and most of the Mopars. Daddy was gone a lot. They were doing real good on the dirt tracks, and there was the big rivalry between Wade and Ned Jarrett. They'd had a big feud and crash at Spartanburg. Daddy and Wade went to Old Bridge, New Jersey, and won from the pole on July 10. Two days later Wade started third and won at Bridgehampton, New York. Three days after that Wade won the pole and the race at Islip, New York. And the fourth straight was at Watkins Glen on July 19 and Billy Wade and Bud Moore did it from the pole again. That's four wins in a row in nine days, and three from the pole!

In one of those wins we didn't stop at the end, and there was a controversy about the gas tank. Ned had hit the pit road for gas and Daddy said, "Screw it! We aren't stopping." We won the race and Ned said, "Oh, they got a big tank."

Four wins in a row was something that had never happened before, and stuff like that goes in the record books and never comes out. When you do something notable for the first time like that, it can never be taken away. It's a first and in the record books forever. Bud Moore Engineering and Billy Wade were the first to win four Grand National races in a row.

Spartanburg promoter Joe Littlejohn, Sr., had captured lightning in a bottle during the famous June 26 race at the Piedmont Interstate Fairgrounds with the tremendous battle between arch-rivals Ned Jarrett and Billy Wade. So he reasoned that a match race between them and the other two primary Grand National antagonists, Richard Petty and David Pearson, would be a can't-miss proposition. Try to imagine a promoter pulling something like that off today. But on Monday, August 24, 1964, Joe Littlejohn arranged it under the lights as the prelude to a 100-lap sportsman race that was equally loaded with everybody that was anybody racing that tour. A standing-room-only crowd of close to 10,000 race fans soaked it all in on a perfect summer evening.

I was there, and the place was packed for the 20-lap match race. Littlejohn put up a thousand dollars, which was pretty good for 20 laps. Daddy and Wade didn't run much in practice, and the son-of-a-gun blew the motor and they only had about an hour to change it. Daddy told them to load it up on the truck. I remember being there and staying there because I knew they were coming back. I don't know if the officials drug their feet a little bit or gave us some extra time, but we only had about an hour. Daddy, Warren Prout, and two or three others were in the truck going to the shop. It wasn't that far to the new shop and they just yanked the blown motor out, put a new one in it, and came back. It had a wet sump oil pan, so you just had a couple of lines running to it and that's it. We had three or four guys, and the motor was just sitting there back at the shop.

NASCAR official Dick Beaty, to the day he died, thought we swapped the doors with the 16 car, Dieringer's team car. But we didn't. It was the 1 car, and we did swap the motor. They did it so quickly that they were gone and back in less than an hour and a half. I remember when they came back in, the fans went crazy. But Dick Beaty swore we swapped the doors. It could have been done, but that isn't what happened. How could it? There weren't any decals, and the doors were hand painted.

They had to change the motor because there weren't but four cars in the race, plus it was for our friend Joe Littlejohn. We played hell trying to convince everybody that the motor was changed.

Petty won the pole with Jarrett second, Pearson third, and Billy Wade fourth. When they got the green, the four of them ran around the track in a wad with fenders beating and banging for a couple of laps. Then, going into three, Wade was moving hard on the inside and passed Petty for the lead. Petty kind of lost it going up high and slid into the rail. It was just bad enough that they couldn't fix it, and he was done. After that was a three-car race, but Wade took off and made it a fight for second, which Jarrett took ahead of Pearson. Jarrett was a good ten or fifteen car lengths behind Billy.

The next day the paper had a picture of Stella Wade kissing Billy with Daddy and Warren Prout standing beside them. It got a lot of publicity to run 20 laps for a thousand dollars.

Just think of it. A 20-lap, winner-take-all match race on a half-mile dirt track between three drivers and a car owner from the first two NASCAR Hall of Fame inductions: Petty, Pearson, and Jarrett, and the first crew chief and car owner Hall of Fame Inductee, Bud Moore of Billy Wade's winning car. It was a fabulous night of racing and a great accomplishment for Bud Moore Engineering that is quickly fading from memory.

Life in the Moore family returned to normal, again, albeit a little uneasily, because there was always another tragedy just around the corner, especially in 1964. That September, likable Jimmy Pardue crashed to his death tire-testing at Charlotte. Testing was as deadly as racing. It still is. In 1964, one of the Moore boys had a strong desire to get behind the wheel of a race car, but it was not to be. The timing could not have possibly been worse for him.

When we lost Weatherly, Fireball got killed, and Pardue went out of the ballpark at Charlotte, Momma told Daddy, "You're not putting any of my babies in these race cars." That was the reason that Daryl never got any family support to drive a racecar. Now, Smoke and Daryl graduated from Spartan High in '65. Daryl was running a go-kart a little bit with Pop Eargle and Daddy when they were fooling with Smith in 1960. Daddy was actually selling go-kart motors and working on street cars. That's the way he made a living. But Daryl wanted to be a race driver real bad. He never got any family support, but if we hadn't lost Weatherly, Daryl probably would have gotten a shot at running a backup car or something. Joe Littlejohn, Sr., had even stated that Daryl was going to be one of our next race drivers when he got old enough.

Daddy got rid of the go-karts and stuff when he got the Lincoln-Mercury deal. But with the tragedies of Weatherly and Fireball and Pardue and the two at Indy, Daryl's timing, as far as being Bud Moore's son and wanting to race, was terrible. Even Maurice Petty, who had polio, got to drive a race car. Donnie Owens, Cotton's son, got a chance and decided he didn't want to do it. But not Daryl. He was disappointed that he never got to drive a race car. He went down to Daytona and chauffeured Miss Teen America around, but never got a shot at driving a race car because Betty Moore said, "You're not putting any of my babies in one of those race cars." The deal they had was, Daddy ran the business and Momma ran the household and the family, and that's the way it worked.

The Moore family would not have a son behind the wheel, and that was final. Also final were the 1964 results, which listed Billy Wade finishing fourth in the points, right behind his old teammate Pearson, who was still driving for Cotton Owens. Wade was ahead of Jimmy Pardue, who was dead. Wade and Moore completed 1964 with four wins (five including the match race), five poles, a dozen top fives, and an amazing 25 top tens in just 35 starts. In contrast, Richard Petty was the champion and he ran every race he could, all 61, as did Pearson. (It was a 62-race season, but you could not run both qualifying races at Daytona in February, so 61 races was the maximum.) Jarrett took second in points and raced 59 times. Needless to say, everything was pointing towards 1965 being the year Bud Moore was back in the championship chase. It was such a relief that the long, deadly 1964 season was over.

CHAPTER THREE

"Stella, There's Been a Wreck"

In 1964 the Moores had endured the loss of not only their own driver, but other racing friends who were actually like family members, too. There is no question that the racing community was closer knit then than now. But in 1965, tragedy seemed to be behind them. Bud Moore Engineering had a new driver and an old hand in potent year-old Mercurys just as capable of winning as the new factory equipment. There were no General Motors entries to speak of, and Chrysler was boycotting because Bill France, Sr., had banned their hemi engine. When the team was not racing, they were testing, and before the season started, extra money was to be made from Goodyear or Firestone. Bud Moore was aligned with Goodyear, and Greg was living it from 500 Fernwood Drive.

I was nearly eight years old and remember this stuff real well. Everything was lovely. Billy Wade was the number one driver and very solid. We'd been going out to the fish camp with Billy, Stella, and all us kids, socializing, and with the off season and holidays, 1964's bad times just faded away.

So we went to a tire test at Daytona for the Daytona 500. Wade's teammate was Darel Dieringer, and he went down there first. He was under contract with Goodyear to test the inner liner in our number 16 car. It was January 4, 1965. They put a spike in the track coming off of four and told Darel to hit it with the right front at 140 miles an hour by looking at the tach. He went by the first time and he missed it. He sped by the second time and hit it, but it didn't blow the tire. They wanted to blow the outer tire and not the inner. We didn't have any two-way radios, and when he came by the third time, apparently he's about half pissed off and going too fast. He wasn't running wide open, but he was running about 160, hit the spike, and blew the outer tire, the inner liner, the whole deal. Then *boom*, he hit the wall, slid right to the end of pit road, and was sitting there with broken ribs, a little bit of a concussion, and the car was totaled. The 16 car and the driver were finished for the immediate future, but the test was not finished.

There was still work to be done, so a phone call was made to 400 North Fairview Avenue.

Goodyear was getting ready to do the construction test for the Daytona 500. The spike deal was over. So Daddy called Daryl at the shop in Spartanburg and said, "Get Wade on an airplane. Tell Delaney and them to put the 1 car on the truck and bring it down here so we can finish the tire test."

Wade was all pumped up, because those tire tests were how you made money back then. Daryl drove him out to airport. Billy Wade said, "Goddamit, I'm going to get some of Goodyear's money this time. Dieringer's been getting all that tire test money and now I'm going to get some of that Goodyear money." Petty was down there, too, but only Dieringer had been running over the spikes. Wade had nothing to do with the spike deal.

Goodyear had a set of tires called the control tires, the ones they already had all the performance data for. On January 5, Wade was testing the control tires. Goodyear wanted Wade to make ten laps on them. Apparently the control tires were last year's tires, but they weren't worn out or anything. So Wade went out and ran.

Daddy always said it was the last lap, the ninth lap. But it was at the end of the seventh lap, because I remember finding the chart at the shop and that's where they quit keeping lap speeds on the chart. It was right about time for him to come in, and he went off into turn one running low and it blew the right front. *Kaboom*! He had a long way to go before he hit the wall, hit it a ton, and slid. It veed the dash. The bar that ran over the driver was bowed. We didn't have the five-point hookup, and Wade submarined underneath the belts when he hit. He hit so directly and so hard that maybe he didn't have his belts tight enough, but it broke the back of the seat a little bit. The back of the seat was loose. From what I heard from some of the crew guys that got down there with the safety people, there was blood in the car.

I don't think Daddy was one of the first that got to him. One of the crew guys said Wade was sitting in the seat. Daddy said he was flopped over the steering wheel. He wasn't. The lap belt was up across Wade's upper chest. He was gurgling like he was foaming at the mouth. The impact took his organs and shoved everything way, way up. Richard Petty said he drowned in his own blood. They took him out through the windshield and by the time they got him on the stretcher, he was dead. It wasn't pretty.

The second tragedy within a year for Gregory and his family took place on January 5, 1965, when Billy Wade lost his life in this Mercury Marauder while tire-testing at Daytona. Here, an official and others examine the wreckage (Moore Family Collection).

Seven-year-old Gregory, who had suffered through the death of his dad's previous driver less than one year earlier, was about to go through it again.

This was the bad part. It was January 5, 1965, right after lunch, about 2:20 P.M. eastern time. I was a little kid. Daryl walked home from Spartan High after school. He had dropped Wade off at the airport earlier that morning. The phone rang and Momma picked it up and Daddy told her, "Get over to Stella's house right now. It's getting on the news. We just lost Wade. He blew a right front and it killed him. Get over there before she hears it on the radio." This was about 30 minutes after it had happened. Daddy also had told Mario Rossi, who was in town helping with the motors and stuff to head over there, too. Rossi was supposed to have already told her because he lived closer.

Momma picked me up from Houston Elementary School and told me what had happened. I could not believe it and didn't comprehend it for a while. She dropped me off at the house and headed on over to Stella's.

When she got to Stella's, Rossi was sitting there and nobody was saying anything. It was like everybody was kind of visiting. Stella said, "Something's wrong. What's going on? Betty, what's going on?" Momma had thought she had been told, but she had to break the news. "Stella, there's been a wreck and Billy's been hurt."

"Is it bad?"

"Real bad."

Stella went into hysterics, and they got Dr. Bonner over there, who knocked her out immediately. Momma said that even with all she'd been through with Daddy, living through World War II, telling Stella Wade about Billy was the hardest thing she ever had to do in her life. And at that point right then, Daddy came real close to not racing again. That was not a cool deal.

Goodyear paid for everything. Goodyear did things they didn't have to do. Months later, I remember Stella came over to the house with the girls and stayed there in Fernwood for about two weeks before they moved back to Texas in the summer of '65.

The closeness of the deaths of Joe Weatherly and Billy Wade, and the other racers of '64 had a lasting effect at Bud Moore Engineering for the next 35 years of its existence.

Because of what happened to Weatherly and Wade, we always had safety in mind. Daddy said in 1972 when we came back to NASCAR, "We can't stand to lose another driver." We never built qualifying engines. We never took chances with tires. We almost always put on four at once. We always put brand new engine parts in because we always had those deaths tugging at our shoulders the whole time. That's the way we raced. We raced much more conservatively than we should have in a lot of cases because of the bad stuff that happened in '64 and '65.

Daddy and Buddy Baker argued about the qualifying engines. Daddy was bad about detuning the engines. We wouldn't run as much ignition timing in an engine as we dynoed it with because that was always tugging at us. We wouldn't take chances. We didn't win many poles, and that's the reason. Daddy, Daryl, and I had those deaths tugging at us from then until the last time we ever ran a race. Even when Larry Pearson missed the show at Daytona in 1997 and Universal Studios were going to give us $100,000 and all we had to do was make the race. When we got back home Momma said, "Well, at least nobody got hurt."

That was about the time the hemi engine boycott started with the Mopars dropping out for the 1965 season. Bill France, Sr., and Joe Littlejohn, Sr., came over to Daddy's shop and offered him some show-up money. France Sr. said, "I need those Mercurys to get out there and run." That's when Daddy began to run those year-old Mercurys with Darel Dieringer and Earl Balmer, because France Sr. needed those cars to offset the boycott.

Incredibly, Bud Moore with his almost superhuman will and constitution managed to be ready in time for the 1965 season. He did it for Bill France, Sr., the sport, and most of all, for his family. For the second January in a row, the Moore Family proved that racing is what they do.

CHAPTER FOUR

Fernwood Farms

Away from the track, it was only natural that Gregory and the rambunctious Fernwood crowd would eventually get around to daring contests of speed on the neighborhood dirt tracks. The first speedway was at the corner of Pineville Road and Overland Drive.

The Wood brothers had that track in real good shape with the bike racing, but I remember a wooden race car Perry and Bill Shoolbred built that looked just like Daddy's Billy Wade car. It had a roof and a piece of sheet metal around the body and across the hood. It had red sides and black over the hood and roof with the white number 1 on it. It had "Bud Moore Engineering" and "Bristol Lincoln Mercury" painted on it like Wade's did. Daryl pulled it with a rope tied to the back of that Honda 50, and you couldn't steer it much at all. If you were in the car, you were just along for the ride. I remember Perry and Bill were flying and Daryl came over a hill beside a little oak tree. They didn't clear the tree, and they hit it with the left front wheel. They hit it so hard that it broke that rope, and Perry's face hit that sheet metal hood and bent it up. I guess if that piece of sheet metal hadn't been folded over double on the edge where he hit, it would have cut his head in half. It was a miracle, but I don't think he even bled that much.

The second track was at Greengate and Applewood lanes and Gregory took a more active role. Maybe too active. He raced!

We had our usual group: Perry, Brenty, Billy Pratt, Bill Dickerson, Bill Shoolbred, Bill Rainey, Sam Forry, John Wilson, Cleve Brown, me, and usually some strangers that jumped in not really knowing what they were getting in to. I had a little Mattell 20-inch bicycle with that battery-powered Varoom motor on it that made it sound like it had a real motor. It came with training wheels, but we

Bill Shoolbred (left) and Perry Allen Wood (seated inside) constructed a racer designed for gravity power based on Billy Wade's Bud Moore Mercury. When pulled behind a Honda 50 motorbike, it flew! (Perry Wood Racing Collection).

took the training wheels off. We'd been racing up there all summer all day, every day. The first turn was banked, and we hauled ass into that turn. We had inverted starts to try to make it even, and usually I got lapped anyway.

One day I was on the pole, and Cleve was beside me on the outside of the front row. Perry and Shoolbred were on the back row. There were at least four rows, maybe five. Well, Brent was driving that Honda 50 for the pace car, and he pulled over and we got the green. I was on the pole, and I got down into one and thought, "Well, I'll hold the inside." By that time I had gotten to where I could about keep from getting lapped in a ten-lap race. I was like an independent. I was a Herman Beam. You know, Herman the Turtle. I was the slow car.

I was hugging the inside and I wanted to lead the first lap. Somehow or another I wanted to hold somebody off. But what I did was, I hit a brick. We had some bricks on the inside so you couldn't cut the corner. I hit the brick on the inside and crashed on my own. Perry and Shoolbred had drafted up on me, and Shoolbred had a nice English bike with little old skinny tires. It had those rat trap pedals that were so sharp, and it hit me right in the back of the head when we all piled-up. It didn't even really hurt. So we got into this pile up in turn one. I always called it "The Wreck." I had really wanted to lead the first lap because I was getting a little bit faster and a little bit stronger. But Shoolbred's pedal gashed my head pretty badly. I reached my hand back there and saw the blood and ran home crying to Momma. I caused the accident. Nobody wrecked me. But I wasn't out of action long.

Shoolbred felt so bad about this because it looked worse than it was. Twenty years later when I was working at the shop dynoing motors he'd ask me, "Your head OK?" I'd say, "Bill, it didn't hurt me that bad. It just bled a little bit. It's as good as it ever was."

Our neighborhood had some serious falls during this period. Gregory remembers:

Billy Hardy fell out of a tree house down by the lower Spartan High parking lot one summer. He used to come down and Brenty would help him with his math homework or something. They lived on Overland Drive, and his daddy was in banking and helped Charlie Bradshaw and Jerry Richardson get the money to start the Hardee's franchises. Anyway, he was nailing something there and went to grab a limb. He fell and was in the hospital about a month. Then there was Mike McGarahan, who had that rope swing over that little creek. He fell off of that and broke his arm so badly it was in a cast for a year. It was a pretty doggone treacherous swing. Brenty might have done it, maybe. I remember going down there and seeing the kids swinging on it, but I never did.

The summer of 1965 was the prime of Gregory's Fernwood years, when he was getting old enough to hold his own in the street and neighborhood. But that July Fourth was one of very special importance that is a favorite memory of those involved.

I remember being at the Castaway Motel, the best place on Daytona Beach. A.J. Foyt was there, *ABC's Wide World of Sports* was there, and all the neat guys. John Locke, his wife, and the Goodyear people stayed there. John came within a gnat's ass of getting General Tire to come into NASCAR.

Everywhere you looked was somebody famous. Dieringer and Earl Balmer, driving our cars, were there. Bob Colvin, president of Darlington Raceway, stayed on the other side and had a room that we didn't know about. They called it the Party Room. It was only in action during Speedweeks in February. They didn't do it in July because too many wives and children came. They had it hid as well as they could with a set-up bar. All the guys pitched in something like 20 bucks apiece. Back then, Speedweeks lasted about two weeks or 17 days. It was ridiculous. Daddy, Colvin, and Joe Littlejohn, Sr., all pooled their money together and set up a bar. The wives never knew anything about that. The men would just go disappear over at the Party Room on the side where Colvin stayed.

On that summer's trip, I remember the number one song in the country on the Fourth of July 1965 was *Satisfaction* by the Rolling Stones. They played it over and over and over.

Daryl cut his head when he jumped off the high dive. I jumped off it, but Daryl dove and he got such a good run that he bumped his head. Momma carried him to the hospital, and I stayed with the wife of the guy from Monroe Shock Absorbers, Dee Dee, who was Italian.

Then there was the night Perry, Brenty, Daryl, Smoke, Colvin's daughter, and maybe some others and me were sitting out on the edge of the motel's sundeck in the dark. Out there at the beach we saw something ... *and it moved!* We all ran down to the beach and there was this huge sea turtle. It had fish hanging off of it. I don't remember if it was Smoke or some other nut, but somebody tried to climb on its back. It turned around and crawled back into the water. Probably a smart turtle!

> There was an amazing feat that was a wonder to behold, performed regularly by a legend, creating an image that will live on forever in the minds of those fortunate to have seen it.

That was when beer cans were about five times thicker than they are now. A. J. Foyt was a pretty tough guy and had some hands and huge arms on him from wrestling those USAC dirt cars all over the place. That son-of-a-gun would squeeze a Busch beer can from top to bottom with his thumb on the bottom and his pointer and middle fingers on the top and flatten it. That beer can couldn't have been any flatter if it had been run over by a car. I'll never forget it. Brenty and I tried to do it later and we had to stomp it with our feet to get it that flat — and I was a stomper! But it was effortless for Foyt to do by hand.

A. J. took a liking to Perry. I remember that he called Perry Pee Wee. I was still only eight years old. A. J. would come and knock on Perry's door and say, "Can Pee Wee come out and play?" We all played the heck out of some shuffleboard at the Castaway that time. Then Foyt won the Firecracker 400 in the Wood Brothers' second car. He said Perry was his good luck charm.

Really, I think A. J. Foyt was a misunderstood person. He was just like any other good race driver. He had a little bit of a temper, but

The Castaway Motel sundeck sported, from left to right, Brent Moore, A. J. Foyt, Perry Allen Wood, Big Smoke Wood, and Little Smoke Wood on July 3, 1965 (Perry Wood Racing Collection).

he could back up what he said. A. J. was coming off of that bad crash at Riverside that nearly killed him. There was blood all over that car, and it messed him up bad. Daddy said it broke his back. That crash was the final scene of the movie *Redline 7000*.

> *Mr. and Mrs. Moore did not neglect their children's need for a spiritual and religious upbringing. While admittedly leaving the home side duties to Betty, Bud Moore had a major influence on Sunday mornings in Fernwood Farms.*

If he was in town, Daddy made sure I had my coat and tie on and my butt was in church. He went to church when he was little and that's the way we did it. Unless you were sick, you went to church. You had to flat be running a fever or you went. I never had a choice and didn't mind it. I enjoyed it. We just took for granted that we were going to go to church. Dr. Ball started Fernwood Baptist Church, and I loved him to death. We knew his son David and all their other kids. We got a little bit angry because we didn't think they did Dr. Ball right at the end. They retired him too early.

The first preacher they got, the assistant minister, lasted about a year. He coached the basketball team the Mahaffeys and I played on and was a pretty good guy. Then he made a couple of remarks that really saddened the old people, things that were just too modern-day for the congregation. He made some statements one time about the old people getting out of the way for the young. For the old people, that was bad to say because it was the older people supporting the church. It wasn't long before they replaced him. They had to go through about two assistant ministers before they ever found anybody. Everybody really got angry over how Dr. Ball was forced out. It was dirty rotten. Churches are like businesses, and when new people come in things change. That hurt Fernwood Baptist, when they forced Dr. Ball out. He wasn't that old.

Dr. Ball would come strolling down to the shop at least twice a year unexpectedly. Daryl or I would know he was coming through the front door, and Daddy would be looking for the back door. Daddy loved him and got mad about the way they treated him, too. Everybody there in Fernwood was like family and a lot of them didn't like what happened.

If Momma ever got sick, Dr. Ball came by the house. If one of the kids ever got sick, he came by the house. He used to always laugh and tell Momma, "I'm still working on Bud. I don't have him yet, but I'm not giving up either."

I went into the Boy Scouts, Troop Nine, at Fernwood Baptist, and I went through all that stuff. I was a den leader for a Cub Scout outfit, the den chief. I did that for about a year.

> *Greg lived in the world of a sports celebrity with access to things the rest of us only dreamed of experiencing. He, Brent, and Daryl never showed it and were as normal as any of the kids in Fernwood.*

Chapter Five

Good Times Return

One of the most popular wins in stock racing history took place on September 5, 1966, in Darlington, South Carolina. The Southern 500 was still the biggest and most prestigious race of the year in most people's minds, and this may have been the proudest moment ever for Bud Moore Engineering. The new, one-of-a-kind 1966 Mercury Comet had already finished second in the Firecracker 400 and won the previous race to Darlington at Asheville-Weaverville. The Comet, sometimes jokingly called "The Vomit," was still a huge underdog, especially at a place like Darlington, but Bud Moore and Darel Dieringer were not. There are so many proud moments in Bud Moore's career, and this is at the top. Gregory was literally right square in the middle of it.

Dieringer and Petty were racing for the win, and Petty snookered us. He came in to the pits and didn't take on tires because his clutch was slipping. We had previously come in and put on right-side tires, so he had a lead. Petty's right-side tires were worn completely out and he was on the cord. We were catching him, but not quite fast enough. He was going to have to wreck or blow a tire for us to win. He was having to go too far, and he blew a tire. So we passed him with seven laps to go and won the race.

I was watching the race with Momma in turn four from the old scoring stand, and they let us in the pits because they knew we had won the race. So we started down the pit road when Dieringer came by headed towards Victory Lane. They stopped him right there at the pits so Johnny Reb could climb on the hood with the Confederate flag. Dieringer started taking his helmet and gloves off and Bill Delaney, who was our mechanic and truck driver, just grabbed me up and put me in the car. I got my picture made with my hand on the roll bar and the crew all got on the top, and we all rode up there to Victory Lane. Speedway president Bob Colvin, Daddy, Dieringer, Johnny Reb, Miss Southern 500, the radio and TV people, Ray Melton the track announcer, and a bunch of others were all crowded in there. I sat on the edge of the car's roof watching all that was going on. That made a pretty big impression on me at nine years old. Really, really big!

Greg ranks that ride as one of the very top moments of his life. Thank goodness someone took a picture.
Away from the races, Gregory Moore had quite an early career as a football player and probably could have made something out of it. He started with the Fernwood Tigers.

I played a lot of football. A bunch! I was one of Fernwood's stars. George Mahaffey and I almost won the state championship. I was a halfback from the third grade all the way through the eighth. Sterling Anderson was the head coach and David Satterfield was the

Visible here with his right hand on the roll bar, Gregory got the ride of his life into Victory Lane with Darel Dieringer after winning the 1966 Southern 500 (courtesy Bud Moore Engineering Archives).

assistant coach. Years later, his son Randy was backup quarterback to Steve Fuller at Spartanburg High School. Fuller went on to star at Clemson and helped guide the Chicago Bears to the 1986 Super Bowl victory.

We had George Mahaffey and me in the backfield and I was fairly quick at running. Brenty ran track and held the record in the broad jump at Spartan High. He, John Wilson, and I had a 50-yard dash set up from Monroe Road down through our yard, Wilson's yard, and down to the other end. Brenty had it measured almost with a micrometer. We dashed down that track with Brenty timing us.

Wilson turned out to be a real good track runner at Spartan High in the mile and cross country. Brent coached Fernwood football for a while, but not while I played.

I played one year in the third grade with the little bitty guys, and Brent coached the bigger bantams. Brent coached Billy Pratt, and he was almost as big a sissy as that other guy. Later, the high school coach, Glen Vick, told Billy to give up football because he'd never amount to anything. Billy ended up with a football scholarship to Gardner-Webb. I also had Brenty helping me out the whole time, rooting me on, and he was like my coach at home.

I had a very successful Fernwood Tigers career. I was a real good halfback in the seventh and eighth grades. George and I killed everybody. We didn't even get scored on in 1969. Nine and zero and not scored on. Wicked! The next year they upped the weight limit to 120 pounds. We put together about the same team we had, and Sterling Anderson was the coach. He had coached the Salvation Army. Jack Welch was a coach. With David Satterfield, those guys were good enough coaches to have coached at Spartan High. They made us want to play. Momma came to all the games and brought the drinks, and she got a little trophy at the banquet.

They devised a playoff system and had regions. We could have had an all-star team by taking players from the other Spartanburg teams. We didn't take anybody. We didn't need anybody. There wasn't anybody we wanted. We *were* the all-star team. I was number 32 and George was 33. We won the first three games. We beat the crap out of Chester 42 to 12. They stopped the game in the fourth quarter because George and me were having to fight everybody. We played Irmo and beat them 34 to 8. You see, these playoff teams were so good they could actually score on us.

The game we were supposed to have trouble with was playing Cherokee County. We played them next at Snyder Field at Wofford College under the lights, which was a real big deal. A pretty good crowd was on hand in the rain. It was pouring down rain! This was to get to the state finals. Sterling and David had a bet of maybe $1,000 with the other coach or somebody they had a grudge with that we were going to beat them. I learned this afterwards.

We won the toss and they kicked off and it got sloshy. (Later, Wofford was mad because we tore the field all up.) I received the kickoff and fumbled it. But I picked it up and got out close to the 20 yard line. We always kept the stuff simple. The first play from scrimmage I ran 82 yards right up the middle for a touchdown. We wound up killing them 34 to 8.

We were doing really well, and we went to the state championship in Abbeville. We came to find out later that they had cheated. Somehow or another they slid these big guys in on us. We noticed when they came over the hill the guys looked a little bit bigger.

We were lucky about winning the toss all season. But for that game, we lost the toss. On the first play from scrimmage, they hand off to this black guy. He's not little, and he goes right up the middle. Our defensive line was so good they usually tackled these guys for two-yard losses, busted the play up, and caused fumbles. But this guy just dragged people, and George and I had to come out of the backfield and hit him at the same time to bring him down. I turned around to George and said, "You know, I believe we got a problem." They beat us 30 to 0, which was very humiliating.

Gregory advanced to Evans Junior High School in what appeared to be the continuation of a very promising career on the gridiron. It was not to be.

At Evans, I was a starter on the team with Fuller. Glen Vick was the coach. Vick knew my history at Fernwood. They had me playing halfback and changed me to wingback. That was all cool, everything was fine.

Well, in about the third game, I hurt my back. I don't think it was any particular play; it just happened. It probably started the year before, playing for Fernwood. My back just went out, and it hurt so bad I couldn't even get into a three-point stance. I went to practice and told Vick that I just couldn't do this anymore. We had a black guy there who was really quick, but didn't know the plays. Vick said, "Hang around here long enough and teach Roy the plays." Roy Miller wound up being a star at Spartan High. All I had to do was show him some of the plays and work with him maybe two or three practices, and he turned out to be fantastic. The team won every game that year. I might have scored a touchdown and played some defense, too. But I stopped and never played any more football. George never played any more, either. We got into smoking cigarettes, drinking liquor, and all that bad stuff. We were just 12- or 13-year-old kids.

Greg entertained the possibility of being a racer himself at one time, but not on four wheels. Just like his brother Daryl, though, he was not going to get in a race car, no matter what.

I wanted to race motorcycles. I got real good at running dirt bikes at local events and had a guy that wanted me to drive one of his bikes. But I never did do it. They had eliminated the 175 Class, and then the guy from the Yamaha place called me and said that he had five bikes come in in a box. They were YZ racers. He sold me one for like 600 bucks. I rode it about twice and sold it to a guy down the street for his kids. I never fooled with motorcycles after that. I had a Yamaha 250 and a Honda 90 cc. We had dirt tracks over there in Hillbrook, and I was kind of interested in running motocross. But I knew that we had had so much tragedy that Momma was never going to go for it. I was really more into football, and that's about the time we got a rock band going. I think I could have driven a race car, no if, ands, or buts about it. I just knew it would never gain any support within the family. Daryl was the perfect candidate and wanted to do it. But when we lost those two race drivers and the other drivers that got killed, Betty Moore wasn't going to have any part of it.

In 1970, the Moore family outgrew the little house at 500 Fernwood Drive and moved to more spacious accommodations in Hillbrook Forest. Along the way, Gregory and his father grew closer, and Gregory began to grow into a new role: Bud's left-handed right-hand man.

When it got to be about 1970, Daddy had done pretty well with the Trans Am thing. Because Spartanburg Country Club was so overcrowded, Hugh Lanier came up with Lan-Yair Country Club. His momma owned the property. Nearby, Daddy and he bought their houses at about the same time. That was a hoot of a deal. Daddy didn't tell Momma about it. That's just how they did things. Momma couldn't complain because it was a heck of a nice house. It was about 3,500 square feet, good neighborhood, so we did the transition over to Hillbrook. Hillbrook was — and still is, nearly 50 years later — Fernwood's rival, half a mile away as the crow flies. Brent was in college and came home and discovered we'd moved!

Brent got married about three or four months before he got out of Clemson, and Daryl got married in 1971. So from 1971 until about 1978 it was just Daddy, Momma, and me. But Daryl, Daddy, and I always ate lunch at home with Momma every day. We always did everything together.

Brent Clark Moore graduated in May of 1968 from Spartanburg High School, where he was a scholar student, track athlete, and legitimate celebrity. His SHS yearbook entry reads: "'Sprint' ... 'off to the races' ... 'helpful' counselor ... coach ... 'it's got possibilities' ... meteorologist?" His accomplishments conclude with "Overall Science Fair Winner."

Brenty got to go to some races in the summer and help part-time. He was the only one with a college education, and he had all the opportunity to get involved in racing if he wanted to. Brenty made a dynamometer for the high school science fair. He had a three horsepower lawnmower motor and a nice display. He took a brake caliper off of one of the Cougars for the load cell, and he would load it and put it on a scale. He ran different fuels in it, like ether, and it would change the horsepower reading and prove that it worked right. He had all these equations on it. Brenty won at the high school, the regional, and then went to the national contest and got an honorable mention or something. He was so smart, and Daddy gives him credit for helping us technically. He really did help a lot. He'd call me up to tell me stuff, and I would apply it where I could.

We actually got with the engineers and changed the correction factor on the dyno that they use today. They call it a friction coefficient. Brenty and I figured that stuff out years before.

Let's say you were making 550 horsepower. We couldn't understand why a motor in the middle of the winter would pull 560 or 561 horsepower, but in the heat of the summer, with all your corrections for the barometer and everything, it wouldn't pull but 542. There was about a 10 to 12 horsepower difference that people couldn't figure out. That's the friction coefficient. It's figured in with the barometer, humidity, carburetor air temperature, and air density. It affects the motor. A thunderstorm can affect it. If you didn't have a correction factor you'd never know what you were doing. On observed horsepower, summertime to dead of winter, there's a big difference, and you're just trying to find three or four horsepower. If you couldn't correct it, you'd be lost. That was one thing we were really big on, dynoing the engines. We were probably one of the earliest to have a dyno — Smokey and us.

We also had a Magnaflux machine, which detected cracks by magnetic charging and sucked the florescent stuff into the crack. Daddy bought the Magnaflux machine when they were still down there at Bud Moore's Garage.

At the 1968 Spartanburg High School Science Fair, Brent Moore took first place honors with his dynamometer (Perry Wood Racing Collection).

Brent was a huge influence on Gregory's life. But Brent went his own way down a different path, and Gregory stayed in Spartanburg, bonding closely with his dad.

Daddy and I got to playing golf out there, and believe it or not, that's when I became Daddy's partner to do about anything. That's the way it was. Years later, if we were going to a turkey shoot or to play golf, it was mainly him, Edmund Rogers, Joe Littlejohn, Sr., and me. They'd give Joe Sr. and me strokes because he was getting old by then and we played the exact same game. We came off the tee box with a three iron, and Daddy and Edmund could hit a wood. Joe Sr. was good at putting and the short game, and I was good for a sixth or seventh grader. Thank goodness for all those rounds in the Fernwood back yard par three.

We were real close to Joe Sr., who had put on the match race and promoted for decades at the Fairgrounds. That was our deal at Lan-Yair, and they were a bunch of good people that we got to know. We sat around in the clubhouse, and I'd have a beer and they'd be pouring their liquor. We knew the Laniers because they were our next door neighbors, with

Fuller, George Wyatt, and all these cool people in Hillbrook. But I'd still come back to Fernwood. Brent and everyone else was in college. Daryl was in the Navy, Smoke was in the Army in Germany, and Anne was there with him.

Even back then, Gregory and his daddy had heroes like most everyone else. All these years later, they still do.

My three heroes were Daddy, Leonard Wood, and Smokey Yunick. Leonard Wood was one of my mentors. He helped me out because he and I were doing about the same thing: working on the cylinder heads and induction systems.

John Wayne—that's Bud Moore's hero. The Duke! Any film he made, Daddy and Momma, with me in the back seat, went to the Scenic Drive-in or the Pine Street Drive-in Theater to see, with the speaker hanging on the inside of the car. Daddy couldn't hear too well out of one ear because of the war, and he cranked that thing up wide open.

Our family was really, really tight. We went to the Beacon, and that was a big thing because Daddy's farm, his daddy Dick Moore's farm, was back behind the Beacon. That's where the old homestead was.

Spartanburg's history is not only thick in auto racing, but its musical roots run even longer and deeper. Who knew that the town's musical scene in the 1970s not only included the Marshall Tucker Band and Uncle Walt's Band, but Gregory Moore and his band?

In the mid–70s, Gregory was a full-fledged rock and roller with his band, "Stairway," seen here posing at a cabin at Converse College. From left to right are Larry Burrell (lead guitar), Greg Moore (lead vocals and rhythm guitar), Phil High (drums), and Len Stewart (bass). Missing from Stairway's group photo is Stephen High, who was the sound and light man. He and 17 others were killed on April 6, 2005, in a helicopter crash in an Afghanistan sandstorm (Moore Family Collection).

During the college years I took guitar lessons from Larry Burrell over on Emory Road in Fernwood. He showed me enough, but I was kind of self-taught. His mother was a schoolteacher, and his daddy was the guy that worked on everybody's TV sets for years. Larry and I put together a band called "Stairway" with Phil High as drummer and Len Stewart on bass. We played Top 40 stuff, like the Rolling Stones. Anything loud. I bought a Rickenbacker guitar and had a Gibson L6S like Carlos Santana endorsed. (You know, you always had a backup guitar.) We bought equipment and stuff and rented a room across from First Baptist Church above McMahan Shoes for $50 a month. We subleased it from the girls that had the hair salon below us. It didn't have any heat, and I'd take over the Salamander — the blow heater from the shop. We kept the place rented because we had a couch moved up there and we needed a place to take our girlfriends. You know the gals were impressed. They just had to meet the boys in the band. We met some of them all right!

We played up at the Branch, which is now U. S. C. Upstate, and two or three weeks at the Sound and Light Lounge, which used to be the DeLuxe Diner. We played at Hooley's Underground at the Franklin Hotel for a week filling in for a band. We played at the National Guard Armory a couple of times for some parties. We went to the Torch Club in Tryon, North Carolina, for a weekend. They paid us pretty well and that place was packed. In fact, the Lynyrd Skynyrd drummer, Artimus Pyle, had been up there, and we had to move his stuff out of the way so we could set ours up.

We went somewhere and dressed up like Kiss in 1975. We had the makeup perfect. Len Stewart was painted up like Gene Simmons. Larry was Ace Frehely, and I was like Paul Stanley. We put the cat nose on Phil High and could hit their songs about dead perfect. It was just a show band anyway, and we'd crank it up loud, bring out the fuzz boxes and the special effects. We had the shoes with the platforms on and had it dead right.

We got us a little U-Haul trailer and played all over the area from about '74, when Follmer drove the car, until Baker in '77. We damn sure weren't Marshall Tucker, but we weren't the bottom rung either. Larry Burrell, my old guitar teacher, was a real good friend of mine. We never had a falling out or anything; people just moved away, and we lost contact after the band broke up. I got to going to all the races so much and lost contact with him a few years ago.

Greg was speeding towards a crossroads where some life decisions would have to be made. He was a rock and roller, football player, golfer, young man about town, and an increasingly closer friend and partner to his father, a great racer. The latter role continues to this day.

CHAPTER SIX

That First Taste of Racing

Bud Moore Engineering in 1967 had a revolving door for drivers. There were two Mercury Cyclones, numbers 15 and 16, competing on the NASCAR Grand National circuit with numerous occupants. These cars complemented the two Mercury Cougars numbers 15 and 98 being run in the SCCA Trans Am Series with another rotation of hot pilots.

Gregory was only ten years old, but he was involved in a little more than stomping out cigarettes. In fact, a smoke butt on the floor of Bud Moore Engineering in 1967 was likely an offense punishable by death! They called it "the shop," but it was literally a factory as much as one anywhere. That had to be one of the busiest years in the Moores' lives, running two different national series with two different sanctioning bodies and all those high octane egos to keep in check. If anybody in the world could handle that job, it was Bud Moore. Meanwhile, somewhere beyond being just babysat at the shop, Gregory soaked in the entire ambiance of a major factory racing operation that he would employ for himself in the not too distant future. What a time to be there! The walls of 400 North Fairview Avenue were bursting with racecars and racers ... and speed.

With the Cyclones in 1967, Daddy had a who's who of drivers, and none of them did all that well. We had some decent runs, but no consistency like we expected. That was especially true after a little Comet the year before had won Weaverville and Darlington back to back and come close at Daytona in July. So here were all these beautiful Cyclones—no more Comets—top drivers, and not much success. In the Grand National cars, Curtis Turner crashed the 15 at Riverside and Gurney led a lot in the 16. He started third and they black-flagged us for something that they didn't need to. Gurney was trying to catch up from the black flag and the motor blew. Bobby Allison ran the 16 car in four races, and Sam McQuagg drove six in the 15, and they couldn't get it done. Gordon Johncock took the 16 for a good ride at Rockingham with a fifth, but he was an Indy driver who had other commitments. LeeRoy Yarbrough raced with us in the number 16 six times with a third at Atlanta at the Dixie 400 that summer. We were free to use whoever we wanted to use.

But the Cougars were outstanding, winning all the time with Parnelli Jones, Dan Gurney, and David Pearson. They didn't have the same paint schemes as the Cyclones. The Cyclones had Bud Moore red sides, and the hoods, roofs, and rear decks were silver. The Cougars had the red sides, hood, and rear deck lids, but they had a silver roof. Lincoln-Mercury boss Fran Hernandez wanted a silver top on the Cougars because it was a luxury pony car. Those cars had these spring towers on them where the springs were on top of the upper control arms. We just had a lousy season with the Cyclones and couldn't lose with the Cougars.

Six • That First Taste of Racing

On the SCCA side of the shop, there was a clutter of checkered flags and trophies.

The Cougars were a very successful, last minute, put-together program. That program got the blessings of Ford Motor Company, but they had mixed emotions because they also had Carroll Shelby and the Mustangs. We had the championship won. Pearson won and was the only stock car driver ever to win a Trans Am race. Parnelli won the Paul Revere 250 at Daytona at midnight on the morning of the Fourth of July before the Firecracker 400. I went to a couple of those SCCA races; that was about the era that Daryl was in the service and Brenty was in school.

The screw-up on that deal was that we had a weight disadvantage the whole time, even though we had the cars lightened up like crazy and had the Camaros and the Mustangs whipped. Easy! We went into the last race with a two point lead and Fran Hernandez came up with the idea of running motorcycle batteries for less weight. Untested! In those days, when you pitted, the ignition had to be turned off. The car couldn't be running. It was just a goofy SCCA rule. Hell, they used to even make the driver get out. Anyway, we put those sorry, lightweight motorcycle batteries in both Cougars with a two point lead in the standings going into the final race of the season in Kent, Washington. Well, Gurney lost his windshield, which messed him up; then the battery quit and the car wouldn't start when we got it fixed. Then Parnelli came in for a routine pit stop and his car wouldn't restart either. Those lousy batteries in both of the Cougars quit. So we ended up losing the 1967 championship by two points. Then they scrubbed the Cougar program all together because they didn't want competition for the Mustang program, and Shelby took the thing alone for '68 like he did in '66.

Bud Moore Engineering changed course in 1968 and took a break from the SCCA, going NASCAR all the way, even if it meant spearheading an entirely new series.

Jim Foster got Daddy together with Bill France, Sr., who was interested in a NASCAR Trans Am–type program to run on short tracks. He wanted to create a pony car championship, and we had all those Cougars. NASCAR called their new series the Grand Touring, or GT, Division. Basically all we did was change the roll cages around a little bit to meet the NASCAR standards and run those leftover 1967 Trans Am Cougars in '68.

Jim Foster had a big hand in getting that GT thing going, and France liked it. It did pretty well for the next few years. In the meantime, we converted either one or two of the '67 Cyclones to 1968 models. There's some controversy about it. I think we had one that was built fresh and the others were conversions from the '67s.

With the Grand National drivers of the week in 1967 being so unsuccessful, Bud Moore settled in on a veteran hard charger: 1963 Daytona 500 winner DeWayne "Tiny" Lund, an Iowan who had long since relocated to his Lake Santee fishing camp in Moncks Corner, South Carolina. For 1968, Tiny was the pony car driver and the stock car pilot and was a proven winner.

Our shop foreman, Ken Myler, came to work in 1966 and had an association with Tiny Lund. Tiny came forward in '68 and said, "I'd like to drive the car." Then NASCAR formed the GT series and Tiny did so well he won the championship.

We had a second car that we put everybody in. A Japanese guy, the top Japanese road racer, Seichi Suzuki, drove it. We had a translator from English to Japanese. Daryl held up the pit board for him with some crazy-looking stuff in Japanese written on it, and the picture was in *National Speed Sport News*. The board was about three times bigger than Daryl. We finished fourth.

That series was really good, and I got to go to a lot of those races. I remember being down at Columbia on the dirt track. I ended up working the scoreboard with my cousin Cecil, who was like a weekend warrior on the pit crew. It was kind of fun to do because I think we ran one and two. There were a lot of dirt tracks, and we also ran Charlotte, Rockingham, and Atlanta. It was pretty successful.

Our biggest competition was a Ross Huggins Mustang that they built for Donnie Allison. He gave us a pretty good run for our money. What was ironic was that Warren Prout, who had left us the year before, headed up that deal. Prout was no slouch and had helped build the Comet. They were tough to outrun.

I got to know Donnie a lot better, and we've always been close since. He came to drive our car in '72. Then Smokey Yunick would show up with his Camaro. If it got through inspection — which it usually didn't — Bunkie Blackburn or Paul Goldsmith usually drove it. Smokey's Camaro was fast, but it seems like the starter would always fall off of it or something.

Tiny did a helluva job. He was a short track driver and super good. Back then, they didn't adjust for weight either. I thought it was because we always had so much left side weight. Tiny did double duty, too. We ran him in the Cyclone 13 times and he had a lot of ninths, sixths, and stuff like that. In the Daytona 500 he started fifth and finished ninth. He really fit in.

A funny thing about Daytona: They got down there and found out in practice that the Mercury was aerodynamically about two miles an hour faster than the Torino. Talk about getting hot! Jacques Passino called down there and raised all kinds of hell. How did they get the aerodynamics better on the Mercury than the Torino? It was a big stink. We were unsponsored except for a little help from Ford and finished ninth.

In the World 600 at Charlotte, Tiny was in the lead pack with a good shot to win and pitted. I think we had a screwed-up pit stop, and when he came back out, he was running fourth or something. Well, it started raining, and he got so mad and was so strong, he smashed his fist down on the steering wheel and broke it — the wheel, not his hand. They had to get a steering wheel from one of the Cougars and put it on there, and he had to finish with that little bitty steering wheel. I think there was another rain delay or two, and it was finally red-flagged and Buddy Baker won it. Tiny finished seventh. It was a frigged-up deal.

Driving a baker's dozen races in Bud Moore's Cyclones in 1968, Tiny Lund had three top fives and seven top tens including a season's best third in the Firecracker 400 at Daytona. All in all, it was not bad for a part time Grand National deal.

Gregory remembers a funny incident back in the dirt track days — an incident that explains why his dad and Tiny Lund actually had some bad blood going back to November 10, 1963:

It was at Concord, North Carolina, on the dirt and Tiny and Weatherly were running good that night. I was a little boy and I was there. Tiny spun Weatherly out late, and Daddy picked up a dirt clod and ran out there to the edge of the track and knocked the doggone hell out of the side of Tiny's car. Daddy said, "That might not have been too smart. That son-of-a-gun could have killed me." Jarrett won that night and Weatherly was second in our last race in a Pontiac. Tiny could have killed everybody in the garage area, probably single-handedly. But he never did do anything but joke around.

The lovable giant Tiny Lund drove Bud Moore's Mercury Cyclones in 1968, once breaking the steering wheel with his fist. Tiny won the 1968 Grand Touring championship in a Moore Cougar and chased Gregory on foot (courtesy Bud Moore Engineering Archives).

Ironically, the Textile 250 was the last race Joe Weatherly ever led or completed for Bud Moore and the first race of the deadly 1964 season.

A typical evening before the big speedway race during the summer of '68 found Tiny Lund in classic form.

We had Tiny's Cyclone and the GT car, too. Goldsmith had the pole in the GT race. That was one time they got through inspection with Smokey's car. We were still staying at the Atlanta Motel like when we were kids. We were all out at the swimming pool. Brenty and I were passing the football. I remember going in the room and Tiny and Daddy were talking about the chassis or something. They were drinking that V.O. out of these big cups. It was the drink back then. Momma was in there and nobody was cussing any more than normal or anything. Tiny set his drink down on the floor between his legs. He sat on the end of the bed. Daddy said something about changing the steering box or what would help the car, and Tiny said, "That's right! That's got to be what's wrong with it!" He stomped his foot down on the floor and poured out that whole doggone thing of pure liquor. He didn't kick it over; he just stomped his foot. He'd probably already had a bottle before then; Daddy, too. Momma fussed that the room smelled like liquor the rest of the time. It smelled like V.O. for four rooms over.

Momma always fussed if Daddy drank too much, which was about every time you turned around. Momma was Momma.

Later, we went outside and Tiny said, "Gregory, I bet I can outrun you. Take off." So I took off and that son-of-a-gun caught me. He caught me! He didn't catch me and tackle me, but I was pretty quick in 1968. I had a head start and he caught me. It was hilarious. I had a full head of steam and remember turning around and Tiny's right on me! So he had to be a pretty good athlete. He wasn't big and fat. John Sears was fat and Bill Venturini was fat. Tiny was in pretty good shape. You had to be in pretty good shape to break the steering wheel.

Tiny had a heart of gold and always got along with the crew. Donnie Allison told me that Tiny would pull up beside him before the start of a race and spit water on him, just messing with him. Tiny was doing something all the time.

Tweety Hylton and Cale Yarborough were also staying at the Atlanta Motel when we were there. It had a pretty good pool. Tiny got drunk and kept pushing Cale under the water. Cale finally had to get mad at him. He said, "Tiny, you're about to drown me, no joke!" Old Tiny just laughed and pushed him down again, just playing. I remember seeing that. It was kind of funny, like the Foyt thing with the beer can at Daytona. Tiny was a good fellow and could drive the car — no ifs, ands, or buts about it.

Tiny Lund would have probably driven for us the next year, 1969, but that's when Ford Motor Company approached Daddy about the Mustang program because Shelby got devastated by Mark Donahue and Penske with their Camaro. The Chevrolet small block motor was so much better. Shelby tried to run that tunnel port deal and that didn't work out. Jerry Titus and the Shelby deal just got completely outrun. We would have done a helluva lot better with the Cougars than they did with Mustangs, with our pit crew being so much faster and having Parnelli and those guys. It jump-started getting Bud Moore Engineering back into Trans Am. It was like one of our Cougar drivers, Ed Leslie, said out in Monterrey recently: "I've never seen a situation where you get fired for running too good." Ford didn't want the Cougars to outrun the Mustangs, but now they had to have Bud Moore back.

Every once in a while you catch lightning in a bottle, and Bud Moore did it just after midnight on July 4, 1968, at Daytona in the Paul Revere 250. That was a road course GT race that got the green flag under the lights at midnight on Independence Day morning. For the Moores, it made for a long day.

Lloyd Ruby only raced our car one time and won the Paul Revere. It was unreal! We actually won the pole with a 289. We ran two cars that night and Tiny had one. We were helping fill the field out with Ruby in our second car, and he won. It was like when we ran Swede Savage at Rockingham. We had Tiny and we had Swede Savage. Tiny won, Swede was second, and Paul "Little Bud" Moore in a car we had sold him — painted yellow, with "Barbeque King" on it — ran third. So you had Cougars one-two-three.

We got to see Lloyd out in Monterrey. He couldn't remember if that race was '67 or '68. By then Lloyd was getting up into his 80s. It was at a Ford Motor Company 100th anniversary celebration. Daddy and I went to that, and we rode to the racetrack every day with Parnelli and Lloyd Ruby. Parnelli was still cussing Firestone tires about what happened in '69. He was cussing it like it happened last week.

That 1968 season had a big influence on Brent and me. Daryl was in the Navy. I participated a lot more in the program and spent more time in the shop learning things.

Six • *That First Taste of Racing*

The 24 Hours of Daytona was scheduled for February 2, 1969, with a star-studded field of international drivers and in some cases, rich sportsmen and celebrities. One such notable was L. Gordon Cooper, Mercury 7 and Gemini 5 astronaut, who was the last man to go into space alone. However, on this date, he was scheduled to co-drive a Bud Moore Cougar number 19 with a driver by the name of Charles Buckley. They qualified 25th in a field of 67, just ahead of none other than Sam Posey and Ricardo Rodriquez, but the finishing results were as bad as it gets. The official finishing order put them 67th and last with no laps completed.

Gordon Cooper was under contract with NASA. They had the big headlines in the Daytona paper about Gordon Cooper driving a Bud Moore Cougar in the 24 Hours of Daytona. He had toyed around in a racecar a little bit. I don't think he drove as much as Paul Newman did, but he obviously had the balls. I got to meet him. He practiced and qualified the car and was running pretty good. Then NASA called NASCAR and got Gordon Cooper up there and said, "If you start that race, your contract with NASA is void!" Like he had really been doing something safe going into orbit, being a test pilot, and Mercury astronaut! It's kind of hilarious, really. You can get on top of a Titan rocket and you don't know if it is going to blow up or not. But you can't get in a NASCAR racecar, which is the safest one. That would have been interesting." But at least the publicity helped to draw people. Gordon Cooper wanting to race was big news. Momma's got it in her scrapbook.

By 1969, Bud Moore Engineering was out of the Grand National business and was a full scale SCCA Trans Am road racing organization again. With high-powered Ford Mustangs and world famous road racers, the most frequent view the competition ever saw of a Bud Moore Mustang was the taillights. Excellence was the standard, and victory was expected as always.

At the end of '68 we sold all the cars and three of the motors and a bunch of stuff to Tom Pistone. He put '69 sheet metal on them and there really wasn't any difference except on the side. Tiny and Tom ran real well with them, too. Tiny would have been our driver in '69, but Ford hired Parnelli and George Follmer. Follmer had done real well with the AMC deal. Winning that NASCAR GT series as handily as we did in '68 was one of the reasons we got the SCCA Trans Am deal back in '69. In fact, there was better competition in '68 in NASCAR GT than the Mustang program faced with Shelby in SCCA. So when Shelby didn't get canned, they just formed two teams. We did all the winning until the Firestone tires started tearing up. Parnelli still cusses that.

We were supposed to have won the championship in '69. We were up in St. Jovite, Canada, and Follmer had the pole. It was a helluva good road course. On the first lap, he lost the engine. Then all the Ford teams came roaring down through there, hit the oil, and it wiped all the Fords slap out. That's exactly the same weekend NASCAR had the tire problem and boycott at Talladega. I've always told Daddy, "It was a bad day for NASCAR and a *damn* bad day for Bud Moore Engineering, but we weren't in on the Talladega tire controversy." We dodged that and I'm glad we did because that was a bad situation.

The St. Jovite trip was pretty neat. The people were bilingual because it was in Quebec. The track was more French-speaking than English-speaking. They had a walkover that went across the top of the track that was a little ahead of its time. Daddy and Brenty got to noticing that everybody kept looking up. There were these gals walking across that bridge and some of them didn't have on any drawers. They had on dresses and you got a pretty good free shot on some of them. That intrigued me a little bit, too, as an 11-year-old.

Gregory was not just playing in the shop anymore. A more accurate description would be experimenting. With bicycle tracks, football, and rock and roll getting increasingly smaller in his rear view mirror, Gregory found a home at 400 North Fairview and never looked back again. Gregory Moore was becoming a racer.

A factory deal back then wasn't but a few thousand dollars a race in parts. They gave us the cars, the parts, the blocks, and a bunch of engineers in the way. Ford engineer Lee Morse was in charge of the induction system, but the guy that really got me tuned in had come to the shop in 1969. His name was Denny Woo. He was the air flow guru and showed me how to work the flow bench stuff and I became fascinated with it. So to keep me out of the way, he let me take pieces of blown cylinder heads and play on the flow bench with clay and bondo and stuff. I really got inspired. I've actually got some drawings of designs I made when I was 12 years old and we incorporated some of it.

We had already had the flow bench a few months. A flow bench is a thing with an electric motor in it that sucks air like crazy, and monometers to check pressure. What you do is flow air through the intake port and exhaust port in the cylinder head to see how much air is going through it. Nobody much liked fooling with that stuff, because hand-grinding a cylinder back then was something that you threw off on somebody. Later on it turned into about a third of the whole equation. That's where I came in. For a while they called me "Mr. Flow." I knew every cylinder head guy from pro stock racing to NASCAR. I'd get this or that one to do stuff for me, and I'd also do my own stuff.

What I got to do was on the intake side because it didn't get so hot. I got my hands on some epoxy resin that came out of Heveron, N.J., called Crown Plastic Mastic. It was a two-part epoxy. You could put it in the intake port of the manifold and it would stay in there. It wouldn't come out. You couldn't put it on the exhaust side. It would get too hot. As for the intake runners and the ports of the manifold, all my stuff had epoxies in it. Later on we used a combination of J. B. Weld and something else. To hold it, we would drill a couple of set screws through the bottom of the intake runner and that would hold it in case the stuff came loose. This was way before the aluminum cylinder head came in. They had high ports with raised exhaust ports because they had to dodge the upper control arm and had a lousy exhaust port. So we started milling the whole doggone thing. We machined the entire exhaust port off and raised it an inch and a half to get a straight shot. Bill Gazaway let us do it initially when we got back to NASCAR in 1972. It was called a high port.

We just carried that stuff even further. I got plum ridiculous. I had it to where I would flow the headers with a cone design. A guy named Jim Fueling got a bunch of publicity for it, but I already had it. I called it an exhaust port tongue that extended a little into the header at the floor. Never dynoed it; it was just an experimentation.

We were the first ones to ever run step headers. That's where you had a pipe come out about an inch and seven-eighths and go into a bigger pipe. It wasn't like a megaphone; the header was actually staged. We got to the point where we were running three-stage headers. That was some of the technology we used in the late 70s.

I worked the flow bench, ran the dyno, and cleaned parts. Even in later years everybody got dirty. Ford got mad at me one day when they called the shop. They said, "What the Hell took you so long to answer the phone? It's getting to where it takes you awhile to get to the phone." I said, "Hell, man, we're busy! I was back there washing parts." The guy said, "You wash parts?" I said, "Yeah, what's the big deal?" I caught overflow gas on the pit crew for a long time, scored, and hauled the gas. Later on, Davey Allison used to help me haul when Bobby was driving just because he wanted to. I did technical articles, too. We had a big argument about high swirl technology in the cylinder head back in the mid–1980's. By the time racing started seriously for me, I had already swept the floors and spent time down there working wherever at the shop with the Trans-Am Mustangs and the 1972 Fords when we came back to NASCAR.

> *Gregory was doing fine at 400 North Fairview, but he was not allowed to go to the track with his dad until the time was right. That happened to be as Trans-Am racing wound down for Bud Moore Engineering and Winston Cup stockers roared back to life. Gregory was an eyewitness to the transition.*

Momma would not let me go to the race track with Daddy until I was about 12 years old. In '69 and '70 I was playing on that football team that was doing so well. We went to Brainerd, Minnesota, on a family vacation and won the race. We went to Watkins Glen and Momma went, too. All this stuff was in the summertime and we didn't run but about 12 races all that year. I got to go to three or four. Then in 1971, Daddy ran the short season with the Trans Am guys. We were leading the points and went to Edmonton, Alberta, and Donahue beat us. We ran second. Ford wasn't spending a nickel, and the promoters were supposed to pay Daddy about $2,000 or $3,000 to show up. Two races previous to that race, the guys quit paying us. So all we had was a sponsor that our driver Peter Gregg had found: S and S Jacobs, a construction outfit out of Florida. We put it on both cars.

Gregory at 15 years old. As he grew from boy to man, he found his place at Bud Moore Engineering, helping to make the transition that allowed the small-block Mustang engine to power their NASCAR return with the Ford Torino (courtesy Bud Moore Engineering Archives).

Parnelli ran the first race at Michigan — or wherever they ran the first race — and sat on the pole. It rained, and he spun off the course and wrecked on the first lap. He got pissed off at the SCCA because they wanted to charge his wife $10 to get a pit pass. So Parnelli gave them the $10 after he had already done two days of legwork promoting the race. He got mad and didn't want to run any more; plus he knew Ford was pulling out, and he had his Indy stuff going on.

In '71, we about won the championship anyway, and we didn't even run the last four races. So on July 4, 1971, Momma, Daddy, and I went down to Daytona by ourselves, and Daddy sat down and met with France Sr. That's when he talked to France Sr. about coming back in with the yellow car in '72, but we didn't know it was going to be yellow then. We were going to bring in a six-liter, 366 cubic inch engine and help NASCAR convert from the factory days to the new days and use the small-block motors. They always went by liters; five-liters were 305 cubic inches, six-liters were 366 cubic inches, and seven-liters were 427 cubic inches. You see, Dieringer's 1966 Comet had a 396 cubic inch engine, but it had a weight break. If you only ran six and a half liters you could take out 200 pounds of weight. What we did was destroke the engine and take the lead out, and that's what made it drive so well. Anyway, France Sr. said, "Look, Bud, if you're going to come in, you do anything you want and we'll help you all we can with a race for race sponsorship."

Before leaving the Trans Am Series, a Greg experienced watershed moment in the summer of 1969 during a family vacation up north.

The Trans Am thing was fascinating. You had the best road racers in the world. There was Mark Donahue, Parnelli Jones, George Follmer, Peter Revson, Peter Gregg, Dan Gurney, Swede Savage, all those great ones.

One thing that made a very big impression on me when I was 12 years old was up there at Brainerd, Minnesota, in July of 1969. I was only nine going into Victory Lane at Darlington, so this is three years later and I remember it better. We won two of the first four races that year and had trouble with the Firestone tires at the ones we didn't win. We had tested up there and were in real good shape. Well, Parnelli won the race. I remember it for several reasons. First of all, Minnesota is the Land of a Thousand Lakes. The water was crystal clear. The whole family was up there at a resort on some lake near Brainerd. They had these mayflies in July and they would get all over the screen doors and stuff. You'd get a fishing pole and you didn't have to buy bait. All you did was take one of those flies and put it on the line, throw it in there, and pull up a bream about a foot long or whatever. It was a neat trip.

Well, Follmer sat on the pole for the race. Parnelli had missed a day of practice because of a commitment with the open wheel cars, but he won the race pretty easily. That was the first time I ever got to go to Victory Lane where they had a podium-type finish. Horst Kwech won the under two liter class, and he got a trophy. You got the first, second, and third place finishers up on stage, very similar to what you see in Formula One now. It was so cool, and the thing was that they gave you these sterling silver cups. We don't have them because the drivers got them. But they got these cups; the winner had a wreath around his neck and a bottle of champagne, and he was pouring the champagne into this silver cup. The team was passing it around and drinking it. I got to get in on that. Daddy handed it to me and said, "Boy, you can have a little bit." Buck Sewell and all of them were real happy and passing it around. It was like a fairy tale. I was old enough now for it to really impress me. I'd got a dose of it since the time I was born and I got a real good dose of it when I was nine with Dieringer, but here I was three years later, drinking champagne out of a sterling silver cup with Parnelli Jones after winning the race beating Mark Donahue and Peter Revson and all these great road racers. We were on top of the world in road racing. That's something that's reinforcing my interest, telling me that this really is something I want to do. And this was right in the middle of when we were doing real well in the football thing. I was playing halfback and George Mahaffey was on the team, and we won every game and weren't even scored on. I was surrounded by a winning atmosphere. I saw the champagne thing years later as a grown man, but Daddy used to just shake it up and try to hit Bill Broderick, the Hat Man for Union 76, and knock his hairdo off.

Look, road racing and podium-style Victory Lanes to me have a bigger impact than putting a thing up there so nobody can sit on top of the car and shaking out Pepsi Colas. That sucks. When I'm in charge, we're going to have podium finishes and kiss beauty queens like Buck Baker and David Pearson did. Hell, Buck Baker would marry them later. He did! And we're going to wave two checkered flags like at Indy. But back then in Trans Am, the competition was so tough, you got recognized if you finished second and third. The first place guy is the one with the big cup, and that's the one we're going to drink the booze out of. The second place guy's got a trophy he holds up and the third place guy's got one and gets his picture taken, too. Formula One does that great. It's exciting. Look at Indianapolis. They got the milk the winner drinks. That milk outfit's been doing that since 1933. That is so superior to a bunch of guys throwing Gatorade or something.

A lot of people have complained about the NASCAR Victory Lane. It's too ... sissy or something. They need to man it up a lot. At the height of Trans Am, they did it the best. The glory years of Trans Am were from 1966 to 1971. It was so big-time back then. The bottom line was that it reinforced racing for me. The crews got skinned knuckles and they got dirty. Parnelli got out of the car — and back then they wore goggles — and he's covered with dirt and grime. They were all men. Really tough men just like Daddy and Big Smoke, guys that fought in World War Two. It's not like today when they get out clean as a daisy with those full-faced helmets and gloves. But don't get me wrong about that.

Anyway, everybody's just so happy, and you got Fran Hernandez and Jacques Passino and all the big wheels from Ford up there. Nothing could ever compare to me going into Victory Lane with Dieringer in the Southern 500 and getting out of the car and there's 80,000 people pulling for us, screaming and happy. And nothing will ever compare to winning the Daytona 500 in a lot of ways. But it's hard to compare being in Victory Lane with Parnelli Jones with the podium-type finish, drinking champagne out of a silver cup with the powers-that-be from Ford right there with the first, second, and third place guys. I wasn't even old enough to drink, but people didn't pay any attention to that stuff back then. And all these mechanics had worked their tails off, and we had beat Roger Penske, Carroll Shelby, Dan Gurney, and got one of the greatest race drivers in the world on our team. Compare that to going into Victory Lane with Benny Parsons after winning the Nashville 420. Don't get me wrong, because every win we had was good. Even that was great because of what happened later that night with a beautiful photographer. A lot of Victory Lane situations wound up with me in the company of some young lady. But Nashville didn't have the impact of winning Talladega or Darlington with Earnhardt. I can remember winning several races with Ricky Rudd or Bobby Allison that just seemed so routine. Just another routine win. Anyway, winning at Brainerd in that super competitive atmosphere with all those great drivers and cars, and being right in the middle of it, has a special place in my heart and mind. It still means everything to me because those Trans Am days will never come back. That might have been the greatest series ever.

For the record, the Trans Am race of which Greg speaks so fondly took place on July 6, 1969, at Donnybrooke International Speedway in Brainerd, Minnesota. That podium ceremony hosted Parnelli Jones finishing first in the family Mustang, Ronnie Bucknum as runner-up in the second Penske Camaro, and Peter Revson third in Carroll Shelby's Mustang. Greg reports that the under two liter winner was Horst Kwech. However, Internet records indicate either Peter Gregg or Bert Everette in a Porsche taking that honor. Greg was there, so it must have been Kwech.

Bud Moore Engineering was rebuilding its stock car program in 1972 in what was now known as the Winston Cup. Bud and Greg took their extensive small-block Mustang motor experience and adapted it to a much heavier, longer, and wider Torino for almost exclusively oval racing. The transition was agonizing, but the engine was developed on the fly.

The big motors they were trying to phase out were where Daddy fell right in place with the small-block Ford from the Trans Am, the 351. A 426 or 427 is seven liters. A 366 is six liters. A 305 is five liters. You run unrestricted if you run 366. But you were still kind of restricted. You couldn't run two four-barrels. You couldn't run fuel injection. They wanted to phase the big motors out and wanted to phase in the six liter engine. When they took the plates completely away from the big motors, they made them illegal. If you took a 429 motor that came from Holman-Moody with a restrictor plate on it, it made 468 horse power the way it was supposed to be fixed. If you took one of our 351s out of the box and souped it up like a 302, it made 520 horsepower and 500 rpms more. We couldn't figure out why the equation wasn't quite working. When they restricted the air on the big motor, it was to kill the horsepower, just like the plate. The big motors in '71 until '74, you could run, but they had to have a restrictor plate. If you ran a 366 cubic inches or under, you ran unrestricted, with a single four-barrel carburetor and a 1¹¹⁄₁₆ inch throttle body, the standard throttle body for a Holley carburetor. That was the key. The restrictor plate was gone until they reintroduced it when Bobby Allison about went in the stands at Talladega in 1987.

> *Bud Moore Engineering fielded an unsponsored, school-bus-yellow Ford Torino number 15 in ten races with outstanding drivers David Pearson, Donnie Allison, LeeRoy Yarbrough, and Dick Brooks. As they laid the groundwork for the future of stock car racing, engine woes plagued the team all year and they missed the biggest race of the season.*

In 1972, with David Pearson driving, we went down to Daytona for the 500. I did not make that trip because there wasn't any sense in it. We got down there and Pearson was one of the faster cars, but we started splitting cylinder walls in the motors. What we had done was take a 351 stock block and bore it 80 over to make it six liters to 366. Well, the block wouldn't stand it. It split the cylinder walls. We had another motor down there that we had only bored 30 over and it was a thin wall block. We thought there was enough material there. We put that one in and Pearson ran really quickly, but it didn't make it either. It split the cylinder wall. Daddy flew back to the shop on an airplane. I remember being in the dyno room with Daryl and everybody was looking over the motor and left it just a standard four-inch bore. We carried it down there, and it was running good until halfway down the backstretch on the second lap and that son-of-a-gun blew a cylinder wall. We knew we had a block problem. There was no Daytona 500 for Pearson and the Moores.

We sat out three or four races and came to find out Ford had made for the drag racing program a limited number of what we call a Siamese square-bore block. Plus it had high nickel content in it. We got our hands on four of them. That's all that were left. Those blocks would stand an 80-over bore. They had thicker walls and higher nickel content. They would still start splitting down the main bearing webbings if you didn't have everything just right, but you could keep the cylinder in it. That's when we took the Mini Plenum manifold we'd run in Trans Am and turned it into the box manifold that we ran all those years in our cars and Donleavy's cars with a single 4500 carburetor on it. It was a two-piece manifold that had a big lid, and it had nine-inch runners in it, which was what you needed for the size of the cylinder head and stuff they ran then. It was a fiberglass piece and Gazaway let us use it because we weren't running for the championship, it was a developmental program, plus we had the high-port heads. The exhaust port on a stock 351 Cleveland head was so messed up compared to a Chevrolet head. The Chevrolet exhaust port just went straight, and the Ford would go out and turn down so it would miss the upper control arms and some of the stuff in the package with the Mustang. We had the exhaust ports milled all the way off with these aluminum plates we had put on it and raised the port an inch and a half. This box manifold on it lived at Atlanta and finished fourth with David Pearson driving. Then Donnie Allison drove it six races and we ran in the top ten everywhere we went until something happened.

The best run we had going with him was Darlington at the Southern 500. We qualified eleventh, but we had the race set up and Daddy and Banjo Matthews changed some stuff around in the front end. I was down there with the pit crew, hanging out and helping. We had one of the fastest cars in Happy Hour. Well, when they dropped the green flag, Donnie moved up about three or four spots. Pearson had moved over to the ride with the Wood Brothers and had to come from the rear. About the time Pearson got to Donnie, Donnie gave him room. There was this slow car, number 03 driven by Tommy Gale, that kept drifting high where Donnie wanted to pass him and he couldn't get around. If he could have got around that car, he could have gone on. He was getting held up and he started around him, and then the 03 drifted up and wrecked him. He just about cleared him and the guy knocks us out. Like Donnie said, "We had the car on used tires to beat that day." To this day he says that was one of the sickest he ever was.

In the '72 Southern 500, the car was right. I think Donnie took a job driving one of Bobby's sportsman cars after that, and we went to Rockingham with Dick Brooks. We qualified seventh, the car ran good, and we led the race, but the car broke a valve spring. That was the only time Dick Brooks drove for us and did a real good job. That was the last time we ran that car in 1972.

During the off season between 1972 and 1973, the 15-year-old known at 400 North Fairview as Mr. Flow was delving into technological experimentation with Ford engineers three times his age. A word of caution: Gregory gets technical.

Lee Morse went through Ford and fooled with Mose Nolan and worked with Buddy Bar, who did a lot of manifold casting on the west coast. He cast those things up to where we could set them. This was at the end of '72 and Brooks actually tested it. We got the first piece from Buddy Bar and tested it at Charlotte at the end of the season. It was the best fiberglass job we had with the lid and all that stuff on it because it was a two-piece manifold to the production model that was actually aluminum and was sellable. Sure enough, it was as good. Dick Brooks ran pretty well with it. We were mainly just testing the manifold. We got a good enough baseline. As a matter of fact, Brooks said the cast one felt a little bit better up off the corner. The reason it did was because the runners in it were a little bit smaller. He said the cast one had a better pop. The lap times were identical. He said when he got on the gas, the cast piece felt a little bit better, but we attributed that to the fact that the internals of the manifold were more consistent.

The whole key to that deal was to have a nine-inch runner. You put a 4500 carburetor on it and it had a lid. People made box manifolds, but the whole idea with the Ford cylinder heads was that the ports were so big that for the 351 on paper, you wanted an 8 1/2 inch to 9 inch runner length. What they did, they had runners and had the openings on the opposite sides. It was kind of copied after the Mini Plenum. It was a big old box and you set the lid on top of it. Instead of the ports running like a scorpion in the intake manifold, they were laid to get the length of the runners. That thing with that 4500 carburetor would make an ungodly amount of torque. That was the staple manifold. The Wood Brothers ran it. Everybody ran it. We ran that manifold until it was made illegal in '83 because it was two-piece. By that time, Edelbrock had come up with some pieces and Ford had made a single plane-type manifold that was a little bit better. What killed it was that NASCAR outlawed the 4500 carburetor. You had to run the regular 830 series, and when you put the smaller carburetor on it, it didn't work as well as with the big 4500 because they screwed the distribution up too much. That was one thing we spent a lot of time on in the shop, getting the distribution straight in that manifold. We started running the cast pieces in '73, and being that it was aluminum, you could grind on it and weld on it. One of the first things we did was straighten the front runner out. That was good for ten horsepower, but we had to offset the distributor because it had an indentation. Chevrolet had the distributor in the back and Ford had it in the front. We just went through all kinds of growing pains with that thing. The trick to make that manifold work that Bud Moore called 'The Maxi-Box' was the manifold lid itself. That was the top part that bolted down with all the little bolts around it. The work that you did up underneath the opening for the carburetor set was dead critical. You had to put in a divider and distribution tabs, which were little flaps and stuff that were pointing the fuel different ways. It was really crazy looking.

Obviously, Gregory Clyde Moore had moved to another plane, both intellectually and in his ability to contribute to Bud Moore Engineering. He was on the verge of manhood on multiple fronts and life-changing decisions were just around the bend. The Baby was a boy no more.

CHAPTER SEVEN

Back in NASCAR and Seriously Involved

In 1973, corporate dollars began to flow into the handsome brick building emblazoned with "Bud Moore Engineering" with the arrival of sponsorship from an engine oil additive company competing with STP. Gone were the oddly beautiful and unsponsored yellow Torinos tenaciously driven by committee. In came the gaudy, gorgeous white, blue, and orange-trimmed Torinos of Sta-Power Engine Conditioners in the hands of the 1970 Grand National Champion.

I started working basically half-time, full-time, and drawing a paycheck in late '72 or the start of '73. We were going to run all the races, which we did, and signed with Bobby Isaac. Sta-Power was supposed to give us something like $180,000, and Petty was getting some ungodly number like $250,000 from STP.

In the Daytona 500 we ran second to Richard Petty. It was a pumped-up deal, a big shot in the arm. This was going to work. Then there was a situation where guys were cheating with restrictor plates and some of the numbers didn't add up on the horsepower thing. If everything had been on an even keel, we should have run better than we did, especially with Isaac driving it. Isaac was super neat. We went to Atlanta, led the race, and Isaac just lost it and finished second. We were running at the front at Darlington in the spring race and broke a connecting rod. That amazed us, because that particular set of rods was the last of what we called the Trans Am rods. It was for the 351 rod length. They were better than the other parts we were running and were the last new set we had. We thought it was a bullet-proof piece because we'd used it so much. We ran them two or three races and this was a brand new set, the last that was made by Ford Motor Company. Ducky Newman and Daryl were scratching their heads saying, "Of all things, why in the hell did it break one of those Trans Am rods when we're getting away running the lighter weight smaller deal?" That was a big disappointment to Isaac. I was at that race and he got disheartened at that. You can see him sitting there on the film with his arms crossed. That was one of a lot of things that happens in racing that wasn't supposed to happen, but it did. How many times was Lloyd Ruby supposed to win Indy and never did? We had some good runs with Isaac with a fourth at Richmond, third at Martinsville, seventh at Nashville, and fourth in the 600 at Charlotte. We didn't win any poles, but usually started in the top five or so.

Tragedy on the speedway once again directly affected Bud Moore Engineering. In what has become a legendary event in auto racing lore, it happened on August 12, 1973.

We got down to Talladega, and that's where they had the bad wreck with Larry Smith. We practiced and qualified over 190, started fourth, and the car was running good. Fairly early in the race, Larry Smith blew a tire and hit the wall. The inertia reel stripped at the back of his shoulder harness. They used to have a lever where the driver could release the pressure on his shoulder harness to move around some, then lock it back in place. Well, the impact stripped the teeth out of that inertia reel that locked the belts in place, and his head hit the roll bar running across in front of his head. He had taken the padding out of the front of his helmet because he had had trouble with headaches from an injury in a modified car where he had cracked his skull. So it threw him into the roll bar and when they got him out of the car, there was blood running down his face when they put him on the stretcher. Pearson said he remembered this, too. When they went by under caution, Isaac was running fourth. You could tell Smith was dead. He was lying there on the stretcher and the drivers saw it. Before they restarted the race, Banjo was on the radio talking to Isaac and Isaac said, "Don't say nothing to Bud, but I'm getting out of this thing. Something's telling me to get out of this thing." He never said what it was. He never owned up to it. We're convinced it had to do with him seeing Larry Smith's crash and seeing him lying there on the stretcher. He was under contract with us and Sta-Power, and we let him walk out of it. So that's when we decided who we were going to put in it to finish the race. Coo Coo Marlin drove it and brought it right back up to the front. But the front end had been damaged and it was moving around on him a little bit. He could still draft and Coo Coo did a helluva job. He ran real well at the big tracks anyway. He won a qualifying race at Daytona in 1972. But we still finished thirteenth that day Smith got killed, with a relief driver.

Under the gun to get a driver, Bud Moore took a chance with rising star Darrell Waltrip. By the same token, Waltrip left his own Terminal Transport Mercury team wrenched by veteran Suitcase Jake Elder to sit in a top-notch seat for the first time. He was also in a heated battle with Lenny Pond for Winston Cup Rookie of the Year.

We put Darrell Waltrip in it for the last five races. I went to almost all the races that year, and Waltrip qualified no worse than eighth everywhere we went. In the first race at Darlington in the Southern 500, Waltrip qualified fourth. We spun out two or three times and still finished eighth. His butt was burning. Daddy cooled him off— he hosed him down sitting in the car. Daddy revived him with the hose. We had all kinds of problems and Darrell said it was a miracle we did finish that high.

Next we went to Richmond, which was a half-mile paved track back then, and had the wreck with Baxter Price when all those cars burned up. Bobby Allison was on the pole and we were outside. The race had just started and they were running down the backstretch side by side. Baxter Price was out there in his usual piece of crap, running real slow, and spun out. Everybody was racing back to the caution flag, and Daddy radioed Waltrip not to come flying through there because the track was blocked on the front straightaway. So Bobby dove into the pits and Darrell stayed out on the race track and piled right into them. The cars caught on fire, but the flames hadn't reached our car yet. Daddy told him to go back and get the radio out of the car. Even if the car was burning up, Daddy wanted that radio back. Back then they were just taped to the roll bar or something, not the sophisticated equipment they have today. That was a nine-car crash on lap four triggered by Baxter Price, who started last and finished last. They stopped the race for an hour.

Another time, we were up there at Charlotte running a strong third or fourth and crashed. They had made Charlie Glotzbach start in the back because they had caught him with a cheater carburetor plate. He came to the front. About the time Glotzbach got there, we were about a hundred yards behind him and Glotzbach wrecked on the front straightaway. The track was partially blocked, but there was plenty of room to get around and Waltrip ran into the wreck. The wreck took place on lap 46 and also took out the leader and pole-sitter David Pearson. Darrell wrecked sometimes and the car let him down sometimes.

Darrell had second thoughts about leaving his own team for Bud Moore. The feeling might have been mutual.

Darrell Waltrip was a good guy. I got to interface with him some then, but not a lot. I wasn't on the radio with him. I got to know him and his wife, Stevie, and we knew he was the best young guy coming up. All you had to do was ask him. But he was!

The nail in the coffin on that deal was that Sta-Power did not pay the last of their sponsorship money which was $80,000. That was a ton of money back then. So Daddy ran the last four or five races out of his own pocket. At the end of 1973, we had fully intended to run '74 with Darrell even though he got pissed and said we lost Rookie of the Year for him to Lenny Pond. Even though there was some friction there, that wasn't the problem. The problem was Sta-Power didn't fulfill their contract. Sta-Power was one of those hit and run sponsors. They got into trouble with pyramid selling because they wanted to compete with STP by selling it like Amway. They had enough money to honor $90,000 to $100,000 of the contract, but not the last $80,000. So Daddy went ahead and finished out the season. I don't think we got any money out of Sta-Power the whole time Darrell drove the car. So they gave the rookie thing to Lenny Pond and not Darrell, and it hurt him. He felt like he would have won it if he had stayed in his own car with Jake Elder.

The off season before 1974 found the Moores seeking sponsorship dollars and wanting to keep Darrell Waltrip racing at 400 North Fairview. It was a daunting task. Hard decisions had to be made, and Gregory was old enough to have more than a casual interest.

We liked Waltrip. Daddy was a little bit hard on him like he was with all the drivers, hollering on the radio and that kind of stuff. Waltrip's biggest beef was that he wanted to drive the car in '74 and didn't get to because we needed a sponsor. George Follmer had Royal Crown Cola and was fooling with the SCCA Can-AM division. The Can-Am division was getting ready to fold up, so RC had some money and wanted to take a look at NASCAR. George had won for us in the Trans-Am Mustangs and had his marketing guy contact our PR guy. RC had good money, which was probably $50,000 more than Sta-Power if they'd have paid all of it. So that's why Darrell didn't get to drive the car. He understands it now. We even tried to get the RC people to accept Darrell Waltrip, but they wanted George Follmer because he had won the Can-Am races. So Darrell and Jake ran their own car in '74, and in '75 Darrell got in the car with Digard with David Ifft. I was right there in the mix of all that.

A hard decision was made concerning Darrell Waltrip, and a soft drink name was plastered across the panels of the white Bud Moore Torino. Now they needed to win races with a road course sports car driver running mostly on southern ovals unfamiliar to him.

So we put George Follmer in the number 15 sponsored by Royal Crown Cola for 1974. We got down to Daytona and ran second in the 125 mile qualifying race, got in the 500, and wrecked when the windshield came out of it. We weren't running all that well and finished twentieth. We had some good runs and led a lot of Talladega in the spring after starting third. Pearson in the Wood Brothers Mercury was on the pole, Bettenhausen was second in Penske's Matador, we were third, and Dan Daughtry fourth. That was by far George's best race for us. Three guys dominated that day: Pearson, Bettenhausen, and Follmer. We all pitted after halfway and I was working on the crew catching overflow gas. Don Miller was doing the same thing I was doing on Penske's car two stalls away. Grant Adcox was a rookie, comes in hot, and slides into the back of Bettenhausen. Don Miller lost his leg. Don's a helluva nice guy. He was general manager for Penske for years. In the end, Follmer led a solid 26 laps, blew, and Pearson won. That was a Talladega thing. Another horrible accident.

RC Cola was getting antsy about not winning, and economics quickly entered the picture. It also became apparent that maybe the road course sports car ace from California was not going to make a good enough oval racer to compete with the established southern stock car stars.

We knew we were in trouble in Atlanta when George went up to Pearson and asked him, "Where do you start putting on the brakes?" Back then at Atlanta you didn't use any frigging brakes. "You don't use brakes down here, man," David told him. We knew right then we were in pretty bad trouble. Then RC got into trouble because of a conflict in Cuba or something and the price of sugar was going to double. So Kent Keesler at RC told us that the car was going to have to do real, real well or they weren't coming back. We had to win a race or the price of sugar was going to cut into their advertising budget. Well, Buddy Baker was fooling with Harry Hyde in that '71 K and K Insurance Dodge Charger, and they were trying to run a hemi with a little old restrictor plate on it. Baker had seen how fast our car was down the straightaway at Atlanta and wanted to drive it. Buddy would mash the throttle. We put two and two together and made one of the toughest decisions we ever had to make. They even had these ads out for RC and our team saying, "Let George do it!" George really did a pretty good job, but maybe George couldn't do it. So basically we kicked George out of the car and put Baker in it. We hated to do it. I love George to death. He ran out of a set of brakes in Nashville in about 15 laps. We canned Follmer trying to keep the sponsor.

When we put Baker in it, the car went to running up front. We won poles, but we still had problems with the car breaking. What really was the pisser was when we got up there to Bristol with him and Cale. Cale spun him out coming off of four leading the race on the last lap and we didn't win. If we had won that race, RC might have come back. We really had some great runs with Baker at the end of '74 in the last half of the races. He was in the top five qualifiers all but once, with a couple of poles at Pocono and Dover, and he took ten top tens with four second place finishes.

One of the weirdest things that ever happened to us or anybody in NASCAR was in the summer race at Talladega. That was when we had rocks put in the rear end that clogged the cooler and made it burn up. That's the reason we didn't win Talladega in 1974. It was a mass sabotage of about 20 cars the night before the race. The rumor was that the relatives of these disgruntled competitors were mad over an intake manifold that was legal one year and wasn't legal the next. They found Speedy Dry in gas tanks and everybody just started checking everything. They cut lines. Now how in the hell were we going to know to check the rear end to see if it had rocks in it? We checked the fuel cell and went over the car with a fine-toothed comb. I think the only thing we didn't check was to pull the gear out. We knew it was from there because Talladega had those little old tiny granite-looking rocks in the garage area lying around.

We lost the rear end with just a few laps to go and lost the race. It cooked! Baker kept noticing that he smelled something, but he was still flying! We took the rear end out and there were rocks in the oil line where it goes to the cooler. The rocks weren't enough to tear that nine-inch Ford rear end up. But it was enough to stop the cooler up and it took almost the whole race to do it. It definitely wasn't doing it any good. We were probably the only ones that the saboteurs successfully hit. We also happened to be the runningest son-of-a-bitch down there that day.

Nobody has ever submitted any proof as to who sabotaged the cars. There are theories, and I'm not even sure they are fair. It almost had to be an inside job. We don't know. I was down there and it was disheartening. I couldn't believe it. We got back to the shop and Morris Cody pulled the rear end out and you could tell it was the rocks from the garage area. We poured out about four Dixie cups full of this real small gravel.

Morris worked with us until he passed away. He had prostate cancer and didn't want to go through the chemo. He loved racing.

On August 11, 1974, Buddy Baker started sixth and led 98 of 188 laps, finishing three laps behind not running at the finish in fifth place.
Other than the sabotage, something else took place that weekend when Greg's football career came back to haunt him.

Down there at Talladega they sent me to the truck to get a rear end. Well, sitting up there in the truck at an angle was a nine-inch Ford rear end. I had done it a thousand times. I'd put it in a buggy and roll it over to the car. So I went to pick the thing up and my back went out and *boom*, I hit the floor. Well, Cale was walking by and he saw me and came and grabbed me. He helped me out of the truck. Daddy and the team were over at the car and Cale was driving for Junior then. Cale walked me all the way to the infield care center to Dr. Hardwick, the track doctor. Cale stayed with me a few minutes and Daddy didn't even know anything about it. The doctor took a needle and shot some stuff in my back, and I lay there for about 30 minutes until the pain eased up and I could go. They wouldn't dare do anything like that now. After that deal, I went to see Doctor Bonner, who had gone into radiology. Doctor Bonner was Joe Littlejohn's physician, my physician, Bud Moore's physician, the Clements' physician, and he lived on Maple Street in Spartanburg right there next to where my apartment is now. I thought I hurt it in the ninth grade playing for Evans, or maybe the year before. I thought I had some broken ribs. Daddy was there and told the doctor to let him know what was going on. Doctor Bonner called Daddy and said, "Look, that kid broke his back at some point in time. It wasn't yesterday, but two or three years ago he broke his back." I knew it wasn't Shoolbred in The Wreck. That was my head he ran over. That's where I suffered the brain damage. That's the wandering eye I've got. But I ground cylinder heads. I lifted stuff. Daryl and I lifted engine blocks. I never let my back slow me up doing anything.

Another angle of running a racing team was more important that one might think.

Buster Bell of Bell Dry Cleaners loved us with all those damn drivers' suits and crews' uniforms. Plus Buster used Sanitone. We found out early on that the dry cleaner you used needed to be a pretty high quality. It was with Buddy Baker that we carried a driver's suit to One Hour Martinizing and got it done real quickly. I don't know if the dry cleaning fluid was stronger or hadn't been changed or what, but it burned parts of his leg where he sweated. So we started using the Sanitone thing at Buster Bell's and never had any of those problems. He was a little pricier, but that's the Bud Moore way of doing things. He wanted it to be the best, just like he wanted the cleanest floor. It was perfection. That was always our trademark.

Buddy Baker was on board full time beginning in 1975 with a hodge-podge of sponsors. There was plenty of speed, poles, front row starts, laps led, and four checkered flags, the most since Billy Wade's four wins in a row in 1964. The faster the venue, the better results for the number 15. The Moores made stockers run, and run fast! But bad luck reared its ugly head right away, on the biggest stage of the year.

It was the Daytona 500, and we had been in the lead off and on all day along with Pearson, Petty, and Foyt. Pretty decent company. Baker had led as much of the race as anybody and was out front when we came up to lap Pearson. We had already pitted, got tires and gas, and were coming up to lap the second place car—and the motor blew! Baker thought it was a timing chain. It spit and it quit. It acted just like a timing chain. He coasted down pit road and the motor was dead. Baker got out of the car and he was as upset as hell. He said, "It snapped the goddamn timing chain." We finished twentieth.

Well, we got back to the shop and Cody's cleaning the car up with a couple of guys. There was a ground wire to the ignition under the dash that shook loose. One of the main deals. When it shook it might have touched once or twice and that made seem like it was spitting and quitting. Just like a timing chain, which was something we'd seen break back then. But Daryl fixed that timing chain problem. So Cody hooked the wire back up and cranked it, and it liked to scared Daddy and them in the shop. He just reached in there and flipped the switch and *brooooom*, it cranked right up. You talk about getting sick. A loose wire and we thought the motor blew with the timing chain? We didn't even think about it because Baker drove enough cars and blew enough motors to know if something was screwed up or not. He was an expert, his foot was so damn heavy.

Bud Moore Engineering was too good for their luck to stay so sour, and they started putting together a fine season. But as good fortune returned in the Moore camp, the fates frowned upon others, especially at Talladega where Gregory and the boys won a thousand miles of races that year.

In 1975 with Baker we had a super year with poles at Rockingham, Bristol, and the spring Talladega race that we also won. But that was bad, too, because that's when Lynda Petty's little brother, Randy Owens, got killed. They even had a trophy named after him. Richard was overheating and was in the pits. They were going to shoot some water in the cooling system. We heard a boom and it threw Owens and the water tank up so high in the air. The water tank had rusted out on the bottom and they didn't have a regulator on the nitrogen tank. It's got about 3,000 pounds of pressure and he threw too much on it. There was a picture of when the tank came down and it just missed Richard Petty. It threw Randy Owens up about as high as a telephone pole, and there were a couple of people under him that tried to break his fall. That's when Daddy made the statement that he wondered if we were ever going to win another race with as much bad luck as we had, with sabotage and wires falling loose under the dash.

We got to be real close with Baker. He even went to Spartan High for a year when Buck and the family lived up the street on Fernwood Drive in the late 1950s and early '60s.

Buck won the 1957 Grand National Championship driving for Daddy, so it figured that Buddy could drive. It was like a family member coming back. We knew Baker had a heavy foot and was a super nice guy.

> *It happens in racing that a special bond forms between racing team members. It takes on the characteristics of a blood-related family. As much as the Bakers were family to the Moores, so were others who had moved on. Such was the case with the gentle giant from Iowa who won many trophies and much glory in Bud Moore equipment. Having had their share of personal tragedy in the mid–1960s, Gregory and the team still had to be the unfortunate witnesses to death from time to time at the speedway. On August 17, 1975, at Talladega, the Grim Reaper came right to their doorstep as a Bud Moore championship driver and close personal friend took his final green flag.*

I had been down there at Speedweeks in '75, and a guy by the name of Terry Link had, to my understanding, bought the leftover GTO stuff from Ray Nichels. He had a purple-looking GTO, and it was good that somebody was out there trying to run a Pontiac, but he was like a Roy Mayne. I'd never heard of him. He was a Daytona fireman and had this goofy looking helmet. Even his helmet looked stupid. I was there and was very familiar with that Pontiac although it had Le Mans sheet metal on it. He didn't have any business being out there. Tiny, who had done so well, was a friend, was running back there, and spun in what should have been just a routine spin-out. Terry Link never cracked the gas and drove right through Tiny's door. We lost Tiny.

Link was about like Jocko Maggiacomo, who ended Bobby Allison's career at Pocono in 1988 in a similar T-bone crash. He didn't know any better. This guy was inexperienced and never ran again after that. I mean, you have to feel about as bad for him as you do Tiny. I'm sure he's sick to this day over it.

Link was hurt, too, and the safety crews didn't do anything to help him. So these two guys jumped over the fence and ran out there. One of them got out his big redneck knife and cut Terry Link's belts to get him out of the car, which was on fire. Otherwise there would have been two dead. And the security came over there and started clubbing on these fans who saved Link's life. The security said, "We got people to do this." It was just the gate guards harassing people.

Seemed like we heard about Tiny during the race, but never said anything to Baker. We didn't want to get the driver upset. Of course Buddy Baker won the race and that took a lot of the wind out of it. It definitely threw a damper on it. They kept it kind of quiet. I remember Brenty cussing. He said, "Goddammit! We win the race. We're starting to run good. Poor old Tiny goes spinning down the backstretch and gets killed." I think that was about the time that NASCAR really took their first real serious look at who was driving, beyond the fact that they had the $500 entry fee. But that was bad.

> *In 1975, Bud Moore Engineering signed on sponsors where they could find them, usually on a race-to-race basis. Lots of one-shot deals adorned the white Torino's fenders.*

We just picked up different sponsors like Coppertone, Army, Holiday Inn, Sunny King Ford, Shoney's, and United Gunite. United Gunite was blue swimming pool stuff, and we won at Atlanta in the fall with them. The guy and his wife were nuts, but they had money. That was the next to last race, and then the last race was Norris Industries. Norris was developing a wheel in the stock cars because of the disc brake situation. You couldn't run disc brakes without air-cooling through the wheel. So Norris developed a wheel with big

Buddy Baker drove the Sunny King Ford to victory in the Talladega 500 on August 17, 1975, but the news of Lund's death was kept from him until afterwards (Perry Wood Racing Collection).

old holes, not the little bitty holes that the other guys came out with. Norris developed that wheel when Hurst-Airheart developed a brake that would work on a 3,800 pound stock car. We got out to Ontario and just outran the hell out of everybody so bad, and the car had Norris on it out there where his business was. So Norris agreed to sponsor the car and ultimately did so in '76, '77, '78, and one race into 1979. We really had a terrific finish to 1975 with back to back wins in the 500s at Atlanta and Ontario totally out-classing the fields both times.

The first full season with Buddy Baker was generally a huge success. They lost the Daytona 500 by a loose wire at the end, always started up front, swept Talladega's two races, and had many other fine runs. The final numbers were four wins, three poles, 12 top fives, 13 top tens, 788 laps led, over $230,000 won, and a somewhat disappointing fifteenth in the Winston Cup point standings. But Baker was coming back, as was funding from Norris Industries. Truthfully, Bud Moore Engineering was approaching the top of its game. In 1976 the Norris Industries Ford number 15 put together a rock-solid seventh place finish in the point standings with the only victory being the normally expected one at Talladega along with two poles, 16 top fives in 30 races, and 1028 laps led. The boys from 400 North Fairview Avenue had a top ten time trial speed almost every time out and were the favorites when it came to the super speedways. There is nothing like hard work to make a race car run.

One particular race that season found 300 hundred miles separating the men at the track and those in the shop trying to find speed. Truth be told, the problem had been identified months earlier.

In 1973 you used to be able to run the cars three years. The '73 Torino, which was still a fastback, turned out to be a better car than the '72 with the big wide-mouth front, and the '73 was blunt and had the bumper that stuck out. Well, we could only run it until

'75. Between '75 and '76, we didn't gain a lot of power. We had changed the ring package around and Mr. Flow had gotten a little bit better with the cylinder heads. It was about ten horsepower better. That wasn't much, but it was a little better.

In '76, Brenty and I knew that they were going to go from the slope-roof fastback and make a notchback. The only thing they did to the grill was put a little bit of a point in it, and that wasn't bad. Everybody's got their expertise, and Brenty sat down and said, "You can figure it any way you want to, but with the dimensions and the way I got it figured, when we go to Talladega, that car with the same horsepower will be at least two and a half to three miles an hour slower." I pretty much agreed with him, and Daddy was like, "Well, I don't think it's going to hurt it that much."

So we loaded up and went down to Talladega. We had won both races there in '75, and this was the first Talladega race of '76 and here we went with a notchback car. I think the notchback qualified fifth and did decent at Daytona, but blew up before halfway in the 500. Now we were down at Talladega, where handling doesn't mean as much.

In '75 with the fastback it was very easy to run and qualify at 190. Baker ran one warm-up lap and got the oil temperatures up and then had his hoof in it. With the other car in '75 he'd warm up at 188.8 until we qualified at like 190. Well, this notchback came by the first damn lap and runs 185.9. This is not in qualifying trim with the front all taped up, but this is what we were stuck running. We warmed up two and a half miles per hour slower with ten more horsepower. I was there and had the stopwatches on it. It did exactly what Brenty said it would do. But NASCAR had made one change. You always had the air cleaner and cowl hook-up with the front of the air cleaner blocked so the radiator air couldn't go straight in. Now NASCAR wanted the air cleaners open all the way around. You didn't have the guard on half the air cleaner. They made us take that off. Instead of having 560 horsepower we had 577. Baker came in and everybody's frustrated. We knew we were going to pick up some when we qualified and stopped the front end up, but we had seen immediately that we weren't going to be as fast as that son-of-a-gun we had in '75 that won both races, because it wasn't a fastback. Baker said it drove good and the little bit of extra horsepower was offset by the aerodynamics. Well, Daddy, Morris Cody, Baker, and I to some degree said it had to be the cowl induction thing. It was screwed up.

We had a motor that Daryl and the others were dynoing at the shop in Spartanburg. It was the second or third motor they built at the shop. The one we had in the car was the best one we thought we could come up with. It was the S31 motor. The folks at the shop had the S25 motor on the dyno, and we'd talked about using it for the race motor. It wasn't done yet, so we were going to qualify with maybe the third-best motor. Hell, you weren't talking about more than three horsepower, but that S25 was the motor that the wire fell off of at Daytona in '75, and we had the two wins at Talladega with it. We knew we had that motor that was getting worked on. It was the block and the crank. We never reused valves or anything, it was just the block. The horsepower is in the block. The S25 never showed any more horsepower. If anything, it showed less!

So Daddy, Morris Cody, Baker, and I sat in a motel room. Cody's got his shoes off and his feet propped up on the bed. They all got 'em a drink of liquor, and I was sitting there, me with a doggone Schlitz. I got a case of free Schlitz off of Trickle or one of the ARCA guys or somebody, and I was sitting there drinking me a free Schlitz. Daddy had already called the shop from the racetrack and told them to get the 25 motor ready because we wanted to bring it down there. "Something's wrong, we're off on speed." Then Daryl made the statement, "Brenty told you that doggone notchback was going to be slower."

Daddy said, "I don't give a damn, we're gonna run the 25 in the race regardless because it's got a proven history." Daryl and them worked and got the motor finished up probably a day quicker.

Back then, I think, we would go in the track on Thursday versus going in on Friday later on. So you had that extra day. Well, Daryl's got the motor together and it was sitting on the dyno. A good number on a heat in the Froude load cell at that time was measured in units. Froude was a guy from England who invented the water brake dyno. Daryl knew how to run the dyno. I wasn't doing but a little bit of dyno work back then. I'm Mr. Flow. So Daddy gets on the phone and tells Daryl, "Don't ya'll go anywhere. Where's that motor now?" "We got it sitting on the dyno." It was Daryl, Billy Burgess, and Jerry Mason. Ducky Newman had just left to go to work for Digard. "Go break the thing in."

We had a break-in procedure that took about 30 minutes. You flashed the valves and did a few things to it, then started doing power runs on it. We sat there talking, and Baker and Daddy and Morris Cody had about three drinks and were disgusted. Something's wrong; we should have warmed up at 187 at least, not 185.8 or whatever it was. Cody and Daddy said it's got to be the cowl. I said, "No. I think that would affect it some, but I think it's got to be in the body." Daryl had made the mistake of telling Daddy over the telephone that they'd dyno the 25 motor, but Brenty had already told him what he calculated and we had seen it with other cars. Daddy said, "I don't want ya'll to leave. I want that son-of-a-bitch power run," and hung the phone up.

We sat around talking about the cowl, what this guy was doing, what Junior had, how somebody warmed up at 188, and we were three miles an hour slower than the fastest guy. Everybody's jaw was dragging the ground. We've got to come up with an answer. We knew Baker was going to hold it to the floor, and he said it drove better. That told me the car was going to be good and tight, getting good air to the spoiler. Baker's got it to the floor and all we could do was knock timing in it, tape the front end up, and we were going to run what we were going to run.

Meanwhile, back at 400 North Fairview Avenue, Daryl and the boys at the shop sweated out the search for speed and the next phone call from Alabama.

Daryl figured the correction factor with the little swing thing. We were using standard SAE correction and were hoping it would pull, observed, 79 units. If it pulled 80, we were all going to have a damn party. Corrected, that was going to be about 590 horsepower. Daddy called Daryl. "What'd it pull?" Daryl said, "Seventy-six units." That wasn't that far off, but it corrected out to be 558 horsepower, not 570. Daddy said, "Oh, Daryl, you figured that correction factor wrong. I want you to go back out there and sling the hygrometer, run the whole thing, and call us back."

So we had another drink. We were still talking about the cowl, and Daddy wanted to know why it didn't pull 78, 79, or 80 units. I don't think we'd ever seen one pull 80 units except in the dead of winter when there's no correction. So Daryl ran it, Daddy called and said, "What did it run?" "Seventy-six units." "Godammit, boy, you aren't doing something right. I know it's supposed to pull more that that. You sure about that?" "Daddy, I'm just reading what the gauge says." "How did you do it? Did you rev it up?" And so on.

So we sat there and had another drink. Then we kind of talked about the notchback and the spoiler. Well, they were still hollering about that cowl and we can do this, do that, and we can still lay the spoiler back. And with Baker, you could lay the spoiler flat! We hadn't done that yet, and we knew that was a little bit of speed.

Daddy called Daryl back. "Did you run the son-of-a-bitch again?" "Yes." "Did you figure that correction right?" "Yes." "What'd it pull?" "Seventy-six units." Daddy got so mad he said, "We figured out it's the cowl. Tell Jerry Mason to put that sick son-of-a-bitch on the truck. I want it down here first thing in the morning." We didn't have time to change the motor. We had to qualify with the one that was in it. Sure enough, we stopped up the front end, laid the spoiler on back a little bit, did all the trick stuff, and knocked a degree of timing in it. Instead of running 190.5, it runs 187.8, which was about twelfth fastest. Now we were even madder.

So here came Jerry Mason pulling up with that sick-ass motor. Daddy said, "Get that sick son-of-a-bitch down off the truck. We're going to try it anyway." Daryl ran that motor five frigging times and it pulled 76 units every time. Daryl said, "If I'd have just told him a lie and said it pulled 77.5, we could have run it the one time, still carried it down there, and I could have been at the Capri Lounge having a beer two hours quicker." We were on the phone with Daryl off and on for four hours, and I drank about half of that case of Schlitz and I know they went through a quart of V. O.

Friday during practice it was a whole new ballgame.

The next day, Baker went out on the track and there were cars doing a little bit of drafting. He started drafting at 192, caught somebody, and blew on by them. It drafted like crazy! He blew by the pole sitter and the top four guys — Marcis, Petty, Donnie Allison,

With an aerodynamically challenged notchback Ford Torino that Bud said "wasn't worth a damn" and had a "sick" engine, Buddy Baker streaked to a world's record 500-mile speed of 169.887 on May 2, 1976, in the Winston 500 at Talladega (Perry Wood Racing Collection).

and Parsons — because he deliberately went out there behind them. He ran one lap and he was leading and pulling away from them. Everybody was happy as hell then.

Well, we went out and ran by ourselves and it was just a tick better, like 188. We tried little tricks with the cowl and it made no difference. Baker got out of the car and said, "We're in good shape. It's going to draft. It's got to be the aerodynamics." He laughed. I said, "That was what I been trying to tell Diddy!" Richard Petty called Lee Petty "Diddy." So by God that's what I said. Baker was *happy*. Lord have mercy, he was happy.

> *No one familiar with the situation at the time could honestly imagine what great things would unfold on May 2, 1976, at the Alabama International Speedway. Bud Moore Engineering only won one race in 1976, but oh, how they did it!*

Daddy had called the motor "a sick son-of-a-bitch" and said, "The car isn't worth a damn." We did see in practice that we might be in pretty good shape, maybe. Baker smiled because he was getting around cars. He could blow by them.

So they dropped the green flag and he passed about ten cars going down the backstretch. On the third lap, he dove to the bottom in the tri-oval, passed the leader, and they never saw us again. All that time we spent sitting in that motel room drinking, trying to brainstorm, and then we broke the world's record for a 500 mile race. Unbelievable! I had never seen Baker come to the front that quick in my life. He was just flying! Baker said the only time he cracked the throttle was to come down pit road. I remember the write-up in *Stock Car Racing Magazine* about the fastest 500 mile race and everything. So we came to the conclusion that that car was down horsepower-wise aerodynamically in a straight line. It turned out that we outran them worse in '76 than we for did both races in '75 at Talladega with that lousy-ass motor in that unaerodynamic car — and it flew!

> *It was a fantastic day. The actual statistics for the race show that Buddy Baker did not get credit for leading a lap until the thirteenth. That does not contradict Greg's recollection because lead changes are only scored at the finish line. Especially at Talladega, there are countless instances of multiple leaders within a lap. But only the driver crossing the stripe gets the credit. Greg is also correct in saying that Baker checked out when he got the lead because he led for 135 of the 188 lap race. Therefore, after he got the lead on lap 13, Buddy Baker led 135 of the last 175 laps of the race at what was then the world's record speed for 500 miles of 169.877. That record held until August 6, 1978, when Lenny Pond won a 500 miler there at over 174. And it all happened in that sick-ass car.*
>
> *In 1977, Buddy Baker topped 1976's fine performance with a sparkling fifth place in the race for the Winston Cup, the highest finish of his career and Bud Moore Engineering's best since Dieringer's third in 1965. That was no small achievement for a lead foot known mostly for flat-out, full-speed-ahead racing, excelling on the super speedways, coping with the mid-size tracks, and hanging on for dear life on the short tracks and road courses. But one thing was sorely lacking. The team went winless in 1977, and unrest found a home on North Fairview Avenue. The Daytona 500 was one of many close calls, with victory within reach again, when something prevented a win.*

Seventy-seven was a real pisser at Daytona because Salt Walther was down there driving and Baker was running real good. Salt Walther was a rich kid and his daddy kept putting him in race cars. Just past halfway, Walther crashed on the backstretch and took Baker and Marcis with him. Baker recovered enough to finish third a lap behind, but Walther wrecked us and Baker got hot over that. That was the start of us beginning to have a bad season.

Greg (far left) helps push Buddy Baker's Torino to the grid at Talladega on August 7, 1977, prior to a rather atypical sixth place finish (Perry Wood Racing Collection).

The Chevrolets started getting that aerodynamic advantage. We'd break motors and stuff and get in wrecks. Baker ran seconds and thirds and Pearson just let him wear his tires out, sat there, and laughed at him. At Charlotte Baker was like, "Ah, I got him now." Daddy said, "Slow up. Don't burn your tires up." "Oh no, hell, don't worry about it." Then Pearson all of a sudden started standing on it, went by as he lit a cigarette, and won with three laps to go. He did that about two or three times. You talk about getting frustrated? Then we ran out of parts. That's when M. C. Anderson got involved in it and wanted Baker to come drive for him.

> *Everybody knew it was time for a change. Norris knew it. Greg Moore knew it. Bud Moore knew it. And Buddy Baker was already doing something about it. He was destined for the M. C. Anderson team, which was basically an independent with bottomless pockets. More than anything, Baker wanted a Daytona 500 trophy, and he thought he had a better chance with Anderson's team of Oldsmobiles. Greg was about to be involved in a monumental hiring and a life-altering decision.*

CHAPTER EIGHT

The Pulpit or the Pits

In 1975, Gregory turned 18 years old and graduated from Spartanburg High School. College was definitely in his future as it was for all the Moore children as they chose their paths in life.

Daryl elected after his hitch in the U. S. Navy to get married, start a family, and join the faculty at Bud Moore Engineering. There he proceeded to build some of the winningest motors in Trans Am and big-time stock car racing history for the duration of the business.

Brent stayed in touch with racing from afar during his four years at Clemson University from which he graduated in 1972. He also got married, started a family, and found employment making power, but differently from his brother and father. Brent went to work splitting atoms, first with Florida Power and Light and then with Duke Energy at the Oconee Nuclear Station on Lake Keowee near his old Clemson stomping grounds.

As for Gregory, he headed north on Pine Street, past the corner where Bud Moore's Garage used to be, to the intersection with Interstate 85. There, within sight of the beautiful Blue Ridge Mountains, sits the University of South Carolina Upstate. When it opened in 1967, it was the University of South Carolina Spartanburg, but everybody in town called it "The Branch." Gregory showed up a few years later ready to learn.

I learned to drive just as soon as I was old enough to get a driver's license. For some reason the highway bothered me, but not initially. I didn't have a bad experience or anything, seems like it just developed. I never liked to drive the interstate highways, just like Richard Petty doesn't. I still can't. Very rarely did you ever see Richard Petty driving a car. But he's won more Daytona 500s than anybody. I've got that highway phobia bad. That's why people never saw me driving a car. I'd run to McDonald's or something, but nobody could figure that out. I came to find out years later that I got it from my grandmother on my momma's side, Ethel Gregory. That was her maiden name. That's where I got my name. She was Ethel Clark later. She had that same phobia. Driving *period* made her nervous. So it was an inherited deal. I don't know if it was visual or what it was.

After I graduated from Spartanburg High School in May of 1975, I went to the Branch for about a year and a half, and I worked at the shop the whole time. I'd just shoot up to the Branch, take the earliest courses I could, and be at Bud Moore Engineering by lunch. That was a close drive. I date myself as first getting a paycheck in 1973 at the shop. That's when they started taking out taxes and insurance and everything.

At the Branch I was passing and everything. I was majoring in history and psychology. What I had actually decided was if I didn't go racing, I was going to get into theology and,

Eight • The Pulpit or the Pits

believe it or not, be a preacher. The Rev. Gregory Clyde Moore. I would have transferred to Presbyterian College (PC) in Clinton, South Carolina. But Daddy wanted me to go to Clemson and get an engineering degree and would have paid for everything. I didn't want to do that. Not because I didn't want to go to Clemson. My brother Brenty went there. I knew I wasn't going to like driving up and down I-85 every weekend because I'd be going to the races and the shop.

So I went a different route. I never knew how all of this would have transferred because I never quite got that far. But my intentions were to go to the Branch for a couple of years then transfer to PC. I was born a Southern Baptist and baptized by Dr. William Ball at Fernwood Baptist Church, but I spent a lot of time over at Westminster Presbyterian Church with Dr. Pettit. There really wasn't that much difference between a Presbyterian and a Baptist that mattered to me. So I knew if I had to drive to and from school, I could go down 56, a two-lane road from Spartanburg to Clinton. We went right by Clinton taking the Woodpecker Trail to Daytona in the old days, and it was close. I'd been going by it since I was a kid. I liked Presbyterian churches. PC was a good school. Just everything. Anne's brother George Dickerson went there on a basketball scholarship. I thought it was a perfect fit. There are a lot of things about the Presbyterians I like better than the Baptists. The biggest thing's just to be a Christian, I guess. To me it's a big thing.

Let me put it this way. It had nothing to do with being against the Baptists. It had to do with not wanting to drive down the frigging highway. Those were my intentions, but I never followed up on any of it. The reason I never followed up on any of it was because that was about the time that Baker was leaving.

With the 1978 Winston Cup season just around the corner, Bud Moore Engineering had sponsor doubts, no car, and no driver. Going without a win for the first time in three years was troubling. There was no question that the cars would be fast and reliable. It was a matter of securing Norris Industries as the sponsor, finding something to replace the Ford Torino, and hiring a driver worthy of the seat. Gregory would turn 21 years old during the next season and was a man heavily involved in racing. Yet a higher calling was whispering in his ear the whole time.

Bud Moore had a left-handed right-hand man in waiting, and the future of Bud Moore Engineering was at a crossroads. A couple of phone calls in late 1977 changed the directions of Bud Moore Engineering and Gregory Moore, and everything came into focus.

We didn't know if Norris was going to come back or not, and Banjo came to Daddy and said, "Look, I'll tell you somebody that I think would be good in the car that really needs a ride bad because he's broke and I know he's who you need. Bobby Allison." Allison had driven four races for us in the Cyclone in 1967 and didn't do much. He was running that old AMC Matador and it had about made him go broke. So we called and told Allison if he wanted to drive the car, he could drive the car, but we weren't sure we could keep the sponsor. Bobby jumped at the chance and problem number one was resolved. So Daddy and I were in a hotel room late in 1977 at some race and called Norris and said, "Baker's leaving." He said, "Yeah, I know that." "We got Bobby Allison to drive the car and we wanted to know if you were going to stay." Norris answered, "Oh, hell yeah! I'm good for next year." Norris was good for one more year, and we went looking for a car to prepare for Daytona.

Where we snookered everybody with the Thunderbird was with an edition in 1978 called the Diamond Jubilee. This is what brought the Thunderbird back, and it was about that time I really started getting full-time involved. We could have run a notchback Torino or we could run a Thunderbird. And back then you couldn't run any side glasses. The Oldsmobiles had this bullet nose and a slope back, but they had to leave it open. All that air would go in the car. Well, Ford came out with this special Thunderbird. So Daddy and I got a catalogue and started looking at it. Then we went down to Pierce Motor Company in Spartanburg and saw it on the showroom floor. This special edition was much more expensive. It had a vinyl roof and the back window was filled in. If you notice Bobby Allison's car only had that one slit back there. There really wasn't a window at all. If we had had to leave that rear window open, it wouldn't have been worth it. So we called France Sr. and told him about the Thunderbird Diamond Jubilee Edition and said they were going to make 5,000 of them. We asked if we could run that car. "If they produce a car without a rear glass in it, you can run it," France said. We had them right then!

So Bud Moore Engineering was secure for 1978 with reliable, familiar, and top-notch sponsorship from Norris Industries. They had the commitment of driver Bobby Allison, a world-class racer with 47 major stock car victories, 48 poles, and a winning reputation known globally. Gregory and his father did their homework well and caught the competition flat-footed on the largest stage in racing. Finally, Gregory now had to decide whether or not to forgo his religious urgings and commit to the family business with all his heart and soul. He even considered teaching history or something. He weighed his options, added it all up, and cast his lot.

I had been at the Branch for a year and a half until the middle of 1977 and working at the shop the whole time. Daddy said, "You can quit if you want to. That's fine. I want you to go to Clemson and study engineering." He never knew I had any intentions of becoming a preacher. My mother knew, but you know how Daddy was. He wasn't paying any attention. All he knew was that he'd pay for my college education and wanted me to go to Clemson, be an engineer, and be more effective for the race team. But when we hired Bobby Allison as our driver, that's what made up my mind, and I told Daddy. He said, "Well, we got this car approved; now we got to make it run." I said, "Daddy, I know we do. That son-of-a-bitch is going to run if I have to get behind it and push it!" Then the Bobby Allison deal was like a Cinderella story. But that changed my mind about finishing college and the Rev. Gregory Moore thing. I was influenced enough religiously that I was interested in going into that seriously, but didn't. When we hired Bobby Allison after such a terrible year in '77, that's when I had to make the decision to wear my car out going to and from PC or try to race. We had to get that Thunderbird running.

In the winter of late 1977, Bud Moore Engineering built the Norris Industries–sponsored 1978 Diamond Jubilee Edition Thunderbird into the beautiful 580 horsepower, white and blue-trimmed number 15 beast that would insure the team stayed at the center of the Winston Cup universe. They loaded it on the trailer at 400 North Fairview Avenue in Spartanburg and trucked it to Daytona to see what the fruit of their labors would do.

We went down there to test the car in December of '77 and rented the racetrack for three or four days. We were there the first day by ourselves. You had to pay $3,000 for the fire crew and safety people, and we split the cost with Benny Parsons and Jake Elder, who brought one of those Oldsmobiles. So we had a gauge to measure ourselves against and split the cost.

We didn't run but a few laps with the Thunderbird, and Bobby came in and told us it drove real well and was running fair. Went back out and burned a rod bearing.

So Daddy and I went out to eat that night and he was kind of down. He said, "You know, we really made a good impression on Bobby Allison, didn't we." I said, "Daddy, everything's going to be all right. We're going to put that other engine in it and be all right." The other motor we put in we knew was a little bit different profile. It was a backup engine and probably wouldn't run quite as well.

So we put the other engine in it and Daddy and Bobby got to talking about fooling with the chassis. We ran about 183 miles per hour and Benny ran 185 or 186. They fooled with it and Bobby said, "We're off on speed a little bit, but this son-of-a-gun drives unreal." Bobby just started flipping out. "There's something about this car that drove better. I've never driven a car that drove like this at Daytona." There was some stuff we did with the Holman spindles versus the other ones. That all goes into Daddy knowing how to set the chassis. The car handled so well that Bobby got pumped up because he knew he wasn't going to have to lift. He could drive anywhere he wanted to. When the car would go into the corner and go into yaw, we didn't have that air getting inside and it got to the spoiler. That's what made it handle so well. So that's where we had everybody snookered. It was a big boxy son-of-a-gun and was a hundred horsepower off aerodynamically to the General Motors cars in a straight line. Those Oldsmobiles got loose with all that air going in the back, and we got our air to the rear spoiler so Bobby could run the corners so much harder. That overcame the 15 to 20 horsepower we were down to the General Motors cars in '78 and '79.

Back at 400 North Fairview, Bud and the boys changed this and adjusted that, Mr. Flow machined some heads, Daryl worked some dyno magic, Brent sent in some scientific figures, and they went back to the Beach in February 1978, well prepared for Speedweeks. However, on the trip down, Gregory enlightened his father on what might have been.

Daddy and I were in the car on the way down and something was said about going to church. "I don't know if you know it or not, but I was seriously thinking about going into being a preacher." "Where in the hell did you come up with that?" "Daddy, you didn't know that?" "No, I didn't know that!" "Well you probably just didn't pay attention. Momma knew it. I am a Christian and I seriously thought about it. If I hadn't gone racing full-time, maybe I would have been a preacher at the track." I don't know. I wanted to work on the race car. I got fascinated with the dyno and the flow bench years earlier.

The time had come for the true test of Gregory and the Moores' long, hard winter of work. It did not really start out all that great in Thursday's 125 mile qualifying race, as television documented for Saturday's ABC Wide World of Sports.

So we went back down there and got the motor better. We really lit up some stuff, and I did a lot of work on the heads and we picked up a good 15 horsepower. Donleavy had brought us some lifters. We were running out of mushroom lifters with a one-inch bottom at the bottom of the tappet. We had some Chrysler lifters that were machined that would fit. Sure enough, we put Donleavy's in there and they fit, and the cam stayed in. So we went ahead and ran those. But the oil hole would barely pass below where it needed to. We measured the bottom, and Daryl and the boys miked the hole. The oiler on the lifter was off about six or seven thousandths, and it would starve the bottom end. We didn't know that, but we caught it. We were so pumped up because we knew we were going to be down in qualifying speed because we had a brick we were trying to race. Remember how much aero straight line horsepower difference there was with the Oldsmobiles that year: a hundred!

That's at 200 miles an hour. At 140 miles per hour or so, it isn't anywhere near that bad. So we knew we were going to be down on speed, but it pulled up and drafted like we thought it was going to and had seen in practice.

We led the qualifying race right out of the box. Bobby drove it to the front and Baker's right in behind him in M. C. Anderson's Oldsmobile. It was so cool when Bobby came straight to the front. We felt so good and said that this thing really was going to draft. Well, Allison and Baker got together in turns three and four with Baker hitting us right around the driver's door. Our car was torn up worse than Baker's. They fixed theirs and we had to fix ours. It was really screwed up — and we had a one of a kind with that Thunderbird.

The new Thunderbird experiment was literally on the ropes in the first round. The car was badly wrecked, there was less than 72 hours to fix it, and the driver was Alabama bound. So Gregory, his dad, and a dedicated team of master mechanics toiled straight through until the 15 was ready ... they hoped.

We saw that the car was going to really draft and had qualified thirty-third because of the wreck in the qualifier. Speedwise, I think we were about twentieth fastest. We jumped on that son-of-a-gun and were bound and determined to fix it. That thing is going to run, in the Daytona 500. That thing is actually going to run and we were going to make it! And it was with the backup engine because we burnt the bearings up in the first one."

Bobby was going to go back to Alabama until he saw all the work we did to get the car repaired. We were going to fix the car anyway because we were on the Winner's Circle Plan. That was a plan paying bonus money to teams that entered all the races and had won a race recently. We got the deal money just to show up. Bobby ran so well in the 125-mile qualifier that he proved our theory. We saw in practice he could hang on and it was going to handle. It was so foggy, and Petty and those guys were having trouble, and we started getting caught up. We saw how many people we could pass in the corners and knew we had a shot at this thing. We really knew we had a shot in the 125-miler. But Bobby crashed and was so disgusted. His health wasn't that good, and he was broke from running that Matador. He came to the garage Saturday morning to tell Daddy that he was going home to Hueytown. When he saw the miraculous repair job we did, Bobby was shocked we had it fixed so well so quickly. He thought it was a different car! We had jumped on that thing and we were *inspired*! We had us a race driver. We had us a good racecar that was going to handle.

I remember I wanted to put some Bondo up on the front fender, where it had a few wrinkles. *Sports Illustrated* said about our car, "Rough trip for a battered luxury liner." After we practiced, I tried and tried to get Daddy to let us rub just a little bit of Bondo in there, smooth it out, spray it white, and stick the decals back on it. Daddy said, "Look, as far as we've come on this thing, I'm going to show you the art of hiding those two or three little wrinkles with these decals. It isn't going to make that much difference, boy." He was right. The front end was so big, blowing such a big hole in the air, one or two little ripples didn't matter. But me being Mr. Flow with micrometers and wind tunnels and all this B.S., I knew that it made a little bit of difference.

The 1978 Daytona 500 was joined in progress by ABC Sports just around the halfway point. Crashes and mechanical woes took their normal toll, especially a crash on lap 60 involving Pearson, Petty, and Waltrip who were running one, two, three. But there were plenty of top-of-the-line cars still contesting the race. It came down to the only two it should have been: luckless Bobby Allison in a furiously repaired experimental car, and

Buddy Baker, the man who left Bud Moore Engineering for a better chance to win this race, who had wrecked with Allison three days earlier.

Late in the race, we had a super good pit stop and ran Baker down with help from Dave Marcis, who was a lap behind in that Osterlund car number 2. I felt at that point that we were finally going to win the race or have a shot at it. I don't believe you could have driven a ten-penny nail up mine or Daddy's butt. We were waiting for the rocks to stop up the oil cooler, or for a wire to fall off under the dash, or something else to happen. I believe the Moore family, along with Judy Allison, Bonnie Allison, Pop Allison, and everybody else, held our breaths for about ten minutes. *Stock Car Racing Magazine* showed a very intense picture of Daddy with a few laps to go.

What happened was, Baker's car had a rod bolt shake loose. He said he saw Bobby catching him, and we just had got to him when he said that son-of-a-bitch was vibrating so bad the mirror was turning. It finally broke the rod and that secured the victory for us. We knew this was going to be the break we'd been looking for. We'd never won the Daytona 500. We'd always run good. Should have won it with Weatherly at least once. Should have won it with Dieringer, but it rained, and should have won it with Baker. We were holding our breaths. This was what was going to put us back on top. And it did!

It was based on a theory. We didn't build a Mercury because we were trying to get

Seen here at Rockingham on March 5, 1978, the Bud Moore–built Diamond Jubilee Edition Thunderbird of Bobby Allison, with its small back window, is contrasted with the larger corresponding opening in the Junior Johnson–prepared Oldsmobile of Cale Yarborough (Perry Wood Racing Collection).

Ford back in racing and that T-Bird was the catalyst. That's the reason Daddy wouldn't get a Chevrolet. We'd been working on this to get Ford back and they were about to come. But that was Daddy's twentieth year of trying to win the Daytona 500, and it was just surreal being in Victory Lane. All those years we came close to winning or were favored to win and didn't. Then finally crashing in the qualifier and having to start so far back and pulling it off. There is no way to describe how unreal it was. Of course we never made it back, but we should have. Anyway, 1978 was a happy time for all of us.

At the checkers it was Bobby Allison first, Junior Johnson's Oldsmobiles driven by Cale Yarborough and Benny Parsons second and third, Ron Hutcherson in A. J.'s Buick fourth, and Dick Brooks fifth in Junie Donleavy's Mercury. It was a proud moment to finally reach the top of the Daytona Mountain and add perhaps the only thing missing from Bud Moore's resume. And now visions of the Winston Cup Championship were dancing in their heads. The rest of the season saw the team contending everywhere, all the time.

We went to the next race and it was *still* running like Jack the Bear. We won Atlanta, Dover, Charlotte, and Ontario again. It was great. We finished second in points. But the Thunderbird had something to do with that, too. You know you couldn't run the rear glass back then. The Oldsmobiles and all had the snout noses on them and slope roof, but had that big opening at the back. We flat snookered them!

The 1978 season was a whopping success. The runner-up points finish was the best since back-to-back titles by Joe Weatherly in 1962 and 1963. They were only 474 points behind Cale Yarborough and took second by a razor-thin margin of 35 points over the three followers, Waltrip, Parsons, and Marcis. The Moore, Allison, and Norris trio won three of the last seven races including the season ender at Ontario for the second year in a row. Altogether in 30 races they tallied five wins, 14 top fives, 22 top tens, a pole, $354,245 in winnings, and 1043 laps led. Needless to say, the 1978 Ford Thunderbird Diamond Jubilee Edition experiment was the best of times at 400 North Fairview Avenue and for the gentlemen who raced there.

It continued into the 1979 season with one of the classic events in the history of stock car racing — one that always comes up when the greatest races of all time are discussed. Unfortunately, the discussion is often between individuals with no idea what took place before 1971. There were scores of incredibly exciting and noteworthy races run before the so called "Golden Era" began that year. That is when R. J. Reynolds and Winston cigarettes came in and chloroformed all the dirt tracks and most of the short ones that were the heart of the sport for its first 22 years.

That being said, one race is without question the most exciting stock car race ever. It took place on February 18, 1979, in Daytona Beach, Florida, and most everyone knows the story. The east coast of the United States was snowed in on that winter Sunday, it had been raining in Daytona, and there was nothing on the tube to watch except the 500. It was a race for the ages and maybe the most exciting ever run, period! Squarely positioned right in the middle of everything was Bobby Allison in Bud Moore's white and blue Hodgdon Thunderbird number 15. Norris Industries had been replaced on the quarter panels by the engineering firm of California's Warner Hodgdon. Bobby started the dreary Sabbath with as good a chance to win as anybody and better than most in seventh place beside Dick Brooks' Bearfinder Olds. It would be two 500s in a row for the big bird from Spartanburg if the leader of the Alabama Gang could pull it off. Actually, this was the race that launched NASCAR's product globally.

Eight • The Pulpit or the Pits

We got down to Daytona and the car was a little bit faster, but it was still a brick. We had a little bit better horsepower and had tricked the aerodynamics up a little more. We had run it a season! It was the same car that we won with in '78. We were another 10 or 12 horsepower better in '79 than in '78. We qualified seventh, and it would still draft and it would still handle.

The three cars that were winning were Bobby, Donnie Allison in Hoss Ellington's Olds, and Cale in Junior's Olds. Well, early in the race they came off of turn two, and Donnie was leading with Bobby right below him followed by Cale, Darrell, and a long line of cars drafting. Bobby dropped back to slip in line and just did tap Donnie in the left rear. Donnie lost it, spinning right off Bobby's front end, and got a little airborne. He caught Bobby in the door as Bobby went by, enough for him to spin, too. Cale dove low and headed through that muddy, wet grass along the backstretch at about 200 miles per hour and of course he lost it as well. Donnie and Cale just got stuck, but our car backed into the big dirt bank that kept the cars out of Lake Lloyd like when Tommy Irwin went in years earlier. All three got stuck in the mud, and ours was the most torn up of the three cars. They got Cale and Donnie going and Cale lost a lap as they just left us sitting there. We had to get towed out and lost a lap. We made the lap up one time, but only held it for a little while and they got back by us. We were in contention for the win and were as fast as anybody. We spent the rest of the day trying to make up the frigging lap.

Try as they might, Greg and the boys were not going to make it two in a row in the Daytona 500. However, the Bud Moore Thunderbird number 15 would be the backdrop for one of the iconic moments in the history of stock car racing.

Towards the end, we were running sixth, two laps down. Bobby had just started kind of cooling it. I noticed that he'd slowed down, and that was why Cale was mad. To all those cars, the draft meant so much more than it does now because they blew the big hole in the air. Bobby was safely in sixth and there was no chance in us gaining a position. Behind Donnie and Cale on the lead lap, much further back, were Petty, Waltrip, and Foyt. Donnie sat there and led ninety-something laps and probably had the fastest car or at least was equal. This was going to be the biggest win of his life, and Cale had done nothing but follow him, waiting to pull the slingshot. That works well if there isn't anybody in front of the lead car to draft on. Bobby was on the same straightaway with Donnie and Cale hooked up and catching him. Bobby was waiting on them. I had put two and two together and figured out what Bobby was going to do. He was going to blow a hole to create some disturbed air. They drove well, but were not aerodynamic. Bobby knew what was going on and hadn't said anything on the radio at all. I noticed on the stopwatch that he was running slower than he really needed to be running if he was wide open by himself. I don't know this for a fact, but it appeared to me — and this is my theory — that he was going to get 100 yards ahead of them and disturb the air. Bobby's bent-up Thunderbird was gone, but the air was still moving. We were the car that was the closest, and we were way ahead of them when they hit the backstretch on the last lap.

Cale could see that happening and admitted that when he went to make his move, he didn't get quite a good enough run. Donnie was not just going to let Cale drive by him. Donnie went to make the block, but Cale was already up alongside of him. So Donnie carried him to the grass. There was no out-of-bounds line back then, and Cale never picked his foot up. When he saw he couldn't clear him, you could plainly see him turn the steering wheel toward Donnie. So they crashed into the turn three outside wall at about 190 miles per hour, still beating and banging into each other and then sliding down to the grass on the inside of the apron.

Bobby saw the caution flag, or we may have told him. The wreck was in his mirror. So he goes all the way around the race track. The bad part was that we didn't complete that lap and finish the race, which dropped us to eleventh. Five positions was a bunch of money.

Bobby pulled over to see if Donnie wanted a ride back to the garage area, and it was a pretty bad wreck. He also wanted to see if Donnie was OK. He saw them outside the cars and nobody was really arguing much at that point. They both had hit pretty hard and might have just been getting their marbles straight. Bobby hadn't said a word. Suddenly, Cale ran over there and swung his helmet at the window net. I don't think Cale meant to hit Bobby. It was just a gesture, but it hit Bobby in the nose. Bobby said he looked down and there was blood coming out and he was still strapped in the car. You know that was going to piss somebody off. Cale was a good guy. I don't think he meant to hit him.

So Bobby said, "I guess I better take care of this." You've heard the story that when Bobby got out and questioned Cale's ancestry, Cale started wearing out Bobby's fist with his nose. Bobby said that was his story and he is sticking to it. So they were fighting, and Bobby grabbed Cale by the leg and took him to the ground. Now everybody knew that in a boxing ring, Cale Yarborough would whip Bobby Allison. Cale was a Golden Gloves boxer. They swung and nobody connected, but Bobby kind of got the best of Cale. Donnie just stood back there rooting it on. And in the background of many of the press photos was our T-Bird.

Postscript to a race finish for the ages.

Everybody was snowed in in the southeast. Bobby was aggravated and mad because we never could get the lap back and weren't in contention for the win. But he sure much rather would have seen his brother in Hoss' car win the race than Cale in the Bill Gazaway car. Gazaway was NASCAR's head technical inspector, and Cale's owner, Junior Johnson, had NASCAR's so-called "house car." Somebody had some t-shirts made up just like those the fans wore for Cale and Junior's team with a picture of their number 11 on it and everything, and instead of saying "Cale Yarborough," in sort of an arch across the front it said "Bill Gazaway." I think what Cale thought was exactly what I thought was going on, but I don't know because Bobby's never owned up to it. I've never asked him if he was waiting to do what I thought he was doing. Bobby drove the car back to the garage area, but there wasn't any argument with us. We had not even realized that we didn't finish the last lap. We didn't realize that until the next day or when we were going home. We figured we ran sixth, but were eleventh. It wasn't much by today's standards, but it was about $11,000, which was a hell of a lot of money back then. There was a big fine, but they didn't fine Cale. They fined Donnie and Bobby $6,000 before the next race.

Cale had an orange visor on his helmet that day. When he swung his helmet, it hit Bobby's nose and the visor came off and landed in the far corner of the passenger side of our car. Daryl and Carol went down there to look at the car the next day in the garage area, and Carol found Cale's visor lying in the car. You can see Cale's helmet in the fight pictures and there's no visor on it. I don't know what this thing would be worth, but Daryl and Carol just took it home and didn't think much about it. They've got it, and it may have some historical value. I'm sure Cale would sign it now. Maybe they should get all three of them to sign it.

Eight • The Pulpit or the Pits

The very next race was the following weekend at Rockingham. Bobby Allison won the pole and had his brother Donnie alongside. Behind them was the third member of the Daytona 500 fisticuffs, Cale Yarborough, with Buddy Baker outside. The racing was furious for the first nine laps, and when Cale and Donnie entered turn three side by side with Donnie leading on the low side, Donnie lost it and hit Cale. Off they went into the rail, taking with them Rudd, Bonnett, Baker, Petty, Earnhardt, and Waltrip. The first car slipping past by diving to the apron was Bobby Allison, with Pearson not far behind. Bobby went on to dominate the day, leading 311 of 492 laps.

That was unbelievable. The same two guys did it again in the very next race, only this time, there was no fist fight and no hard feelings that I know of. It was so amazing that those two did it again in the very next race and you never hear anything about that. Of course, Bobby ducked low and missed the crash, and he went on to win from the pole. We won the pole at the next race at Richmond, and that was two of the first four poles for '79. It was a real good recovery from Daytona, and we just went back to running well all the rest of the year.

Sometimes things happen in racing that shake you up when complacency has set in and things have been taken for granted. During the Atlanta 500 on March 18, 1979, the sport of stock car racing had one of those shake-up moments. On lap 123, leader Dave Watson, possibly excited over his stellar showing that day, drove into tragedy and straight out of the sport. Greg saw it unfold a few yards away.

Watson was a new guy and was leading the race, and he came into the pits just like anybody else would. He didn't look too fast to me, but he was leading, and we were right up there, maybe even moving into the lead because he was pitting. Well, he came in and his crew ran out there like they all do, and Watson crossed his car up. A young man — I believe he was about 18 years old — was standing in the pit road with the jack in his hands, and here came this racecar sliding sideways right at him. There was nowhere for him to run even if he'd have had time to, and *boom*, the car hit him at the passenger door. It knocked him way down pit road, and he hit his head hard on the asphalt. He wasn't moving. An official came over and straightened one of his legs that was bent back under him. It was terrible. He never made a motion to get out of the way.

It wasn't that far from us. Daryl and Carol's daughters, Missy and Candy, were in the pits. They were only about nine or ten years old. I saw what happened and ran down there and grabbed them and told Carol to get them out of there. I didn't want them to see that. We finished second to Baker in that race. That was another example of how dangerous the pits were back then. Hell, they still are.

The boys on North Fairview Avenue recovered from the disappointing, but spectacular, Speedweeks to record a third place finish in the 1979 Winston Cup Point Standings, which was great by anyone's standards. That was true especially considering the level of the competition from the other Ford and General Motors teams who seemed to have shops full of Mercurys, Chevys, Pontiacs, Buicks, and the super speedway terrors, the Oldsmobiles. It was hard to understand Bobby Allison's growing discontent since he had scored five wins at Rockingham, North Wilkesboro, Talladega (of course), Riverside, and Richmond. He took poles at Rockingham, Richmond, and Darlington. He led 1,855 laps (still today the most laps led in a season for Bud Moore by far), 18 top fives, and 22 top tens again in 30 races. The team pocketed almost $363,000, also a record for Bud Moore Engineering.

Bobby Allison excelled on any track, anytime, anywhere, but was becoming restless as the team embarked on their third campaign together. He wanted something done to shake things up, whether it meant Bud, Greg, and the boys building him a Chevy or commuting from Hueytown to some shop other than the one in Spartanburg. Indeed, changes came in 1980.

The novelty of the Thunderbird experiment was long gone. I said, "Daddy, we're driving ourselves crazy trying to fight horsepower. We were down to the Oldsmobiles about what I said we are. We're fighting the aero. If you want it to run faster you got to build a Mercury." We finally did, but only after Bobby had thought he was going to quit and got offers from Ranier. We built him a Cougar. That son-of-a-bitch hauled ass every time we carried it to the race track. Like Bobby said, "The Cougar's slicker." It was one full second faster with the same engine in it at Daytona. One full second! The whole object of the thing was that we were trying to get Ford Motor Company back in racing. We never built the Mercury until 1980. We built the Cougar just to qualify better. So we converted one over to a Cougar and only raced it a handful of times, and it ran well everywhere.

The first time Bobby raced it was in the Busch Clash, and he ran fourth. He said it was faster, but not quite as tight as the Thunderbird. It was a tick looser. The rear roof line was a little gentler, and it had that little tiny porthole in the back. In a draft, that car was not quite as snug. It was the Thunderbird chassis under it. That was how sharp Bobby was. But we didn't race the Cougar everywhere. The Cougar was a limited running car.

No controversy at Speedweeks 1980. Buddy Baker smoked everybody and finally got his dream victory, dominating the 500 in Harry Ranier's Oldsmobile number 28. Greg and the boys did just fine themselves.

We ran second at Daytona with the Cougar, and Baker had that black and silver Ranier Oldsmobile. The Cougar ran well. We had to get the fenders out of a junkyard. It was actually a 1976. Daddy keeps saying it was a Montego. It wasn't. That's what the Wood Brothers were running. Ours was actually a Cougar. The Cougar and Montego were basically the same thing. Daddy, Banjo, Bobby and I took the same engine and the same chassis set up in the Cougar. As a matter of fact, we changed the sheet metal so it was the same car and took it down to Daytona. It warmed up six-tenths quicker the first lap by.

We built the Cougar to try to pacify Bobby because we were getting into the situation of qualifying badly at Daytona. We held off with the Thunderbird for so long because the Thunderbird was a big seller with Ford and we were doing everything we could to get Ford involved. We heard rumblings they were looking at it. Daddy was in contact with Lee Morse. We knew that they might come back. We told Bobby we weren't going to build a Chevrolet. That was our whole object. The Thunderbird handled fine and it won races. It hurt you aerodynamically a little bit at Atlanta, but that wasn't like Daytona. The Cougar was definitely a much faster car. Daddy said, "What difference does it make?" The Wood Brothers had the Mercury. Donleavy had a Mercury. We knew they were faster. We wanted to run the Thunderbird for the brand recognition. We knew Ford was getting ready to come back, and sure enough, in '81 they had their first meeting. I was in on that meeting at Ford with SVO. They'd get to squabbling. They cussed everybody out and gave us all leather jackets. But we succeeded. At Atlanta in the fall, we went down there and sat on the pole. Allison was winning going away, then a guy blew a motor and we hit the wall.

A young man who was often a welcomed guest in the Bud Moore pit area in those days was destined to carve his own name into the sport. Greg got to know him well.

In seven races with the "Junkyard" Cougar, Bobby Allison's best showing was on the Fourth of July at Daytona in the Firecracker 400. After starting fourteenth, he led off and on for 63 of 160 laps, edging Pearson and Earnhardt for the win (Perry Wood Racing Collection).

Davey Allison was four years younger than me. I used to haul the gas and all that stuff, and if Davey showed up, he would haul the gas. Davey was just a little guy, and I was real good friends with him. To us he was just like part of the team when he came, and he came when he could. We had a real close organization. His Daddy let him drive the Matador. He snuck in and got to drive a couple of laps. That's how Davey got started. When he got old enough, Bobby let him run that thing a little bit. His daddy was grooming him to be a driver. Davey loved racing and had it in his blood. They went testing somewhere with the Matador, and Bobby ran that thing because he was getting some show-up money to run the Busch Series a little bit. We'd even help pit the car. Davey got in it when there was nobody looking and drove it some laps and ran it faster than Bobby wanted him to. You knew he had the nuts to do it.

His brother Clifford was even younger by seven years and hung around some, as did their sister Bonnie. It was like a family deal. We had Pop Allison, who would keep the laps and hand Bobby a drink of water. Donnie always stood by or came to most of the races. He drove for us in '72. He relief-drove for us and about won Rockingham. He's still pissed off about that race when Pearson just did beat him in 1978.

As the cliché goes, all good things must come to an end. Any way you look at it, the Bud Moore–Bobby Allison relationship accomplished just about everything it could except a championship; but a lot of other teams missed the championship, too. As always, integrity, quality, and success were imperative and never in question at 400 North Fairview Avenue.

Winning was expected as it had been since the 1950s. The main variable was the driver, and the better the pilot, the better the results. At 23 years old, Greg Moore was the man beside the man and the other face of Bud Moore Engineering. Greg was in high gear and involved. The year of 1980 was the end of one sweet ride and a fabulous era.

Bobby didn't understand what was going on. We kept telling him that Ford's coming back. "We'll build you a Mercury because that's a Ford product. We're not going to switch to Chevrolet because Ford's getting ready to come back. We've succeeded in our mission." In a victory lane Bobby said we got the car out of a junkyard. Well we did get the sheet metal out of a junkyard, but he wasn't meaning it derogatorily. A lot of people took it that way. He said, "I tried every way in the world to get Bud Moore to build me a Chevrolet, but mean old Bud Moore wouldn't build me a Chevrolet. He did build me a Cougar. I guess I'll have to be satisfied with a Cougar." Bobby wasn't truly convinced that Ford was really coming back. He didn't believe it was as serious as we knew it was, and Harry Ranier offered him a bunch of money up front. They had Waddell Wilson, Jake Elder, and money. He later said he didn't know how he ever won a race with that bunch. They were the most disorganized people in the world. But Harry Ranier's a great guy. There's not a damn thing wrong with Harry Ranier. They were spending money hand over fist, and they did run good. Then Bobby won the championship in '83 with Digard, another disorganized bunch.

It was probably a good move for Bobby to leave us, but Bobby now says it wasn't. He said it was the worst mistake he ever made. I think the reason Bobby feels bad about it is not because it wasn't proper, but because everything came to fruition, from motors not blowing to cars being aerodynamic by the time we got Ricky Rudd. It was finally Ford's serious commitment, and Bobby missed out on it. He was sarcastic at the time, talking about the Cougar coming out of a junkyard, but later he had problems internally as far as harmony within those other teams. He looks at it now and questions the move, like, "Bud and Gregory were really kind of right about this." He did win a championship elsewhere so it's a coin toss. We got along with him great.

The final season of the Bobby Allison relationship was the worst of the three, but still very competitive with a ninth in the points. Four wins were notched: Dover, Daytona in July, Richmond, and North Wilkesboro. There were poles at North Wilkesboro and Atlanta and a dozen top fives, 18 top tens, but only 948 laps led, about half as many as in '79. The three Bobby Allison years garnered 14 wins and over a million dollars for Bud Moore Engineering, and the future would be fraught with changes. However, Bud Moore had surely gained a right hand man in Greg to help navigate the rough racing rapids ahead.

Chapter Nine

Changes

Things could not have been much stranger if NASCAR had told the racers to run backwards. For 1981, the cars were downsized in wheelbase from 115 inches to 110 inches, and they really looked smaller. But they were fast! When they were fast and sliding backwards, they almost always became 3,500 pound kites without strings or tails. Daytona in February got ugly, and apparently none of this was detected during the teams' winter testing.

If that wasn't enough to keep up with, Greg now had a small brick that ran 200 miles per hour to engineer, with 1973 Winston Cup Champion and 1975 Daytona 500 winner Benny Parsons as the new employee. Benny was a proven winner, a veteran champion, and after his driving career was over, he became a beloved television personality. But at the time, one almost had the feeling that Bud Moore Engineering had settled for less than the best. In retrospect, nothing could have been farther from the truth.

We were real disappointed at Bobby's leaving. Jake Elder came to Daddy and said, "I'm gonna tell you something. Benny Parsons is a good race driver and you got to set the car up a little bit different. You can win races with Benny Parsons. His style is just a little bit different. He's good at Daytona. He's got nuts." Not that he wasn't aggressive, but he had a little different feel than, say, Bobby or Cale. Benny came to Daddy and had that Melling deal. It was only $250,000, which was borderline, but Harry Melling liked Benny and wanted to put him in Bud Moore's car. We liked Benny, too, and knew him well.

When we went to Daytona in 1981, they had downsized the cars. You could convert an old car, but it wasn't real practical. Only a couple of people tried it because you had to cut so much stuff. We never did convert one. The Wood Brothers took one and converted it, and I think we tried to cut one. It just made the car drive so much worse with no wheel tread.

We had one car built and were working on another and went down there testing. The car was squirrelier, but Benny said it drove pretty doggone good. Benny had fewer complaints about our car than Darrell Waltrip had about the Chevrolet. Once again you had a boxy car. It wasn't as far off on speed, even though it was a small brick, and the biggest thing was working out the front fenders. It had those ugly front fenders initially, and the first attempts that everybody had were pretty crude.

We got out there at Daytona, and it had rained one night and the track was still damp on the second day of the testing. We got the car out, shaking it down and making a few changes which weren't too bad. Then the fire department guy that we had known for years went out and rode around the track and said it looked OK from what he could see. "You're good to go." There was one of those corners that was always the last to dry because of the shadows, but it looked like it was good. We weren't in qualifying trim, but Benny dropped it off into one and two. The track was still a little bit damp. He spun twice, never touched anything, and wound up halfway down the backstretch with four flat tires. Never ... touched ... anything! That's how good Benny was. We thanked God we didn't tear it up and Benny was OK. Benny said, "Man, that was close."

We changed the four tires and killed another hour, and then the track was actually dry. Benny went back around and backed off a little going into the first turn just to make sure, and we didn't much blame him. He came back around again, hammering on it, and we ran 191. We felt pretty good about it. We didn't have a problem with looseness as bad as the Chevrolet guys did. They were coming in with white knuckles. Plus Daddy and Banjo were the world's best with a rear-steer car, and we're still on bias-ply tires.

Back to Daytona in February 1981 for Speedweeks and time to go racing with Benny.

We drew the dead last starting spot for the Busch Clash. Dead last. They dropped the green flag, and Benny came all the way up through there and got to Darrell Waltrip. He had easily passed everybody else, but he never could get a run on Waltrip for some reason, and we finished second. We went to the 125 mile qualifier and the car ran up front. We led a few laps, and on the last lap Benny pulled out and drove by Waltrip and another car. He got such a good run he had a two or three car length lead going into turn three. He held the lead through three and still had it coming off of four. We were feeling real good. We had already finished second in the Clash, and here we were, going to win the qualifying race.

Waltrip got a little run on him and dove to the apron. Benny said he couldn't believe it, and Darrell said it was kind of a daring move, but, "I thought I'd be all right," he said. Well he wouldn't have been all right, but Benny went ahead and gave him room to keep from wrecking both of them. Daddy got kind of hot and made it clear to him how we liked to race. "Don't ever do that on the last lap again! If you'd have torn the car up and not brought back anything but the steering wheel, as long as you were OK, fine—but don't *ever* give somebody room like that."

We didn't run that well in the 500. Maybe something broke; I don't remember what the deal was, but about six cars got by on the start and we never could make up ground. I didn't think the motor was as good as the other one, but Benny thought it was. Benny, being Benny, said it was fine. Daddy and I wanted to put the other motor in because it had a little different piston in it. It had dynoed OK, but you can't race a dyno. It just wasn't quite as good as what we had in the Clash and the 125 miler. We had two more we could have put in.

The record shows that Benny Parsons in the Melling number 15 started the 500 in fourth place and did not finish by overheating for thirty-first after 135 laps.

The rest of the year with Benny Parsons would have been a dream year for other teams. Greg and Bud went up to Dearborn to discuss the brick they were racing and what to do to fix it.

In '81, they had downsized it and left it boxy. It was a little brick instead of a big brick, with big, ugly fenders. In the middle of '81, Ford's suits told the designers to design the Thunderbird any way they wanted to do it. "That prick better be aerodynamic because we're getting ready to come back racing." They had the new Thunderbird on the drawing board. The whole idea was to keep running the Thunderbird. We even looked at a Torino. We looked at some different body styles and really didn't want to run a Mercury product. We wanted to keep running the Thunderbird for brand recognition. We had only run the Cougar to keep Allison, but at the same time we didn't want to piss Ford off because they were tickled to death that we took the Thunderbird and ran so well. It was all a plan. By that time, Ford had made their mind up they were going back racing.

In 1981, we had the meeting with Ford. Daddy and I went up to Dearborn, and there was Edsel Ford, and they brought in Michael Kranefuss to head up the thing. For the next in command they hired Lee Morse, who was the engine engineer under the Mustang Trans Am program. Daddy got him his job. He said, "You got to have Lee Morse." We had Mose Dolan, who designed the 427 single overhead cam motor that NASCAR threw out in '66. They ran it in drag racing where Dyno Don Nicholson ran like hell with it, but NASCAR threw it out because it didn't have push rods. But Daddy and I were heard, the right people were brought in, and we left feeling Ford would get us a better race car.

About everywhere else we went, we ran well. We won Nashville, Richmond, and the last race ever at Texas World Speedway. We had them covered like snow and had come up with a new deal. A rev kit was borderline illegal and it was made for drag cars, but NASCAR would never make a ruling on it. We were having trouble breaking valve springs. A rev kit is like having double valve springs for the rocker arm and stuff. I did not come up with this idea. Believe it or not, Bud Moore came up with this idea. We actually made a rev kit and loaded the push rods. That allowed us to put this camshaft in that was so wild, the rate of lift on the mushroom lifters made it to where it should have blown up in 200 miles, but could run 500. The Texas track was bumpy, the car ran real well, and Benny easily won that race. That was one of the few races Earnhardt ran worth a damn with that Stacy deal, and he saw how well Benny ran.

The race cars might have been downsized, but the fun wasn't. Greg recalls the twice-a-year road trips to the North Carolina Sandhills.

Raymond Williams was Captain America and a pretty darn good racecar driver. He had a place up at Rockingham called the Silver Bucket. We'd go over to Raymond's place and eat so many oysters and drink so much liquor that we'd be drunker than hell when we came out of there. There's something about oysters — well, let me put it this way: Between the liquor and the oysters, there were women involved somewhere before we got back to the motel.

Daddy has said this since I was 12 — and there was probably a time he needed to tell me this — he'd say, "Don't be getting into that beer too much." I've always known when to drink and when not to drink. I never drank on the job and never, ever touched any drugs.

The last three races at Rockingham, Atlanta, and Riverside were dismal for Benny and the Moores. However, by the end of the season, once again change was in the air.

The word was out that if Benny Parsons could run at Texas like that in Bud's car, that car was pretty darn good. There had already been some talk about stuff, but Earnhardt was going to have to leave J. D. Stacy. Stacy was trying to push Joe Ruttman and said, "I don't need Wrangler. I'll do whatever I want to do." He loved Joe Ruttman and didn't give a crap about Earnhardt. He had on his team, at one time or another that year, Ruttman, Earnhardt, Richmond, Labonte, Ridley, Sauter, Pond, and some others, and about half of them never got paid. The only one that got paid every nickel was Junie Donleavy, Jody Ridley's owner.

Benny Parsons' first of three wins for Bud Moore took place on May 9, 1981, at Nashville International Raceway, where Parsons led 209 of 420 laps. In the back row are Greg (with the beard) and Brent (with the glasses). Holding the trophy are (left to right) Bud Moore, Benny Parsons and Buck Trent from *Hee Haw* (courtesy Bud Moore Engineering Archives).

The Wrangler people knew that Earnhardt should be a good commodity because in the previous two years he had been Rookie of the Year and Winston Cup Champion. He ran so bad in '81 that I knew he could run better in our car than he'd been running, but we kind of got to liking Benny. This sounds crazy, but we actually asked Wrangler what they thought of Benny Parsons. They said, "Well, Benny Parsons is a good driver, but Dale Earnhardt looks a whole lot more like Wild Bill Hickok in blue jeans than Benny Parsons does in blue jeans. We got our marketing around Earnhardt." We knew he could probably do it.

Benny Parsons had worked out all right in this year of drastic changes. However, the possible acquisition of an available Dale Earnhardt put the wheels in motion to make it happen.

Bob O' Dear was the president of Bluebell, which owned Janzen bathing suits, Wrangler, and some other company, and they had to move Earnhardt away from Stacy. There was nothing wrong with Stacy—I liked him, and he was always nice to Daddy and me—but he was arrogant and was a coal man. He was in love with Joe Ruttman and said he didn't give a damn about Wrangler, he had his own money. Earnhardt and Wrangler weren't even wanted much. Then Childress took Dale for three or four races and gave him $10,000 a race if they qualified. Childress said they sweated making the races. We also still had another year on the contract with Melling. So we had to approach Melling and see if he would release us from the contract. After we found out that Earnhardt was part of the Wrangler package, we had to make a decision. The Wrangler sponsorship was going to be double what we were getting from Melling. To us, it was a ton of money. It was $400,000; $450,000; and $500,000 for three years.

So we finished out that season with Benny and we told him, "Benny, Ford's getting ready to get back in, and we can't run a full season on $250,000. We'd love for you to be the driver, but we got to take this other deal. It's not that you're not a good driver, it's strictly a financial thing." As it turned out, he got the ride with Ranier and the next year was the first person to qualify at 200. He didn't get left out of the shuffle, and that fact made us feel a whole lot better about it.

Benny Parsons departed North Fairview Avenue after a one-and-done season with no hard feelings, a fine year to add to his resume with a top tier team posting three wins, ten top fives, a dozen top tens, and tenth in the final standings. Benny's bright future never approached that 1981 production; he racked up only one more victory, three years later. But he never had raced less than winning equipment, and he went on to a fabulous career with CBS and ESPN until his death in January of 2007.

Chapter Ten

Earnhardt

The Dale Earnhardt Era at 400 North Fairview saw flamboyant blues and yellows adorning all things Bud Moore. The hopes and enthusiasm were sky high and the pockets of Wrangler deep. Speedweeks 1982 could not come soon enough!

Sid Morris was a super good marketing guy who came up with that color scheme where the 15 blended in. In fact, originally it blended so well it almost didn't look like a number! NASCAR made us put some distance in there on the door. Sid came up with that paint scheme, and it was revolutionary. It made a pretty car. We tested with Earnhardt a couple of places, and he loved the way the car drove, and we knew he was going to be OK. Our confidence level was a whole lot better now. It was the car. He couldn't drive that other thing in 1981 for Stacy. We went down to Daytona and ran the 125 miler. We were not in the Clash because he did not sit on a pole in '81 and we didn't either with Benny. We started eleventh and finished fourth in the lead draft behind Baker, Waltrip, and believe it or not, Joe Ruttman in Stacy's car. But anytime Earnhardt went out and drafted, he was super-duper good. We knew we were all right.

All was well, and the Daytona 500 was to be the return of Dale Earnhardt to prominence with a legendary winning team. It started for real on Valentine's Day 1982.

They dropped the green flag in the Daytona 500 and he came straight to the front. We were feeling so good about it because he was talking about the car driving great and he could do anything and there was no problem. He wasn't pulling away from anybody, but he was pulling the train. I remember David Hobbs on CBS TV said that it was "about past time for them to start pitting." It was lap 34 when he came by and I told Daddy, 'Call him in this lap.' I made that call. Daddy told Earnhardt, "Pit next time by. This is a green flag stop for four tires and gas." He got halfway down the backstretch and it ran out of gas. It burned a piston when it did—the number five cylinder, the lean cylinder at the front. He came in and made the stop and we got it fired back up. He made about two laps and could tell the motor was hurt, so we parked it.

When you burn a piston it actually melts the top of the piston a little bit and gets it down to the ring lands and scuffs the cylinder wall up. If it blows a hole all the way through it, the motor will start missing, and it will self-destruct if you run it anymore. Earnhardt couldn't have loped along out there with it. We knew it wouldn't make it. It didn't bust the block, it didn't throw a rod, but it was terminal and we had to park it.

We were still about the first car to hit pit road. I think one other car had pitted before us. It wasn't like we were out there doing anything that much different than anybody else.

The Dale Earnhardt Era saw a major national brand colorfully and imaginatively adorning sheet metal of the Bud Moore Engineering Thunderbird, seen here on March 28, 1982, at Rockingham in the Carolina 500. The result was a dismal twenty-fifth (Perry Wood Racing Collection).

It just so happened that in our gas mileage that day, I was off half a lap. One and a quarter miles. It's just that simple. Missed it by half a lap. If it had run out of gas coming out of four when he was backed out of the gas, it wouldn't have burned a piston. But he was halfway down the backstretch, it leaned out, and it went. It was that close. The way I had it figured, he should have easily made 35 and a half, 36 laps. A few seconds on the watch. We felt like we had a cushion. For some strange reason, though, it only made it 34 and a half laps.

To figure the gas mileage, you know how much you put in it. You fill the tank up. You've already warmed the car up in the garage area. You push it to pit road and you leave pit road wide open. Then you go out there and run and count the number of laps. You take into consideration if he's drafting, if he's by himself, and a lot of factors. When he comes down the backstretch, he cuts it off clean. It's kind of a seat-of-the-pants thing. You get a plug check. They come flying into the garage and all you hear is the wind rushing. It's real easy to get run over because you can't really hear them coming. You pull up there to Union and fill it up. You know how many laps you ran. That way you can get a fuel mileage estimate. It was not an exact science in 1982 and it's not much better now. Just look at the frequency of races that come down to fuel mileage today, especially if there's no late caution flag to let the guys pit. But after the 500, nobody was all that bent out of shape about it. We finished thirty-sixth in the 500, fourth in the 125 miler, and were leading the Daytona 500 right out of the box. We felt pretty good.

Daytona behind them, the Wrangler team forged ahead with no less enthusiasm.

We went to Richmond, where we ran third or fourth about all day long and it rained. Everybody hit pit road, and Dave Marcis stayed out, and we were fourth. Marcis won the race in Stacy's car because it rained and they called it an official race. That was his last win.

Next was a second at Bristol behind Waltrip and a pole at Atlanta. We led most of the race and burned the rod bearings out late and finished twenty-eighth. We had a good chance to win because the crew was on top of it. By then, we knew Earnhardt was Earnhardt. We knew we had a driver better than Benny. We knew by then we had at least a good a driver as Bobby Allison. We had us a horse. A heavy-footed one, too, which was what we liked. Earnhardt was smart for a mill hill guy and real aggressive on the track. Daddy told him from the get-go to be aggressive. Daddy had gotten on Benny a few times for not being aggressive enough, like when Waltrip slid under him at Daytona. Daddy would say, "Look, when you run a guy down and get to him, figure out what you're going to do. Hit him, knock him out of the way, whatever you got to do, go by him. If you're faster than him, don't sit there and wait on him. Go on by him. If he won't get out of your way, knock him out of your way." We didn't have to tell that to Earnhardt. We reaffirmed it.

There was still great optimism for the Wrangler team, but there was also an underlying problem that weighed on Greg's mind. The reliability of the motors was in question, and reliability was the hallmark of a Bud Moore race car. Greg and Daryl worked overtime to figure it out. By April 4, 1982, they did, and it held together. In their sixth race, that one-of-a-kind feeling was back in the CRC Chemicals Rebel 500 carried live on ABC TV.

As Donnie Allen waved Earnhardt on with his Wrangler hat, Dale and Cale went by with less than a lap to go. The winning margin at the finish line was about a foot at the CRC Chemicals Rebel 500 on April 4, 1982 (Perry Wood Racing Collection).

We qualified fifth, and if there was anywhere Daddy knew how to set up a car, it was at Darlington. It was a race-long fight and no matter who took the lead, Earnhardt took it right back. We were fast on the track and the pit stops were perfect.

Now, Darlington was Cale's backyard and maybe only Pearson drove it better. So in the end it came down to us and Cale, who was now driving M. C. Anderson's number 27. Earnhardt took the lead with about ten laps to go, but Cale was all over him. The crowd was going wild because Earnhardt was so popular and Cale was related to everybody else down there. When they came off four and headed for the checkered flag, Cale pulled out to pass, but came up a

A winning Moore family celebration in the South Carolina sunset on April 4, 1982, with (front left to right) Greg, Brent, and Bud (Perry Wood Racing Collection).

foot or two short. Man, were we happy! Not that we had a monkey on our backs; we just needed to show what we had, and we did just that against the best at the toughest track on the circuit, Cale's home track, and in front of the whole country on TV. It was an exciting Victory Lane. As far as I was concerned, Darlington was our home track, too. Daddy had been coming there since it opened in 1950 and won the Southern 500 three times. It was a fantastic day.

The numbers show that Dale Earnhardt led ten times for 181 of the 367 laps. It was his first win since October 5, 1980. The leaders in the last 140 laps were Earnhardt, Bonnett, Earnhardt, Richmond, Earnhardt, Parsons, Earnhardt, Yarborough, and Earnhardt. As for Bud Moore Engineering, it added to Southern 500 victories in 1957 with Speedy Thompson, 1960 with Buck Baker, and 1966 with Darel Dieringer. Joe Weatherly also won this race in 1963 for the team. By the way, that winning Wrangler Thunderbird sits proudly today in Alex Beam's Memory Lane Museum in Mooresville, North Carolina.

After that race, Earnhardt sat seventh in the championship standings, but there was still the shadow of an internal engine weakness to correct.

We had a 300-mile engine. We led the most laps in '82 and '83, but after about 300 miles, we would break a valve spring. At Atlanta we burned a rod bearing, and we didn't know what happened on that deal. We think the Babbitt came off of it. It held together at Richmond and Bristol and at Darlington. We qualified decent enough and led a lot, but kept breaking valve train pieces mainly due to the valve springs. That was the Achilles Heel

Wrangler Team winning portrait at the CRC Chemicals Rebel 500 on April 4, 1982, with bearded Greg, Bud (center, next to trophy), and Dale (white suit) on the back row, Brent (third from left) on the front row, and Danny Fowler (fourth from left) (courtesy Bud Moore Engineering Archives).

of a Ford. You just couldn't turn the RPMs in them. They made the rev kits illegal — the double valve springs that we used when Benny smoked them at Texas in '81. That's what we fought the whole time. They got a little bit better in '83 with the valve spring, but it still wasn't up to snuff. They didn't get the valve train problem fixed in the Ford engine until about '85. The Wood Brothers were having the same problems. Also, we learned that we could run a little bit different camshaft profile in the thing, but then you had a fifth place car. If we ran the camshaft profiles where he could lead the race and run real well, the engine was borderline living. It was too much velocity on the lobe of the camshaft for the valve train. The valve train was heavier in the Ford. The oiling system wasn't as good on the top end of the Ford as it was with the Chevrolet.

Ralph Dale Earnhardt, Sr., is arguably the most popular personality in the history of racing. Greg Moore was his teammate for two years and his friend until the last lap of the 2001 Daytona 500. Greg spent a lot of time with Dale, and he has volumes of Earnhardt tales. However, Greg said, "What happens on the road stays on the road." Greg is to be respected for his integrity in keeping things we would all love to hear about Earnhardt to himself. Yet, there are plenty of Dale Earnhardt yarns that he will relate.

As far as getting along with Earnhardt, we had a blast. The guy was pulling stunts all the time. He was about like a Weatherly. He was raised on a mill hill.

Bobby Allison was always sensitive about a drive shaft vibration. Anytime we'd go out and run, Bobby would say, "Turn the drive shaft 180 degrees to smooth it out." Cotton Owens was balancing the drive shafts, and we had them perfect. Cotton balanced the drive shafts for just about everybody. It was just something Bobby did to get somebody to do something. So, the first time Earnhardt went out and drove the car I asked him, "Do you notice anything about the drive shaft compared to those Chevrolets you've been driving? Any vibration?" His exact words were "Gregory, this is a race car. It's supposed to vibrate. Race cars vibrate." I said, "No, you don't follow what I'm saying, Earnhardt. I'm asking you a question. Bobby used to gripe from time to time about the drive shaft vibrating. We'd usually turn it 180 degrees and smooth it out, or we'd put another one in it." He said, "I'm telling you. A race car's supposed to vibrate. I don't pay that any attention to that. No! It doesn't have a bad vibration!" He was balls to the wall. Ran real aggressively. Probably ran a little bit too aggressively.

Right off the bat, Dale Earnhardt needled Greg, regardless of who his daddy or boss was. He flat out didn't care.

He messed with me from the get-go, aggravating the hell out of me. We would go out drinking and do stuff on the circuit, going out to eat. He wasn't married to Teresa then. He was between wives, a single guy. He was running women in and out. He was just a typical liquor-drinking, hell-raising, single race driver. One of the things he did to me was down there in Atlanta at the race in '82 when we sat on the pole. I had my beard and long hair, and Earnhardt took a long piece of duct tape and walked up behind me and wrapped it around my head and my beard. Made about two laps before I could do anything. They had to carry me down to the nurse's station and cut it out. I had about half a beard and a clump of hair out. He was laughing like hell.

The Dover Dive:

"We were going to the Iron Gate up there at Dover in '82. It's a real nice restaurant we'd been to a thousand times where everybody used to like to go. They had a good steak, and it was within five miles of the motel. We got in there and got about half drunk. We got out of there, and Earnhardt and I were in the back seat, and Daddy and Harold Stott were in the front seat. We pulled up to the driveway to the motel in this rent-a-car running about 20 miles per hour. I made a comment like, "You either got some mill hill redneck in you, or you're related to one of them Bodines up there in New York." When I said that and before I could do anything, Earnhardt reached over and opened up the door and took his foot and shoved me out of the rent-a-car. I cut about three or four flips. It was a wonder it didn't bang me up bad. It skinned my elbows up and tore my pants and the whole thing, and everybody laughed like hell. It was a wonder it didn't kill me. Earnhardt was laughing like crazy."

The Daytona Dip:

"We're down in Daytona in 1982 at the Howard Johnson's pool. Harold Stott gets on Doug Williams' shoulders, and Earnhardt puts me on his, and we have chicken fights. Well, Earnhardt isn't going to lose and he's got ahold of my legs, and Harold Stott is a lot stronger than I am. We're out there fighting and people are laughing, we're half lit, and we're yanking and doing this and doing that. I don't know who officially won. You're supposed to win when somebody splashes in the water. Earnhardt wasn't going to turn loose of my frigging legs, and Harold has ahold of me and he's got big old arms. Nobody's trying to hurt anybody or anything, but it got pretty doggone serious. He was not going to go down, and I'm the weak one up top. The others were pretty strong guys, too. I said, "Earnhardt, let go. Please let go." He had locked his arms around my legs so hard, it about tore my balls off. I think we won the chicken match and got out of the pool. Man, I was hurting. Bad! It was like getting racked with a helmet or something in football. "

The Pocono Problem:

"Up there at Pocono, we were always getting out to the track at six o' clock in the morning. Earnhardt said, "Practice isn't until nine o'clock, so come back and get me at 7:30." So we get to the race track and get the crew out there, and I get in the car to go back and pick Earnhardt up. I go inside and he finishes eating breakfast. We get in the car and head for the track. I thought he was going to drive. "Nah, you're going to drive." So we were going down this two-lane road on Highway 115, and there were deer jumping out in front of us and all kinds of hazards up there in Pennsylvania. I was running about 70, and there wasn't any big hurry. We had an hour to get there and it was only about 20 minutes away. He said, "This son-of-a-bitch won't run any faster?" "Hell," I said, "I'm running 70 in a damn 65 mile per hour zone. How fast do you want me to run?" He took his left foot and just reached over and put it on the top of my right foot and just held it to the floor. I didn't say a thing. I was just steering and steering and steering. We were catching some other cars. The thing just kept getting faster and faster, faster, faster. I looked at the speedometer and it was off the doggone dial. I finally told him, "Look, if you don't get your foot off my foot, we aren't going to make it to the race track. We're going to be dead!" He waited until we got right up on the ass end of a car and there were cars coming the other way. All I could do was get on the brakes. I didn't squeal the tires too much. I just did get stopped. Earnhardt was watching the whole time and laughed like crazy. When we got to the garage area he told everybody I was a pussy-footer because I wouldn't drive the rent-a-car fast enough. It was a Ford Fairmont or some car Hertz had back then. We were running as fast as we could with it."

The next day, perhaps the biggest non-winning moment for Dale Earnhardt and probably the most spectacular of his Bud Moore period occurred on July 25, 1982, in the Mountain Dew 500 at Pocono International Raceway. He and Cale Yarborough swapped the lead furiously early in the race, and past halfway Dale was dueling with his pal Tim Richmond just behind the leaders. On the 135th lap it happened.

Earnhardt was having brake trouble. He had to pump the brakes. Pocono has the longest straightaway in NASCAR, and you were carrying 200 miles per hour into the first turn where they had that famous boilerplate wall. Earnhardt and Richmond were battling, and you had to use a little bit of brakes back then, but Dale didn't use brakes much. They wrecked, and I can remember hearing the fans reacting and seeing Richmond go out of sight. There was a car upside down with a gray bottom. I knew that was us. Daddy's on the radio saying, "Caution! Caution! Come on in. We're going to change all four." I hadn't even had a chance to say anything to Daddy and Earnhardt was on his damn roof. Earnhardt keyed the mic and said, "Yeah, Bud. If you come down here to turn one and two it'll be real easy to change them because all four wheels are off the ground." That's how conscious he was. Then he limped off the race track with Richmond helping him to the ambulance. You could see the oil poured all over the race track out of the dry sump tank. It was a spectacular crash, and it was ironic because Richmond was in Stacy's number 2 car, the car Earnhardt got out of to come drive for us. Earnhardt went to the infield care center, and

Dale Earnhardt hobbles away from his demolished Wrangler Thunderbird with help of his close friend Tim Richmond during the Mountain Dew 500 on July 25, 1982 (courtesy Bud Moore Engineering Archives).

we flew back to Spartanburg on a private plane together. We played cards on the airplane, laughing and talking about it.

Two days later Earnhardt came down to the shop hobbling on crutches with a buddy of his. They looked at the car and he said, "Look how the roll bars held up," and he laughed about it. A lot of drivers wouldn't have wanted to look at it. Daddy had already checked Dale's leg, and Earnhardt pulled me off to the side and told me it was broken. We didn't want NASCAR to know that, so we never said a word to Daddy. Dale never said a word to anybody. Only he and I and some doctor knew it. So before we went to Talladega, his leg was broken. Talladega was where Bodine pushed him high in the tri-oval and wrecked him. But he was scared NASCAR wouldn't let him race. I remember he was on crutches doing an interview and he about slipped up and said his leg was broken. He said he had to go to some more therapy. We kept it secret that his leg was broken until months later. Daddy didn't know it. Nobody knew it. They thought it was torn ligaments. If NASCAR had known his leg was broken, they would not have let him start the race. If Daddy had known it was broken, he would have probably gotten a relief driver and wouldn't have let Earnhardt start. But Earnhardt didn't want the old man to know. He didn't want Daddy to know. He didn't want the crew chief to know. He told me in confidence, and I kept it to myself.

> *Dale Earnhardt was at home at North Fairview Avenue, and even though the results could have been better in 1982, all parties were pleased. One win, one pole, seven top fives, and a dozen top tens brought in $357,270, the second highest amount in Bud Moore history. The twelfth in the point standings was rather so-so, but everyone was optimistic for 1983. Then as now, February meant Speedweeks, and the crew was off to Daytona with a new look all the way around.*

Just about everywhere we went, Earnhardt was the leading lap leader in '82 and we were really looking forward to 1983. Back in about 1981, the Ford executives told the design people, "When you make this next Thunderbird, you do whatever you want, but that son-of-a-bitch better be aerodynamic." That's when they came out with the football-shaped thing. We had tested over the wintertime and the '83 seemed to be a good seven or eight tenths faster than the '82. We had the same engine; same horsepower, same everything. We had to get it where it drove right and we had to work on the front fenders. It would run a 46.87 and the boxy one wouldn't run but about a 47.85 at Daytona. We went to Speedweeks and took the new '83 car and the old '82 for a backup. We had a brand new hauler, the first of the big haulers other than Warner Hodgden and the Wood Brothers with Neil Bonnett in '82. The Pettys had one that was one of ours. They had it on display at Charlotte that year.

> *The first preliminary race of Speedweeks was always for drivers and car owners who had won a pole position the previous year. It was called the Clash, and believe me, it was properly named in 1983.*

We received the biggest fine in NASCAR history at Speedweeks that year. We had worked with Ford and the rev kit. They knew we had valve train flex, and they still hadn't straightened the valves up in the head. So Lee Morse—and this was pretty ingenious—made some cast valve covers. You couldn't run a stud girdle where it ties all the rockers together, which was a common drag race piece. So he came up with these valve covers that were real strong and lightweight. They were magnesium. The valve stud actually came through the top of the valve cover, and a nut went on top of it and held it dead solid to the valve cover. So it wasn't the rev kit like we had in '81, but it wasn't a stud girdle either. They don't use that now because we have shaft rocker arms. Now this is where we made a screw-up. When we made the valve covers, we put the breather pipes a little too low on the valve cover. You had to vent the thing because you weren't running a vacuum in the crank case. One of our guys did it, probably the way we told him to.

Everything was fine in the Clash except they all tangled up and crashed. We were running up front and we started blowing smoke. It was coming out of the breathers and getting on the headers. Gazaway was watching. I sat there listening to NASCAR with my little spy thing — I was one of the early ones to have a scanner. They watched him and said it was clearing up. It blew smoke for a lap and quit. It was spitting a little bit of oil out of the valve covers, barely getting on some windshields. We were right up there in front, third or fourth, in good position. Gazaway didn't want to black-flag us. With about four laps to go, finally it really puffed, really badly, going down the backstretch. Gazaway told Beaty to give us the black flag. We needed to get off the track, but the thing cleared back up. We raised hell that it had cleared back up. The motor was running great. The oil was just coming out of the breather cap. They put the black flag on us. They gave you a couple of laps to observe it. Finally with two laps to go, Gazaway yelled over the radio, "*Gregory! Tell Bud to park that son-of-a-bitch because it's already cost him more than he's going to win!*"

"Daddy never said a word to Earnhardt, and Earnhardt hadn't paid any attention to the black flag. Earnhardt knew it was smoking. He saw the black flag and his number displayed, but he knew the motor hadn't blown up, and he kept his hoof in it. It was a match race! They came down with about a lap to go, and they all went to wrecking. And the reason they wrecked was that Earnhardt had oiled up some of the windshields. They all went spinning. The Wood Brothers' car with Baker in it and everybody got screwed up. I think Bonnett went on to win it.

Earnhardt was in the wreck, got out of the car, and the reporters came over. CBS TV was down there with Earnhardt, and the first thing they said was, "Dale, didn't you see the black flag?" He said, "I wasn't looking for the black flag. I was looking for the checkered flag!"

It was a $10,000 fine. World record fine of NASCAR of all time! They only fined Bobby Allison $8,000 when Penske and he had the roller camshaft in that Matador. This was the all-time biggest fine. That really went over well with Earnhardt and them. So they had this big meeting. It got all over the TV. *Record fine!* I mean, it was ungodly, and on CBS on top of that. This wasn't on ESPNU, or whatever. Here we were, looking like the villains of the whole doggone thing.

We had to fix some of these cars. There were about two other Thunderbirds involved in it. I know the Wood Brothers were. So we called Phil Harris at the shop. He loaded up parts, fenders, all kinds of crazy stuff. The wreck hadn't bent frames up or anything too bad. Back then you fixed stuff.

The next day, Ford had this meeting. Daddy, Earnhardt, Gazaway, Bill France, Jr., all the higher-ups were sitting in there. It was the biggest cuss fight you ever heard in your life! NASCAR said they were going to wait a week or two and reduce the fine to $3,000, but they didn't say anything to the press about it. About a year later they said something about a $10,000 fine that was later reduced. Well, it was reduced the next day, but it still went on record up to that point as being the biggest fine ever. Back then, $10,000 went a lot further ... about ten times further! Now they don't hesitate to fine somebody $100,000 for shooting the bird. As great as A. J. Foyt and Bud Moore were, there is no way they could even be in the garage area for more than about 15 minutes today without getting fined at least $20,000. That's a fact!

The first meaningful competition of the season took place on February 17, 1983, in the first Uno Twin 125 Qualifier. It did not pay points, but paid off in research and development data—and confidence. Then they ran the 500.

We ran in the 125 miler and Earnhardt dominated it. He caught Foyt just right. Foyt ran well, and if it hadn't been our car behind him, Foyt would have won. We drafted by him, and I remember my sister-in-law Carol in the pits said, "Earnhardt's pulled out and just now drove by him." We knew we had Foyt set up. Man, we were getting right then!

So we got in the 500 and the car's running like a son-of-a-bitch. We go back and forth. We led a little bit, and then ran second, ran third, ran fourth. Did all these things and the car was flying. Then all of a sudden on lap 63, the mother blew up ... again! This time it didn't break a rod, it didn't burn a piston; this time what happened was the hardened tip of a brand new valve broke. Some people ran these valves twice, but we never would. TRW had a fused tip that would go on the end of a titanium valve that was super-fused. It was hard steel so the little roller on the rocker could sit on it. We caught one on the dyno that had broken right before Speedweeks, and we thought it was just a freakish thing. We thought when we had changed valve springs we had hit it on something. Come to find out it was a defective batch. It was a brand new part. It failed! It cost Earnhardt another Daytona 500.

Now that one was not Greg Moore's fault. We checked everything, even new parts. When we went back, we made sure that never happened again. We had a special test we put the valves through. We always looked at them under Zyglo. That's like Magnaflux only you soak it in fluid and look at it under ultraviolet light. All that was checked. Every new part that went into our motors. And some people ran these parts two 500-mile races. All the stuff we carried down to Daytona was brand new. So we screwed Earnhardt out of another Daytona 500—and Bud Moore, too!

There was a whole season to go with 29 races left and no time for losing sleep over a thirty-fifth at Daytona. A second at Richmond the next time out helped, but that was followed by a dismal stretch of seven races littered with blown engines and crashes. Then Greg came up with an idea, and beginning at Dover in mid–May, the team came alive, reeling off a string of eighths, ninth, fifth, fourth, eighth, fifteenth, and ninth. Finally, the sun broke through the clouds and shone brightly on the boys at 400 North Fairview.

We finally got the valve spring thing under control. We were getting the motor to live a little bit better. The RPMs were coming up. We got on this gig that Daryl and I had talked about back in the engine room. Daryl kept going on about that camshaft. That was a flat tappet—smaller tappet diameter. We were running mushroom lifters. Chevrolets really had to have a mushroom lifter where the bottom of the lifter was bigger. The Elliotts were running well, too, and we knew they had something figured out. I knew what camshaft the Elliotts and Chevrolets were running. It was a real high velocity camshaft with that mushroom lifter. We had those mushrooms in '82 and it was real high velocity.

You could run a one-inch. That was the rule. A Ford stock lifter was 8.875 in diameter. A Chevrolet stock lifter was smaller—8.40. My reasoning was that NASCAR caught Bobby Allison with a roller camshaft because they couldn't pull a lifter out and they got to looking.

That was like getting caught with a big motor. You don't get caught with a roller camshaft. That was very bad cheating.

This was my scheme, but I'll give Daryl and Daddy the credit on it. I told Daddy on the way to somewhere, "You can get Gazaway to do a whole lot of things. I got an idea. We really need to win a few races to hang on to this driver even though we got him signed through '84." I knew where we had them. "You go to Gazaway. Get them to ban the mushroom lifter. You've got to be able to move the lifter out during an inspection. You've got to run a stock diameter lifter. We'll cripple the Chevrolets for six weeks, and we'll win some races."

NASCAR did it. The very next race after they banned the mushroom lifter, we smoked their butts. It just slowed the Chevrolets and those guys up. We got down there to Daytona on July 4 and they were cussing me badly. Ernie Elliott said, "I'll get you, you S.O.B.," because they knew we were the ones that got that rule changed. But it really was a good idea and NASCAR's always stuck with it. They never went back to a mushroom lifter, and they made Chevrolet and everybody run the same size. So we got that rule fixed and the Elliotts couldn't run, and we qualified better. We led 19 laps, didn't blow, and finished ninth. Then we went to Nashville and beat Waltrip in his own backyard. We ran like Jack the Bear. Earnhardt ran great. That wasn't a problem.

The Chevrolets were crippled up for about five races. Even once they got caught up, we were a little more equal. We were leading all the races, running well, and went to Talladega. Now that was a fantastic win. Earnhardt qualified fourth and led about 40 laps, beating Waltrip, Richmond, Petty, Gant, and Bodine all in the lead pack. Man, we were feeling great!

> *But the chilly winds of change began to blow through the portals of Bud Moore Engineering, and winning with Dale was done. There were lots of good runs, a ton of laughs, and no hard feelings, but the handwriting was on the wall. Dale laid it out for Greg.*

The cars ran good, the motor reliability had gotten better, and we were getting things squared away. Ford came out with a new manifold instead of the box manifold. Everything was falling in place from Ford Motor Company in '83. This was what was frustrating. Earnhardt told me when we were sitting out there in a rental car or something, "You know I love you to death, but it's my dream to drive a Chevrolet for Junior Johnson. I'm just a Chevrolet guy."

"Well, that's great," I said. "We're Ford guys."

He came to me with about five races to go. He didn't tell Daddy because he had such mixed emotions about leaving anyway. It was real complicated. "Gregory," he said, "I'm going to just tell you right now. Y'all go ahead and start hunting because I'm not going to drive for y'all next year. I got something else worked out."

I said, "Well, that's OK. You go ahead and drive for Junior. We'll take Waltrip back. That'll work. You can go on over there." Boy, that pissed him off real good. It really did. I caught him perfect on that. I was really just being sarcastic. He led with his chin on that one. He stepped into it.

I told Daddy, "I think we're going to have to find another driver." "Well," said Daddy, "that isn't what he told me." I said, "OK." So it kept going on and on.

The sad part was that he really loved driving for us, but he wanted to be in a Chevrolet. His dream was to drive for Junior Johnson. He liked Richard Childress a lot, and they built a program around him. Hats off to them. I love Richard Childress, but he did go a long way pretty quickly. Now look at him. He still runs great. Plus he was a good guy, old school.

Actually, Junior was supposed to get Earnhardt when he left us. That was the deal! This was the kicker. Junior had the politics and everything all worked out, and Budweiser didn't want him! *Budweiser didn't want him!* If Junior Johnson had had Dale Earnhardt, he might have won 500 frigging races! But things got jockeyed up, and Chevrolet bought him out from underneath us and he went back to Childress. That was like Plan C. Childress knew this, and away they go.

Good things often happen in life when you least expect it. You find a $20 bill in a pair of jeans you haven't worn in a while. There's one more beer in the fridge hiding behind the orange juice carton. You're out killing time at the mall and run into an old best friend you haven't seen in 30 years. Or your mind is miles away from the thoughts and worries of life when the phone rings with a surprise on the other end of the line. It was like that with Greg.

There were a few races left in the 1983 season and out of the clear blue sky, Tim Richmond called me on the telephone. He and Raymond Beadle, Richmond's car owner with the Old Milwaukee Pontiac number 27, were squabbling about money. We knew Richmond would be able to drive the car with Earnhardt leaving. It was so obvious he had balls as big as soccer balls. Plus he was extremely marketable. The guy was handsome, and he had a wide-open lifestyle that got a lot of attention. It killed him, too, I guess. He died of AIDS. But this was way before he ever got sick or anything. He wanted to drive our car, and we considered him a top-notch replacement for Earnhardt.

Well, Earnhardt knew Richmond had called us, and one day Earnhardt and I are in a car driving down the road somewhere and he says, "I think Ron Bouchard would make a good driver for y'all." I said, "Earnhardt, are you kidding?" Those were the exact words. We were sitting in the front seat of a rent-a-car. He said, "No, I think Ron Bouchard is a nice guy. I think he'd make you a good driver."

"Look," I said. "I am not putting that no-driving son-of-a-bitch in that car. Bud Moore won't. We're going to put somebody in it that can run with *you*!"

He knew that Richmond was wanting to get in the car. He had caught wind of it. That's how the thing got all queered up. Then a marketing guy went to him, someone who had been handling a lot of Earnhardt stuff over the years, and he talked to Richmond enough to screw the deal up. "God, you don't want to drive for Bud Moore. That son-of-a-bitch will drive you nuts." We'd already talked to Richmond when he came down to the shop. He was going to drive the car. They were going to do a Wrangler commercial with him. That was one thing he wanted. He wanted to do a commercial.

We had a three-year deal with Wrangler *and* Earnhardt. So we went to the lawyer's office and got into it: If the driver tells us he's going to leave, and we had Wrangler another year ... what are we going to do? We came real close to keeping Wrangler in '85. But they threw all their money toward Earnhardt and Chevrolet.

So Richmond called back after he had been to the shop and met with us and the Wrangler people. He agreed to this, agreed to that; supposedly it was a done deal. Then he says, "You know Beadle owes me some money, and so-and-so told me so much crap that I think I'll just stay here and try to get the rest of my money next year." And he did. Richmond drove for Beadle another two years before he went to Hendrick.

You know, you put the power of suggestion in somebody's mind; it's the power of the mouth. You get somebody badmouthing somebody, and the power of the mouth queered that thing. Anyway, that's business.

So there was uncertainty at Bud Moore Engineering. The Richmond deal came and went on the fickle fall winds like the leaves that swirled around outside the shop door at the close of every racing season. Earnhardt was running out the string, and a driver worthy of the blue and yellow Wrangler Thunderbird was yet to be found. Greg reflects on what went wrong with Earnhardt.

Earnhardt ran hard the rest of the season. Sometimes it was a problem because he would rather go hunting than make a public appearance, but he made them. On the track he never cracked the throttle. As far as a lame duck driver? That son-of-a-bitch wasn't any lame duck! I think he got faster. He's a racer! He wasn't leaving because he disliked our team or was mad at anybody.

Now, he did blame Ford for being a little slow reacting to some of the technological stuff that they said they were going to do. Junior Johnson has always said, "If we're relying on the manufacturers to do something, back in those days, it took too long. You had to talk about it for a year, and then it would happen." Otherwise, you just did it yourself—like the rev kit. Do this yourself. Do that yourself. That 351 motor we had? We just built it off the technology of the 302 we had in the Trans Am. The whole frigging motor was done by ourselves.

The Earnhardt Era at 400 North Fairview Avenue came to an end with the Winston Western 500 at Riverside International Raceway on November 20, 1983. Dale Earnhardt time-trialed ninth in his last ride in a Ford race car, led four laps with 27 to go, and

It is not hard to tell which one is Greg as the Wrangler Jeans Machine is pushed to the grid on August 1, 1982, for the Talladega 500 (Perry Wood Racing Collection).

ended it with Bud and the boys with a solid fourth place finish. On that trip, for one last time, Dale Earnhardt had to get Greg's goat ... and his beer, too.

Out at Riverside, Earnhardt stayed next door to me at the motel. He always stayed next door to me because when they got the card game going, he'd come take my beer out of the trash can. He'd say, "Go over there and get Greg's beer. I want a beer." If he did it once, he probably did it a hundred times. Harold Stott and the crew were in there getting the card game going, and they'd go get my beer.

Icing the beer, that was the big thing. Everybody did that. You brought beer from the racetrack, it's free, and it's hot. You want it to get cold quick You took your trash can and scalded it out in the shower, then you put the beer into the trash can, you poured your ice on top of it, and threw a little salt on it. That was the trick. Like an ice cream churn, it would make that beer get real cold.

So Earnhardt said, "Go get Greg's beer." That left me about two beers. Earnhardt stole my beer for a card game, and I had to go get some. I hopped in the rent-a-car, and it was not far to buy some more beer. It just now had gotten dusk dark.

I was driving down through there, and all of a sudden I see blue lights. I was half lit! So I turned down a side road because I knew it looped around and I wanted to get turned around. The cop saw me turn. It was a rent-a-car that Earnhardt had about knocked the durn fenders off of.

The police got out, and I got out — me with hair down to my shoulders and my beard. They thought they were going to get me for drugs or something, and I *never, ever* messed with that shit. The police said, "Let's go back and talk about this." I sat there and I had to sweet talk until I got myself out of there. I don't know what I said, because that cop had him a drunk. I had it in the championship groove that night.

Out of the woods on the drunken driving rap and safe at the motel, Greg was confronted with another headache courtesy of Mr. Earnhardt.

I got back to the motel and took the beer to the room and iced it down. Then I heard knocking on a door. There was this gal, drop-dead gorgeous, knocking on Earnhardt's door. Drop dead gorgeous! She lived out there. Earnhardt told her he would take her out to eat. But Earnhardt had gone out to eat with Daddy and the Wrangler people.

I heard her crying, and I went out there and she said, "Dale was supposed to meet me and take me out." I said, "Honey, he went out to eat with the Wrangler people and he's been gone about an hour. He may be coming back soon." She says, "Can I stay here and wait on him?" "Yeah, you can stay here and wait on him." Now, Earnhardt's not married to Teresa yet and she's not in Riverside!

So this doll came in the room, and I sat there and listened to her and really babysat this girl. She waited around about an hour and a half, and Earnhardt didn't show up. I think she drank about three of my Budweisers or something, then finally she got in her car and left. She was really a pretty nice girl.

Earnhardt and Daddy strolled in about ten o'clock or ten thirty. It wasn't late, but you had to do things kind of early because you had to get up so early, plus you had the time change. I told him about it and Earnhardt said, "Who was over here?"

"That good looking girl that was out at the racetrack." "Aw, I'm not worried about her. What'd she do? I had to go out with O'Dear and Bud and them. She probably had a good time with you." Then he wanted to get mad, accusing me of taking advantage of her. I said, "*No!* Listen, I haven't done anything. I sat here and babysat that girl!"

Now this is what really took the cake. These were the best words I've ever heard. "Well," he says, "she's not but 19 or something like that. She needs to be home with her daddy. She doesn't have any morals."

I said, "Oh, I do not believe you said that. You're talking about morals? You're talking about *morals*?"

There was stuff like that going on that I wouldn't dare say. This was all pre-marriage and pre-children with Teresa. Teresa Earnhardt was fantastic. We loved Teresa to death. Earnhardt came to me one time and said, "I think I'm going to marry her."

"Well, that's what you need to do."

"She's from a racing family, you know."

I said, "If you love her, of course you should marry her. You got to act like somebody."

Teresa would catch Earnhardt with another young lady and Teresa would be gone for three or four weeks. They'd been dating and in love with each other forever. He'd come to me all the time asking me what he needed to do. How in the world am I going to tell him what to do? I think he was five or six years older. Asking me all this silly stuff and he's not even going to drive our car anymore. And I'm getting in trouble for babysitting his women. I mean, what the hell's going on here? Telling me he was not going to drive. Hiring another driver and queering the other deal. I got to live with all that the rest of my life. Still, you can't help but love the guy.

I still say to this day that David Pearson is the greatest race driver that ever lived. Earnhardt would have to be number two. But he's right there with him. It might be a tie. Call it a frigging tie!

Bud Moore and Dale Earnhardt had their best year together in 1983 with two wins, nine top fives, 14 top tens, 1030 laps led, a Bud Moore record $401,991 in winnings, and eighth in the final Winston Cup Championship Point Standings. By any standards, not too bad. The best compliment a racer can pay another racer is to say that he was the best that ever lived. Make no mistake about it. Greg is steadfast in his opinion that David Pearson is the greatest stock car driver that ever lived, and that opinion is shared by a very large number of people qualified to speak on the subject. David Gene Pearson and Ralph Dale Earnhardt, both Hall of Fame drivers, raced for Walter Bud Moore, a Hall of Fame owner and crew chief. Gregory Clyde Moore was right there in the middle of it all with them.

Chapter Eleven

The Roosters

Dale Earnhardt was all but gone. At 400 North Fairview Avenue in Spartanburg there was about to be a very desirable seat available in a championship-caliber, factory-backed Thunderbird with a top notch, nationally respected sponsor, signed, sealed, and delivered for the 1984 Winston Cup campaign. Greg had to find a race car driver deserving of the assignment. With a couple of races left in the '83 season, a great driver slipped through Greg's fingers due to rumor, innuendo, and interference. Then Greg went from One Tough Customer to One Just As Tough Customer.

The number one guy was Tim Richmond. That deal was already handled. Wrangler had agreed to do a TV commercial, which they had never done. They had done advertisements in magazines with Earnhardt, and now they were going to do a TV commercial with Richmond. Wrangler was tickled to death with the whole deal.

They questioned the drug thing a little bit with Richmond. The movie *Six Pack* or something was made and Richmond kind of got a bad rap on that. Nobody went into particulars, but they were pointing the finger at him a little bit wrong on that whole thing. I knew that. But this is what got me. We had this meeting with Wrangler and Richmond wasn't even there. One of the guys at Wrangler — and it wasn't O'Dear, it was the second guy — said something about cocaine. I spoke up and said, "Whoa, whoa, wait a minute!" There weren't any drugs that I knew of in racing, except there were a lot of alcoholics, especially in the engine room. The paint room was bad, too. The whole shop was bad!

I said, "Look!" I stopped him right there. "To run like that son-of-a-bitch does, if cocaine helps, I'm going to start taking it, too. I'm not worried about what he does." Seriously, who cares? You're hiring a heavy foot. That was something you heard about in Hollywood.

We could start throwing some very big-name drivers in on some stuff I saw. Let me put it this way: I've always said, "What goes on on the road, stays on the road." That pertains more to the old days than it does now because there's too many TV cameras, too many sponsors, and it did start changing about the time all the sponsors started coming in. Everybody had to start watching what they were doing. The biggest thing back then was to get caught drinking by the cops or coming out of a room with some woman or something that looked a little bit too fishy. Now, if you suspiciously look doped up ... if you *think* about being doped up, they test you.

Anyway, the Richmond thing got screwed up and I don't think I even had a conversation with Ron Bouchard. I said something to Daddy about it. "Do you believe Earnhardt suggested we hire Ron Bouchard?" Daddy said, "Ron Bouchard? Good God! I'll drive the son-of-a-bitch before I put him in it!" But there were a bunch of drivers wanting to get in our car.

Bob O'Dear, the head guy at Wrangler, liked Ricky Rudd. Rudd was getting fired from Childress so that Childress could take Earnhardt, and Rudd was starting to run well in that Piedmont Airlines car. I knew Rudd could run short tracks. He qualified on the pole down at Daytona one time, and I think he stayed up front about half a lap. Ricky was fantastic everywhere except Daytona and Talladega. He admitted that himself. Ricky Rudd wasn't scared of anything!

I loved Ricky. I thought that in a lot of ways he might have been the best-suited driver for us all around. He was mean, aggressive, and ran well on handling tracks. But he had signed a deal with the UNO people. UNO had been left out in the cold as a sponsor, so they were hunting a car. They were a sponsor with a driver and no car. Rudd had signed a letter of intent with them. Now, a letter of intent you can wipe your butt with. That doesn't work, period. Ricky had a real sharp lawyer, a friend of his, who handled some of his stuff. So Ricky and his lawyer got that thing spit out real quick. He got out of the contract with Bob Tezak and UNO, making him available to us if we wanted him. We wanted Rudd, we got Rudd, and we were tickled. Daddy said, "Got him!"

With several hot shots wanting to climb in the window of the number 15 for a couple of years, Ricky Rudd got the call and was maybe the best driver Greg ever hired.

Rudd came down to the shop, put on a Wrangler hat, and said, "Yeah, we got a deal." We were happy as hell. We really were. We got Wrangler coming back, we got Ford, we got a driver that's won some races, and he's fast and runs great on short tracks. Anything old — Martinsville, Bristol, Darlington — we loved. Rudd could run real well everywhere. So he was leaving the Piedmont Airlines Richard Childress car (which they had got running well, and my hat's off to them.) The shop loved Ricky immediately. Everybody fell in love with him.

The future was now and his name was Ricky Rudd from Chesapeake, Virginia. Not the tallest guy on the track, but just maybe the toughest. Wrangler was one tough customer, according to their famous advertising campaign, and Ricky Rudd more than filled the bill. He proved it quickly — as in, immediately.

We got Ricky ready and went down to Daytona and tested with him. He ran well. We took the car that we'd won Talladega with in '83. That was a special car we'd fixed aerodynamically. We had taken our Daytona car and rebodied it. That was the car with the long trailing arms and all that stuff that I'd always told everybody about. I've always said that stuff was the trick to why our cars always handled so well at Daytona. I'd gone back there with the body guys in the shop before Talladega in '83 and showed them the voids where the fender's contours went in and out. I wanted them to put Bondo in the fender. I didn't want flimsy-ass metal. I didn't want any deflection. I wanted that curve just like a flow bench. I knew all that stuff — Mr. Flow, remember? I wanted them to straighten it as straight as they could and still fit all the templates, which they did, and we got the sides straightened out on that thing. It had very little of what we called "oil can effect" because we put it in the wind tunnel at Lockheed and that was where I caught this stuff.

The Lockheed wind tunnel in Marietta, Georgia, was a top-secret area, but Greg offers some fascinating insight as to what went on there.

I've slept through more wind tunnel tests than you'd believe. What you did was, you let the guys test all the stuff they wanted to, then you went in there and fixed the car. We were at Lockheed with the Trans AM program. I think were the first ones who ever went to a wind tunnel because Ford had it contracted. You know that little wing on the back of the Trans Am cars? That happened because we'd already been at Lockheed.

We were going down there all the time, and we did it on Ford's nickel. We weren't paying any money for anything like that. We went all we wanted, but the problem was having the time. I'd say we went at least twice a year the whole time we were with Ford, and I mean we had two-day sessions. We'd sit there and let these guys give us all this gibberish, and we'd start looking at drag numbers and down force. Then we'd run those guys out of the room and fix the son-of-a-gun. We had our body people there to Bondo and sand and paint the car before we went back to recheck the results.

They had a guy called Don, and he was the guy that did the smoke wand. We called him Don Wand. There was another guy with the clay that was shaped onto the body.

One time we went down there and they said the numbers on one of our cars were good. Well, I knew they *weren't* good. Bob Riley with Ford was there. This was the second year with Rudd in '85. Elliott was really running well. I looked at his car and they had some tricks on it. They had the rear end changed around and were able to run less spoiler. It was something besides the ten horsepower he had. Ten horsepower didn't do anything. It had to be a combination. It was always a combination of things. It's *really* a combination of things now.

We left there and we'd clayed some stuff up. I asked Bob Riley, "Is this car good?" He kind of hesitated and said, "Yeah, yeah, yeah, this is a good car." I said, "Is this car even close to Elliott's?"

"Damn," he said, "I can't tell you that."

Oh boy, I got hot! I told Daddy, "Let's get this car out of here."

"No! They said it's good. Boy, you don't know what in the Hell you're talking about. Bob Riley —."

I stopped Daddy and said, "Look, you see Don out there with that wand? That smoke? It's going up over that car and it's blowing right straight up your ass! Let's get out of here."

So we got out of there. Later we found out that that car was down about 20 horsepower on drag. It had good down force, so later on we got all that fixed. That was just this one particular car.

Another time was about two years later, in early '86, before we went to Talladega. That was the race when Ricky Rudd got sick and Rusty Wallace got in and came to the front. Before that, we noticed that some air was getting on the inside of the car. We were testing other things, and we saw the window net flapping and were trying to stop that. So the guy got on the A pillar. (That's the one that runs down along the windshield. The B pillar is right behind the window net, and the C pillar is alongside the back glass.) The guy kept claying it up, but it didn't change enough because air was still going in the car. They shut the wind tunnel down and, no joke, the wind was still coming in, probably about 40 miles per hour. So Daddy went out there and took the clay out of this guy's hand. He said, "Son-of-a-bitch, this is the way I want it," and put it on the A pillar. Daddy wanted it shaped a certain way and the guy kept doing it wrong. When Daddy did it, it didn't really look that good. But he put it on there, they blew it at 200 miles an hour, and the car was fixed! I nearly fell over. Bud Moore fixed it. The net quit rattling and the drag numbers got better. And the first thing Rusty Wallace said when he got out of the car down there at Talladega was, "You know, there's no air coming in this car. In that Pontiac, I'm used to hearing that air coming in and buffeting around. This car is dead silent. You could smoke a cigarette in this son-of-a-bitch." Rusty still talks about that. That race was Bobby Hillin's only Cup win, with Tim Richmond second and Rusty Wallace third just a few feet behind, relieving for Rudd.

Daddy was good for doing stuff like that. I have to take my hat off to him. He had a very crude way of approaching things, but it also had a very strange way of working, like about 98 percent of the time.

In the fall of 1968, the Ford Motor Company introduced the slogan, "Ford has a better idea." In Greg's world, their own ideas and innovations were the lifeblood that kept Bud Moore Engineering at the front of the field. From the dirt floor garage next to the beauty salon at St. John and Pine streets, to the cutting edge scientific cleanliness of 400 North Fairview Avenue, the common threads of genius, muscle, sweat, and confidence sustained what was literally a Hall of Fame operation for 50 years.

We came up with a lot of innovations. Some with employees and a lot just with Daryl and me. Daryl was the one who came up with the idea of balancing the camshaft. If Daryl hadn't figured that out, these motors wouldn't be turning like they do. That was what stopped timing chains from breaking in 1990. Daryl had talked about it, and I said, "Go tell Daddy." "Aw hell," Daryl said. "He isn't going to listen to anything." I said, "He will this. Daddy, come here. See that camshaft? See that centric on the front? Daryl's got a good point. You balance that centric and you'll balance that camshaft."

Nobody had ever done any camshaft balancing. That's a common thing now. Daryl invented it. Daryl said that if you balanced that son-of-a-gun, it would cut down all that vibration in the valve train. So Daddy, Cotton, and Daryl spent about two days up there in 1990 and '91 spinning the things and they just smoothed it right out. We put it in the motor and even the timing light settled down. Smoothed it right out.

Preston Miller was Ford's liaison for years. He was our spotter, and he saw what we'd done. He said, "I know you'll want to keep this for yourselves, and you've had it for yourselves for a few races, but it's really too big a technological gain not to tell the other Ford teams, with you all being sponsored by Ford." They had different ways they did it, but we made three kits for every Ford team. We made three kits for Yates, three kits for Donleavy, three kits for Elliott, and so on. We made three kits for every Ford-supported team, and by that time there were about ten. Everybody got three kits. Daryl didn't ever get mentioned. It was a Ford Motor Company "Better Idea." That's fine. We didn't give a damn, didn't even get Honorable Mention. Matter of fact, I don't even think we got credit for it. But people at Ford Motor Company know it. Everybody else knows it. Cotton balanced all our drive shafts — Cotton knew it!

The Busch Clash got things started for the Winston Cup teams as usual for the annual Speedweeks in February, but the 1984 edition will be cussed and discussed from now own. If nobody believed it yet, they were about to find out that the new Wrangler One Tough Customer was as tough as the old one — if not tougher. And his car owner would perform the kind of act that is the stuff of legend. Toughness meets toughness.

The winter testing was successful, and all we did was massage the car Earnhardt won Talladega with in 1983. That was our number one car, and back then we decided to use the Richmond car, which was fair aerodynamically, as the backup. That was the way people did it back then in 1984. The super-duper car was the one we were going to run in the Clash, too.

We got out there and that car was quick right off the truck. At that time, nobody got that much practice. Some of those Clash cars didn't get but about 20 laps of practice because of rain or something. Rudd said our car handled well, but we didn't get to do a long run. And we didn't quite have enough rear spoiler on it. It wasn't quite tight enough, and he drifted up in the corners. Earnhardt would have just let the tail end hang out and gone on.

It was a 20 lap race, and there were about five laps to go when they came off turn four. We were running real well, just hanging on the draft, biding our time before making a move to the front. Baker was leading in the Wood Brothers' car, Bonnett was second, Yarborough third, Geoff Bodine was fourth, Rudd fifth, and Jody Ridley was sixth in an independent car and was able to hang onto the front five. Those were the only cars it was coming down to.

Our car was loose and kept getting closer to the turn four wall. Ricky tried to take the lead two or three times, holding it on the bottom, and he couldn't hold it. Richard Petty was doing the race for CBS TV and said — and he calls Ricky "Ritchie" — "Ritchie's running real good, but he looks a little bit loose to me." I think three degrees of spoiler might have fixed it and he could have won the race. There was just not enough practice time in race trim. Nobody talked on the radio much, he said just very little and was hanging on to it. They were all white-knuckling the crap out of it. Ricky had about lost it the lap before, just drifting up and drifting up.

Ridley tried to go under Rudd, who was running high, and just barely tapped him in the left rear — but it didn't take much to get you out of shape at over 200. They started to come into sight in the tri-oval, and I never saw the car for more than an instant before I heard the stands get quiet. I heard the fans go, "Whoa! *Oh!*" So I started running up toward there, and I got there just about the time the car set back down on its wheels. We couldn't see all the twirling and all that stuff it had done. By the time we got there everybody was telling us that the son-of-a-bitch had flipped and it was the damndest they ever seen. And it was! It was a mess. Some of the officials had stopped us, but we could tell Ricky was alive. He had those Banjo seats in that thing and got to flopping around. He had the driver restraints and his arm still flew out the window. He was just hanging on to it. He was addled and wasn't really hurt that bad. I don't know how the hell it didn't kill him.

Daddy turned around to me and said, "There goes our Daytona 500 effort, doesn't it?" I said, "No, not necessarily." So we went flying to the hospital, and Ricky was sitting up. They had done an MRI on him by the time we got there, and he said, "I'm OK." He was faking the hell out of it, because he wasn't OK. He was still dizzy. He was bound and determined he wasn't going to get out of that car. He stayed overnight and bullshits his way out of the hospital the next day.

Ricky walked around with sunglasses on. His eyes were black at the bottom and his eyeballs were blood red, and he said, "I'm dizzy, but I think I'll be OK." That shows you what kind of balls that guy had. We got out the very next day — the *next day!* — *and* he made a couple of laps in the backup car. He said, "Bud, my eyelids are pulling down. I can't see." Daddy said, "You can't see? I'll fix that." Daddy took some tape — either masking tape or duct tape — and pulled his upper eyelids up and taped them up, and pulled the lower ones down beneath his eyes and taped them down and said, "That'll fix it." Rudd put his bubble goggles on and said, "Hell yeah, that fixed it!" And that's the way he ran.

Ricky did take time that day after the race to look up Jody Ridley. He got pissed at

Ridley over the Busch Clash deal. He jumped on him the next day. He got in the backup car and everybody was fighting for that 200 miles per hour mark. We qualified at 197.8 or something, and Yarborough took the pole at 201.8 miles per hour. We taped Rudd's eyes open, and he ran seventh in the 125 mile qualifier and seventh in the 500. He said all he could do was keep his eyes on Ron Bouchard and follow him. He said, "I was dizzy as hell," but he hung on. Now that's tough! Ricky Rudd is as tough as they ever came.

Ricky Rudd did not have to prove he was tough to live up to his Wrangler advertisements as One Tough Customer, but he did it anyway in his very first race for Bud Moore Engineering. It will always be a cornerstone of Ricky's personal legacy—and he still had four years to go racing out of 400 North Fairview!

After that, Rudd and the boys headed to Richmond, Virginia. It was a home game for Ricky. Bud Moore already had six wins at Richmond, and three of the first four ever run there with Joe Weatherly when it was dirt. Bobby Allison won there twice and Benny Parsons once on the pavement, so Ricky Rudd was in the best of situations, except for his beat-up body.

When we got to Richmond the next week Rudd's eyes were still black and blood red. In this day and time they wouldn't have let him race. He had a mild concussion, but he wasn't going to let on. Linda Rudd said, "I've seen him with broken arms, and he's tough. Don't worry about it. He'll be all right." She said he didn't have any sense, and he didn't!

At Richmond he qualified fourth and smoked by Waltrip on scuff tires with 20 laps to go and won the race. In Victory Lane, Rudd's eyes looked like something out of one of those movies where the monster is possessed—blood red eyes with huge black pupils. Wrangler's One Tough Customer could not be any tougher.

Ricky Rudd did have something to say about Dale Earnhardt that was forever true.

He told me something about Earnhardt, and he finally proved it at Wilkesboro in '91. He said, "I don't know what it is about Dale Earnhardt. Anybody else on the track, it was a whole different story. You cannot rub fenders with Earnhardt and come out on top. The only way you can get him is to take yourself out with him." You don't want to do that. But Ricky did it up there at Wilkesboro in '91. He was driving for Bernstein in that Quaker State Buick. Earnhardt said, "If NASCAR doesn't throw that son-of-a-gun out...." Well, Earnhardt had been rubbing on him all day long, and Rudd finally had enough and took him out! Took himself out, too, of course. Geoff Bodine won the race, and that got Hendrick going.

As much as any driver who ever crossed the threshold at Bud Moore Engineering, Ricky Rudd was at home with the Moores. It was like he was surrounded by family. With that family, he enjoyed four high-octane winning years of the Rooster, innovations, and confrontations. But first, Greg gave Ricky some advice.

I always told Ricky—and this happened every race we ever ran—"Daddy's going to holler on that radio and I know it's going to get on your nerves, but don't pay it any attention. All you do is you cuss him back and he loves it." This is true! "About the third time he hollers at you and it's getting on your nerves, tell him you're driving the son-of-a-bitch and you won't have any more problems, and it gets a little better." The next race he does the same thing. For four years, thirty races a year, 120 races, it happened every race exactly that way! That is no joke. The car ran and the pit crew was great. Back then we had a super pit crew. We were on top of everything. But Ricky Rudd was just fantastic.

Then there was another Better Idea from Ford.

We were the first one to have that big, tall scoring stand, where the guys sit up there with the computers. Motorcraft made one of those in '86 when all those fancy postcards came out. I called it the Lunar Lander. Bill Burrell hated that son-of-a-bitch. We had to sneak it through. We had to talk to Beaty about it. It had two seats, and we had Linda sitting up there scoring the car in the pits. It had a little hood on it. I think we had a crude lap counter or something. We put a sponsor up there next to Linda. The head guy at Motorcraft or Edsel Ford or somebody sat up there next to her. It was a big thing. Bill Burrell had to put it together and disassemble that thing and put it on the truck. The pit crew guys and I would all help him put it up and set up the pits. There were a couple of tracks that wouldn't let us put it up because they thought it overcrowded the pits. Dover was one of them. They got a skyscraper now with ten people on it. But that was the very first one, so help me. Motorcraft made it. That was one of Ford's better ideas. Bill Burrell thought it sucked.

It was about that time that Greg taught his driver to relax and have a cool brew or two. It also came to light that the team had a couple of roosters on it, and a pair of Fernwood boys found work on the road.

First of all, Ricky didn't drink. Well, about mid-season of '84, Ricky got in my motel room and into my beer. I got him messed up. But really, Rudd didn't drink, and Linda went to about all the races and sat right there with us the whole time. It was a dead perfect fit for Bud Moore Engineering.

I was the first one to ever get Bill Elliott drunk. That was out at Riverside in '81. He went out there and hung around with us and Benny. He hadn't run Riverside before. It was right before he got the Melling deal. Elliott and I were going out to the race track, and we got a Ford Fairmont rent-a-car and threw the belts off the motor. I don't know how we did it on the highway going to the race track from the motel. Elliott and I got out there and put the belts back on it. Elliott didn't need to be at the race track. He had taken a look at it once and had it figured out. That was how good he was. We went to a bar and I got about three beers in him and he didn't even know where he was. He laughed, acted up, and everything.

Somewhere along the line we put the nickname "Rooster" and Ricky Rudd together, and that was a perfect fit, too. I mean, that little sucker would get mad. He was like a Chihuahua jumping on a Doberman Pinscher. He went for it. He was not afraid to get in another driver's face. By God, he'd usually come out on top. "Rooster" came about because Rudd liked it and that was the term we always called Momma. Daddy always called her either "Baby" or "Rooster." Why he called her Rooster I don't know. Maybe his daddy called his momma Rooster. It was in a nice way, a term of affection. Rudd and even Earnhardt used to say, "Where's Rooster at?" Momma was real little and would hardly say anything. But when the time came, she could sure get on Bud Moore's ass. That was at home behind closed doors. Not at the race track.

Nearly nothing could rattle Greg Moore because he had pretty much seen and done it all at this point in his career. But there was one incident that scared him, when he saw some Hall of Fame tempers flare.

There was a famous confrontation between Richard Petty and Darrell Waltrip when Richard stuck that long finger in Waltrip's face at Daytona. I was in the middle of that by accident because you got put in the garage area in order of points. Richard was on one side and Waltrip was on the other. We were in the middle.

What happened was this: Back then, you could race around to the caution flag. Richard saw it, but Darrell was trying to make up a lap and pass before they got to the flag. Richard saw him coming and didn't like him and sort of moved up in front of him like, "Slow down, asshole, there's a wreck up here!" Waltrip probably saw the wreck, too, but he was going to get by Petty, so Richard just crowded him a little bit.

After the race, I ran up there to Rudd in the garage and hadn't even thought about that incident in the race. All the cars were just now pulling into the garage. Waltrip hopped out of his car and Richard jumped out of his. We were right in the middle. I told Ricky, "You sit right there." Rick said, "What in the...?" I said, "Just sit." I was standing a few feet away and those two were getting ready to go for it. Darrell said, "Richard! Richard, I'm not playing with you this time!" I mean, they came *that close* to somebody getting hurt. Now, I don't know who would have been hurt, but somebody would have. Dale Inman went up there and grabbed Richard, and an official, a pretty big one, jumped in between them. They saw what was going on and just ran over there. It was getting ready to be nasty. All this happened in about 45 seconds, but that was the worse deal I can talk about. Back in the old days, before I was there, somebody got hit with a lug wrench or something all the time. It took a lot to scare me back then, and that right there kind of got my attention. I didn't want in the middle of that because Baby would have been hurt! One of those two were getting ready to get hurt. I don't know which one.

It did happen occasionally, though. One time at Darlington, Pearson was on seven cylinders. I think he was in the Osterlund car. He was out there just running and trying to stay out of the way and finish the race with a few laps to go. He was looking in his mirror; he was smart. Well, Richmond was about fourth, and he thought Pearson might have been in the way a little bit and blocking him. Pearson was two laps down, just trying to finish. Richmond went by and gave Pearson the finger when he passed. So they came in the garage area after the race and Pearson got out of his car. Pearson wasn't thinking too much about it, but probably still had it on his mind. Richmond jumped up in his face and said, "Let me tell you something, old man," and *blap*! He was flat on his ass! Pearson flat knocked him down. Hit him in the face.

With all the controversy about the drugs and everything, Richmond wasn't real popular with the drivers anyway. Dick Beaty walked over and said, "What happened?" Somebody replied, "Richmond jumped up in Pearson's face and called him an old man, why the fuck was he in the way, and Richmond wound up on the ground." Beaty said, "Ah, it's even. Forget it." Dick Beaty had seen so much of it. He was an old racer himself from the '50s. They would fine somebody a million dollars if they did that today.

Dick Beaty and his inspectors were not beyond creating a little turmoil themselves. Imagine this happening today:

We were out there at Riverside in 1985 on race morning. Beaty and the other officials always got there an hour before they opened the garage area. What they did was roll Ricky Rudd's car out of our garage and put the pace car in there and put the Motorcraft car cover back on it. Those car covers had just come out — the pretty ones with the sponsor names on them. They had the cover pulled down, and it covered the wheels and we didn't pay it any attention. They had the race car hidden behind one of the buildings.

We were always some of the first ones to get there, and we go strolling in early that morning about half hung over and half asleep and take the car cover off. There isn't any damn race car! Daddy and me are looking around saying, "Where in the hell's the car?" We haven't panicked yet, but we're getting close. Then all the inspectors come around the corner laughing like hell. Beaty and Buster Auten and the rest of the inspectors were over there dying laughing. Then they went and pushed the racecar back around to us and said, "We didn't mess with it." But I've always wondered, in the back of my mind, if there was something they were looking at. But I don't think really think so, because it was the last race of the season and we won it on my fantastic two-tires call on the last pit stop. That was how to do it.

> There was a short period in the Ricky Rudd years when the patriarch of the family took ill and Greg had to fill his shoes in the most harrowing of all pit road duties. Bravery and a piece of wood were all that stood between the crew and two tons of speeding steel and rubber in the oily, slippery pits of stock car racing.

In 1986, there were three races Daddy couldn't come to because he was sick and running a fever. Doctor Bonner suspected he got Hepatitis B off some bad seafood. So I had to hold the pit board. The way Rudd and I did it, Ricky said, "What I want you to do, Gregory, is you put that board where you want me to put that left front tire. I'll put it there." By George, we hit her dead right every time. Beginner's luck. I did it at Bristol, Darlington, and North Wilkesboro. We ran second up there at Bristol when it rained. It was spooky because the pit road was damp. You get out there and you're watching what you're doing!

I figured out a way for me to do it. The pit board is big. I was a young man then and had some arm strength and I could do stuff. The board had "Motocraft" on it and a big 15. It was identifiable and as big as a guy could stand to hold it. You go way out in the pit road and you're waving it. Like, "Look at me, man. This is your pit." The guys are coming in and they're hauling ass. The driver has got to look. Then you slide back in the pit box and you motion the driver with your head a little bit. I put the board right there on his left front and he would run right up to it with the car. I held it off to the side. I only had had a few feet to get out of the way if I had to. *Olé*! *It's* exactly like landing a plane on an aircraft carrier. I did it three races in a row. They're coming at you and going by you. It isn't for weak-hearted people. I didn't have any problem doing it.

Junior Johnson was against the pit road speed limit. The driver's got to be partly responsible for that. I mean, Junior drove a race car and Junior Johnson isn't scared of anything! And he had a point. I had seen people hurt even with pit road speed limits.

> Make no mistake about it. The Ricky Rudd years on North Fairview Avenue were ultra-competitive. Rudd was as likely to win each and every race as anybody else out there.

Greg on pit road during the 1985 season (courtesy Bud Moore Engineering Archives).

Everything was good — almost. Except for those suits. Those Dearborn suits and their better ideas.

In '87 we won the Atlanta 500 going away. We had to race Rusty Wallace in the Kodiak car and Benny Parsons in Hendrick's car. Ricky outran the hell out of them. He got on top of the steering wheel, and we were doing it.

We always just signed Ricky year to year, and he had offers. That's the way Motorcraft was. Ricky and I talked about it. Right there towards the last few years, we tried to sign a good driver to a three-year deal so everyone could plan for the future. This was so the driver didn't have to worry that he was going to have the rug pulled out from underneath him.

Somewhere along the line in 1987 Ford had switched the marketing guy. They were constantly changing about every 18 months. I went through 11 racing directors who would actually come to the race track. The racing director was the guy between Ford headquarters and me. Well, this new guy got the idea that he didn't like Ricky Rudd. It all came over a deal about Rudd missing an appearance. That was where it started, and it wasn't Ricky's fault. We were up there at Pocono and they wanted Rudd to make an appearance in Hershey,

A very satisfying Victory Lane after the Atlanta 500 win on March 15, 1987. Linda Rudd on the left and Bud Moore on the right flank the Roosters — Ricky Rudd and Betty Moore (courtesy Bud Moore Engineering Archives).

Pennsylvania. Rudd thought it was somewhere else in Pennsylvania that was three hours away. It was a mix-up and it wasn't Rudd's fault. We had told this marketing guy that the night before any race, outside of going to out to eat, you are not going to run our driver to death. We always limited drivers to a certain number of appearances. If it's the off-season and you're going to pay him a ton to do extra, that's OK. But the driver is *not* to do anything the night before that race. Leave him alone!

Ricky said, "I can't drive three hours over there and come back." That's all that happened, but Ford got all pissed off about it. But the misunderstanding was with the new racing director. He was a screw-up. It wasn't Ricky. That was the only time Ricky ever did anything wrong in their eyes, and it was all over Ford's own mistake. We won two races that year! So Rudd got pissed off and was already going somewhere when we went up there to Dover and smoked them. Leonard Wood said, "How in the hell did y'all let him get gone?" I said, "Shit, I don't know! Go ask Ford."

That Hershey deal started souring it with the Ford people. This new guy and some of the marketing people up there at Ford got the ass at him. Then the guy at Ford decided they were going to cut part of our deal, and there were two or three sponsors that were going to pick up the other half of it. That was when they put part of Motorcraft on part of Elliott's Coors car. They split the deal up a little bit. But Ricky did his job, and Ricky and I were always best of friends and still are. No if, ands, or buts about that thing!

> Now the handwriting was clearly visible on the wall. Into their fourth year together and having enjoyed a very successful relationship, Ricky Rudd was leaving. He had lasted twice as long as Earnhardt, who lasted twice as long as Parsons. It looked like the next driver should be around 400 North Fairview for about eight years. Greg went back in a hiring mode and then some. The back-biting business side of racing reared its ugly head again.

We were going to put Ken Schrader in the car. Ford had been schooling him along. He had been driving for Donleavy. They said he was ready to move up, and Michael Kranefuss was going to put Schrader in our car. We had a deal set up. Daddy told them that day that we better sign a contract. The Ford guy said, "Ah, don't worry about it. We got him handled." We came to a gentlemen's agreement and offered him a super deal.

Well, we got hung out to dry on the Schrader deal. We got down to Darlington and Daddy comes up to the truck and says, "Well, Schrader isn't going to drive for us. You got to find us another driver."

I said, "Do what?"

"Yeah, you have to find a driver and about $700,000."

"We already had all this handled!"

Under the circumstances in modern-day terms, anybody would have done what Schrader did. He didn't jump a contract, but he jumped a handshake. Daddy said, "Schrader, we want you and we want to do good for you. But if a man's handshake isn't any good, your contract isn't any good either." Schrader said, "I guess when it comes to money in this business, it isn't." What could he say? He could talk a line of crap, I know that. He was a pretty good comedian. We hadn't signed a contract with him. It was a ton more money, too. Then he screws us and goes to drive for Hendrick. He still didn't win much, and he would have with us. He knows that now. He set on about a million poles and won one race at Atlanta.

Ricky Rudd told me who he was talking to. Rudd was talking to Quaker State and Kenny Bernstein's Buick number 26. He was talking to the people of Morgan-McClure's

Kodak Olds number 4. He had four offers, and all of them were about the same as our ride. He wasn't going to get left out. He'd call me on the phone and say, "I talked to so and so. What do you think?" We'd talk about it. That's how good a parting it was with Ricky. We were worried about him getting taken care of, and he was worried about us getting taken care of. Ricky settled on the Quaker State deal because it was about the best opportunity.

Ricky, Daddy, and I had talked to Quaker State about coming to us. We turned them down for Motorcraft. I had the choice of four sponsors in '86. I could have had Zerex, Quaker State, Quincy's Steak House, and Folger's. Ruttman thought he was coming along with the Folger's deal, but he wasn't. He was getting real friendly. I liked him, don't get me wrong. Like Daryl said, "We don't need that character." We about put Scott Pruitt in the car one time in '93. He was a road racer running Indy cars that Ford liked. Daryl said, "Screw Scott Pruitt!" Quincy's didn't have enough money and I threw it Kulwicki's way. Alan Kulwicki drove the Quincy's car in 1986.

The young Rooster left the roost at 400 North Fairview after the 1987 season, and you get the idea that neither the Rudds nor the Moores were very happy about it. It also felt like Ford had pulled a few too many strings, maybe over-stepping their boundaries a bit with people who didn't know the business well. They paid the bills, so they called the shots.

The final numbers on Ricky Rudd's four years were 126 races, six wins, 41 top fives, 65 top tens, five poles, nearly 2,000 laps led, almost $2,000,000 in purses won, and points finishes of seventh, sixth, fifth, and sixth. It had been a very good four years with Ricky Rudd, but another change of direction was in the offing, and it came from the north.

Chapter Twelve

Cooking with Crisco

Greg had his work cut out for him with the ride- and sponsor-swapping for 1988 already underway. This time, Greg's hard work and the chance to drive one of the premier cars on the circuit brought not an established veteran to the seat, but an up and coming Yankee kid and a new sponsor for 1988. This was a challenging season all the way around.

Now, not only did I have to find another driver, I had to find about another quarter of a million dollars. It was costing about $1,250,000 to run a season. They had cut our Motorcraft deal in half. We knew that was going to happen. Another sponsor was attached to the Schrader deal — I don't remember who it was — and that got messed up when he went to drive for Hendrick in the number 25, taking Richmond's place. I pieced this together and that together, and Brett Bodine had come up to us at Talladega after he got in Junior's car and looked pretty good. He came up to me and said, "I'd really like to drive that car." He'd run pretty doggone good in Busch. He ran the double zero, the Sam Ard car. He was really a good prospect going in. He was the first guy that approached us after the Schrader deal fell apart.

Daddy and I were working underneath the hood, changing the valve springs or something, and I said, "Brett says he might want to drive the car." Daddy said, "Well, let's go talk to him." We talked to him for a few minutes and Daddy said, "Try and put the thing together." Brett ran well in Busch and we didn't have anybody! When the time came later on I said, "Hell, let's just put him in it." Then I went to Brett and said, "Daddy said you could drive the car." Then we were talking about it and I said, "Brett, there's one thing we've got to do. We've only got half a sponsor." He said, "Well, we'll get looking for something."

Sid Morris handled the Crisco deal because Buddy Baker was closing up his Oldsmobile team number 88 and they had been with them. Crisco was the sponsor without a home and still wanted to race. I called them up and said that we had Brett Bodine, who ran third in the Busch Grand National points. "Yeah, yeah, we'll go for that." Crisco became the main sponsor because they paid more money. Kirby Boone was working for Sid and came down to the shop. Brett knew these people, and we got that deal put together pretty doggone quickly to be that late in the year.

Crisco was spending $800,000 and Motorcraft was spending $500,000. That was a million three, about the fifth best deal in the garage area at that time. Nowadays, that won't even hire a driver. Crisco was the easiest sponsor I ever got. It belonged to Procter and Gamble. Easiest in the world to work with. They didn't give a rip how the car ran. It was all about show cars. It was a good thing they didn't care about how it ran, because that son-of-a-bitch of ours was in the wall! So we hired Brett Bodine and we got Crisco. It was a pretty good money deal after it was all said and done. The deals we had with Brett Bodine for '88 and '89 were real good in money, and we felt fine about it.

Ricky Rudd had some real good choices and got a ride. How the timing of this thing happened I don't know. Like a lot of things in racing, it was just luck. Ricky and I were talking about it and I said, "This is pretty neat. We got us more money than we had last year, kept our deal, didn't want to lose you, but you got a good ride, too. You had a choice of four rides, so everybody was happy about it." It was a win-win deal and nobody felt bad.

Lame duck Ricky, before he left for the green Quaker State Buick number 26 of Kenny Bernstein, threw in some bonus help in the form of a free driver evaluation of his replacement.

Ricky followed Brett when he drove Hoss Ellington's Bull's-Eye Barbeque car. They ran a limited schedule. Ricky followed him around up there at Dover and said, "I think he can do it. He's diamonding the race track. He's not doing it right, but he can learn. He'll be all right." Brett was fast, he just wrecked a lot.

The winter testing ritual was different for Bud Moore Engineering in the north Florida cold of 1988. A new driver, a new car, a new sponsor, a new season, and new hopes fueled the furnace at 400 North Fairview. All went well enough and Speedweeks, as always, was full of promise.

We went and tested at Daytona with Brett and were in pretty good shape. We returned in February hoping he'd surprise us, but we went to qualify and sucked, which gave us a lousy starting spot in the second qualifying race. There was a big crash in the 125 miler involving us, Yarborough, Martin, and bunch of others. Obviously we were not all that hopeful for the 500, starting next to last in forty-first position. We couldn't even see the front from there.

It was just past halfway that all hell broke loose. If you saw the wreck with Petty, it was so bad without having any help that you thought it would have killed him. Our spotter at that race was my brother Brent. He was on top of the truck. This was right about the time people started using spotters. Brent couldn't even see all the way around the racetrack. There wasn't any of the spotter saying, "Clear," or any of that. Brent couldn't even see what was going on, and he was hollering, "Caution!" way before Brett got into the tri-oval. He could holler "Caution," but that was about as far as he could go. Well, Brett came sliding in there. He had hit a piece of debris that punctured the left rear. It was partly his fault and partly because he had hit a piece of Richard's suspension and blown the tire. If he hadn't blown the tire, he might have missed him. The fact that he did blow the tire meant he couldn't control it and knocked the hell out of Petty. After Richard did all those rolls on his nose along the grandstand fence, he landed down on the track and spun around a couple of times, and then Brett T-bones him right square on the left front wheel. Everybody felt real bad about it.

Brett took a lick and got banged up, too. He was carried to the infield care center. The people in the garage area did not know that Brett had a flat at the time that he hit Richard. A lot of people still don't know that. It looked like a completely rookie mistake. But he wasn't a rookie because he drove too many races in '87 before coming to us.

That crash made us infamous. Brent got a lot of airtime when he plowed into Richard. He about killed Richard Petty. He about killed Bud Moore. He about killed all of us financially. Tore up every frigging car we had. That was another one of my great decisions.

Hopes weren't particularly high after returning to the shop with a car that resembled a squashed Crisco can and a 35th place finish in the 500. Unfortunately, there would be other occasions when the Bud Moore Thunderbird would assume a variation of that same unpleasant shape. Greg and the boys pressed on.

We went to Richmond. Brett was good at short tracks, and we were running pretty doggone well. We came in on the first or second stop, and we were going to put on all four tires. Back then we pulled the lugs off the left side — Ray Harris did it — while they worked on the right side. Then the tire changer would come around and they'd just pull the tire off. That was common practice for a pit stop back then. Well, as soon as we dropped the jack on the right side, Brett drove off. He went down into the corner and the wheels fell off of it. Brett felt so bad about that. Just awful. Brett said he was so used to just taking on two in Busch, but that was his screw-up. I said, "Brett, don't worry about that. Everybody's done that at one time or another. Shit happens. We aren't worried about it."

An all-star race at Charlotte called the Winston Open showcased Brett's skills on the tricky mile and a half layout as he qualified second and ran up near the front the whole race. Racing furiously at the end of the hundred lap sprint, Brett edged across the finish line just nipping Ken Schrader by the narrowest of margins—for sixth! But he didn't hit anything, and there was promise for the big event four times as long a week later.

We ran the preliminary race, and you had to win it to get into the Winston. We outran just about everybody at one time or another in what we called the Dummy Race. It's now kind of a big deal. I'll never forget Tony Glover came over and said, "Brett really had them covered. Running that good in a race like this would be just about enough to piss me off." I said, "We *are* pissed off!" We ran so well in practice and were supposed to win the son-of-a-bitch. Just wait until the 600.

Brett Bodine ran exactly 58 points-paying races for Bud Moore Engineering and made his two biggest impressions in the first ten. In fact, they occurred in the first race at Daytona with the big Petty crash and in the tenth race at Charlotte. That was the Memorial Day running of the Coca-Cola World 600. Brett had without a doubt his finest outing in the Crisco Thunderbird. He also came Lord knows how close to ending the career of a legend.

We got in the 600 and he hauled ass! He started fourteenth, but came immediately to the front. He was running real well. The car was real strong. There wasn't a pit road speed, and a guy two pits up from us blew a motor and had oil all over the place. It had just happened. Back then, somebody came out there with two 50-pound bags of Speedy Dry — which is actually cat litter — spread it over there, swept it a little bit, and that's about as good as you're going to get in 1988 for a cleanup. It was an improvement from 1968, but it was still not what we needed.

Brett had led a pretty good ways into the race, and we knew he was going to come in hot. We wanted him to come in hot because we had a good pit crew, but he came in just a little bit too hot. Daddy was out there with the big old pit board, motioning him in. Daddy's done it ten thousand times and put the pit board down on the pit road for Brett to stop. Brett got into that Speedy Dry and just couldn't get whoa'd down. That happened a lot. He got it locked up, hit the Speedy Dry, the crew got out of the way, and Daddy did make a little attempt to get out of the way. He had the big board, and it looked like the car was going to get stopped. But by the time we realized it wasn't going to get stopped,

Deep in discussion are NASCAR Technical Inspector Dick Beaty, Crisco Team Manager Greg Moore, and the driver of the number 15 Bud Moore Thunderbird, Brett Bodine (courtesy Bud Moore Engineering Archives).

Brett was on him. That was pretty damn quick. Daddy made about one step to get out of the way, and the nose of the car caught the board and the board acted like a scoop. It bumped his leg and scooped Daddy up and threw him over into the Wood Brothers' pit, and Eddie Wood stood there holding two tires. When Daddy came down, his leg hit the guard rail; luckily he didn't hit his head. He knocked one of the tires out of Eddie Wood's hands.

I ran down there. I could see that they were pitting Kyle Petty, too — he was just getting to the pits. That was how far we were ahead of them. Well, Eddie looked down and saw there was no blood coming out or anything, so he went on with Kyle's pit stop. Daddy was starting to try to sit up. That just went to show that Daddy was still pretty doggone tough. He had broken a leg but hadn't hit his head. He just landed perfectly! He got all 10s from the judges for sticking the landing!

I stood there looking at him and said, "Are you OK?" "Yeah, I'm OK." I took the headset off of him. We stood there for a few seconds and we didn't know what to do. The paramedics got right on it. I didn't have much time to react, but I could see there was no blood. I was panicking. I didn't know what to do. I was in shock. I remember Daddy said, "I'm all right. I think I'm OK."

The crew rolled the car back and changed the right side tires, but they didn't get enough gas in it. They only got in one can. Brett went back out, and he was still in pretty good shape. I didn't know what to do. Daryl was there, and they had Daddy on a stretcher. Momma was also there with Carol and the family.

I knew he wasn't dead. I knew he didn't have a head injury. I hadn't seen any blood. It wasn't anything serious. I did know his leg was hurt and might be broken. At that point in time, the way he was acting, it was like he didn't even know his leg was broken. But I had seen him go up — he got up in the air good. His leg hit the guard rail two pits down. There was only one film I ever saw of it, and it was a Charlotte station that showed it. Hitting Eddie Wood's tire and knocking it out of his hands helped to break his fall. We had all this stuff working together. Thank the good Lord. The good Lord was looking after him — again!

Meanwhile, in the infield hospital, a steady stream of drivers was coming through, thanks to the excessively poor tire wear on the super-fast Hoosier-shod race cars. Harry Gant, Cale Yarborough, Neil Bonnett, Dave Marcis, Buddy Baker, Rick Wilson, and others were getting checked out after blowing tires and banging the walls.

We were up front and I had the headset on, and somebody said something about the gas. I said, "Forget the gas! We're going to leave him out there and lead some laps. We'll get out of sync with them. We'll use this to our advantage." I ran down to the infield care center to check on Daddy, and he was OK. That was where Daddy made the statement, "Just tell the son-of-a-bitch he's got to win the race now!" That was the race where Harry Gant and all the Hoosier guys were blowing tires. It was, "This one's hit the wall," and "That one's hit the wall." They're all lying in the hospital, and here they come bringing Bud Moore in, and it was like, "What in the hell are you doing here?" Everybody was in there, and they were all laughing about it — except Momma. It took Momma a week to calm down. She cried for a week. It scared us pretty badly, but you knew that in racing that stuff was going to happen. It upset all of us.

The show must go on, and in spite of all the chaos in the pit area, Brett Bodine and the number 15 Crisco Thunderbird actually had as good a chance as anybody to win the 600. Then Bud Moore Engineering's seemingly exclusive curse returned to alter an outcome once again. Greg's trained ear picked up on it before anybody else noticed. He was like a mother knowing her baby was sick just by the sound it made. Greg knew they were done right away.

I got back to the pit and the son-of-a-gun was running like hell, leading the race. Then, with about 50 laps to go, he came by and I heard the motor change pitch. I knew what it was. It was one of those goddamn valve springs! I asked Doug and Harold, "Y'all hear it?" They didn't. I said, "Listen to him when he comes back by. It's got a valve spring gone off of it." He came back past and I could just tell by the sound. I heard it. It was like it was on seven and half cylinders. It just didn't quite have that tune to it. It was a little bit of dull sound. Brett came on the radio and said, "We're on seven and a half." I said, 'We got a pretty good lead. Keep your hoof in it!" Rusty and Waltrip were battling it out behind us, and initially we were still holding our own with a good lead. Then they caught word that Brett's blowing up; the motor's going sour. They quit racing each other and get nose to tail. They caught us with 31 laps to go. Right before the finish Kulwicki slipped by and we ran fourth. That was getting ready to be a Cinderella story, and then one of those lousy valve springs did it again. Dave Despain said on his TV show that night — I don't know why — that I was the hero of the race because I didn't panic. "I have got to give hats off to Greg Moore for not losing his cool." I've known Dave for years, and I got mentioned on TV that night.

But we were more worried about getting Momma calmed down. That was bad. They put a cast or something on Daddy, and Daryl and Carol had the station wagon and drove him back that night. Then we took him to the doctor in Spartanburg. He was gone several races. I know he missed four. It should have killed him. It could have been a gross, gory situation, a two-month stay in the hospital, but the good Lord was looking after him. That's the scary part about it: what if, what if. There are no guarantees that any of us are going to be here tomorrow — especially for him, after going through World War II and everything. As fragile as my bones are, it would probably have broken half the bones in my body. And he was 63 years old at the time! That shows you how tough Daddy was. He was tough just like his friend Big Smoke, the policeman from Spartanburg. Big Smoke would sometimes come home from work with blood on him and think nothing of it. Just sit down, light up a cigarette, and ask what was for supper. Those were some tough guys. That's the breed of people that made NASCAR. Big Smoke, Daddy, and Dolph Vermont, Cotton Owens, all went through the Depression, and the wives did, too. They're just tough! If the same thing happened to me right now, I would not survive.

Banjo had a little plaque made about a week later saying, "The Purple Heart Award, given to Bud Moore for time and dedication given above and beyond the call of duty."

Ultimately, disaster was averted for the sport in general and the Moore family specifically as the powers that be in Daytona rewrote the pit road rules. They had learned that Momma knows best.

Ford, the Frances, and everybody was calling and checking on Daddy. Momma said, "There isn't anybody else going over there. We're going to use a stick! The man isn't going to stand in front of that race car anymore." And they didn't! They came out with the rule that there would not be any more pit boards out there. Momma got that handled somehow. The Rooster got that rule handled — It was the Rooster Rule! Seriously, it was within one or two races. It was real quick. I'm not saying that NASCAR didn't already have that running through their heads. But Momma said — in between crying — that nobody was going to use a pit board anymore. "That isn't going to happen." I knew it was pretty scary because when Daddy got sick for a few races in '87 and I used the pit board for Ricky Rudd, I got a dose of it myself.

In the very next race, without the patriarch of the family at the helm, the Crisco team slides on up to Dover and Brett runs well again. As luck would have it, an incident occurred that sticks in Greg's craw to this day.

Brett was running real, real well at Dover. The left side tires weren't wearing, and our stuff always ran real well at Dover. Then Doug Williams, the crew chief, made a stupid call that I'm still mad to this day about. It was a green flag stop and we were a strong fifth, I think. Hendrick's cars had some distance on us. We're not running bad, easily top ten. Doug said, "Lefts aren't wearing. Let's just put on two." I said, "Whoa! Wait a minute! You can't do that up here!" He kept going on: "Let's just put on two."

I said, "Doug, you can't put on two tires. Up here at Dover you got to put on four tires! We got too many laps on the left side."

"But they're not wearing! I know Wayne Torrence, the Goodyear tire engineer, said they aren't wearing."

It was true that with the depth gauge, the lefts weren't wearing as badly as they normally did. But you can't do that at Dover on the pavement. Two tires don't work. That isn't the time to pull the two-tire trick. We pulled it with Benny at Richmond. I pulled it with Rudd. Evernham pulled it at Charlotte with Gordon and they thought it was the greatest thing in the world. It's the oldest trick in the book, but you have to do it at the right place at the right time. That isn't the place you do it. Not in the middle of the race.

I said, "All right, godammit! Go ahead and put the son-of-a-bitches on." We put the two tires on and the car's screwed and he hits the wall and tears it up. I got back to Spartanburg and Daddy said, "I want to ask you one question. Who in the hell made that call?" It was a bad call.

Greg and the boys at 400 North Fairview, as well as the suits in Dearborn, were still committed to Brett Bodine as 1988 wore on. However, the results weren't there. The record shows that the last two-thirds of that year beginning after the Dover crash saw only two top tens the rest of the way. They took a sixth at Michigan and a third back at Charlotte, where Brett led 50 laps. But the other 15 races saw five engine failures, three crashes that took them out and others that didn't, and a string of very poor finishes resulting in a sad twentieth in the final standings — the team's worst result since 1974 with George Follmer and Buddy Baker splitting the year. A change had been in the wind with the design of the car and name of the sponsor, but not the name of the driver.

It was about mid-season 1988. Motorcraft was encouraged enough with what they saw and decided they needed their own car. "We don't need Crisco on it. We want it all Motorcraft." Crisco knew that the ante was going to go up. They had their $800,000 and knew that to sponsor a front-running car they were going to have to cough up a little over a million. They were completely satisfied with the program the year before and by no means did they pull out. What happened was, Motorcraft stepped up to the plate with more money than they and Crisco had offered together in '88. Crisco wasn't a player because the racing budget that they gave us in 1988 was actually 20 percent of their entire advertising budget. One fifth of their entire advertising budget went just to the race car. So racing was getting a little bit too rich for their blood, just like eventually it got too rich for some of the rest of them. Procter and Gamble were still in there with the Tide brand. Motorcraft stepped up before Crisco stepped down. I think Crisco just got out because they knew they couldn't cough up another $600,000 or $700,000. They wanted to be involved somewhere in racing, but it wasn't a Melling deal where it was something we had to try to get out of.

Greg and a skeleton crew, with renewed enthusiasm, loaded up for an off-season testing session 200 miles away with the newly designed T-Bird. Sometimes it is just your day.

It was Doug Williams, Bill Burrell, Brett Bodine, and me. We took the sorriest motor we had. We had brand new motors sitting around there. "Well, we're going to Atlanta." Daddy said, "Which motor you going to test with?" I said, "Take the 21 motor. It'll run." It didn't show anything on the dyno. It wasn't that far off, but it was a few horsepower off. We just stuck it in the car. It was a race motor. It wasn't any qualifying motor or anything. We were testing the new body. It was all about the aerodynamics. In '89, that's when the car had the white down the side of it and the little stupid-looking black 15 that looked like crap. We went and tested before the '89 season, and it was funny as hell down there in Atlanta in the new Thunderbird. We dropped it off the truck and ran six laps and went quicker than anybody. Brett didn't know any better. I guess he was just out there running fast. The other guys had been down there two days testing. Waltrip was tire testing, and we warmed up three tenths quicker first time by. We didn't do anything to the car. We might have put one little piece of tape on the grill. We didn't stop it up or anything. There's about four or five real good cars down there and they're scratching their asses. They said, "What in the hell's going on?" We go out again and run another three tenths quicker. We ran six laps on that test. When we left we were a half second quicker than anybody. That was a big-time test! Daddy didn't even go. I was talking to him on the phone. He said, "Oh, that's pretty good. Load it up and come on home." I think I got cussed out because we ran too many laps. I think we ran six. That was a long way to go to Atlanta, but those six were pretty quick laps.

The Atlanta test was fast and encouraging for Greg and the team. As a bonus, they witnessed a scary—now funny—impromptu test drive.

Rudd and them were out there running and his car owner, Kenny Bernstein, said he was going to make a couple of laps. He said he was going to follow Ricky. Bernstein wanted to get a little bit of experience, and he got a little bit too much too quick. He was following Rudd around, and that wasn't too smart. Rudd said he wasn't even running. "I wasn't even running hard. I know not to. I was going to let him follow me a couple of laps and *boom*!" You ought to have seen it. It messed that car up. I'm not throwing off on Bernstein because that son-of-a-gun isn't scared to go fast. Kenny Bernstein has won hundreds of drag races and championships. He's just isn't used to turning left worth a damn. Bernstein about got himself killed. That was the end of Bernstein's oval track career. About the end of his life!

So it's off to Daytona for Speedweeks and the optimism it always brings, especially with a new car. And besides, 1989 could not possibly be as dismal as 1988—or could it? Once again by July, the handwriting was on the wall and change was again in the air.

They did the model change between '88 and '89. A lot of those were the Rudd cars with the Crisco white on it. The 1989 T-Bird was a better aerodynamic car, period. That test at Atlanta had been so encouraging. Motorcraft had their own car now with different promotional deals. Brett had done gone and got him some contact lenses. Everything was just going to be better. It *looked* like it was going to be better, anyway, but it wasn't. We got eighth in the 600 at Charlotte, and Daddy didn't get run over, but by mid-season we had all come to the conclusion that Brett wasn't getting it done. We had to figure out what we had to do to keep Motorcraft. He had had a one year deal with Crisco, and we rehired him and he had one year with Motorcraft. So Lee Morse at Motorcraft said, "Here's what the deal is guys. We're going to sponsor you for next year, but you got to get another driver. We don't have any confidence in him." Brett was great at doing public appearances. We didn't have any of that trouble like we had with Earnhardt out there hunting and stuff. Brett thought everything was going real well, that everybody was happy. I said, "Well, keep it in the back of your mind that they aren't real happy right now."

By football season, Greg was out shopping. The first phone call went to Florida.

We all got to talking about what it was going to cost to get a driver of better caliber without breaking the bank. We were 90 percent sure we weren't going to keep who we had, so we started driver shopping. It was right around "Silly Season." Well, I said, "I can get you some numbers pretty quick." So I made a couple of unofficial phone calls, and one was to Rick Wilson, who at that time was running one of Morgan-McClure's Kodak cars. I liked Rick. I'd heard the number from some other teams because he was shopping around. I called Rick and said, "We're not quite sure we're going to get rid of the driver we have, but we are looking. Now hypothetically, give me a ballpark figure as to what it would take to hire you." We knew we were going to have to get some more money out of Motorcraft to hire somebody better. He said, "Oh, I'd love to drive that car." Sure enough, his price was going to be about another $100,000 to $150,000 more than we could have paid Brett. So I went down and relayed the message to Daddy that it was going to cost more money, about $150,000 more. "Well, we got to think about that." We had not offered Rick Wilson a job. It was all supposed to be hypothetical and under wraps.

The very next race we go to, Brett comes up to me and says, "I thought y'all had faith in me."

"What are you talking about?"

"I've got to tell you this. My feelings are kind of hurt."

"Well, what are you talking about?"

"Rick Wilson's told everybody that you and Bud had offered him a job."

"He did what?"

Brett said, "You know how these guys get out here talking and everything."

I said, "Brett, we haven't made up our minds what we're going to do. I needed a price range and his name was brought up up there at Ford. You're still a candidate to drive the car if you want to."

He said, "I still want to drive the car."

I said, "Well you better be looking at other options."

He talked to Quaker State. He talked to Morgan-McClure. He had two offers and he pursued them. Rick Wilson went with Bob Rahilly and Dinner Bell Foods, and they were late making their payments. He didn't run worth a frig in that car. Quaker State was interested in either Brett or Dale Jarrett and decided to go with Brett, which was probably a pretty stupid move. We were still floundering around with Ford about the prices. Now we had to get a decent driver or we'd lose Motorcraft. We had a deal, only they weren't going to sponsor it with Bud Moore as the driver. Let's put it that way.

The second time was the charm as a brief conversation in the Sandhills of North Carolina yielded an acceptable new employee.

I caught through the grapevine that one of those becoming available was Morgan Shepherd. He was driving for Rahilly and Valvoline and they were fighting like cats and dogs. They weren't running all that good. I went up to Morgan at Rockingham at the end of the season and talked to him. I said, "You haven't signed anything yet, have you?"

"No."

"You going to be staying where you are?"

"No, it doesn't look like it."

"Well, you want to drive this thing for us?"

"Yep."

I said, "I'll go to work on it and see what we have to do." We get back to the shop and call Motorcraft and say we think we got somebody, Morgan Shepherd. Lee Morse up there said, "All right. Now we got somebody who will mash the button. He's a journeyman driver and we'll find out now if that car's going to run with Morgan Shepherd in it." I told Morgan we had to go up to Ford. "We got one meeting we have to go to and introduce you to the people and present a program to them. It's a formality." I had to write out what we were going to do and what our changes were and corporate-type stuff. We got up there and did all that stuff and signed the deal. We were walking out of the thing and Morgan looked over at me and said, "We got them."

He was a little cheaper than Rick Wilson. Rick Wilson had priced himself pretty damn high for somebody that had never won a race. And he never did. But Ford's happy now. We got a deal. We got Morgan Shepherd and Ford for another year.

Everybody said Bud Moore and Morgan Shepherd would be in a fistfight before you know it. "There'll be a killing!" Sportswriters Mike Mulhern and Steve Waid and Tom Higgins and those guys were laughing. They knew Morgan was kind of hot-headed and Daddy was also kind of hot-headed, and they said, "We have got to see this! These two will kill each other by the second race. Morgan can't get along with anybody. Bud Moore can't get along with anybody. This is going to be interesting."

Although they managed a position higher in the final standings with a nineteenth, the year 1989 was actually worse than 1988. Brett brought home one top five and six top tens, led only two laps, and did not look very impressive doing it. But as always, the outgoing driver left 400 North Fairview on good terms with Greg and the boys.

I told Brett that we had this deal worked out and we were going to put Morgan in the car. He said, "Well, I been talking to this one and that one and I think I'm going to drive for Quaker State and Bernstein." I said, "That would be a good choice." I thought, "Well, Ricky Rudd left us to go to Quaker State. When you leave Bud Moore you go to Quaker State." And that was when Rudd went from Quaker State to Hendrick.

Brett went on to win a controversial race at North Wilkesboro for Bernstein in 1990 and had a solid second to Jeff Gordon at Indianapolis in the inaugural Brickyard 400 there in 1994. After six extremely poor finishes, another five DNQs, and a bad practice crash, Brett hung up his helmet for good in 2003. Then as luck would have it, he landed a plum position with NASCAR in the research center where he assisted on the Car of Tomorrow development and became the Sprint Cup pace car driver. You can bet that the basis for whatever Brett Bodine learned as a racer was acquired at 400 North Fairview. Greg has a final thought on the Brett Bodine Experiment and recalled a recent encounter.

Brett Bodine ran for us in '88 and '89. By the middle of '89 he was on the way out, but he finished the season. He was run off, he just didn't know it. He could be fast. I'm going to tell you what messed that guy up. That was when he wrecked that Quaker State car down there in Daytona. Remember he won Wilkesboro, which was a fluke because the caution flag got screwed up and he was out there on new tires and the rest of them weren't. I can't say anything about the way Brett raced. The only problem was that every car we had he tore up, especially the good ones. I got to where I would only buy one side of the headers. Those things were expensive and you had a set for every car. He'd crash them and I'd just order one side instead of ordering a whole set because I knew he was going to knock the right side off of it. Then I really got smart. Instead of getting them made out of stainless, I just told them to make them out of mild steel. Same horsepower. I said, "Hell, he's going to tear them up anyway." I got tired of buying them. I was the one ordering all the parts. I don't know how I did it.

He wasn't a race car driver — he was a *pace car* driver! We went down to Darlington to some appearance at a recent race and they were taking big wheels for rides. Brett took me and my cousin in the pace car and held it wide open. He never ran that fast around Darlington! We got three laps wide open and were running about 120. He never lifted. I knew what he was doing. They don't carry you that fast. The CEO of Ford doesn't go for that fast a ride. Brett knew the line. I wish he'd have known it when he was driving our car! There are two years of good laughs out of Brett Bodine. Morgan Shepherd could be another whole book. That's no joke!

Greg reflects on his day-to-day duties around the shop and those of others around this time.

I ran the dyno, dealt with the driver, hired and fired the driver, dealt with the sponsor, did the R and D for the engine room and helped them back there, ported the cylinder heads, talked to the press, kept Bud Moore from killing somebody, ordered the parts, and supplied the beer. Ken Myler did a lot of the stuff with the frames, and when Donnie Wingo came on he would handle the car parts and I would handle the engine parts with Daryl.

It was Bud and Greg the whole time. Nothing ever changed until we started to sell the team. Donnie was there even when Doug Williams was, too. Donnie had worked for Satterfield and had come to a few races. We put him to work and we knew he could get it done. He was crew chief material really before he was old enough. Doug Williams was crew chief and he did us a real good job, but when he left we immediately put Donnie in there. That was during the Bodine times. We slid Donnie in there and he just did great, so we gradually started giving Donnie more responsibility. But it was always Bud and me. When we were selling the team it was still just us.

Trying to have a personal life in his line of work was a most daunting task. Modern conveniences, or inconveniences, did not necessarily improve his life. One in particular was a first.

Every time we'd go out there and try to drink beer, the phone would ring and it would be some race driver. That phone drove me crazy. I had an answering machine way before anybody else I knew. I was dating this girl and she started leaving me instructions on it: "You do this and you do that." I got rid of the answering machine. I got rid of the girl, too. I didn't need anybody leaving me instructions. I didn't have that much time off. I ripped it out.

I was the first person to come to the racetrack with a cell phone. That's another screw-up!

When it came to Bud Moore Engineering, it was either Daddy, Daryl, Ducky, Strawberry Davis, me, or the fabricators that were the absolute firsts with stuff. I've heard people say they were the first ones to do something that we did two years earlier. It's whoever gets written up in the damn books first that is first, but this book's true. This is 100 percent true.

Bud Moore Engineering was poised for the last decade of the century, sporting new colors, new driver, new sponsor, and a fresh outlook. Bring on 1990.

CHAPTER THIRTEEN

Skating Back to the Front

A new decade, new hopes, new expectations, new math (actually geometry), and new cars filled the handsome brick walls and shiny gray floors at 400 North Fairview Avenue. Morgan Shepherd requested changes to Bud Moore Engineering's fleet of Thunderbirds, putting his stamp on the team right off the bat. There was an air of cooperation, especially since one of the changes was long overdue.

After the last race of '89 at Atlanta, we had the race track rented for that Monday. We went out there just to break Morgan in a little bit with the car. He ran a few laps and was good even on a dirty racetrack. He wanted the car set up a little bit differently and Daddy, Donnie, and Morgan got their brains together and handled things. Everybody felt pretty good about it. During the winter, Morgan came down to the shop and said, "I know you and Banjo are really great friends, but with this radial tire, we're about going to have to run a front-steer car." Daddy said, "Well, if that's what you want, that's what we'll do." Morgan said, "Now, you don't have to throw all your cars away at once. You can reclip them." That's what a lot of people were doing — putting Laughlin front clips on Banjo's cars. So initially that's what we started doing.

Greg explained the difference between a front-steer and a rear-steer race car.

In a rear-steer, the steering linkage is back behind the center line between the front wheels and works on the spindles and tie rods from that direction. In a front-steer, which is a typical Ford set up, all that stuff is up front. Mike Laughlin gave the simplest, best description of it to me back in '78. He said, "Gregory, if you take a bent stick and push it through the sand, that stick is going to try to go all over the place. It's liable to hit a rock and go everywhere. But if you turn it over and drag it through the sand, it'll go in a straight line." Basically, it makes the car feel better to the driver going into the corner. The trouble was, everybody had the rear-steer cars worked out so well with the bias-ply tire that the front-steers tended to be a little on the tight side. The real good teams had the rear-steer, and when the radial tire came about, it forced everybody to the front-steer deal. That's when we had to eat crow, even though Laughlin had offered to build us some cars for nothing. We said, "Mike, we need you to help us." He said, "I'll help you out all I can." All Banjo's stuff was rear-steer and becoming obsolete. Daddy had already told him, "You're going to have to swap these things over because of the radial tire."

There were people who tried to hang on. We hung on longer than most. A lot of people converted over in '89. A lot converted over long before that. A properly set up rear-steer car like one of Junior's or the Wood Brothers', or ours with the bias-ply tires, was an excellent chassis. But with the radials on and especially with the body style Ford had come out with, you were going to have to put a front steer on it. Luckily, Morgan knew a lot about that. He knew how he wanted to make it feel. That's what he had at Rahilly's. He said he had driven rear-steer cars that were good. But this whole thing was about this radial tire coming into being.

It was a busy winter for the Moores between 1989 and 1990. A new broom sweeps clean, as the saying goes, and the broom would be tested as new things always were for over a generation: at the beach during the winter.

We converted some cars over and went down to Daytona to test. We ran fairly decently. Then we came back in February for Speedweeks, and what was ridiculous was the Clash. Morgan had sat on the pole the year before in Rahilly's car at Watkins Glen, so that put us in the Clash. We got into that deal and didn't have a whole lot of practice. Morgan went out there and drafted and looked pretty good. He said, "Well, I don't think we're turning enough RPMs." We were running a restrictor plate and it had a 300 gear in it. You don't turn much with a plate motor. We had a gear that was just a tick lower, a 305, and put it in, but didn't try it. It was too low. They dropped the green flag and it wouldn't pull up like it had in practice. Even five points made that much difference. We finished next to last in the Clash, and it was a joke. We lost the draft and everything. It was pitiful. We got in the 125 miler with some of the better cars in it and were decent, but finished fifteenth. We didn't have to use a provisional spot. We still didn't feel like we were running as well as we needed to. After the 125 miler, we caught wind of what was going on.

A full-blown emergency blindsided most of the top teams and a cross country scramble ensued. Warning: Greg gets technical.

That's when we were doing all that crazy stuff with the restrictor plate. Somebody had let them slide through and do something different to the plate that we thought was totally illegal. They were allowing them to seal off the center hole with a sleeve. On the carburetor, the hole was supposed to be open in the middle. Then you had the cloverleaf, the other venturi holes around the center hole, underneath it. You had this staub [a short metal pole NASCAR inspectors used to check for cheating] that was to pass through the middle hole and sit on the floor for the inspector to keep from making it a solid pull. Around it you had your cloverleaf stuff. Some of them made a sleeve to go in the center hole so then the inspector's staub would go in it, but it sealed the system off. Then you had direct pull from those other four carburetor venturis from underneath the plate an inch below.

We had talked about doing this. We did it and tested it on the flow bench and saw that it was about 15 to 18 more horsepower. A helluva lot more air flow. Mr. Flow! I never did dyno it. Daddy said, "There is no way they're going to let us get by with that. There is no way we can take a thin cylindrical piece of sheet metal and put it down in there just to miss the staub to make it direct pull. All that's going to do is get Dick Beaty and those guys mad at us." We went down there with ours the way we thought was legal. There were two cars that slid through and they let them pass inspection. One was Waddell Wilson's car. Everybody else had their stuff open. Elliott hadn't done it, this one hadn't done it, that one hadn't done it. I had noticed that we weren't as quick in the second test session as we had been in the first that year. I'll never forget it. I told Art Kreb, one of the inspectors, "Art, you might as well take that staub, no more than what it's policing now — and I know what its intentions were for — and stick it up your ass because you're not measuring anything."

With an "I don't have time for this" look for the photographer, Greg toils with his first love: a race motor (courtesy Bud Moore Engineering Archives).

I called our machinist and told him to meet us at the shop. I told Daryl to bolt a set of heads on the fixture. "I'm coming with the manifold off the car. We have to fix this thing and make it direct flow." He said, "Surely to God they didn't let them do that."

"Yep," I said. "That's the reason we were off a little bit."

"Well what the...?"

I said, "I don't know what these crazy son-of-a-guns are thinking about."

Ernie Elliott was mad. The Pettys were mad. The Wood Brothers were mad. We were all out there at the airport cussing because we had to carry our manifolds back and get them fixed. We got on an airplane to Spartanburg, and Elliott was going back to Dahlonega, and everybody was going back to fix the manifolds. We had a day to fix one. I put it up on the apparatus and flowed the air and everything. Sure enough, as soon as I fixed a little staub and put it down in there, you could hear it squealing. The airflow was going supersonic over the short-turn radiuses and all that stuff. So without even dynoing it, we carried the manifold back down there and bolted it on. We went out in the first practice session, and the first lap by, it picked up a half a second. Half a second! We still didn't have it exactly fixed right. We didn't have time to massage it. From then on, every time Morgan went out, he drafted fine, and we wound up finishing tenth in the Daytona 500 with a manifold that was partially compromised. That was the race that Derrick Cope won.

A big secret to their success was a result of some ingenious body work back at 400 North Fairview during the winter between seasons. Hats off the boys in the fab room.

We really nailed them good in 1990 with that C pillar. That's the reason Morgan Shepherd looked like a hero. We really laid a screwing to them then, but there wasn't a template back there where we massaged it. It was an idea that Phil Harris and Daddy came up with in the back of the shop. We pulled those C pillars in, one inch on each side. That was such a drastic difference that it gave it a hundred more pounds of down force on the rear than the other cars. It was at Atlanta when we finished second that it really showed. It didn't matter on the super speedways where you were trying to lay the spoiler down, but at Atlanta and Charlotte it made a huge difference. If the car got into a few degrees of yaw, we got a helluva lot more air on the spoiler and a hundred pounds more down force than the others. That gave us a handling advantage. It was a couple of years before they figured it out. Elliott and all of them were always hollering, "Loose! Loose! Loose!" We had them snookered.

Greg and the boys had Morgan in position to win the Atlanta 500 in their fourth start together. He had been leading for six laps late in the race with victory in sight when Bobby Hillin spun in turn three. Greg had to take a gamble to stay out front because the Bud Moore team was up against the best. Then a wild card came into play.

It was time to come in and get tires. Our tires were a little fresher than Earnhardt's, but I kept noticing water spewing out of the overflow and there weren't but a few laps left. I got to thinking about it and said, "Well, let's make him have to pass us because there's only going to be two laps to go when they drop the green." The thing was squeaking a head gasket because we were doing some welding on the heads and everything. Sure enough, the head gasket wasn't blown, but it was just enough to where it wasn't really running real hot. I could tell it was losing a head gasket, and I told Donnie, "We can't do any worse than second." The problem was Kulwicki was in the middle between us and Earnhardt a lap down. He wouldn't get out of the way. He just flat got in Morgan's way. We might have lost the race anyway, but we never got a chance to race Earnhardt. We should have had a clear shot. If anything, Kulwicki, driving another T-Bird, should have got up in Earnhardt's way. The bastard had us blocked! That's when Preston Miller said, "Man, it doesn't get any better than this. We're second in the points, about won the race, and still got somebody to be mad at." Alan Kulwicki wouldn't get out of the way, so we could blame him. We never even got a chance to get a jump on Earnhardt because he went to the inside. Kulwicki pushed us all the way to the top. Of course Earnhardt beats us by three tenths and Kulwicki still gets seventh a lap behind.

So the 1990 season was off to a fine start, and the Motorcraft Team got better with each race. In the first 11 races, Morgan and the Moores never finished outside the top ten, and they raced to the points lead after Dover on June 3rd. Then came the road course race in the California wine country, and an unusual and costly mistake came into play.

We went from the penthouse to the outhouse. Some of these sevenths and eighths should have been better than that. Things happened. At Sonoma, Morgan was racing Geoff Bodine for second place with only a few laps to go. He was going over the dirt and Bodine was mirror driving. Morgan had run him down and caught him. Bodine was driving for Junior, and Morgan couldn't get by.

We burned a rod bearing with a few laps to go. It starved it for oil pressure. We must have mistakenly started with the oil level in the dry sump tank too low when we put the race engine in. When the oil got sloshing around, it sucked air. It had run all day long, and it wasn't until Morgan got into this dogfight with Bodine for second place that it sucked

Perry Allen Wood (left) renewed an old friendship with Brent Moore at 400 North Fairview beside a Morgan Shepherd Thunderbird during the 1990 Christmas holidays (Perry Wood Racing Collection).

enough air to burn a bearing. We found the oil level in the tank was significantly low. Those moon tanks weren't very high, and you don't want to get it too full. We calculated that it used about a quart per race. We didn't get enough oil in it. It's just that simple. It was sickening! We were going to get by Bodine and finish second and pad the point lead. Instead we fell out with four laps to go and finished twenty-ninth.

That bad break at Sonoma started a free fall through the standings for the next 15 races, punctuated by crashes, engine problems, and just plain bad luck. Half the season was destroyed.

Then we hit some tracks and had some bad things happen. We just didn't run all that well. I think of a football team like Clemson losing a tough game and it knocking the wind out of their sails. In the Firecracker 400 we got caught in that big pile-up early and came back out and made about two laps. As the year went on, we still stayed close enough in points. We had a good combination. We had good communications with Morgan, and everybody was pumped up because we had led the points. Morgan and Daddy got along pretty well on the radio. By that time, Donnie Wingo was doing most of the talking. Preston Miller had perfected the spotting thing real well. So you got Donnie and Preston talking on the radio more than Daddy was. Donnie and Morgan got along well. The team jelled around Morgan. I've never had anything but nice things to say about him.

It's like Morgan's always said: The best season he ever had was 1990. That was one of the better seasons for us. Still, it's like anything else in life: What if...? What if...? If we'd have gone ahead and finished second or third at Sears Point, there's no telling what would have happened the rest of the year just from the attitude of everybody. Instead, we were disheartened. That bad patch was disheartening as hell! We'd had two lousy seasons with Brett Bodine and now, for awhile, we had we've got something going. Ford was happier than all get out. Then we hit that group of races where there were wrecks or Morgan just didn't run well or the car didn't run well. This was about the time that Daryl came up with the timing chain balancing and Daddy and Cotton put that into use. That's when the centric was throwing it off. The camshaft balancing kept the valve springs from breaking and from breaking timing chains. The RPMs went on up.

Three of the last four races found number 15 coming home up front. On November 18, 1990, Greg and Bud were in Victory Lane for the first time since Ricky Rudd won at Dover on September 20, 1987, a span of 92 races. They clambered back up to fifth in the final Winston Cup Point Standings, their best result since Rudd was fifth in 1986.

We came on like gangbusters and finished second at Charlotte, third at Phoenix, and won Atlanta in the last race of the year. That felt real good. But ... it was another win where somebody got killed. I didn't see that one. Ricky Rudd slid in the pits and hit the Speedy Dry like Brett did when he hit Daddy. Mike Rich was changing the right rear tire on Elliott's car and he was hit. Rich was one of the weekend guys for the Elliotts and I did not know him that well. As tragic as that was, we were unfortunately kind of accustomed to winning races with bad news attached to them. Morgan led a lot of laps that day and we weren't challenged at the end. The win let us slip past Rusty Wallace into fifth place in Winston Cup points, and that was a great way to build momentum for 1991.

The team's new car for 1991 was debuted to the public before the Atlanta race, and that might have been the good omen the team needed to spark the victory. Greg sheds some light on Morgan's "office" comforts and his savvy in race car design.

They had the newly designed car shown on TV before the start of the final Atlanta race. The design went back to the full red. That's what we ran with Morgan in '91 and Geoff in '92 and '93 until Quality Care came on board. That was closer to the original Bud Moore colors. The Ford guys came down to Spartanburg and had their design people with them to talk about the new scheme. This was about two or three races from the end of 1990. They were going with an all-red design and wanted to get that white off the sides. So they came up with all dark red with a big white 15 on it. The deep color of red was a little bit different, and they were going to put a white stripe at the bottom. We had a car there that we had painted up, and it looked better than the old car, but it didn't look right.

Morgan was down there because we were fitting him into another seat. Morgan had a certain seat he wanted. He had a pad he always wanted on the driver's door, a place where he could rest his arm, on top of the pad that was already there. Morgan had his own little kit he always brought with him — his own little bag of tricks. He always checked his own belts and had his helmet fixed a certain way. We called it "the Morgan Shepherd Package." When he went up to drive for the Woods after he left us, we just shipped them all our seats since they were already fixed.

So Morgan's down at the shop, and Sam Scott with Ford and a design engineer were rolling out the new design there. Daddy said, "You know, something's not right with this thing." They were looking at different color wheels and stuff. Morgan walked up to the front of the shop and said, "Can I do something? Can I show you my opinion?" We had this black vinyl tape, and Morgan and the guy with Motorsport Design put this black tape at the bottom on the rocker panel instead of white. Morgan said, "Now stand back and look at it." As soon as we did Sam Scott said, "Now, that's a Bud Moore car there." Morgan said, "That it is. That's the way it's supposed to look." That's when the car really went to looking good. Good looking son-of-a-gun!

Morgan Shepherd made the stage in the Grand Ballroom of the Waldorf Astoria Hotel at the 1990 NASCAR awards ceremony and addressed a national TV audience while Greg, Bud, and Betty Moore observed proudly as honored guests. Making the stage at the Waldorf was the unofficial goal of every team. Naturally, the championship was the official goal. But the stage was ripe with benefits. Happy days were here again, and the Christmas holidays in New York City were sweet. They were not on top yet, but they could finally see the top again.

Greg offers this glimpse of their man behind the wheel:

Morgan had a reputation for being one of the harder guys to get along with. He was tough, but in 1990 we didn't have any problems with him. He could write his name, but we didn't know how literate he was. He had something like a fifth grade education. There were a lot of guys back in the old days who didn't have much more than that. He knew how to work on a car. He could build his own engines. He could weld. And it helped that he quit drinking about two years before he got to us. I said, "Morgan, why did you quit drinking? You won't drink a beer with us?" His exact words were, "Gregory, I'm going to tell you what. I flat couldn't handle it. I'd get two or three drinks of liquor in me and I was one of these types of people who wanted to fight everybody in the bar." He said, "I got religion." He was into the church.

When we'd go to Wilkesboro, he'd invite us up to this old timey dance hall. It was a barn that had a buffet line and you danced. It took us about 45 minutes to drive over there, and he'd pay for everybody's food. No drinking, of course. They didn't serve alcohol. Harold and I would go out to the car to fix us a drink and go back in there. It was a lot of fun dancing, and the food was good. Morgan was fun. Morgan had a sense of humor.

In '91 we were worried about being able to go the distance on the gas mileage, and Morgan was warming the car up. We knew we were going to be close on going the distance on one stop. We had oil warmers on the tank, but those earlier ones didn't do that much. Morgan had the car sitting there running, and Daddy reached over there and shut it off. It was cold that day. We didn't run but a lap in the race and it burnt the bearings slap out of it. The oil wasn't hot yet. Morgan was pretty mad when he came wheeling in there. We were laughing about it the next day. I said, "We were just trying to save gas." Morgan said, "Bud did save gas. Bud saved a helluva lot of gas. Bud saved 22 gallons of gas." We didn't run but a lap and it blew up. We did save gas! So he had a sense of humor to him.

Morgan was cool. He could drive you nuts changing shock absorbers. He said, "Change the shocks" a million times. He was always putting on something that was wrong. He had the fastest Busch car in practice one time and changed all four shocks right before he qualified. He missed the show. He came over there to Daddy and he's got four shocks in his hands and he said, "Bud, we've got to put these on. They work great." Daddy said, "You had the fastest car and missed the show." Daddy took them and threw them in the trash can. So help me God. I was standing right there. When he had our stuff on, he run fine. Then there's the roller skating thing. For the most part, the garage area, the competitors, and the other drivers laughed at that. That wasn't really a plus. That might have been OK during a rain delay to show Morgan on his roller skates a few times as they would do, but that kind of stuff didn't help.

We had others in our traveling road party that were not beyond livening things up a bit.

Henry Benfield was a major prankster. Once we had a card game going on in my room with some of the scoring women going in and out. He took a full row of Black Cat firecrackers and threw them in the room lit, and it smoked up the whole wing of the motel. They had the police and everybody out there. They thought the place was on fire.

It always seemed that after a couple of years, one side or the other got antsy or restless and the grass looked greener on the other side of the rail. In mid-season 1991 it happened again.

In 1991, we weren't running quite as well, and Jack Roush offered Morgan a job. When Jack Roush offered him a job, that's when his attitude changed. Roush had talked about hiring him to replace Mark Martin. Seems like Morgan also had another driving offer. And when a driver gets another offer, he gets screwed up. It turns him into a kind of a lame duck driver. Up there at Dover, I think he crashed the car out of frustration. He was pissed off because we took one car instead of another one. It was a damn good car. He crashed it in practice, and I heard through the grapevine that he'd do crap like that so he could get the backup car off the truck. I think he thought the backup car was the one he wanted. He was a funny guy.

We got back to the motel room and were sitting there about half lit and Daddy said, "I'm going to tell you one thing, boy. You better find me a goddamn race driver or we'll park this son-of-a-bitch and we won't ever run again." I said, "Well, I guess that sums that up." And it did! He said, "This Morgan thing's getting pretty aggravating with Roush trying to hire him. He's got a lot of good ideas and he's got a lot of messed up ideas. We just need to do something else. He's getting older."

Morgan had some good runs. The year 1990 was better than '91. Both seasons were a helluva lot better than Brett Bodine. We just felt like Morgan's heart wasn't in the right place. But he got us through the transition of the front- and rear-steer cars. The difference between the haves and have nots was getting bigger, too. We were getting further back on the money compared to the bigger teams. There was a bigger deficit even though we got an increase every year. We still weren't getting enough money to hire any more people.

But the folks punching the clock at 400 North Fairview Avenue reached back and achieved an honor many a team never won no matter how hard they tried. On October 19, 1991, the Bud Moore Engineering Motorcraft Team won the Unocal 76/Rockingham World Championship Pit Crew Competition at Rockingham, North Carolina. It was and still is a big deal.

We got into a discrepancy about the scales back when Bobby Allison was driving the car, and we never entered that thing for a long time. But when Motorcraft got involved in it, they started making us compete. This was only about the second or third time we'd competed since we started boycotting it in the late '70s. I think we'd run it in '89 and got screwed up with the scales and arguments and stuff. But this time, we got in it and had a good stop. We didn't know if there were any penalties or not. They came over and said, "Bud, that looked like a good stop." Daddy said, "I hope we don't get any penalties or anything. It seemed a little slow to me." Well, there weren't any penalties and it broke the world record. I nearly went into hysterics. I called Ford. I called Brenty. I called up there at the shop. That fell right into my hands. I could put it right on the truck: World's Fastest Pit Crew. We had that truck painted up fancy and had that pretty car.

More than twenty years later, Greg still wonders how his 1990 trading card photo captured him licking his fingers while eating an ice cream cone (Perry Wood Racing Collection).

That was a great bunch of guys and I remember them clearly. Of course Donnie Wingo was the crew chief and front tire changer. Harold Stott was the rear tire changer. Danny Fowler was the best jack man in the business. Charlie Gibson was the tire carrier. Phil Thomas was the gasman. Bill Sharp was the catch can man. And Ray Harris took off the left side lugs. Remember, back then, you could take the left side lugs off before the crew came around from the right side to change the tires. I remember our time, too. It was 22.565 seconds for two cans of gas and a four-tire change. We beat Tim Brewer and Junior's boys by over two seconds. There was a big banquet when we came back to Rockingham in February of '92. It was a tremendous honor.

And it is still is a great honor. By the way, the banquet was held on Leap Year Day, February 29, 1992, and the dinner fare was French onion soup, chiffonade salad Florentine,

In 1991 at the peak of their game, Bud, Greg, and Brent Moore sit atop the pit wall, ready to race (courtesy Bud Moore Engineering Archives).

filet mignon wrapped in bacon, baked potato, broccoli spears with hollandaise, and the crowning touch was Mrs. Henning's raspberry sherbet with chambord, a raspberry liqueur. Greg remembers it as "tasty" and adds a postscript:

The very next year we broke the record again and they tried to say Donnie left one lug nut loose. So we watched the official with the torque wrench that checks for loose lugs. It's got a clicker to show if a lug was loose. It never clicked. We were three or four tenths quicker and if it hadn't been for that lug nut, we would have broken the record—*our* record—again. But they couldn't have that. That wouldn't have been good politics. I'm telling you, that deal right there was fixed. They penalized us five goddamn seconds for a lug nut and we were fifth. Donnie and I really looked at it. Donnie said the torque wrench clicked before the lug nut ever moved. The official went ahead and made it move. We were four tenths quicker than before and set another record. Once again, we kind of lost interest in it.

And once again, Greg began the hunt for a new right foot to push the pedal in the Motorcraft Thunderbird. And as always by mid-season of any year, racing folks start exchanging glances and business cards. That's why it is called "Silly Season." An old hand at hiring drivers at the ripe old age of 34, Greg Moore went after only one guy and landed him. But it was not before he had to enlighten him a little.

I found out through the grapevine, before the press knew it or anything, that Junior Johnson was going to run Geoff Bodine off and put Elliott in the car. I found that out through our pilot, Bill Carr. He'd overheard some stuff. We got to doing some checking around and knew for a fact that the deal was done. Budweiser wanted Elliott and wanted Bodine out, and Bodine did not know it. He didn't have any idea at all.

So help me, I'm at the Corners Apartments and I got his phone number and thought about how I'm going to approach this. I called him and said, "Geoff Bodine, Greg Moore. How you doing?"

"Oh, great Greg. What's going on?"

"Blah, blah, blah, blah ... Would you entertain driving for me and Bud next year?"

He said, "Well, I've got a ride."

"No you don't!"

"Junior hasn't come and told me anything."

I said, "Well, Geoff, trust me. You're fired. Your ass is gone. I got you a ride.' There's a witness that heard the conversation — my next door neighbor for all those years. I said, "I've done some research. We're definitely going to get rid of Morgan Shepherd. Morgan Shepherd is gone. We're pretty sure he's going to go drive for the Wood Brothers. From what I can tell, you haven't got a ride." He said, "That's hard for me to believe. How do you know?" I said, "I know for a fact that Elliott's bought some land up that way. There's been some meetings going on and the deal's done. They just haven't told you yet." He said, "Let me check into this and figure out what's going on."

Sure enough, he went to Junior and talked about it and kind of forced their hand. He's got a ride now and Junior isn't going to have him. I talked to Daddy about it, and he said that I had to look at the road courses, short tracks, and everything. I said, "Bodine is a little bit younger, and he's going to be an aggravating Yankee. He's going to get booed and not be real popular. But Ford liked him, and he had that history of winning all those modified races and got Hendrick going in the Levi Garrett car. He was the Bodine brother that could drive.

I talked to him a couple more times and after he found out he wasn't going to have a ride with Junior. I said, "Look. What's this going to cost? I know I can get you $500,000 up front."

"It's going to cost you more than that. It's going to cost you at least six."

I said, "I can probably handle that."

In the meantime, Geoff got to talking to the Wood Brothers, even though he never really considered driving for them because our car was better. The Wood Brothers hadn't run well for a while. A bidding war went on. The Woods coughed some money up, too, and there was one other team in there somewhere. But they got bumped out pretty quickly when the bidding war went on. The Woods told me that their budget couldn't stand more than $500,000. I just went in and told Geoff, "We'll get you the six." This was about the third conversation with him. Ford said if he or a better driver was going to drive the car, they would sponsor it.

I told Daddy, "Well, I got him." I didn't say too much about the money at that point. "We got him, and he's going to come down here and meet with us and Sam Scott and Ford and everything." Daddy had heard somewhere through the grapevine that we'd offered him $600,000. He said, "Where the hell did this $600,000 come from?"

"Well, you wanted to get him, didn't you?"

"Yeah, yeah, yeah, you're right. But I thought I told you to stop at five."

"I didn't have any choice."

Geoff got down to the shop that day and got to laughing and Daddy said, "Gregory got a little bit above our budget. We were thinking more like $500 or $550." Geoff said, "Bud, I'm going to make you the money on the race track. You might as well pay me." And Daddy said, "Well, you're right." Everything just started off good.

Meanwhile, the latest edition of lame duck driver was playing out the string in the number 15 with mostly lackluster starts and finishes. Morgan Shepherd had made Bud Moore Engineering a major factor on Sundays again, and the parting was cordial. Besides, Morgan would not be unemployed for a single minute.

The changeover was friendly. Morgan was going to the Wood Brothers because they were losing Dale Jarrett to the new team formed by Joe Gibbs. We were shipping the Wood Brothers Morgan's seats. Remember, Morgan specially designed all these seats for himself. The Woods were tickled to get him because they had no other options. Their budget was actually a little bit less than ours. They knew Morgan had run well in our car, and they felt like it would be a good deal for them, too. He drove for them for two years. The first year was pretty good. The second year went all to hell, like it did with everybody.

One time at Daytona they had "Morgan Shepherd" written above the door like they had always done, but they had it outlined funny where you couldn't see it real well. It was like an outline with some streaks through it or something. I said, "Eddie, what's the deal with that?" He said, "You see that 'Morgan Shepherd' right there? That's going to be just fading away." They had about made up their minds by the second race of '93 that they were going to do something else.

The final numbers for Morgan Shepherd show a big drop-off in 1991, but the improvement from the previous chauffeur's two-year stint was substantial. In 58 points-paying races, Morgan won once in their fourth race together, took 11 top fives, 30 top tens, won no poles, led 288 laps out of about 17,800, copped over $920,000 in purses, was running at the finish 46 times, captured a fifth and a twelfth in the final point standings, and not a single time did he hit Bud on pit road. Seriously: Morgan Shepherd of Conover, North Carolina, with his skill and knowledge was the catalyst the boys at 400 North Fairview Avenue needed for the blood-red number 15.

Chapter Fourteen

The Yankee Speedster

To paraphrase an old adage, if at first you don't succeed, hire the guy's brother. Having suffered through two miserable and sometimes comical years with Brett Bodine, Greg went after and secured the services of his better brother, Geoff Bodine of Chemung, New York. (He wasn't billing himself as Geoffrey yet.) Yes, he was another Yankee, but this one had a proven track record. By the time he arrived at 400 North Fairview for a fitting, the 42-year-old had already been racing in the big time a dozen years with 11 wins, a whopping 29 poles, and a finish as high as third in the Winston Cup Point Standings in a Rick Hendrick Chevy. With a top-notch driver and the fastest pit crew in the world, Bud Moore Engineering was poised to take it all in 1992.

We had that pretty car. He loved the number 15. Geoff was a hot-headed little Yankee, but a much better driver than his brother. Tim Brewer couldn't put up with him and Junior got rid of him. Brewer told me, "There is no way in hell you and Bud are going to be able to put up with him, but he can drive the car. If your nerves can stand him and you can listen to his bullshit, you'll be OK. But I'll bet y'all kill him in two months.

In the annual preparations for Speedweeks over winter, the Motorcraft team actually had to craft the motors with their wits and imagination due to another one of those pesky British invasions. The last time Bud Moore built an engine this way, Greg was dividing his time between playing football and rock and roll.

By 1992, I felt like we'd been racing a hundred years because I'd been born into it. We had done some routine maintenance at the end of '91 on the dyno with the hard drive and data acquisition system. A guy from England came over and did it. He said the dyno was working perfectly. He changed this and he changed that. And right before the guy was scheduled to leave, he fooled around and got into the data acquisition system and erased everything. By accident! Erased everything! All the records I had in there. Everything! The dyno would still run, but we were back to running it like we did in the '70s. It was about like Daddy and Mario Rossi running a 427 in 1966.

The data acquisition system on the dyno was down for about six weeks. By that I mean we had all the manual gauges like we always did, but we didn't have the two computers hooked up that gave you the real precise readings. You had to have somebody standing there writing something down. You had dial gauges. You had your oil temperature and your water temperature and it would run, but it put us back in the dark ages. Plus, all we had was a little box that measured the torque. It was accurate, it just wasn't as precise. We had to build our Daytona motors with those tools. We were also playing with the carburetor plate thing that we got better at.

Greg Moore (standing) and Perry Allen Wood (in car) with the car Geoff Bodine would use to win the Busch Clash in his first start for Bud Moore Engineering during December of 1991. Note there is no steering wheel and Wood's "steering" arm pose is being faked. After Speedweeks 1992, Greg wanted Wood to come back and sit in all the race cars for good luck (Perry Wood Racing Collection).

Sunday, February 8, 1992, was the date Greg and boys added another line to their resume for an event that had seen wins snatched away by their driver's conservative style in 1981, a world record fine in 1983, and a devastating aerial ballet in 1984. With a new driver and a motor crafted 1970s style, Bud, Daryl, and Greg went rather blindly and skeptically into Speedweeks' first real test of the season.

We had record fines with Earnhardt and finished second with Benny. In '92, the Busch Clash qualifying was rained out or something and we drew for starting positions. Bodine started third. They dropped the green flag and Geoff hung on good, but he said it was too loose; we had to tighten it up a little bit. He slid back to about third from the rear and let them finish that segment out. It was run in two ten-lap segments with the field inverted for the second one. When he pitted between segments and we could work on it, we put a round of bite in it and bolted on four new tires. When they went green flag again, he blew by Rusty quickly, and there was Ernie Irvan and Mark Martin. Once he got rolling, Geoff passed them and they couldn't get back by him. He pulled that train fast. We'd seen that in practice. We looked at the stopwatch, and he was leading as fast as any laps had been run. So he came by on the last lap and the speed was still up good and they started down the backstretch. The guys in second and third place pulled up alongside each other and got racing, and we just went on. When we crossed the line we were ten car lengths ahead of

The shop's dynamometer was serviced prior to the 1992 season, and years of engine performance data were accidentally erased. The cars ran great anyway, thanks to Greg, Daryl, and a strong team (courtesy Bud Moore Engineering Archives).

Irvan. It worked perfectly! Made Ford happy. Made me happy, too. We came right out of the box and won the Busch Clash in a car that really wasn't that good. That was not the same car we ran in the 500, and it was with one of the motors we built with the dyno broken.

A first-ever Busch Clash win with a brand new driver was an eye-popping start for Bud Moore Engineering, especially considering they used an engine built on a prehistoric dynamometer to do it. How they would fare in the qualifier and 500 was a whole different matter. Bud and Greg got another Thunderbird out of the truck to find out. A ho-hum seventh in the 125 mile qualifying race produced a sixteenth place start in the Daytona 500.

We ran two cars, and that car we used in the Clash wasn't nearly as good as the one in the 500. I remember this was the last race A. J. ran at Daytona and the first for Joe Gibbs. Geoff and Morgan got into each other early, and we had some damage on the left front, but it didn't slow us down at all. Then we got caught for speeding on pit road, and that got us hooked up for a lot of drafting with Davey Allison. The race was stopped for rain a little while, and of course they had this huge crash that wrecked a bunch of good cars like Marlin, Irvan, Elliott, Martin, Schrader, Earnhardt, Jarrett, Petty, Wallace, and Waltrip. It didn't matter because nobody could catch Davey that day and he beat Morgan at the line. We were third, which we were real happy with.

It was only a few races into season when unexpectedly, words of discontent began flowing from the mouth of Geoff Bodine. Greg had fought this regularly over the years, but never this early in a driver relationship. Maybe Tim Brewer was right. Maybe they would kill Bodine before two months passed. Then Ford got another of their "Better Ideas."

We finished third in the Daytona 500 and everybody was happy as heck. So we went to Rockingham and ran fourteenth. Bodine never had run well there. The third race was in Richmond, and in practice we were flying. We knocked timing in the motor and should have sat on the pole and everything. In qualifying, instead of turning 8500, it turned 8800 down the backstretch to take the green, and Bodine lost it in three and four and backed it into the wall. He felt real bad, and I said, "Don't worry about it. We'll get the backup car.' He took the backup car and ran second day fastest and about half-assed in the race, finishing sixteenth. By then he said the car wouldn't do this and wouldn't do that, we didn't have enough gear, and the motor wouldn't run. It was the same stuff he'd done with Junior and everybody else. That's one of the reasons Junior got rid of him. He was aggravating. Well, every driver we ever had was aggravating. The least aggravating driver was Ricky Rudd.

Bodine had a bad habit to take the steering wheel off the car. If he came in and he didn't run a good lap or something, he'd take the steering wheel off and throw it against the windshield. He'd crack the windshield and we'd have to put a new one in it. Stuff like that. Little Yankee tantrums. Bodine would get moody, but you had to work with him. He and Daddy did not communicate well, but I could put up with him. Besides, like our other drivers, he only had a one-year contract. And he was pretty fearless in the race car. He'd bump a guy.

He was throwing off on us, and Daddy's hollering at him on the radio. Brett told me, "Don't pay him any attention. That's exactly what he does everywhere he goes. He runs good at Daytona, then goes to these other tracks and don't run worth a damn." Now, Brett's a fine one to talk, but he knows his own brother. Then Geoff started whining like hell and went crying to the sponsors. Sam Scott from Ford came to me, and Sam Scott was one of the better guys they had of the seven or eight who were the racing directors over a 12-year period. Sam said, "We want you to start calling all the shots because we know you can do it and Bud's getting a little bit older." I said, "Whoa, whoa, whoa, wait a minute. I am not going to do that." They wanted me to be completely running the whole thing. They said, "Why not?"

I said, "For one thing, Daddy and I work as a team. I'm not a crew chief. Let's let Donnie Wingo do it."

"Nah, he's not old enough. We want you to do it. Are you saying you can't?"

"I'm not saying I can't. I'm saying I won't!" They kept messing around, and I said, "Let me tell you something, I'm not going to do that. I agree with Daddy about 98 percent of the time. He can't hear well out of one ear and might holler on the radio and everything, but we work as a team. You've got to get somebody else."

I went to Daddy and said, "Look, we're having trouble with the driver. He's hollering about this and hollering about that and we got to try to keep the deal. Ford asked me to call the shots."

Daddy said, "Well, you can do it."

"I know it, but we got to try and find somebody else. They said Donnie isn't old enough." So Daddy and me were sitting back at the motel about half lit and he said, "You know, Travis Carter isn't doing anything." I said, "That's exactly what we need to do. Call Travis."

Greg had a fierce loyalty for working with his father, pooling their ideas in running the team together as father and son. That was much preferable to "calling the shots" alone. But he and his father agreed that nothing was wrong with bringing in a fresh, calming influence. Travis Carter's resume was impressive. He was crew chief on the championship runs of Benny Parsons in 1973 and Cale Yarborough in 1978. He won the Daytona 500 with Benny in 1975, among many other races. The talented, soft-spoken Travis Carter hung his shingle in Spartanburg in mid–1992.

Travis Carter had been with Harry Gant at Skoal. He had been with Junior and had been sitting on his rear end. We called him up on the phone and said, "What are you doing?"

"Nothing."

"Come down to Spartanburg. We need to talk to you."

"About what?"

"Just come on down here. We think we can get you some money."

We sat in the office with Travis and I said, "Look. We got a communication problem with

Greg Moore in a very pensive pose as he no doubt ponders how to cope with driver discontent and the pressures of managing the team (courtesy Bud Moore Engineering Archives).

the driver. He's a good driver, but he's a Yankee. We ran good at Daytona, then we blew some motors and he tore up some cars. He's giving us a fit. Ford wants me to take over. I'm an engine guy and I don't want to do it."

Daddy spoke up and said, "We got to do something." Travis looked over and said, "How in the hell am I going to tell you two how to race?" I said, "That isn't the problem. We just have to smooth things over."

Then Daddy and I talked about it. Donnie did us a good job changing the right front tire. After all, we did win the pit crew championship at the end of '91, and he was a helluva good guy. I told Daddy, "This is how we're going to do it. I'm the team manager. I'm going to give Travis my job." I talked Ford out of a hundred grand to pay Travis. That's nothing compared to what it is now, but it was a bunch of money then. I decided to let him have my job, and I would go back to the engine room and hang around there with Daryl.

Travis was an easy guy to get along with. He didn't want to talk too much, but he knew the chassis and we loved the guy to death. So we hired him.

We had Travis and Donnie fooling with Bodine instead of Daddy cussing him out and me kissing his ass — good cop, bad cop. Bodine said it didn't make any difference about anything. Then we went to some tracks where we ran well anyway and he changed his tune. We were fourth in the Firecracker at Daytona, but we had engine trouble at Talladega. We had one of the fastest cars there and had one of those tips come off a valve — and they were brand new valves. We ran pretty sorry until we got to those two rain-outs.

> *With Travis Carter on board, Greg dedicated himself to finding out what could be done to improve the power plants under the hood of the blood-red Thunderbirds. Daryl, Strawberry Davis, he, and the guys in the engine room toiled through frustrating hours of trial and error, searching for the right combination of airflow, valve angles, and micro-differences to find even a slight improvement in performance. The hard work paid off, and the checkered flag flew over number 15 again. Maybe they should run all the races on Monday afternoons.*

There were two rained-out Sunday races that were run on the next Monday. We won them both. That's when we won the first Manufacturer's Championship for Ford in their history. Oh, they were tickled to death about that.

The first win was at Martinsville and was kind of funny. Here's the story behind us winning again. There were one or two races I didn't go to because I was running cylinder heads on the dyno. We were running two sets of cylinder heads a day. Here's how bad it was. I had the best stuff. I'd poured it myself. The flow bench didn't tell you anything. Mr. Flow was back! If the valve seats were just a tiny bit off, it was 50 horsepower. It was that touchy, how that stuff got when you got past 700 horsepower. In a two week period, I ran ten sets of cylinder heads on the same block assembly. One of the sets of cylinder heads where we had spent about as much money as anything pulled 657 horsepower. The best set pulled 710. There was 680, 693, all kinds of stuff. That's ten sets with brand new valves and everything as perfect as we could do it. I was talking at the racetrack to Keith Dorton, Randy's brother, and said, "Something's going on with these damn heads." He said, "It's crazy. Whoever figures that out first will have an edge." I said, "I'm seeing something." You couldn't measure it. I always walked around with a dial, an indicator, measuring stuff. I'd change valve seat angles one degree even half a degree. You do something like that and it might mean 20 horsepower in the motor. The motors were getting that refined. That's the trouble they got with them now. It's like you breathe on a cylinder head and you lose 20 horsepower. I'll bet you're talking about $100,000 in cylinder heads of different configurations of the same design. Ernie Elliott said he'd seen it, too, and it was crazy. Nobody had a handle on it, and this was the trick to the whole thing.

Peter Guild, who owned Pro Motor Engineering, had one up there in Mooresville that pulled 700 horsepower, and they were cheating the hell out of it. We carried one up there that we had lying on the floor that only pulled 670. That's where the dyno thing came in when that English guy erased our data. I was using a manual gauge. It took us to midseason to get that thing back up and running. The plate motors like we won the Clash with, we got all that stuff right. Probably for the first six races we were off 30 horsepower on the very top end.

This is what we did. Peter had a motor up there that pulled 701 horsepower. I noticed when he ran his motor it had no torque. On the graph it would go up and keep going. I had a manifold with $5,000 in it. It was made from three manifolds and it had been welded on so much, and this was the secret to the whole deal. It was an Edelbrock AH2. Nobody else would fool with it but me and another guy up there at Yates who went to work for himself. It was on their parts record and would always pull in the bottom end.

I told Peter, "Let me show you something." Daniel Fowler was up there with me and I told him to go get our manifold. I said, "I think I've got this thing figured out." The manifold was stock part numbered and everything, and he never had even seen one of them. We bolted it on his motor and it gained 40 foot-pounds at 6,000 rpms. It only made 688 horsepower. I said, "We put that manifold on something with the cam that you got and we got something that's going to run." He said he'd never seen that big of a change in his entire life. He hadn't been building motors as long as we had. We bought one motor off him, and that kind of got him going and put him in business.

We ran our motor in one race, and that's when we went to Martinsville and it ran well. Then after we won Martinsville with it, we went back through it, changed the pistons around, put the other goodies in it, stuck our manifold on it, and it started making 710. Then it did haul ass. Everybody thought we were running Peter's motors, but we weren't. But we did buy one from him, I'll admit that. His assembly and pistons and stuff weren't right. When we took off stuff he had wrong and put on stuff we both had right, it really would run. We ran that stuff the rest of the year and we just did better.

The Martinsville win on Monday, September 28, 1992, was a solid victory for Bud Moore Engineering. Geoff qualified seventh and swapped the lead all Monday long with his principal adversaries, Rusty Wallace, Kyle Petty, and brother Brett. But the final 42 laps belonged to Geoff Bodine, and he slipped under the checkered bunting two-tenths of a second ahead of Rusty. It was Bud Moore Engineering's first win in 54 starts. However, the patriarch of the team remained in Spartanburg, watching on ESPN like most of us.

Daddy didn't go. He was very disheartened by the whole thing. He said, "Y'all go up there and handle it." So we go up there to Martinsville and once again, the key was a combination of several things. Bodine said getting Travis Carter didn't help. Well, it did help because he didn't have Bud Moore hollering in his ear and pissing him off. Kind of a communications thing. Brett Bodine didn't pay that any attention. Allison didn't pay it any attention. Earnhardt—we never had to say anything to him. You didn't have to tell him anything except, "Remember, if you run too hard it's going to blow up after 300 miles." That was the valve springs and all that bum stuff back then.

We came down to the last pit stop with a few laps to go. We had a good pit crew, but

At Daytona's Pepsi 400 on the Fourth of July 1992, not only did the Motorcraft Team record an excellent fourth place on the lead lap, Greg was photographed with the President of the United States, George H. W. Bush. Brent (left) and Bud (right) await their turns (courtesy Bud Moore Engineering Archives).

some of those other guys started getting better. When we won that pit crew championship, it pissed a bunch of people off. We never practiced. Jake Elder said, "They broke the record and we rehearsed a hundred pit stops with these young guys. Those mothers should be on social security, not out here doing this stuff." Anyway, it was time to put on tires. We got to thinking about it and said, "If we screw up in the pits, whoever gets in front of us is going to win the race. Let's put on two tires." The left sides only had about 30 laps on them. Bodine's good at Martinsville, and the motor with that damn manifold would just jump out of the corners. *Boom!* It was like a rocket to the flag stand. We put on two tires. For the last several laps Bodine just drives off and leaves everyone else behind.

We got back to the shop and I doubted myself a little bit. Daddy said, "Why didn't you put on four tires?" I said, "Well, we wanted to make sure we were out front. There weren't too many laps left and we were running well. We wanted to win the race."

"I'd have put four tires on it."

"Daddy, we had two other pit crews that were a little quicker than us. We probably would have run third."

"Yeah, but I'd have put four tires on it!"

"Daddy, I would have, too, but we wanted to win the race."

These other guys had stepped their programs up. That's when they had started getting these college athletes. We were falling behind a little bit, but not much. We figured if we came out fourth with four brand new tires and they had four brand new tires, we wouldn't

Geoff Bodine (back row, center — under the oo of Goody's) and the Motorcraft team celebrate in Victory Lane on Monday, September 28, 1992. Their success was greatly due to Greg's heads-up, two-tire pit stop with a few laps to go. Greg is kneeling fifth from the left (courtesy Bud Moore Engineering Archive).

have enough time to get around them. That's the reason I've always said a two-tire deal isn't a secret. We did it with Benny. We did it with Rudd at Riverside in '85. I take more pride in Riverside in '85 than anything I ever pulled off. And we pulled it again at Martinsville in '92. You got to pull it at the right place at the right time with the right number of laps left and with what the tires are doing. You don't do it at Dover. Not with Brett Bodine!

I have to agree with Daddy. If we'd put four tires on it and come out second, we probably could have won the race, even if we'd come out third. But at Martinsville you can block. You got to get by the guy or knock the hell out of him. We came out in front and had a clear race track and went on.

> Those two Sunday rain-outs amounted to a brief eight days in the fall of 1992 that were reminiscent of the years with Buck Baker, Jack Smith, Joe Weatherly, and Billy Wade — the years when winning was expected every time out. They loaded up the car in Spartanburg, went to some weekday short-track race, took care of business, and brought the hardware and cash back home. At least for a while, the boys at 400 North Fairview could do no wrong. Once again, Greg and Travis took the team into moonshine country, this time in North Carolina for a 400 lapper at North Wilkesboro. And once again, the boss stayed home and watched it on ESPN.

Daddy had set the car up, had the springs right, got even a better motor, and got a 500 ratio rear end, which is a little bit much to be turning it for a Ford. We took the manifold and a modified motor with the other stuff in it, and we put it on the dyno and it pulled even more torque, more horsepower. We went up to North Wilkesboro and qualified third. Bodine's on top of the steering wheel. We outran them so bad, I think we lapped the field about twice. We outran them so bad it was a joke. Like Mark Martin said, "There wasn't anybody going to do anything with that 15 today." The manifold had just enough hesitation off the corner. Like Dick Trickle said, "That thing's got a hot spot." What happened, you don't spin your wheels when you first put your foot in it. But once you started off the corner, it went like a rocket because of the torque curve. Some of those guys were spinning their tires. Bodine had that full one-inch drop-snout car that turned in the corners and everything. If we ever dominated a race in modern times, that was the one. It looked like Weatherly at Hillsborough in '63. Martinsville, Wilkesboro, Daytona, Darlington, Talladega, Atlanta — these were tracks that were very good to us.

The record shows that 1992 was a success, with three wins including the prestigious Busch Clash, seven top fives, 11 top tens, $618,515 in winnings, but a disappointing sixteenth in the final point standings. It seemed that the Moore-Bodine relationship was a fragile one at best, with Travis Carter being the glue holding the Motorcraft Team together. But the negotiating of another one-year deal went without a hitch, and hopes were high during the winter for better results.

It is hard to describe the tragedy and disappointment that lay ahead in 1993. As in 1992, the campaign started well. The second 125 mile qualifier for the Daytona 500 found Geoff right on Earnhardt's tail at the finish, providing a solid sixth place start for the big race. The main event on Valentine's Day brought to mind that infamous 1929 Chicago massacre at the Clark Street garage. Car-rending crashes took out potential winners, with the highlight being Rusty Wallace's backstretch lift-off as he flipped and rolled more than a dozen times. When it came down to the wire, there were 18 cars on the lead lap, and pulling the train were Dale, Dale, Geoff, Hut, and Jeff the rookie.

We pushed Dale Jarrett by Earnhardt, and our front end's crumpled up from an earlier bump. The one that screwed us was Hut Stricklin driving Junior's number 27 McDonald's car. We had it all set up. But something got on the grill. The water temperature went up. The oil temperature went up. Bodine called over the radio, "This son-of-a-bitch is getting a little hot. What do y'all think you ought to do?" Travis turned to me and said, "What do you think?"

"Look," I said, "there are six laps to go. This is the Daytona 500. Run it until it blows! We aren't pulling into the stinking pits to take a piece of debris off. We're going to try to win this thing. It'll stand it."

In turn two of the last lap, Bodine pulled out and Hut Stricklin got about 20 feet too far back from him. Bodine was trying to get him lined up. So we pushed Dale Jarrett past Earnhardt, but Hut isn't on his bumper. We've got the in-car camera, and Bodine's motioning Hut to come on. Well, that got Dale Jarrett past Earnhardt and we get right up to Jarrett's left rear quarter panel, but Hut's too far back to help us draft by and take the lead, which we could have done easy. So we come to the finish, and that's when Ned Jarrett is broadcasting the race on CBS TV and coaching his boy to the win. Bodine held off Hut easy and Jeff Gordon fell back to fifth. That was as close as we ever came to winning anywhere that we still didn't win.

After Daytona, the good times kept coming as the Yankee Speedster captured ninth at the Rock, twelfth at Richmond, sixth at Atlanta, and eighth at Darlington, and headed

At the finish of the Daytona 500, with his father, Ned, urging him on from the CBS broadcast booth, Dale Jarrett edged Dale Earnhardt for the win, with Geoff Bodine's Motorcraft T-Bird in a very close third place on February 14, 1993 (courtesy Bud Moore Engineering Archives).

to Bristol holding down second in the championship standings. All was good and things were on schedule. April Fool's Day 1993 holds a special significance for Greg and me. I proposed to my wife Yaneth on her birthday that night at the fanciest restaurant in Coconut Grove in Miami. She said, "Yes." We went to my house afterwards to call our mothers and I flipped on the television and naturally ESPN popped up, but without sound. The scene on the screen was a rainy, rural road with blurred images of flashing red and blue emergency lights. As Yaneth and I spread the word of our engagement, I gathered that an unspeakable tragedy was unfolding in the cold, icy rain of the mountains near Bristol, Tennessee. Greg was within earshot of the unfolding horror that night.

Donnie and Harold and I were driving up that way. It was drizzling rain and real cold. We were staying at the same Holiday Inn with the Pettys and lots of others. It was about ten o'clock at night when we heard sirens start going off. I thought, "What in the hell is going on?" We thought there was some big interstate crash. It was unreal!

Later we found out there had been a plane crash. Bob Brooks, the owner of Hooters, had given Alan Kulwicki and his team a plane called a Merlin. It's got Gardte engines on it. They're real high horsepower motors and super-fast, but they're tricky to fly. That's what our pilot, Bill Carr, told me. The plane of choice then and now is what they call a King Air. That's what we flew in. Cale had a Merlin for a while and got rid of it.

Kulwicki had a guy who was not a full-time pilot. Bill said, "The only thing a part-time pilot will do is be a cowboy and drive you straight in the ground." Imagine the difference between someone who files an airplane every other week and somebody who flies them all the time. A full-time pilot will stay on top of things.

What happened was that the guy let the plane ice up. He wasn't watching what he was doing and the plane got heavy. It didn't have motor failure or anything. But it crashed, and Alan Kulwicki got killed on the way to Bristol. It killed everybody and it was terrible. Maybe the guy didn't make a mistake. I don't know. They said Kulwicki was the only person still intact. He was sitting in a seat thrown clear. It was a terrible scene.

We got out there to the racetrack the next morning and found out all about it, and it was awful. Kulwicki's crew was up there with the race car. The guy had won the championship the year before. Everybody liked him. He did it on his own. Now the team hasn't got a driver. They haven't got the sponsor's son. They've lost five people. Kulwicki had a nice shop up there in Charlotte and everything. If there ever was a modern-day Smokey Yunick, Bud Moore, or Cotton Owens, he was it. He did it all and was kind of a small-time deal. He had a bigger shop and more people than we did, but compared to a Hendrick or something wasn't much.

Kulwicki's parents, who were super-nice, got left with a race team. They didn't want it. The parents wanted to unload the race team.

The Kulwicki nightmare faded away. Nightmares always do. Stock car racing historically has fewer tragedies than, say, open-wheel racing. During the good times, those nightmare periods are few and far between. During the worst of times, they seem to overlap. This was a time when they did overlap, and true personalities and ambitions came to the surface. It soon became apparent that the team at 400 North Fairview was going to need a new wheelman, and they fought hard to sign a contender. The year wasn't half over and Silly Season was under way.

Bodine and Waltrip and some of them had said they wanted their own race team. They thought that was the way to go. Many who tried it regretted it. If Kulwicki hadn't died, the opportunity wouldn't have happened for Bodine, and things with us probably would have been pretty doggone good. But the Kulwickis really wanted Bodine to buy the race team. Bodine's wife, Kathy, was against the whole thing, but he had the money and thought he'd get his own team.

Kathy—we loved her. She finally told him, "Look, I'm tired of you being ugly to people." Kathy got along with our folks real well. She was funnier than hell. Kathy was on our side. She said, "I don't know why he's buying this race team. He's done spent $800,000."

I said, "He's getting in your pocketbook, isn't he?"

"He isn't going to get in it much more! I told him to drive for you. Don't do this!"

Geoff ran through a bunch of money, and she got tired of people booing him. She took her money. She loved him, but she couldn't take the son-of-a-gun not getting along with car owners, so she just got real mad. Still, we had a ball with Bodine. He really wasn't that bad. Kathy died of a heart attack at 51 or something like in 2001.

Bodine went ahead and committed to purchasing the Kulwicki team around midseason of '93. We were trying to keep our deal, but Bodine was planning on taking our sponsors, buying that race team, and there we were going to sit with no driver, no sponsor, a shop full of people, and some awful good race cars. This is when I got on the phone and raised $10,000 worth of hell. I called everyone short of Edsel. I said, "Y'all want to give Bodine more money to take the deal and start something, and you don't even know what's going on."

Now it's up to me to get a driver. Bodine wanted a million dollars or half a million dollars more than we wanted or needed for the next year. So we got in this big sponsor battle, which was nothing new. It was already Silly Season. Bodine said he knew Bud and Greg were probably mad at him. Ford said to Bodine, "Yeah, we'll sponsor you. We've got the money invested and we know you can do it. You won the Manufacturers' Championship." So I got to thinking about it. Here they are going to pull our deal. They'd already said they were going to change to Quality Care with the blue car for '94. Then Ford says, "We are going to stay with Bud Moore." We said we'd do the deal, but they said, "You got to find a driver."

So the Bodine deal with Motorcraft got nixed. I got Quality Care for '94. Ford took Sam Scott and moved him over to another division and hired a super-nice guy named Dave Arnie. He said, "We're going to change the car. We're going to change the color, we're going to do this, and we're going to do that. But we've got to have a driver." This is where the Ted Musgrave thing comes in and Roush and I had the big falling out. I'd already got into it with him a few times when he first got into stock car racing. Daddy and I kept saying we needed a multi-year deal. We'd say, "Y'all want to sign a one-year deal with the driver. We get to mid-season, and if we do worth a damn, everybody wants to hire the driver. Y'all start shopping the sponsorship around. We can't hire anybody and can't do anything else except do the best we can with what we've got because there's no other future." Like with Wrangler for three years when we had Earnhardt, Earnhardt, and Ricky Rudd.

So we get Ted Musgrave down there to sign a three-year deal to drive for Bud Moore, Greg Moore, Quality Care, better money, a future — but Musgrave was driving for Ray DeWitt. He was like an independent with some money. Ford was schooling Ted Musgrave up. So we were going to put Ted Musgrave in the car, get Quality Care, and have a three-year deal. But Jack Roush grabbed the Family Channel and hired Musgrave away so Bud Moore couldn't get a three-year deal. Ray DeWitt said, "I ought to shoot the mother. I let him out of a contract to drive for you, not to drive for Jack Roush." There are no ifs, ands, or buts about that. Roush formed another team just to keep us from getting a driver that Ford liked. So there I am, stuck again.

As Geoff Bodine was trying to buy the late Alan Kulwicki's team, his employer of the present was full-bore into the 1993 season with one of their best tracks and chances to win coming up way out west in wine country. Everybody was up to the task even though their hearts and minds were mostly elsewhere. It would be an extremely special race in the storied history of Bud Moore Engineering.

We won our last race in 1993 with Geoff Bodine, and Daddy didn't go out there. We had our game plan and the car ran great. We qualified third, outran them, won the race, and knew Bodine was leaving. I was not mad at Bodine or anything. I knew we were going to win the race with about ten laps to go unless something bad happened. Travis Carter came over there to me and said that Bodine wanted to do a Kulwicki Victory Lap, which was to circumnavigate the course in the wrong direction with the checkered flag. I thought that was pretty stupid, but OK.

Then I got to thinking about it. Daddy isn't there, and Bodine is going to start spraying that champagne, and we're going to be getting on that little charter plane to fly home. Momma had just bought me a brand-spanking-new black, lightweight Members Only jacket for $600. I don't want to get that champagne mess all over my new jacket! I didn't want in any pictures or anything. I mean, I was in a great mood, it was a great win, Bodine drove his heart out, but I didn't even go to Victory Lane and the jacket was the main excuse.

Later, I'm at the back of the truck and here comes Mike Mulhern, Deb Williams, a bunch of reporters, and I have my own press conference. Then the crew guys came up and said, "Why didn't you go to Victory Lane?" I said, "I didn't want to get champagne on my

Momma's jacket she just bought me." Seriously! I just stayed out of the way. I'd do it the same way if I had it to do over.

It would have helped if I'd liked the driver a little bit better or if Daddy had been there. Daddy was not at our last three wins. He was not at Martinsville, he was not at North Wilkesboro, and he was not at Sonoma. The last Victory Lane he was in as a car owner was the Busch Clash at Daytona in February of 1992.

After all those nasty, dimly lit dirt tracks of the '60s, after the twisty road courses of the Trans Am glory days, and after scores of wins from coast to coast that came home to 400 North Fairview Avenue, Gregory Clyde Moore and Bud Moore Engineering were done winning. They were not nearly done trying, but the checkered bunting would never fly across the nose of one of their cars again.

Then, on July 12, 1993, came another horrible tragedy involving one of the superstars of the day. Davey Allison was the driver for Robert Yates' Racing in the Texaco Havoline number 28 Ford Thunderbird. In the infield at Talladega International Speedway Allison's Hughes 369HS helicopter crashed as he was attempting to touch down where the occupants could watch Neil Bonnett's son David test a Busch car for his upcoming debut. In the helicopter with Allison was his friend and fellow racer Red Farmer. Farmer survived, but Davey died the day after the accident. As Greg continued to try to ink an A List driver, another top Ford team suddenly needed one, too.

We got into a deal with Jimmy Spencer. He was driving for Bobby Allison in the number 12 Mieneke Mufflers car. We offered him $100,000 up front. We had a meeting scheduled with him, but Davey Allison got killed the day before Jimmy was supposed to come to the shop. Jimmy wanted to drive the car. He said, "Bobby's had a lot of bad things and he's just lost Davey, so I'm going to have to try and stay with them." That deal went down the tubes.

Greg was undeterred despite the disappointing driver search so far. He still had a couple of heavy negotiations to come with a former employee and a previous Cup champion. First, the former employee.

I was trying to re-hire Ricky Rudd. He saw how we ran out there at Sears Point. Rudd was in behind Bodine and Ernie Irvan. Bodine was out front, and when they got through the short stuff they could get to him. They could out-brake him. When they'd round the corner and come through the high sweepers and go down that straightaway, so help me, he'd drive a hundred yards ahead of them. So Larry McClure, who had Ernie Irvan driving his car at that time, laughed and said, "We can do something with him up there on the short stuff, but if he's leading at the top of the hill and around the corner, you can forget it."

We had changed the motor around a little bit with a different camshaft. Daddy set the chassis because he knows all about the road course stuff, and it had a 500 ratio rear end in it. On top of that, we put a spark plug in it that was like a dyno plug. You couldn't run it at a speedway because it was too hot a plug, but it was perfect for short tracks. It was called Autolite 501. We gave that car all the goodies. They dropped the green flag and he was a bad son-of-a-gun. Ricky Rudd said, "The only way I could have won the race was out-brake him in that short stuff and knock him out of the way. I might have been able to do that." That's the turn where Rudd did put Davey Allison out in '91.

Well, Ricky was trying to take Tide from Hendrick, but he hadn't quite done it. He'd hired a few people. He wanted to get away from Hendrick because he'd seen he was the second-rate driver and didn't like that. It was the same as when Earnhardt never liked it when Childress got Mike Skinner as a second car.

I called Rudd on the phone, and he was pretty impressed with the Sears Point race and said he was working on this Tide deal. I said I could get him three years at $650,000, and we got real buddy-buddy. He was going to bring the Tide deal to us for $2.8 million and I only had $2.4. He calls me on the phone and says, "Look, Gregory, we can do anything we want to with this." I had Ford for three years and a little bit less money.

We got to Bristol and we're getting desperate. We don't have anybody hired. We thought, "Let's offer him eight, eight fifty, and a million for the third year. Ricky still doesn't have that Tide deal totally handled. It isn't signed." I told him, "I think I got us handled." He said, 'Why in the hell didn't you tell me that a month ago? I'm too far into this thing now. If you'd told me that a month ago, I'd have scrubbed this whole damn deal. Do me one favor. Keep that ride open for three weeks. Don't hire anybody. If the Tide thing doesn't get signed up, I sure want to drive for y'all. If I'd known that's what they were going to pay me, I wouldn't have fooled with all this other stuff."

Well, it was four weeks and we hadn't signed a new driver. Even one of my nieces said, "Uncle Gregory, why are you letting Ricky use you?"

"Baby, he isn't using your Uncle Gregory. He stood in my corner for four years. Don't you think Uncle Gregory can stand in his for four weeks?"

"Well, yeah."

If Tide had gone ahead and signed with Hendrick and not gone with Ricky, we were like plan B+.

Greg approached a former Winston Cup Champion looking for a new home as the final shot.

Then there was Terry Labonte. He was with Billy Hagan and Kellogg's. They didn't run worth a damn. He was pitiful. We got him to come down and talk to us. He came down to the shop and had already looked at Hendrick and all that big stuff. He looked at our shop and said, "I never figured this place to be so nice, to be so little and everything. This is cool as hell." But before he, Daddy, and I went into the office and sat down, Terry said, "I think I got a better chance of winning the championship with Hendrick than I do with y'all. Kellogg's will follow me." I said, "OK, Terry. I've been trying to get you something set up to get you in his car." Same thing I offered Rudd. About the same as Hendrick was offering him. Bud Moore was sitting right over there, and we were talking. "If you go over there to Hendrick with Kellogg's, what about taking Billy Hagan's sponsor? You drive for us, we're going to do good, you'll have a good car, Ford engineering will be behind you 100 percent, and you don't have to take Hagan's sponsor." Terry didn't give a damn. I said, "OK. You go up there and drive for them. You're going to run pretty well. But if you don't, he'll de-nut you." So he did go up there and he did run well. He won a championship. What can I say? But he put Hagan out of business, and it was Hagan who had given him his first chance. Put Hagan out of business! Billy Hagan took a chance on him years ago. I didn't operate like that. I'd have much rather had Ricky Rudd or Ted Musgrave than Terry Labonte, even though I liked Terry Labonte. He would have been in a much better car than Billy Hagan, but not as good as Rick Hendrick. Where does all this leave me?

The season was racing toward fall and time was fleeting. Not to cast any aspersions on the remaining candidates, but it seemed Bud Moore Engineering would end up with less than they had hoped for to pilot the number 15's new colors and sponsor for 1994. Call it hard feelings, bad feelings, or whatever. The Bud Moore Team went to a crucial test at the Indianapolis Motor Speedway where the First Annual Brickyard 400 was scheduled for August of 1994. Relationships in Gasoline Alley were strained and strange for Greg and the boys. Amid all of the racing and testing, Greg was still putting his heart and soul into filling the seat of the number 15.

We go up to Indy for the test session for the first race, and Bodine is supposed to drive the car. Bodine won't even get in our car and drive a lap. It's a test session, and he's over there with that number 7 car of Kulwicki's old team, white, no sponsor or nothing on it. He's cut a deal with Hoosier tire or something. I said, "Geoff, we need to make a lap or two."' He wouldn't help. So I went over there and I asked Morgan. Morgan went out there and ran a couple of laps and ran better in our car than he did in the Wood Brothers.' There's about 20 of us up there testing. Nobody had run up there at Indy at that point except Daddy and Smokey in that test deal they did in '61 with Pontiac.

Lake Speed got in there and drove for a couple of laps. It just shows you how cutthroat all that stuff was — and still is. It's probably worse now than it was. When Davey Allison got hurt, they put Lake Speed in his car and ran a few races, and he ran fair. He didn't run like Davey Allison did, but he was pretty fair. Daddy said, "We got a driver out of a contract with Ray DeWitt and Roush hires that one." Then Lee Morse at Ford says, "What about Lake Speed?" I have to admit he ran well. He started fourth for Yates in the number 28 at Watkins Glen and did OK, and at Michigan he started second and finished seventh — and he's available.

Lake ran one more race for Yates at Bristol before he came over to us. Lake Speed was going to drive the number 15 Quality Care car for Bud Moore. Bodine had already bought Kulwicki's team, and we were going to let him go. Lake joined the team in time for Dover in September to finish out the season and gear up for 1994's new colors and sponsor. At Dover we were the fastest before qualifying, but we finished bad. Lake ran the last seven races, and the best we did was an eleventh at Charlotte. He was bad about not qualifying any good. That was the end of '93. We get a Lake Speed. Didn't I really get a good one?

Greg Moore reflects on the frustrations of knowing they had a top factory team and not being able to land a comparable driver for the seat. All the while they still were the standard bearer for the Ford Motor Company and its Motorcraft sponsorship and upcoming Quality Care rebranding.

There's so much stuff that happened in that period. I didn't have a life except just trying to find money. I don't know. The Lake Speed thing—I just about had a nervous breakdown. We didn't leave on perfect terms with Bodine. When he got his own team, he saw how much money had to be spent. He won a couple of races on those gumball tires with Hoosier. Then when Roush took his sponsor Exide away from him, he knew what we went through. He got QVC and that wasn't enough funding. So he ran through a bunch of money. I get along fine with Geoff Bodine now.

I'm going to be honest with you. The screw-up that got Bud Moore Engineering was when Alan Kulwicki's plane crashed. That set off a chain reaction of a lot of things. Here's what's ironic: We had had our share of tragedies that affected us directly, and then two tragedies affected us more than losing our own two drivers. That's because they also affected so many other people, like sponsors and drivers and their connections. With Kulwicki's plane crash and Davey Allison's helicopter crash, there were people who gained things and lots of people who lost things. I've never seen a point in history over a period of a year where things happened to other teams because of sponsorships. It's like we got hit harder over those deals than we did when we lost Weatherly after two straight championships and Wade who was doing real good and headed to the top.

Of course it was a bigger emotional thing if we lost a driver who drove for us. Daddy always said he should have never listened when Weatherly told him to put that transmission in that car. And Wade wasn't scheduled to be down at the tire test, but Dieringer didn't do what he was supposed to and got hurt. All this stuff that we blamed ourselves for tugged on our shoulder the whole time. All of them were bad, all of them were sad. But business-wise, everything that happened as far as those 1993 tragedies had a direct financial stability effect on Bud Moore Engineering. Anybody who was racing back then saw it. It was terrible. I liked Alan Kulwicki. I liked Davey Allison. When all was said and done, we missed Musgrave, we missed Jimmy Spencer, we missed Terry Labonte, we missed Ricky Rudd, and we got Lake Speed. Can you believe that?

The story mercifully closed on 1993 with a second consecutive sixteenth place points finish for the Motorcraft team. Again they had fallen far short of their own expectations, let alone those of Ford. The year's numbers showed 23 races with Geoff Bodine including a pole, a win, two top fives, eight top tens, $586,750 in winnings plus seven starts with Lake Speed which added virtually nothing to those figures. Sadly, that pole at Martinsville on April 25 and the win at Sears Point on May 16, which came only three weeks apart, were the last of their kind for the proud history of Bud Moore Engineering.

Chapter Fifteen

Quality Care and the Factory Farewell

The 1994 season was approached with guarded optimism. A new driver with a different outlook was on the way. Greg had worked tirelessly to hire a replacement for Geoff Bodine, and after missing some more attractive replacements, he settled on Lake Speed, who had finished out 1993 for them. They met to sign the deal at 400 North Fairview.

Lake was kind of a hard sale because he had just had his own team with Purex for a sponsor. He even won the spring race at Darlington in 1988 on gumball Hoosiers in his own Oldsmobile driving for Wynn's K-Mart. Basically, there was nobody left. He was the best shot we had, and Lee Morse kept going on about him. At one time Lake was worth some pretty good money. He had inherited some business holdings down in Mississippi and was world's karting champion. He had quit drinking about four or five years before he came to drive for us, and his wife Rice and he got religion. That was partially what screwed him up. Lake and I got along great. Fantastic! Lake sat there in our office and said, "Look, I know y'all have a good car. I know it's going to run good. I'm behind y'all 100 percent, but I'm not good at taking criticism. I'm not good at that because I'm used to running my own show." I could see that. I understood it. It was another one year deal for $600,000.

The colors on the number 15 Thunderbird were new, a mostly sky blue scheme with red and black stripes on the rocker panels reminiscent of the previous Motorcraft schemes. White numbers and lettering included a big QC on the hood for Quality Care, Ford's equivalent of General Motors' Goodwrench brand. Ford was still funding the operation, but Lake Speed was essentially plan C at best. Good results were expected and the new team rolled south to Daytona.

We went to Daytona and our top speed wasn't all that good. We got in the 125 miler and finished eleventh. In the 500 we started twenty-second and moved up near the front and had just passed Earnhardt for third. But we had to pit for gas and the rest of them didn't, and we wound up fourteenth. I told Lake, "Man, I hate that." He said, "We had a good car. The car drove perfect. I'll never get down on y'all as long as y'all never get down on me."

The next couple of races were so-so, but then we got kind of hot. At Atlanta we were sixth, Darlington was a fifth, and Bristol third. We ran fantastic at Bristol. If we hadn't adjusted on the car we would have won the race. He was flying the whole time. He wanted to adjust on the car and we wound up third instead of second. That got us to fifth in the point standings. We were twelfth at North Wilkesboro, had a bad run Martinsville, and came in seventh at Talladega, after which we were still fifth in the standings. Then we had some more so-so to bad races and went to Daytona in July for the Firecracker tenth in points.

Actually all was going very well, probably better than expected. The Quality Care team had battled as high as fifth in the standings, but had fallen back to tenth for the mid-season trip back to the beach. Greg had fought hard to massage Lake Speed's fragile ego by balancing his roles as cheerleader and boss. For Bud Moore Engineering, the winds of discontent soon came blowing in off the Atlantic.

We went to Daytona in July. We had the fastest frigging car down there, using a Yates rent-a-motor. Lake couldn't get it running. It wouldn't run worth a rip and we had that good special Daytona car. We had used a Yates restrictor plate motor in February in Daytona and were fine. So in July we used another Yates restrictor plate motor and it wouldn't run worth a damn. I had griped about the gas mileage the whole time in February. Rain hit us and we had to qualify the next day. I had a motor that had been sitting on the truck for a year. We called it the 46 motor. It was the one Geoff had run third with in the 500, and it had all our goodies on it. Daryl and the guys in the engine room had freshened it up. I told Daddy, "We got to do something." He agreed. "Go get 46 off the truck." So we did, and we stuffed the thing in. Everybody knew we were taking that Yates motor out and putting our motor in. Our restrictor motors had always run so well. Lake went out, got warmed up, and got the green to qualify. Going down the backstretch wide open, it started raining and he came in. I asked him what he thought and he said it was a ton better. "I can feel it through the gearbox. I was turning more RPMs going down the backstretch than I was with the other motor." We didn't do anything to it and it ran six tenths quicker on a hotter day. So here we are starting at the rear in thirty-third.

They dropped the green flag and here he comes. He was passing one or two cars a lap. He was coming, and everybody in the garage area was watching Bud's old used motor move up. He finally got all the way up there to the lead. He hollered to Preston Miller, who was doing the spotting, "Preston! This son-of-a-bitch is loose. Get me out of here!" All the crew and I heard that. We had been down there trying to run up front all week. Lake Speed drove from the rear to the front and then hollered for Preston to get him out of there. Get him somewhere where he can drop back. Once he got up front and the train got to pushing him, he wanted out of there. So he dropped back to about ninth or tenth, and that was where he rode and finished.

From that moment on, the team got down on him. They flat got down on him. Lake started hearing and feeling a lot of negativity towards his driving. And he doesn't like criticism. They said that this man can't qualify all that well. He can't do this, he can't do that. He had bragged on our motors but said the car didn't drive quite as well as the Yates car did. That pissed the guys off in the back and they all got down on him. Lake and I had a discussion after that when we got to Talladega. He said, "You know, Ernie Irvan told me that his set up was tighter than what we got." I said very sarcastically, "Yes, Lake, that's correct. That's because Ernie Irvan was planning on leading the pack. It's real simple. If you're going to lead the train, the car's got to be tight because you don't have air on your back spoiler, you don't have anybody in front of you, and it's just lifting you up. You've got to be tight to lead. He's got 30 cars pushing him. If you're in the midst of the whole train, then you're taking air off the front of the car, which hurts the front end from sticking, and

Rarely going to the track, Daryl Moore preferred to stay at the shop and build the race motors that powered the Fords of Bud Moore Engineering for more than a quarter of a century (courtesy Bud Moore Engineering Archives).

you got air taken off the back, so the car can be about anything you want it to be. You get up front and the air plants the nose down and the ass end gets jacked up with all the cars pushing you." Lake sheepishly said, "Oh I didn't know all that. I didn't understand." Lake was a race driver, but he couldn't figure that out. To run out front, the car's got to be tight. He didn't know because he didn't ever run up front. He just didn't know.

Later we carried a motor up to his dyno. He had his own dyno. The best Ford motor he ever had was 705 horsepower. I took the lousiest motor I had, which showed 694 on our dyno, and put it on his and it made 740 with 50 more foot-pounds torque. Lake said the motors in these cars were fantastic. These were our motors. But he said he drove that Yates car of McReynolds and you could drive it anywhere you wanted to. So we had the ingredients of a good combination. The engine room was behind him, Daddy didn't give a damn, and the guys in the back, the pit crew, thought he was a wuss. I said, "Look, we got to keep this guy another year. We've done pretty well with him. Y'all have pissed him off."

About midseason, a national advertising campaign for Ford Quality Care hit the tube, featuring a comical little skit starring Lake Speed and the Bud Moore pit crew. Playing mostly during races and sporting events, it included Lake's only line, which came back to haunt him.

Ford spent a whole bunch of money on a commercial. They spent a lot of money on marketing Lake. They used actors and some of the crew guys. It was real cool, Quality Care. In it, everybody's working away on and around our car in a shop, and it's supposed to be real intense and quiet. Lake gets him a cup of coffee and knocks a wrench off the bench, and it hits the concrete floor real loud, clanging around, making a lot of noise. All the crew guys stop what they're doing and glare at him because they've been interrupted, and Lake says, "Sorry, guys." Then everybody pops busily back to work like nothing had happened. There's some announcer talking about Quality Care, but that was basically it. Lake's line was something we used when we ran badly. "Sorry, guys." Lake was a super-good guy. A very good friend of mine. I was glad he drove the car.

Gregory Clyde Moore in his Sunday best. Life was good even if the driver left something to be desired (courtesy Bud Moore Engineering Archives).

Three more races with Lake Speed saw mid-pack finishes and a lap led at Talladega. Then came one of the signature events in stock car racing history, if not auto racing as a whole. Since it was first laid out in 1909 by Carl Fisher as a testing ground for American auto mak-

ers, the two and a half mile rounded rectangle at the corner of Georgetown Road and 16th Street west of downtown Indianapolis has been the preeminent shrine to auto racing. Its resurfacing with 3,200,000 ten-pound Culver paving bricks in the winter of 1910 spawned the Inaugural International 500 Mile Sweepstakes in 1911 at the most famous racecourse in the world, the Indianapolis Motor Speedway. In very short order the facility became known as the Brickyard, the race as the Indianapolis 500, and both were and still are sacred to racers around the world. It was considered near blasphemy when the thought of running stock cars, or "taxi-cabs," there was proposed in the early 1990s. Nevertheless, on August 6, 1994, the inaugural Brickyard 400 was run on that hallowed plot of Indiana real estate. Greg Moore saw it for the first time in race trim with over a quarter of a million crazy race fans cramming the double-deck grandstand across from him and others all around the huge speedway. They were united in witnessing history.

It was so unreal. It wasn't just another track. It was awesome. I was there for the test the year before, but I'd never seen it full of 300,000 people. One of the biggest things that got away with me, more than its size and the crowd, was that super-good announcer they had, Tom Carnegie. He'd say during qualifying, "And heeeeeee's on it!" Or "And it's a neeeeew traaaack record!" That guy was the best. He was like Ray Melton at Darlington. "Clap your hands, stomp your feet. All the colors of the rainbow...." They were super announcers and represented their tracks.

What was also amazing about it was the way they knew everybody. I don't know if Tony George had done the research on it, but I went down to get a time sheet and the people in there knew me. I thought, "How in the world do they know who I am?" It was just, "OK Greg, here's your sheet." They had the electrical timing there and the other tracks didn't.

Also, Indy was wickedly fast down the straightaways. It was very difficult for a driver to drive it, and it was much narrower. I never dreamed the track was that narrow. And the sound! Darlington had copied this and used to have the covered grandstands. When you come down that front straightaway with that thing running 200 miles an hour, if it was running right, you could just tell it. It was making that perfect noise. They had the people, they had the noise, they had a spooky race track to drive, and the crowd control that was fantastic. They could get half a million people out of that place faster that North Wilkesboro could get out 10,000.

It was so professional. Tony George said, "Winston Cup sponsors this series and all these guys can smoke in designated areas in Gasoline Alley." They limited the number of tickets sold because they didn't want to outsell the Indy 500. His grandparents didn't want that to ever happen. I really didn't see a damn thing about it I didn't like. Tony was a super-good guy. Momma, Daddy, and he went down to the Bahamas and stuff. He walked over in the pits and said, "Where's Bud at? Where's Bud at?" Of course old, old Mary Hulman was still saying, "Gentlemen, start your engines." Tom Carnegie would announce, "Here's Mary Hulman to say those famous words," and they'd wheel her out there and hold her up to the mic and she'd say, "That's my name, that's my name." She was confused and it was sad. Finally after some prompting she'd say, "Gentlemen, start your engines."

Lake Speed was dreadful, as usual, in time trials, anchoring the next-to-last row — forty-first in a field of 43. But to his credit, he turned in what has to be considered an overall splendid performance on an enormous international stage. Lake actually rose to the occasion.

We didn't qualify well, but we came to the front again. He couldn't qualify on new tires, and that was one of the things we got down on him about. He was a pitiful qualifier. The car was handling fine; we had good pit stops, and a very decent run. Lake put it in the lead for five laps from lap 42 to 46, and it wasn't under the caution either. We actually thought we had a shot to win. They have grandstands behind the pits. The first time we came down pit road for a green flag stop with Harold and them running around changing tires and everything, the people were going nuts. They had never seen anything like it. They were so thrilled at seeing a stock car going around there. People were going berserk behind the pits in the grandstand over us while we were doing the pit stop, and we were running sixth or something. We were up there fifth, sixth, twelfth, tenth, a good run. We had run better all day than the fifteenth place finish we wound up with on the lead lap. That should have been an easy top ten. When we left Indy, we left pretty satisfied.

Greg and the boys left Indianapolis a solid tenth in the standings. A pair of thirteenth at Watkins Glen, where Lake led two laps, and Michigan dropped the team a spot to eleventh in the standings going into the Bristol night race. The earlier trip to the Smoky Mountains in the spring saw them finish third with a good chance of winning. The return visit was eagerly anticipated. The result and ramifications were miserable.

This is where the shit hit the fan! The first Bristol race, everything was great. Almost won. We had the same car with the same motor. We had worked on it and it had a little more horsepower, but nothing drastically changed. Lake never tried to drive the car. He deliberately tried to make us look stupid. It was that obvious. Dick Trickle said, "What in the world is wrong with that driver of yours? He's done wrecked us all once and he's in the way." How do you go back up there and can't get out of your own way? He was mad because he'd heard the crew calling him a no-driving son-of-a-bitch. They called him names like "Lake Lack of Speed" and "Lacka Speed." "Sorry, guys." I started having doubts about him at Daytona when he got up front and told the spotter to get him out of there because he was loose. In my opinion, Lake did not drive the car at Bristol when he knew he could make us look stupid because at exactly the same time he told Ford, "I am not going to come back to drive for those guys because they're down on me."

Ford already had it in their minds, "We're going to be on the stage in New York. Lake needs to come back another year before we sponsor you all." Well, we didn't particularly want him, and I don't think he particularly wanted us. I liked him. I hadn't given up on him. Daryl and I were 100 percent behind him because we knew that after they had done the marketing there was big investment there. Ford got mad at us for running through too many race drivers, which we did. But we blamed the running through too many race drivers on not having multi-year contracts. They said, "Bud and you all can't get along with race drivers." That was not accurate. We got along with drivers from year to year before like Bobby Allison, Buddy Baker, Dale Earnhardt, and Ricky Rudd — who was a guy they chased off. We just can't get along with one that doesn't run. Lake could not qualify a lick. His own wife, Rice, told him, "You got to tighten up your nut strap and run a lap on new tires. You can run in the race, but you're screwing everybody up on starting at the rear." His own wife told him that in front of God and everybody. He knew that we were comparing him to all the drivers we'd had before, like Earnhardt and Allison. The bottom line was he wasn't even a Bodine either. He was just a so-so. He was an also-ran, but a nice guy. He heard negative input from the crew chief. You have to blame Donnie, too. Have to blame some of my key crew members. I said, "We need to keep this so-and-so if we're going to re-sign the deal." I told Daddy, "You better quieten some of these son-of-a-bitches up."

Things were not looking too good for a continuing relationship with Lake Speed, and Greg went after an up-and-coming star. Complicating the matter were the near fatal injuries that Robert Yates' driver, Ernie Irvan, suffered in a practice crash in Michigan on August 19, 1994. Again Greg was looking for a driver kind of behind the scenes, and all of a sudden Yates needed one, too. It was 1993 all over again.

This is where I about get my ass whooped up at North Wilkesboro. We got Bobby Labonte out of a contract with Bill Davis to hire him for a three-year deal. Davis had caught wind that we were going to hire Bobby. Davis was mad, man! I went up to the Wood Brothers' truck and they said, "We hear Bill Davis is a little pissed at you, going to hire his driver."

I said, "Well, I just came up here to hang out."

They said, "You can come over here to hang out, just don't come over here to hide."

I said, "Bill's all right. We've helped him out, but I'm going to get his driver because I have to keep my deal."

We'd helped Bill Davis a bunch. We had given him all our V6 stuff we were working on. We were going to buy Bobby's contract out, and he wasn't exactly a proven commodity. Bobby's daddy, who actually worked on race cars, called me on the phone and said, "I really wanted him to take that job with you and Bud. I told him that's what he needed to do." Ford was going to take Dale Jarrett out of the Joe Gibbs number 18 Interstate Batteries car. I also had a deal outside of Ford worked out with Dale and Hooters to drive our car for two years. So Ford fooled around and gave Dale Jarrett money to drive Robert Yates' car in place of Ernie Irvan because they've got the fastest Ford. So Ford takes Bobby Labonte and gives him to Joe Gibbs to replace Jarrett to keep the coach from getting pissed off. It left us sucking wind again. They did that. We already had it handled. It was just like with Ted Musgrave. I got him out of a contract. Bill Davis still lost Bobby Labonte. We sit again with nothing!

Suddenly, as the last half of the 1994 season wound down, Lake Speed still had a golden opportunity to be on the stage in the Grand Ballroom of the Waldorf Astoria in New York City in December. A Bud Moore driver had not enjoyed that honor since Morgan Shepherd's fifth place in 1990. In a desperate attempt to salvage the season with about five races to go, Ford had another idea.

This is where things really started getting bad and serious, bad enough that Ford Motor Company sent in a consultant named Larry Ward. He was the best consultant in the world. I can't stress this enough. Here's how good he was: There was a big rift between Lee Iaccoca, who invented the Mustang, and Henry Ford II, who said once in *Motor Trend Magazine*, "I just don't like him." Ward was the one who settled it. He was a mediator. They were trying to settle the whole thing because Ford didn't want to fool with us anymore and was going to go to Yates or somebody, or even just sit out, if they couldn't overcome this problem.

Ward moved to Spartanburg in an efficiency apartment and stayed two months. He went to races with us and got the full picture before he made any comments about anything. He was looking at the whole thing. He was super-nice. He saw that Speed wasn't exactly big nuts. We were going to bring in all the technology we could to rectify the situation. I finally told Lake, "You have got to drive the car now. We might lose the deal. I know you got money. I'll get these people to shut up. You have to hang in here another year or we're going to lose the deal. You made a bunch of money. I know you heard some things you didn't like, but we saw some things we didn't like. We went pretty easy on you. Real easy on you compared to most drivers."

Larry Ward said, "We think Lake's a good driver, we know he's got a good car, but we've got to resolve this because we have too much money tied up in marketing. You were supposed to finish in the top ten in points and there's too much dissension among the team. Let's see if we can correct this." He saw where our weaknesses were and where Lake's weaknesses were, which were a bunch more than ours. So we started having these private meetings: Daddy, Lake, the consultant, and me. At one of the meetings, Ward asked Lake, "What would it take to get you to stay here with Bud and us pump a little money in the thing and stay at least one more year?" Lake said, "Well, I want to have total control of the team." His exact words. I started laughing. Daddy said, "I'll tell you what, Lake, we'll do it just like we always did, only you can have more say in it than you did. I'll meet you fifty-fifty and give you the best things we got. Nobody will criticize you any more or anything." The consultant said there was no way we could give him that. He saw it was mainly the driver. I understood the whole thing and thought we had it all worked out. I think part of the thing was that Daddy was about half tired of fooling with that crap. We had never really even needed lawyers to draw up contracts, much less bring a consultant in.

Lake finally came down there and was supposed to make a decision. If he was going to stay, they were going to re-sign the contract for a two-year deal. I had talked to him that morning. I thought everything was going to be cool. He gets to Spartanburg and says, "You know, I didn't know what I was going to say before I came down here, but I'm not going to drive this car anymore." This was with about two races to go. I go, "Oh no! Here we go again." I'd have sworn he would have done it for Daryl and me.

I think Lake was just in over his head. That was the most car, most sponsor, most pressure he had ever been under. That was one of the reasons he had run his own deal. But we needed the money. We needed to keep the people employed. We wound up eleventh in points. We didn't get on the stage. And neither of us ever got that close again.

The second half of the season, Lake hardly ran a lick. We led 11 laps at Martinsville and Rusty took us out. He was fifth at Charlotte and fourth at Atlanta because he was showcasing for a ride. So I go to scrambling — again! Larry Ward, the consultant, saw the situation, too. He said, "Ford's going to sponsor you at least another year if you can find a decent driver." They had been in discussion with Robert Yates. They liked Dale Jarrett and wanted Yates to form a second team, or have Lake stay with us, or stay with us and we get a different driver. They didn't tell me about it, but I knew it. Ward said, "I see what's going on here. You all are a good team, but a little bit behind the times, with a driver a little over the hill that never was worth a damn anyway. We'll get another driver and get Ford to sign this thing up for another year." This decision came in December when we were getting ready to go to Daytona.

All of Ford's expertise and labor relations experience over the past 90 years were no match for the gap between Lake Speed and Bud Moore Engineering. They missed the stage by a lousy 52 points behind Bill Elliott driving Junior Johnson's Budweiser Thunderbird. Lake Speed raced four more years and never sniffed a season as good as the one he had in 1994 with Greg and the boys. Their final numbers were no wins, four top fives, nine top tens, a best starting spot of tenth in the next-to-last race, and $732,405 in winnings, an

On May 25, 1994, Greg and Lake (right) present Bud Moore with a cake to celebrate his sixty-ninth birthday behind the hauler at Charlotte (courtesy Bud Moore Engineering Archives).

all-time high for both up until that point. In all, 1994 was an enormous disappointment considering how close they came to a really good year. Lake Speed moved on and once again, Greg was searching for a driver with very slim pickings. Then something took place that had been floating around under the radar for nearly 20 years. This would have set the racing world on its ear had it materialized.

I came up with an idea. We've only got a one-year deal. So how could they get the biggest bang for their buck?

A couple of years previously, David Pearson got in the Wood Brothers' car at Charlotte and tested and his back was bothering him. He never even tried to run hard, and Leonard said he ran real well. I asked Daddy, "I wonder what Ford would think if we got one of the greatest race drivers of all time, David Pearson, on a one-year deal for some big money driving for a Spartanburg-based team." He said, "I don't know. Call them and see what the deal is."

I made a couple of phone calls, and the people went nuts. I said, "OK, what can I offer him?"

"I can't tell you a multi-year deal. But let me run something by the higher ups."

He called me back the next day. "You are authorized to guarantee him a million dollars up front." That was big money back then. A million dollars up front, a lot of publicity, and a possibility of another year, even though he was getting on up in age, around 60 years old. He'd get 50 percent on all merchandise. Daddy and I always did 50 percent. Can you imagine what the merchandising would have been on that?

Ford pieced all this stuff together in a couple of days when the light bulbs went off in the heads. They said, "Do you reckon you can get that handled?" I said I would try.

This is where I screwed up: There were a couple of eating places where Daddy and David ate breakfast every day. I told Daddy, "Now look, this is handled. Ask Pearson if he's interested. Get him to stop talking about his girlfriends and ask him. I felt like it is better for you to do it than me because you're the man and he's the man. Tell him it's a one-year deal with Quality Care, motors from Yates or anything we want, and a possibility of driving some more if he wants to. He's in the driver's seat. All this marketing can be done around it. It isn't like he never drove for us before. He was Ford's number one guy once when he won the championship in '69."

So Daddy approached him with it. I don't know how he really did it, but he couldn't have put a very hard sell on him. The end result was — and Pearson admits this later — he thought it was a joke! You see, back then, even Jeff Gordon wouldn't have gotten that kind of money. Pearson never took it seriously at all. Looking back on it, we might have run half-assed. Pearson never rode in an ambulance. He might have taken his last ride in an ambulance. That kind of had me a little bit worried. There was Weatherly and Wade tugging at my shoulder again. But it was the real deal. He would have been one of the most highly paid drivers except for Earnhardt. He would have been the highest paid Ford driver — and he thought Bud Moore was pulling his leg.

Greg's pipe dream might have come true with a harder sell, but once again he had nothing to put a driver in the seat of number 15. All there was to do was take the best of who was left again. Greg was on it.

We went driver shopping and talked to several, but Dick Trickle stood out. He had a black car, some independent's car, and had qualified real well a few places. He'd been running pretty decent and had a legacy of all those hundreds of races he'd won in the Midwest. Trickle's biggest problem was that he got into NASCAR real late. He was going on 53 years old. Believe it or not, we also talked to Hermie Sadler. That had to have been a joke. Randy LaJoie was discussed. That was a joke, too. He said, "All I want to do is race on Saturdays." Of the ones that were left — and there were no drivers left in early December — Dick Trickle looked pretty doggone good. He was down to earth, could drive the race car, and we loved him. We got it all signed up for Dick Trickle to drive the car for $550,000. He wasn't all that interested in the price. He said, "I am not worried about the money."

With another year wrangled under the factory banner of the Ford Motor Company, the Bud Moore Engineering team loaded up the Quality Care number 15 Thunderbird at 400 North Fairview Avenue and headed for the Beach in February. The results were, as always, encouraging.

As usual, we went down to Daytona and had a good Speedweeks. Dick ran well, and we were very competitive in practice and knew we'd be OK. He finished ninth in his 125 mile qualifier, giving us a decent seventeenth place start in the 500. Hell, we won it from thirty-third, so seventeenth was OK. The race was pretty routine, and Dick ran in or around the top ten all day. Then, under the final caution with about ten laps to go, he was scrubbing his tires running third and zigged when he should have zagged and hit Robert Pressley, who was doing the same thing. It tore the side of our car up. We finished eleventh in the Daytona 500, but it should have been a win or a second, easy. That's about all you can ask for is to have a decent shot at winning, and we did in the biggest race of the year. It was a good start.

Dick Trickle was old school all the way and really a fun guy. Greg reflected on one of Trickle's trademarks and a signature moment that took place right off the bat for all the world to see.

I'll never forget down there at Daytona in February. This was the race where we were supposed to run good and have a shot. We had the in-car camera for CBS. John Erp, the Ford liaison, said, "I heard Trickle smokes in the car." He's about to panic. I said, "Yeah, he smokes in the car. What's the big deal?" Erp said, "We've got the in-car camera. What if somebody sees him do that? Ford will have a fit." That guy was so nervous. He was about to mess up his britches. He was going to have a conniption. I said, "I know the camera people. Let me go get Trickle." Trickle came over and told Erp, "Look, I won't smoke a cigarette in the 125 miler, but the 500 is a different story. We'll talk to the TV crew and make sure they don't show me smoking a cigarette in the 500." Well, they've always got those cameras running the whole time, and the tape shows exactly how he did it. The caution came out and he slowed down. He pitted and got tires and gas and went back out, and CBS turned the camera around. He reached into his uniform and got a cigarette out. He had cut some of the fingers out of his gloves so he could use a lighter. He lit up and smoked for about a lap. We called and said, "All right, Dick, get ready, one to go." He started speeding up and threw the smoke out the window. I've got the tape. He was a tough guy, and we loved him.

Into the meat of the 1995 season, there were flashes of good things, lots of misfortune, and mostly mediocre runs. Trickle was ninth in the standings after three races, but he never got any higher, dropping back to the mid–20s where he stayed. Through all of it, there was harmony between the veteran Trickle and the battle-hardened and aging team. Then came the dreaded day that Greg and the boys had hoped would never come.

At Darlington in the spring race we chased Earnhardt for the lead all day long and finally hit the wall. We weren't down on him for that because he ran well. Trickle led five laps at Michigan, but finished sixteenth. That was a key race. We were leading, and John Erp from Ford was there and called me up into our truck. I knew some stuff was going on because they were deciding if they were going to stay, leave, sit out, or whatever. We were listening to it on the radio, just us. He wanted to let me know what was going on so I could break the bad news to everybody else. He said, "Gregory, I'm just here to tell you. It doesn't matter if y'all win five or six races, we are not coming back."

I picked up the phone after the race and called Daryl. He said, "What's going on? We were running pretty well." I said, "It doesn't make a damn now. The man told me, as I suspected, that it doesn't matter if we win five more races, they aren't going to be with us anymore." The first excuse that we could come up with was that we always had a different driver and never had a multi-year deal. You might keep a driver for two years, but you had to renegotiate and you could commit only so much money on rebuilding. You got the next year not knowing if you had a sponsor.

With the bad news delivered, it was full steam ahead with 17 of the 31-race schedule still to go, more than half the season. Who knows? Maybe they would win five or six times. It sure wouldn't hurt the selling of Dick Trickle and Bud Moore Engineering for 1996 if they did. Actually, the word from Dearborn may have been a relief. Sure, Ford was leaving, but the sport was booming and there were sponsors to be found. Truth be told, it wasn't as dreadful as it seemed. Maybe the jug was half full instead of half empty. Greg made a phone call to see if a previously turned down offer was still on the table.

The guy that helped me with the Igloo deal went to work with me on the Pennzoil sponsorship. We were offered that deal three times with Michael Waltrip and didn't take it. The time when we were getting ready to take it, Michael was up at Indianapolis with his Busch car and had just signed with Chuck Rider to run one more year for him. We were all sick.

So with still a lot of season to go and a chance to make some noise, Dick Trickle took time to remind everyone exactly whose name was on the front of the brick building at 400 North Fairview Avenue. He was a seasoned veteran and realized he was employed at a legendary location by an iconic figure.

We loved Dick Trickle. There were times that Donnie wanted to do something to the car and Daddy wanted to change something around. Donnie would say that Bud didn't know what he was doing, and Trickle would say, "Whoa. Wait a minute! Bud wants to change something on this car, let him change it. His stuff works! Y'all are cutting the old man a little bit short because of some other things. Besides, he's the boss." It didn't happen that often, but when it did, Trickle would go out there and run better. He was really behind Bud, Daryl, the team, the whole situation, and me.

It was weird. He crashed a bunch and the pit crew sucked. The "world's fastest pit crew" had left Dodge City. But we battled on, doing the best we could. At Daytona in July we were running third under the caution with a lap to go when the green flew again. Sterling Marlin was in front of us and missed a shift. Trickle backed out of the gas to keep from hitting him, and they freight trained on by him and he wound up twelfth. At Pocono, we finished tenth. Incredible as it might seem, that was our only top ten of the whole year. That is unbelievable, but true.

Now at Indianapolis we were hauling ass. Daddy had a guy from Bilstein build some new shocks. We were running those Penske shocks and kept fooling around and fooling around, and Daddy said, "I know what we got to do to fix that car." He goes down to the Bilstein truck and a guy builds them. Daddy said, "Bolt these shocks on it."

"Ah, nah, that isn't going to —"

"Bolt the son-of-a-bitches on there!"

We put the shocks on it and picked the car up a full second. One second! We tested a second quicker than any other car there. They talked about us being the fastest test-wise for three or four weeks and thought we'd be a shoo-in for a top five to start. For the race we qualified eleventh and stayed on the lead lap near the top ten until the end. We broke a valve spring and finished eighteenth on the lead lap.

Watkins Glen was a bad deal with a twenty-eighth place finish. Trickle told us before he ever came to drive, "When we go to Sonoma or Watkins Glen, put in a road course driver." Daddy said, "What do you mean?" Dick said, "I can't drive them." Daddy said, "No, you're our driver. We're not going to do that. We're sticking with you one way or the other. If you're going to drive the car, you're going to drive the road courses." Dick said, "I'm not worth a rip at it. Get you a hot shoe like Boris Said. I don't mind it. If I need to start the car a lap for the points I'll do it. Get a road course driver. I cannot drive road courses." So Daddy sent him to Bob Bondurant's Driving School. He goes to Bob Bondurant's, and the end result was he still couldn't drive a road course. He just couldn't do it.

We had back-to-back crashes at Bristol and Darlington and another at Charlotte. There was bad qualifying everywhere. It was terrible. What was so strange about it was that the car around the race track, even with the bad pit stops, was faster than it was with Lake Speed. Even though Dick might have qualified badly, the car was running closer to the front, even though the record doesn't show that. We were pretty tickled with Trickle, but we knew the guy was old.

> *Dick Trickle was a graybeard as race drivers go, having won hundreds of the midwestern American Speed Association races and outlaw events before some of his competitors were even born. The road trips were endless, and the Wisconsin native was not opposed to having fun. But there was a cloud hanging over the team — a fact of life they could not ignore.*

Trickle was fun as hell. We went out there to Sears Point, and they had one of those bungee jumps. It went way, way, way up in the air. He had been over-served too many adult beverages and said, "Hell. I'm going to do that." I watched him do it. He said in a painful whisper, "That was fun, but it racked my nuts."

ESPN loved to mention him every week no matter how he did. "And Dick Trickle was twenty-third. Dick Trickle qualified nineteenth." Dick Trickle and Bud Moore Engineering were a very good fit, but there was one problem: age. Daddy was too old, Trickle was too old, and for the most part, the team was too old. So we were just falling back. We got to thinking, "What are we going to do?" We hadn't thought of selling the team yet. We just trudged on. What if I had hired a 33-year-old Dick Trickle instead of George Follmer in 1974? Or even Dick Trickle at 47 instead of Brett Bodine? Guess who was the 1989 Winston Cup Rookie of the Year at 48 years old. Dick Trickle! It is just too bad they never hooked up before it was about all over for all of us.

> *Maybe the end was at hand. Maybe it wasn't. The sad statistics for the Dick Trickle season were no wins, no poles, no top fives, one top ten, five laps led, and $664,720 in winnings — which goes to show how much money was at stake, when you could finish twenty-fifth in the standings and have your second best year financially. The direct Ford sponsorship was gone for the first time since before Ricky Rudd and Motorcraft signed on in 1985. Greg and the boys at 400 North Fairview had their backs to a very cold wall in January of 1996.*

> *But back in mid-summer, a super-secret negotiation had gone on, one that has only recently come to light. Greg and Bud have been extremely reluctant to talk about it and never discussed it publicly until it was mentioned in July 2012 on the weekly racing-themed radio show that Greg co-hosts called Droppin' the Hammer on WSPG-AM/FM in Spartanburg. (More about the radio show itself later.) During the legends segment, the guest was Don Hawk, Dale Earnhardt's closest confidant, who has been a friend of Greg's for 30 years. What happened is undeniable. How it is interpreted is a matter of personal opinion. Here is what Greg says:*

Fifteen • *Quality Care and the Factory Farewell*

It was right about the time we got up there to Michigan and Ford told us they weren't coming back. We'd heard some rumblings and knew kind of what was going on through some of my spies and sources. At the same time, Earnhardt and Childress were negotiating their next contract. Well, Don Hawk is a very good friend of mine. He used to call me at two o' clock in the morning and tell me stuff. He was Earnhardt's PR man; eventually he went to work for NASCAR. He was a powerful guy and worked for Earnhardt, not Childress. He's fantastic! This was Earnhardt's guy who had really gotten close to us and the Wood Brothers. He still is really super-duper.

Some kind of decision was going on with Earnhardt and Childress over their contract. A lot of it apparently had to do with the marketing or that two-car team thing with Skinner. Earnhardt sells a ton of souvenirs, and they made more money off their marketing than they did racing. Earnhardt and Hawk got to thinking about it and Earnhardt said, "You know, I could go over there to Ford and be their number one guy again, just like that."

So Hawk said something to me, and Earnhardt got with Daddy and me, and we talked a little about it. Daddy said, "Well, hell yeah!" It was very secret, completely tight-lipped for several weeks. Nobody in the shop even knew it except Daddy, Daryl, and me. A few folks got wind of it right at the very end when it fell apart anyway.

That negotiation went on for about six weeks. To keep it secret, Earnhardt and Hawk flew up to Michigan to meet with two of the heads at Ford in an airplane hangar with no people and no cameras around. Earnhardt told them, "I'll come drive for you. I've got to have this much money and I want to drive for Bud Moore in a three-year deal." He was going to make big money. Ford said, "Yeah, whatever we need to do. That sounds great!"

It was a decision that Earnhardt was making on his own. We never approached him. He was aggravated with something at Childress. When it finally leaked out and people started hearing about it, word was that Ford said, "What about driving Robert Yates' car?" The only thing Earnhardt said was that he might drive for the Wood Brothers, but he would rather drive for Bud Moore if we could put this thing together.

Hawk and Ford finally got this preliminary contract, and Hawk went into Childress' office and tossed it on the desk in front of Childress and said, "You need to look at this and see what you think." Oh Lord, Chevrolet went nuts, of course. Earnhardt ended up getting a heck of a raise from Childress or something. Everything got smoothed over and we didn't get him. You can imagine the heartbreak on that. I don't think he used us. What messed the thing up, we heard later on, was that Ford got to screwing around on it a little bit. Ford hesitated, and I heard somebody wanted to push him over to Yates. But he didn't want to do that. Chevrolet got into the act, and Earnhardt got a lot more money. He earned it. Ford blinked and Chevrolet wound up keeping him. That was enough to make somebody want to break down and cry. The next thing you know, you got to run half a season with Trickle, then you don't have a sponsor and you don't have a driver either.

You read it here first. Dale Earnhardt had a problem re-signing with Richard Childress for whatever reason and made a run at Ford. Instead of pulling the trigger with Bud Moore Engineering, Ford muddied the water with talk of Robert Yates' team instead of realizing what Dale Earnhardt knew. He knew that the only reason he had not dominated 1982 and 1983 with Bud Moore's Wrangler Thunderbirds was because of screwy engine problems that had long, long since been corrected. Earnhardt and Hawk knew that with Dale's incredible driving talent, the perfectionism of Bud Moore Engineering, an infusion of sponsorship dollars, and the resurrection of the good chemistry from before, there was every reason to believe that a black Ford Torino number 15 from 400 North Fairview would be a formidable combination to reckon with every week. Unfortunately, those suits at Ford Motor Company were school kids 25 years earlier and had no clue how close Earnhardt and Moore were back then to winning on a weekly basis. History is a wonderful teacher, but only if you pay attention.

CHAPTER SIXTEEN

Wally's World and Beyond

The uncertainty that seemed the norm rather than the exception at Bud Moore Engineering had an extra added feature as 1996 approached. Homegrown crew chief Donnie Wingo had departed for Travis Carter's Smokin' Joe Team with Jimmy Spencer. Greg and Bud added longtime independent racer Jimmy "Smut" Means to take Wingo's place as crew chief. Means had been a fixture in the garage area for a dozen years and had 455 Cup starts as a driver. His best year was 1982, when he finished eleventh in the standings, 21 points ahead of Bud Moore's driver, Dale Earnhardt, and 28 behind Morgan Shepherd in tenth. He very nearly made the stage at the Waldorf. For the seat behind the wheel, Greg had his eye on a young veteran road course specialist who might just be good for at least two checkered flags. He and Greg hit the bricks on a dizzying sponsor search.

Donnie Wingo left because we didn't have a sponsor. So we got Jimmy Means because he needed a job and he'd been down the year before to help us. But Jimmy was too used to running at the rear and worried about tires and different things. We got along with Jimmy OK, but that was a bad deal. He didn't know how to race up front. When Michael Kranefuss was at SVO, we had come very, very, very close to putting Wally Dallenbach in the car, and that didn't happen. He had gotten into a ruckus with Petty in 1994 and they fired in him in the middle of the season. He couldn't drive Petty's car. Nobody could drive Petty's car at that point in time. Richard made sure of that. I got to be good friends with Dallenbach, and we were going to put him in the car instead of Trickle. Ford somehow got down on that and didn't want to do it. He went up there to Watkins Glen in '95 and had the race won in Bill Davis' car, and they threw a caution and he finished second. So I told him, "Look, you got the ride in the car, but we have got to find a sponsor."

A marketing guy named Jim Bachman, a super-good guy, came along. He got Felix Sabates' sponsors and really liked us. We worked real, real hard on the Browning Rifle people, and Dallenbach and I went to Salt Lake City. They didn't quite have the budget, but later on they did put a sticker on Earnhardt, Jr.'s car. That thing got fairly close, but didn't make it.

We got really committed to Dallenbach when Remington Arms came into the picture. The CEO of Remington wanted Michael Waltrip, and Michael Waltrip was all for it. But meanwhile, the Wood Brothers had become fed up with Morgan Shepherd, and they needed a driver because Citgo wanted somebody younger. So they hired Michael Waltrip — not to mess us up or anything, but because Citgo wanted him. They had Citgo in the bag, and Remington hadn't signed yet. So Michael Waltrip had to go to the Wood Brothers instead of us, and we plugged Dallenbach into the equation with Remington. Remington liked

Dallenbach because he was a good hunter. All that was falling into place and we were talking to the CEO, but a guy by the name of Milner went to Raymoc, and they cut a million dollars off the deal and wound up getting it. We were sicker than hell over that, too. Now, that deal was close! If Michael Waltrip hadn't jumped, that deal would have happened. We'd have been Michael Waltrip and Remington Arms in 1996.

We also had some marketing help that came to us that didn't really give a rip who the driver was. A guy named Dennis Hayes said he'd give us $100,000 to run Daytona if we could make the race. He was in Chapter 11. Dan Emery and another marketing guy had been trying to get Hayes involved in racing somehow or another to do some advertising with NASCAR. Dennis was from Spartanburg and knew my family, liked racing, and had a company, Hayes Modems, down in Atlanta. He was supposed to have been like a Bill Gates, but he got screwed. At the Spartan High Science Fair when Brenty built the dyno and won the thing in 1968, Dennis Hayes built a ruby laser and was runner-up. I remembered meeting Dennis two years before when they brought him around the pits at Atlanta. He came up and reminded me about that contest. This was when Bodine was driving. He said, "I went to Spartanburg High School and I own Hayes Modems." I'd heard of them. He said, "I was runner up to your brother in the science fair." I said, "I remember exactly who you are. You built the ruby laser." He said, "Yeah, I shined it all the way from one end of the gym to the other." Dennis Hayes was and still is a super-nice guy. He committed $100,000 for us to take Dallenbach and go down there to Daytona. We went down, and they'd already come up with a paint scheme. It was a solid white car with a black 15 shaped like it had been, black Hayes Modem writing and logo, with blue, yellow, and purple stripes down the rocker panel. To me that made a much better car than the purple one that came later. We were working on it as we went down there.

When we got there the son-of-a-bitch ran great! We finished fifth in the 125 miler, hanging right with the leaders, and the car flew! We started the Daytona 500 in ninth place and stayed in the lead pack the whole time. Real early on, about the 30th lap, we hit Ernie Irvan and messed the car up. Dallenbach got into the back of him in the short straightaway going into the first turn. Ernie bounced off the wall and kept going, but he was done as far as being a contender goes. Wally slipped under him and went on with a little nose damage. We had to tape the front end up a little bit. That tape was flapping, but our motor was screaming, and everything was going fine. That was a full Bud Moore white car, non-sponsored, with a last-minute $100,000 deal thrown on the side of it. We could have won the race. We should have won that race. That's another one where we pushed somebody by somebody and they went to Victory Lane. We had a better shot at winning the Daytona 500 with Wally than we did either time with Geoff Bodine. I was having so much fun with that thing. A Cinderella story if there ever was one. Wally pushed Dale Jarrett past Earnhardt with about 20 laps to go, and Jarrett stayed there. Jarrett even thanked Wally on national TV in the Victory Lane interview. Wally did a great job, but we got shuffled back to sixth at the end. We ran so much better than sixth. Everybody wanted to race with him because we were so fast that day. When we left Daytona Beach, Dennis said, "You got the deal for the year." It was a very satisfying Speedweeks. So we signed Dallenbach for $350,000 for the season.

Greg explains what amounted to a secret weapon they had for Talladega and especially Daytona for six years.

This was our Daytona car, and there was a secret to it. You'll notice a trend starting in 1990 with Morgan finishing tenth in the 500 its first time out. Even though the finishes weren't that good except with Bodine's two thirds, we had this car, this same car, that always ran up front whether it got wrecked a little or not. Lake Speed, who never runs up front at Daytona, passed Earnhardt for third and ran out of gas. Then he started at the rear and was getting ready to take the lead in the Firecracker race in July and starts telling Preston to get him the hell out of there. The year before, when Dick Trickle was eleventh in the 500, Trickle said he'd never driven a car at Daytona like that in his life. He was in a perfect position to win the Firecracker, and then Sterling Marlin missed a shift on a restart and caused him to back out of it with one lap to go, and he lost his momentum. Dallenbach and he said they could drive that car anywhere on the race track. After Dallenbach ran so well at Daytona, Trickle came up to me and said, "Was that my Daytona car he was running?" I said, "Yeah, that's our Daytona car." He said, "Anybody can drive that race car! That is the best driving race car in the world at Daytona." We blew motors sometimes, and Bodine did not win the Clash with that car. That was a lesser car.

By 1996 the beard was gone, but Greg still had the unique look that was his trademark for over two decades in the NASCAR garage area (courtesy Bud Moore Engineering Archives).

This special one had had some sheet metal changes on it, but it was one car. There was a trick to it and it wasn't cheating. What we had done was put rear trailing arms underneath the car that were seven inches longer, running closer to the front. These are the things that hold the rear housing in place. Most everybody had the trailing arms moved back a number of inches. It's pretty simple the way it worked. What it compromised was that you couldn't make the exhaust system as dead perfect as you wanted to make it with the secondary pipes for the car. It made it feel like a longer wheelbase car. Made it drive like a Cadillac. You wouldn't think seven inches made that much difference. It put the pivot points of the trailing arms closer to the front of the car, and it had a real secure feel to it. Everybody bragged on that car — Morgan Shepherd, Geoff Bodine, Lake Speed, Dick Trickle, Wally Dallenbach. At Talladega it ran well, too. Dallenbach wiped it out there. Nobody else would try it because you gave up three tenths qualifying. We had to play stupid about qualifying bad. But as soon as that was over and they got out there in Happy Hour, here we'd come, picking them off one at a time. Bodine said that there must be something aerodynamically wrong about the car. "I get out here in the draft and I can blow right by them." We sat there and said innocently, "I don't know what it is." We kept our mouths shut about it for all those years. It was that much different. Dallenbach crashed the car at Talladega and we thought about fixing it, but it was too badly wrecked. So we reproduced the long trailing arm car, and that was the white one Larry Pearson drove at Daytona for us in 1997.

The run Bud Moore Engineering put together at Daytona was no small achievement. Greg and his dad crafted a last-minute deal and came up with a rocket ship disguised as *a vanilla Thunderbird. They raced and outraced the best their entire time at the beach. The records show that they brought $96,720 back to 400 North Fairview, and it was certainly more than that with contingency awards. They had only a fraction of the support given the other front-running teams, but whatever they lacked, Greg and the boys had made up for with determination, experience, tenacity, and a hungry and somewhat experienced driver.*

The subsequent Hayes Modems paint schemes were by far the wildest ever to adorn the sheet metal of Bud Moore race cars. The earliest was mostly purple with a yellow stripe along the rocker panels and a dark-tinted aqua nose, roof, and rear deck. The hood was purple with a large global sphere being orbited by a yellow flash and "Hayes Modems" in white across it. The numbers were white, styled as their numbers had been recently, and the rear quarter panels were adorned with another global sphere with three orbits crisscrossing it. In later versions, the car was an all medium blue with the other items as previously described. They were out of the gate sixth in points, and from the cold uncertain winter of late '95 and early '96 came the fresh hope of spring and one more sponsored season. Things looked so good, Greg's thoughts ran wild with dreams of possibilities.

I had some newspaper reporters ask me what we were going to do. We were so confident on the Hayes thing that I was toying with adding a second team and getting another sponsor. I had my hooks out almost in a sponsor and we were going to put Steve Grissom in the other car. He was running good and hard back then and had been the '93 Busch Series Champion. I had him lined up and talked to him about driving the second car. It had leaked out at Talladega that Bud Moore was going to put on a second team with Steve Grissom. In '96 I was feeling pretty doggone good. By the end of '98 I was ready to shoot my goddamn self.

A racing season is a long, hard road. Unfortunately, that road had a concrete wall alongside, and Wally Dallenbach crashed into it regularly. Quickly dreams of a second team evaporated and the underfunded team found the going very, very tough. The lowest of several low points in 1996 was a first in Bud Moore Engineering history.

The results were not as good as expected, but the Bud Moore Hayes Modems Thunderbird and Wally Dallenbach had without a doubt the flashiest race cars to ever roll out of 400 North Fairview Avenue (courtesy Bud Moore Engineering Archives).

We crashed in three of the next four races at Rockingham, Richmond, and Darlington. Then a couple of so-so races led to Martinsville. That was a bad deal. It wasn't Dallenbach's fault. We needed a 620 gear in the car, but Daddy and them wouldn't put one in it. We went out there and qualified. You only had one set of tires. So the next day, in second-day time trials, we put the 620 gear in it with the used tires. The goody was out of the tires when you qualified on the second day. So he missed the lap a little bit and barely missed making the show. It was hot, too. It got hotter. It was bad. It was very bad. Of course Daddy loaded up one with Billy Wade over the brake ducts, so this wasn't the first time we left Martinsville before the race started. But it was the first time we ever failed to qualify anywhere ever.

Finally we got to Sonoma, where Wally excelled on the road course. That was a brand new road course car that we had built and tested at Road Atlanta. We ran two seconds faster than a stock car had ever run around Road Atlanta. Two seconds! But the pit crew cost him that race. Every time we came out of the pits we'd be twelfth. Wally was flying. We had pitted running second and came out running twelfth. Then he had to pass everybody again. We had tire changers that weren't worth a damn. They were old. We just hadn't concentrated on the pit stop stuff enough. Wally did his job and was all over Mark Martin for second. Third wasn't bad, but we expected to win the road courses.

There were more sorry finishes until Talladega. There he was running third, hanging onto Gordon, came into the pits under caution, and came back out about eighteenth. Then they had the big wreck, and that's when we wiped that special car out. He ran pretty well at Indy, finishing seventeenth. He should have, since his father ran there so many times in the Indy 500. We finished on the lead lap all three times we ever went to Indy with Speed, Trickle, and Dallenbach. We were supposed to win Watkins Glen, too, and finished tenth. I don't know what happened at Watkins Glen. We started way back in 31st. That was Earnhardt's last pole and Geoff Bodine's last win. Earnhardt was still beat up from the Talladega wreck that wrecked our special car. Several races later, Dallenbach and Jimmy Spencer crashed at Dover, and Spencer came over and tried to punch Wally through the window net. A NASCAR official pulled Spencer away. It's on You Tube. He would have clobbered Wally, but I don't know that Dallenbach did anything really wrong.

After that, we did nothing much at all and wrecked in two of the last three races at Rockingham and Atlanta. Dennis and I talked, and he wanted to stay on. He had actually committed to another year. But the fact that he went into Chapter 11 again wouldn't let him. Dallenbach went on to drive for Felix Sabates and First Union Bank in 1997 with less success. He drove the number 50 Budweiser car for Hendrick. He called me from out there in Sears Point in 1998. He couldn't get running or anything, and he called me on the phone. "This thing won't run worth a damn. I told them that Bud and them's got a car sitting down there on jack stands in Spartanburg that'll run better than this that hasn't even got a sponsor. We could drop that car off the jack stands and smoke this one." But that whole thing with Dallenbach was a good deal. If we could have run just one more year, we would have been real good, I think.

Something happened toward the end of 1996 that lifted Greg's spirits and has kept them lifted ever since. It seems that the right person usually finds you when you least expect it and are not even trying. It usually happens out of the clear blue, and that is how it happened to Greg.

I'd known Roberta since 1978. When things fell apart towards the end of '96, I bumped into her at Gerhardt's Restaurant near my apartment. I never did have any time to put into a long term relationship. I tried it a few times, but let me put it this way. When you're single at a race track, unless you're planning on having kids or something, you don't need a regular girlfriend too much. Berta was the best thing that ever happened to me because I was about to go nuts. I really was. I owe an awful lot to Roberta.

The 1996 Winston Cup season was over. The team won no races, captured one top five and three top tens, took no poles, led no laps, finished 25th in the point standings for the second year in a row, but pocketed a Bud Moore Engineering record $791,551, which was their zenith for purses won. That was a tad better than the $40,000 of Bud Moore's inaugural 1961 season. After a David and Goliath start, 1996 spun into weeks of poor finishes and piles of colorful scrap metal. It was a lethal combination of bad driving, poor pit stops, sorry luck, indifference, and age. The World's Fastest Pit Crew, the winning of back-to-back races, and the Manufacturers' Championship with the Ford house car had long since disappeared in the rear view mirror.

It might have looked like the season was over across NASCAR's North American footprint, but a super project of epic proportions had been boiling under the surface the whole year. NASCAR was going to run an exhibition race on November 24, 1996, at Suzuka Circuitland, Suzuka City, Japan, for 100 laps on a 1.394 mile road course there. Not everybody was invited, but one of the signature Winston Cup teams had been, and a huge overseas shipping container was dropped off at 400 North Fairview Avenue for the trip. There was enough to do keeping Wally Dallenbach between the fences on a weekly basis, but now Greg was the ramrod of a Japanese trip, making sure the equipment of a whole race team fit into a large tin can, and he had to wing it. And Wally was really expanding his world.

NASCAR had been working on a deal with the guy that owned the Suzuka track over in Japan. They had started talking about it at least a year earlier. They went, I think, three times and we made the very first one. Wally was a super-good road racer, but the only one who had tested over there was Rusty Wallace. They needed to see what to do to change it around a little bit. They invited only so many teams. They invited some Winston West guys because of logistics. We were one of the invited teams because Dallenbach is a good road racer, Daddy was in good with the France family, and they knew we might be getting into a little sponsor trouble. Our longtime secretary, Diane Christie — the greatest secretary of all time — and I got to work on it nine months early, about the time we were going to Daytona. There was a big thing about what you could ship over there and what you couldn't. They gave you one shipping container with room for one car, your wheels, a spare motor, and everything you were going to need. That was a hat trick. There was some stuff they were really funny about, like chemicals. I had to get Material Safety Data paperwork on every chemical, everything. Plus, I was trying to finish the race season, so I knew I had to start on this thing early.

The guy handling the operation was with Nippon Shipping out of Atlanta. He was an American. He said we'd better not carry any brake cleaner — "and don't carry any liquor. It's all got to go through customs." But they were on good terms with these people because they'd already shipped a car over there and Goodyear went, too. They were going to carry all these railroad containers by train to Charleston, put them on a boat, and carry them to Japan. We had to have everything ready a month in advance of the race to give it time to get over there. NASCAR had probably been working on this about two years. Dennis Hayes was all pumped up about it because of the electronics and marketing.

We knew we were going to Suzuka before we knew we were going to lose Hayes or Dallenbach. It was probably a month before Suzuka that we knew Wally was talking to Felix Sabates and had to do something. Anyway, we started working on it earlier than anybody else did. I got to talking about it around the race tracks in April, and no one else even had their containers yet. I was one of the first ones to get a container. They shipped it in and set it down outside the shop. So Diane and I got to work early, and when we weren't busy racing, that's when I would call a company and get stuff faxed in. It was a nightmare, that first trip.

Well, we're about two months away and I'm about set. I've already got the spare motor and the carburetor we're going to carry. The last thing we were going to put on was the car with the motor we wanted in it. We had Ray Harris, a real good carpenter, come in there with wood to wedge stuff in the container. We had to figure how to do it. We gradually worked on it and sorted everything out. I had the guy from Nippon Shipping come up from Atlanta. He didn't go to anybody else's shop, just Bud Moore Engineering. He used us as a case study. For about the last month we were getting ready, he was writing stuff down. I'll bet he made ten trips to Spartanburg. He took pictures, documents, stuff I had.

Then all of a sudden it's about a month before the containers had to be in Charleston for the teams on the east coast. There was a little bit of uncertainty on a lot of things, lots of gray areas. I had a program of all the materials and what all the containers contained. So I talked to the Wood Brothers; I talked to some of Hendrick's crew; to Roush, to everybody. All these teams were calling, and they hadn't received half the paperwork I had. The Woods were pretty prepared, but these other teams would call and I told Diane to give them whatever information they needed. I thought, "These other teams had four or five secretaries and all this stuff, and Diane and I had it finished." There was a lot of effort in it. We took our good road race car. We didn't carry our best motor, just a decent motor, a road race engine. So away it went, over to Japan.

The NASCAR road show went international, off to the Land of the Rising Sun for the 1996 Suzuka Thunder Special. If they thought a yearly trip to New York City was a big-time happening, a journey to Japan had to be off the charts for this assortment of red, white, and blue-blooded Americans. Think of it: Bud Moore and some incredibly brave men stormed the beach at Normandy on June 6, 1944. He and another group of tough guys invaded mainland Japan 52 years later on a much more docile mission. Winning was always the objective. While overseas on this trip, one person went on the attack and it was Greg. The recipient was a famous competitor.

We flew a 747 out of Chicago and landed in Nagoya, Japan. They sent several flights because everybody couldn't go on the same flight. All of our crew went except for Phil Thomas, our gas man, who worked for Holly Farms. Daryl and Brent didn't go. Just Daddy and me, and they requested that Momma go, too. Earl Davis — we called him Strawberry — went with us. Wormy Hayes went with us. Wormy has been a pal since we were kids growing up and was the brother of Dennis Hayes, the sponsor. Wormy went to a bunch of the races with us, most of the big ones. He's a great guy. He always rode with Daddy and me. Wormy was pretty doggone sharp. He caught on to some things and came up with some real good ideas.

After we landed, we went on a shuttle to Suzuka about 30 miles away. The motor man, Daniel Fowler, and I roomed together. I found out later that we were the first ones to get there and the last ones to leave. We were out there nine days and it was tiring. Suzuka's got something like a Six Flags park outside the race track, and it was a pretty neat place. NASCAR gave the invited Cup teams some free plane tickets and $50,000. That was the deal. It still cost us. When all was said and done, I figured up it still cost us probably $20,000, but NASCAR was good on it. We got treated very well. They had us at a resort.

They had an American embassy-type place there and two lines. They had a Japanese line where they'd eat their breakfast, and they had an American line. They had us situated so that we didn't have to go anywhere if we didn't want to. The biggest problem we had was finding us some American beer. So we found where they had brought in a whole bunch of Budweiser. It was a place for the NASCAR teams to go sit and watch TV and get refreshments. It was unbelievable how they had it set up. It was about like a Formula One deal. They probably modeled it after that.

Later on we dropped right off the truck and people were out there warming up. Four, five, six, eight cars, two or three good cars, were on the track, and we were looking at the speeds. Wally went out and ran a second and a half faster on the first lap. Goodyear gave us the tires. They were free. Then something happened out there that I'm still sorry about concerning Rick Hendrick.

It started back awhile before, when it came out in the newspapers that I was saying bad things about the multi-car teams, tearing them all to hell. Multi-car teams were running all the single-car teams off. Darrell Waltrip's team went out of business about the same time we did. About 30 single-car teams went out of business over a five-year period. I was mad because I thought it was bad for NASCAR. I went off on Rick Hendrick. I don't know why I did it because Rick really is a nice guy and a good friend of the family. He thinks the world of Daddy. I don't think he thinks too much of me, though. I need to apologize to him. But I cited him out. So this thing hit the headlines. It was on the front of the sports page of the *Winston-Salem Journal*. There was a smaller article in the *Charlotte Observer*. I saw the article, and it got some publicity. I was a little bit concerned about it. I knew I might have overstepped my bounds a little bit with somebody who was pretty powerful in racing. Rick and Daddy had always gotten along well. At Daddy's Hall of Fame induction, Hendrick bowed down and said, "There's the master there." Rick's a great guy. I shouldn't have done that. So he went to Daddy and said, "Bud, Gregory was pretty hard on me in the newspaper. What's the problem?" Daddy said, "Yeah, I heard he said a few things, but don't talk to me about it. He's grown. Go talk to him about it."

Well, I'm standing out there on the pit road in Suzuka and I am not in exactly the best mood. I'm worn out. We had just got through qualifying twelfth instead of fourth or fifth like we thought we would. We had to make a pit stop during qualifying, and we didn't even have a regular gas guy. So Rick came up there to me and said, "Greg, I talked to your daddy and you were a little hard on me in the newspaper." Well, I lit into him again, and I don't even want to repeat it. I said, "You don't have to worry about us anymore. We're gone. Y'all can have this son-of-a-bitch. You came in here and bought all my drivers out from underneath me. Every time I try to get a little bit ahead, somebody comes in with money and pushes me back out of the way. But we're gone. We won't be back probably. Thanks to sons of bitches like you." He didn't respond. I think he just walked off. I just let him have it. It's a wonder he didn't deck me. I'm afraid I would have hit him back. I was over in Japan. If I had been in Charlotte with the Rainbow Warriors standing around, I would have probably toted an ass-whipping. That's one thing I really regret. It wasn't his fault. Look at how well he's done. Hell, we would have five cars if we could. Who wouldn't? But we didn't. I was beat. I didn't like it. I don't like losing. I didn't like losing playing kids' football. I don't like to lose, period. I never took it back, and I've never talked to him since.

Yes, there was also a race in Japan, and a whale of a race it was. You can take NASCAR out of the country, but you can't keep them from getting it on southern style a half a world away. Unfortunately, there was also an extremely unfortunate incident that cast a pall over the whole trip and everyone who took it, as well as the fans 9,800 miles away in Charlotte.

The bad thing was with Elmo Langley. He was on the flight we were on. He had a little blood pressure problem or something. I think the doctor even warned him about getting on an airplane and making that long trip. He was an inspector and drove the pace car. He had been driving the pace car for years. Buddy Baker, who was one of the TV announcers, and Elmo were out riding around the race track before the race, and poor old Elmo just slumped over the steering wheel, and the Good Lord took him like that! They were going about 60 miles an hour in the pace car. Baker reacted quickly, reached over, turned the key off, put his foot on the brake, and got it stopped. Poor old Elmo just left. That was bad, real bad. It cast a pall over everything and everybody. Elmo won the last Grand National race they ever ran in Spartanburg and it was also his first win. That was just too bad.

Anyway, we qualified twelfth and we were running in the top five the whole time. We ran third, second, but I don't think we led. We were in pretty good shape. All I know is, Wally comes up on the Smokin' Joe car of Travis Carter, and it's hometown Japanese hero driver Hideo Fukuyama. He started mirror-driving Wally, and then we came around to a caution flag. We were the only car that pitted, and we bolted on four tires and came out about eighteenth, the last car on the lead lap. For some reason, a car had gotten stuck in a sand trap with about 20 laps to go, which is a pretty good bit of time on a road course. We thought they were going to clean the track up in about two laps, but they ate up about ten laps under caution. Wally was hollering over the radio, "They're using up my laps!" Every lap that goes by, our chance of winning goes down. So we didn't have many laps left to do what we had to do. They got the green, and Wally passed three or four on the first lap and three or four on the second. Then he came up on Fukuyama again. Wally's got four brand new tires, and now he's turning it 9400 a shift. He said, "How the hell that motor took that punishment, I don't know." Dallenbach was coming. He had turned it loose! Here he came. Then Fukuyama started mirror-driving Wally again. There were about ten laps to go. Wally had used up too much of the goody on his tires fooling with him for about two laps. Donnie Wingo, who used to work for us, had gone to work for Travis at Smokin' Joe's, and they knew we had put on four tires. I'll never understand why they didn't tell him to get out of our way. They kind of got a little bit mad about it. They came down the short chute in front of the pits and I saw him doing it to Wally. I told Daniel Fowler right then that Fukuyama wouldn't be back. Sure enough, it wasn't 20 seconds later that the caution flag was out. Wally took that son-of-a-gun Fukuyama out, but it wasn't payback from Dover towards Smokin' Joes. We started laughing and looked up on one of the screens and saw it.

They restarted and we just ran out of time and finished fifth. Rusty won. He had tested there and is a heck of a good race driver, good road racer. He might have been a little bit stronger than us. It's hard to say. We had an awfully good car. I was pretty proud of our effort for Suzuka.

The final rundown was Rusty Wallace, Dale Earnhardt, Jeff Gordon, Terry Labonte, Wally Dallenbach, Johnny Benson, Bobby Hillin, Mike Skinner, Rick Carelli, and Butch Gilliland. Other notables further back were Dale Jarrett (thirteenth), Ernie Irvan (fourteenth), Sterling Marlin (sixteenth), Robby Gordon (seventeenth), Ron Hornaday (twentieth), Fukuyama (twenty-second, courtesy of Wally), ageless Hershel McGriff (twenty-fifth), Michael Waltrip (twenty-sixth), and Joe Bean (twenty-seventh and last). Joe Bean?

Joe Bean was in it. He was a rich guy with a Winston West car. He was cooler than hell. Butch Gilliland was driving Willie Stroppe's car, Bill Stroppe's son's car. He's a great guy. They were west coast racers.

Before the flight home, Greg and friends had some races of their own — at the amusement park.

Wormy and I had about two days before our flight to come home. We killed some time at the amusement park. They had go-karts that would run about 70 miles per hour. You had to sign a waiver, show a driver's license, and put on a helmet. They didn't have governors on them. You had to use brakes and everything. It wasn't one of those deals where you hold it to the floor and the governor kicks in. These things had two-stroke motors in them. These were governed at about 80! You got ten laps on this pretty good-sized road course. It wouldn't be anything the insurance people would allow here in the States. Wormy, Wally, Sterling and I went over there to race those go-karts. I started out right behind Wally and stayed three or four car lengths behind him for about three laps. He was running his and I was on top of it. I finally over-drove it in one of the turns and spun off the track. I drove on around and came on in.

We had so much fun on the trip. It was tiring, but I'll never forget it. I came home from the Suzuka trip, turned into the driveway at the Corners, got in my apartment and thanked the Good Lord. "You let me get through this, let's see where we go from here." It was exhausting, but it was an experience.

A really amazing meeting took place toward the end of 1996. That meeting, more than anything else, probably shaped Greg's course from that point on. It was the word from above. It was the Great Father taking aside one of his beloved children and giving him words to live by. The message was clear and has never faded from Greg's conscientiousness.

It was after we lost Hayes and Dallenbach, Bill France, Jr., called me down there to Daytona and told me, "We want y'all to get a sponsor. If you don't have a sponsor, don't bring any primered race car to the race track. Don't spend all your daddy's money to do this. That isn't going to be real smart. We need Bud Moore, we don't need you. We like you, but don't spend your daddy's retirement trying to run a race car. If you do, we aren't going to like it at all." He didn't want to see me destroy Daddy's finances. I've always compared myself to Kyle Petty. I couldn't fill the son-of-a-gun's shoes. I had mixed emotions. I did what I was told.

This wasn't the end of the road for Greg and the boys at 400 North Fairview Avenue, but they were hitting the rumble strips when the end came. Brent's pal Dennis Hayes and his modems had done their part to perpetuate the cause, and Hayes Modems went down in history as the last full-time sponsor for Bud Moore Engineering. They had the wildest paint job and went to Japan, too.

CHAPTER SEVENTEEN

Looking for a Savior

The year was 1997, and Bud Moore Engineering was prepared to go to Daytona for Speedweeks as always. Feelers and rumors and conversations with potential sponsors had come and gone since the trip to Japan, but nothing had materialized to put the team on the track. Nonetheless, Greg and Bud acquired the services of a multiple champion right in their own backyard to go to the Beach and make something happen. Larry Pearson, the 1986 and 1987 Busch Series Champion, signed on to make the trip south and get the ball rolling. A huge potential sponsor stood offstage with pockets bulging full of hope, publicity, and money.

We had built a brand new car because we destroyed that good Daytona car with Dallenbach. Before we left the shop, we knew we had a hundred grand if we could make the race. Universal Studios was going to give us a hundred grand if we could make the 500. So we carried a white race car down there and already had the decals made and everything. NASCAR kind of helped us with that deal, but we had to make the race. Once again, we just weren't quite fast enough to make it on speed. We were fifth fastest on the sheet. Larry in the draft was wicked good. It was impressive. Larry was working really well with us. When he went out there to practice, he'd jump on Gordon and those guys and just sit right there with them. Larry and another car ran the pack down. When he got to them he just sifted right through them.

We qualified poorly the first time on pole day. Then we tried to requalify, which was a mistake. I let Jimmy Means and those guys make that call about trying to requalify. I said, "Look, it doesn't matter if the speed's a little bit better, it's going to put us behind about ten more cars." So that was one mistake we made. I fault myself on that. We were stuck starting in twenty-third. That put us a little bit far back in the 125 mile qualifier. Then there was a crash right in front of him and he missed it. Larry got on the brakes and flat-spotted the right front tire. There wasn't time to pit and get caught back up, so we stayed out. The tire was messed up so badly that he couldn't run. So Larry's back there fighting for all he's worth with a bunch of guys we should have been way ahead of, and the laps ran out. There were only 50 laps, and we finished on the lead lap in sixteenth. All we had to do was make the race. We didn't make the race. No Universal Studios decals went on the car, and that was that.

It was a premature exit for Speedweeks 1997. For the record, Larry Pearson finished behind Gary Bradberry, who did not make the 500 either, but ahead of Kenny Wallace, who did. Go figure.

History repeated itself, as in a quarter of a century earlier when David Pearson and

Bud brought the school bus yellow Torino to Daytona in '71 to test the bored-out 351 Cleveland and kept blowing them up after a screaming-fast lap or two. Once again, there was no Daytona 500 for a Pearson and the Moores. It was a long, cold haul back to 400 North Fairview.

Back at home, the team prepared cars almost the same as usual, since their next race was known only to God. An answer to Greg's and the team's problems could be just as far away as the ring of the phone on Bud's desk. It rang from the Beach.

We got to helping out with Daytona USA. Momma, Daddy, and I went down there and helped them open that thing up. I got to know the marketing guy real well, and we built them a show car. They came up with the deal and France OK'd it. They paid us around $50,000 to build this thing, and it was beautiful. We were so tickled with it. We took one of our cars and built them an actual show car, a race car. It had a race motor in it, but we had dropped the compression. We fixed it dead perfect. It had a special radiator, everything. I had a clutch made with softer discs so they could run it in parades and stuff. They actually assigned a guy from Daytona USA to be over that car. They loved it! It was a real race car. We were super-proud of it, too. I think they had to fire a couple of guys because they were out there running it around the race track at 140 miles per hour, just playing with it.

It was not exactly the NASCAR house car, but it wound up at the Charlotte Motor Speedway to run in the Coca-Cola World 600. One of the hot-shoe, balls-to-the-wall pilots of all time was inked for the deal when Greg Sacks came aboard.

Daytona USA came up with the deal, and once again France and his people OK'd it. I told Inspectors Buster Auten and Gary Nelson to come down there to the shop and bring the templates. I said, "Tell me what we have wrong with this car. I don't have time at the track because we're so far behind." There was only one thing they didn't like. It was a little too narrow back towards the C pillars at the roof. So we had to widen that out. We had our tires free again, which was a pretty good deal for the World 600. All your tires free? That's a big chunk of your budget. They were going to give us $35,000 just to run up there at Charlotte. It was a car identical to the show car we built. So we went up there with Greg Sacks on a night test and we were second fastest. Sacks was a doggone brave race driver, and we got along with him great. I always have liked that guy.

We went back up there for the race with one of our motors that had 15 more horsepower. We were ready to cut us a lap. Sacks went out, but the conditions had changed. He was loose as hell coming up off of four, and we fought this condition the whole time. When they went to qualify that night, we got screwed. We weren't in as good a shape as we were on the test, but we were still pretty good. Sacks went down into turn one and two really trying to flat-foot it, and the car bottomed out. The sparks flew at night and he had to back out of the gas and drifted up. It blew the lap. You didn't get to use but one set of tires. If you messed up you had to requalify the second day on that used set of tires. In the heat of the sun the next day, we qualified, and Kenny Wallace beat us by one one-thousandth of a second. So we missed that deal and got pretty doggone disgusted. If I'm not mistaken, though, they still paid us the money.

Another near miss at the track meant another disappointing trip back to 400 North Fairview Avenue. Morale was low, to say the least. No steady driver, no sponsor, no luck, and no prospects to speak of. The phone was still working on Bud's desk, but when it rang, it rang hollow. Finally, Greg and Bud pondered the inevitable. It was time to go fishing for a buyer of the storied team. Pretty much as soon as they dropped their line in the water, the cork disappeared below the surface. Bud's phone started singing.

Our main goal was to find a sponsor and keep racing. The second option was to unload the stuff to somebody who wanted to go racing. The third option was to have a yard sale.

I had already let the auction people walk through with nobody knowing who they were. I knew what the stuff was worth — the land and everything. The last thing we wanted to do was have an auction of the race equipment. You can do well with that, but then you're stuck with the land. Still, Brett Bodine did pretty well with Junior Johnson's stuff. So we toyed with the idea of selling the thing, if possible.

Once the word got out, we got busy. The first attempt to sell it was with K. C. Spurlock. Donna Dixon, who was doing marketing out of Charlotte Motor Speedway, hooked me up with him. Spurlock used to run funny cars and always wanted to own a Winston Cup team. He was a super-nice guy and came to Spartanburg often. He was going to buy all the guts of the team. This guy was pretty sharp and had something figured out. He had an investor who was going to go in with him for something like a million and a half dollars on his part. We inventoried everything in the shop and came up with a price. He was going to run a few races out of the shop and then move the stuff to Charlotte. It was some good money, too. We told him we'd help him any way we could.

Spurlock was buddy-buddy with J. C. Agajanian's son, who was representing Tony Stewart. K. C. and Tony were buddies. And they were talking to a sponsor: Home Depot. Spurlock just about had the deal put together and wanted Daddy and me to come along and help him. I said we might and we might not. We'd decide that later. But that was the formula he had. I was hoping and praying he'd do it. It was an option out, but fell through because the guy who was going to go in with him must have had financial problems and couldn't pull his end of the deal. At the same time, Spurlock couldn't get Home Depot signed right away.

That was a good, but false start. Fortunately, the phone lines at 400 North Fairview were scorching and potential buyers were lining up. This might just work out after all.

At the same time that the Spurlock deal fell through, I got a hold of another guy, and Jim Foster helped us with negotiations. It was a man by the name of Dave Robinson, who lived in Florida. He loved racing. One of the nicest son-of-a-guns you ever met in your life. I got to talking to him, and he was kind of interested in partnering the team. He had pretty deep pockets. We were going to call it Robinson-Moore Motorsports and get everything going. Also, I had some other good marketing people working on a deal with Brett Farve and some other things. That was how the Tim Steele deal came about. This other guy that had been working with Brett Farve, Tim Steele, and H. S. Die to come in and have them buy the team. So they got in on the act. The Robinson thing was going on, and the Tim Steele thing came along. The Steeles were going to pay Daddy, Daryl, and me big salaries to stay there. Well, Daddy and I sat down and said, "Which deal do we need to be doing?" We toyed and toyed with it and went and talked to our attorney, Mr. Bill Terry, about it. He is a great guy and a close friend who had done all the contracts since the early seventies for Daddy. We had preliminary contracts from two people of a selling deal with the potential to partner with them. We looked at both things, and I really wanted to go with the Robinson thing, but there was a problem: Robinson didn't have a sponsor lined up, which was going to put him out on a limb, and we didn't know who was going to drive the car. With Tim Steele, we had a driver with the package, and it looked more promising for them to buy the team because it was going to take a few million dollars. So just on paper that appeared to be a very good option. They were Ford people, and Tim Steele used to win every single ARCA race back then in that red number 16.

> *Bud Moore Engineering was going in the direction of Michigan's Harold Steele and his hot-footed son Tim. Tim Steele came with impressive credentials. He was the Auto Racing Club of America (ARCA) National Champion in 1993, 1996, and 1997. In 146 races, he won 41 times, 24 of which were on super speedways. Tim Steele captured 86 top fives and 101 top tens and took 31 poles.*
>
> *On November 5, 1997, the prospective teammates tested at the recently redesigned, freshly repaved, and newly renamed Atlanta Motor Speedway. It was lightning fast on the day that changed everything.*

We went down to Atlanta and tested with Tim when they just had reconfigured the track. It was the same car Greg Sacks had at Charlotte. It was an excellent mile-and-a-half car. It still had "Daytona USA" painted on it. Man, it was fast, and Atlanta was always a good place for us.

Tim ran a real good lap the first day. He was by far the fastest car down there — and there were a lot of good cars there, too. Then we went out the next day and he was really going to bust off a good one. He couldn't run it flat-footed through three and four. They wanted to loosen the car up and put a piece of a spring rubber in the right rear. They were used to running Banjo cars with front-steer conversion. We were running Hopkins cars like the Laughlins. The Banjo cars were flexible. Our cars were a lot stiffer.

Daddy said, "No, no, no. Don't do that! Don't put that spring rubber in it. That's too much. When you stop the grill up, and knock another degree of timing in it, it's going to be just right through one and two because you're going to be running faster. You put that spring rubber in there and you're going to be too loose." We sat there and argued over that, and I finally told Daddy, "They got their own guy they want to use as a crew chief because Tim and he get along. They're buying into the team, the boy is running well. Go ahead and put it in there." Daddy was adamant. "It's going to be too much. It's too big of an adjustment." He tried to explain that they were used to these other cars. This went on for about an hour. But they did it anyway.

Everybody was getting on top of the trucks to watch Tim run. He went out there and flat-footed it in three and four with the front end stopped up. I'm on the truck with two marketing guys who helped put this thing together. I said, "If he'll stick through three and four this will be pretty good." He went through one and two and, man, he did get through there better. He had to crack it a little bit. It was just a tick tight. He flew down the backstretch and that thing was honking. Tim dropped it off down in three and he isn't going to crack the throttle. I never heard the motor change in three. He got right in the middle of three and four and I saw that thing get just a tick loose. As soon as it started drifting, you could just see it. I thought for a second he was going to hold it. I said, "Stick!" That was all I hollered. "Stick! Stick! *Stick!*" It didn't stick. It snapped. It turned and hit the wall on the driver's side running wide slap open. *Boom*! Flat on the driver's side. It didn't go any distance, and he couldn't have hit it any more perfectly to pancake it. He had to have hit it 100 miles an hour faster than Weatherly did at turn six. All I could think about was Weatherly hitting on the driver's side and running fast with Wade. I thought, "This shit can't be happening to us. What's going on?"

We jumped down off the truck. Everybody ran over there, and I told the marketing guy, "By the way, I've done this before, too. This comes with the program." The fire crews were already on it, bringing in the Jaws of Life, when we got there. They cut the roof off the car and took him out. The crash drove the steering wheel up against the side door roll bars. That's how hard it hit. Tim wasn't bleeding or anything, but he suffered a concussion and appeared to be unconscious. I didn't see how he could have survived. They pulled him out of the top of the car and carried him to the hospital, and we drove over there."

By the time we got there, they had sent him through MRI, and he had come to his senses pretty well. Tim was sitting up and said, "How bad did it tear the car up?" I said, "Well it's fucked up. We were concerned if you were OK." That was a good race driver — worried about the car! I think he could have done it. Somebody clocked him on the backstretch instead of the front stretch because he didn't make it all the way around and it was going to be four tenths quicker if he'd made it.

We had to break the news to his daddy and get on the cell phone. Harold said, "Well, he's OK, isn't he?"

"Yeah, they had to cut him out and run an MRI."

"How bad did it mess up the car? How much is that going to cost?"

Harold was worried about the car, too. He had seen Tim crash before. Harold was also a racer.

> *All the horror and tragedy of the past had flashed back through the collective psyche of Bud Moore Engineering. But it appeared that they had escaped the worst of it this time, much more so than with Ricky Rudd in the Clash of 1984. A high speed driver's-side pancake ranks right there with the T-bone or head-on crash or fire as a racer's worst nightmare. But this Tim Steele guy was a proven champion and was worried more about the car than himself only an hour or so after his wreck. So it was full speed ahead. Let's make a deal.*

Everything looked like it was going to be OK. The marketing people had a pretty good line working with Brett Farve, Nike, and Sony. It looked pretty good but hadn't quite gotten done. We went down to Daytona and tested during the winter of 1997–1998. The car wasn't quite right. It was running fair. That wasn't the problem. They just had starting getting those cars to pull down a little bit with the shocks. It made the car stiff. Our car needed a little more ground clearance, and we were going to correct that. But the problem we got into after about a day of testing was that Tim started to get headaches. Just the vibration in the car gave him headaches. We didn't run all that hot because we were bottoming out. We tested so-so. The Steeles had not committed to buying the team, and they had four or five of their people down there helping. But Tim was having headaches. They spent a bunch of time at the shop and Harold told Daddy, "Bud, I really don't need to be buying this thing outright right now until I see if my kid's OK." Daddy said, "I understand. I don't blame you." Harold said, "We don't really have that sponsorship thing done yet and we're getting closer to Daytona. I've been funding this thing through my H.S. Die. We're just getting cold feet on whether we need to be doing this. I know I signed a preliminary deal with y'all and everything, but he's having headaches and trouble." Daddy and I told Harold that we understood. "That's fine."

We had the misfortune of a crash, but once again, that's Daddy and me. I know Tim ran a couple of races after that and didn't run as well. There were some things said that maybe the crash had something to do with it, and I think it did. I haven't ever heard the official opinion. I think he had some substance abuse problems later on. I don't know. I didn't see any evidence of it. We had a ball with him. I remember us going into some Japanese joint down there at Daytona during the test and it was a fun thing. Harold made good on his end of the deal financially up until that point. We both took a pretty good lick on it. Definitely not as much as the lick Tim Steele took. Once again, here came Weatherly and Wade creeping into our minds. That would have been real nice — number three. It was creeping through my mind when Daddy told them, "No! Don't put that spring rubber in it." Like I said, it was a mutual agreement to part, and it was an unfortunate set of circumstances because I think that would have worked out well for both the shop and the Steeles. It would have taken some of the financial load off Daddy and me, and it would have been a way to continue. The car was trashed, and Harold made good on that. We spent a few hundred thousand dollars and Harold spent a few hundred thousand dollars. That's exactly what wound up happening.

The following quotes attributed to Tim Steele were copied verbatim from the website autoracingsport.com and sum up how close the Moore-Steele relationship came to being a huge force in the money-driven universe of NASCAR stock car racing:

"I was 10 days away from signing a Winston Cup contract when I crashed; and we were going to run for the 1998 Cup Rookie of the Year. My dad and (Green Bay Packers quarterback) Brett Favre were purchasing the team from Bud Moore, and we had Nike and Sony lined up as sponsors. Looking back in '98 when I was at the Mayo Clinic, I now know the doctors were right when they told me I should probably find a different career. I just wasn't willing to accept that. It was like admitting defeat. Racing was my life; it's how I earned my living, and the only job I ever had since I was 20. I didn't know anything else, so it was so hard to walk away from my life. I had worked so hard to get where I had gotten. I just couldn't give up on it now."

Like the Steeles, the Moores had a lifetime investment in racing, only with a significantly longer and more storied history. The Steele family escaped death. The Moore family suffered it twice. As far as keeping Bud Moore Engineering on the speedway in a multi-million dollar, competitive situation, this golden opportunity perished with an ill-advised chassis adjustment in Atlanta. So did a brilliant driving career.

The year 1997 was the first since Bud Moore became a car owner in 1961 that none of the team's cars qualified for a single points-paying race. Even further back than that, it was the first in Gregory Clyde Moore's 39 years that a car his father was tuning on failed to qualify. In fact, in 1957, the year of Greg's birth, Bud Moore won his first Grand National Championship as the winning crew chief for Buck Baker. Bud even won the Southern 500 that year wrenching Speedy Thompson's Chevy. But the cars at 400 North Fairview had speed, and nobody there had given up. Not even close. A proposed arrangement that came and went a few years before was out there again, but died on the vine as did others. So in 1998, the other major suitor for the purchase of the team had stayed in the background all the while as the Steele situation played itself out. Fortunately, Dave Robinson was still interested, and discussions were resurrected in an oily kind of deal.

Pennzoil came back into the picture in a competition of huge proportions and ramifications. They considered only two proposals out of 185. One was from Earnhardt, Inc., with Steve Park, and the other was from Bud Moore Engineering. They had to go with Earnhardt because he had a proven Busch driver and we didn't have one we were committed to. We had a Hooters deal that died, and Conseco Insurance wound up with Foyt and Hornaday in 2001. But even after the Tim Steele thing, Dave Robinson was still interested, although a little bit disgusted. He said he'd try it, but really needed to get a sponsor. He went ahead and signed a basic agreement. We scrubbed going to Speedweeks because of Tim Steele's wreck and his health. Daddy and I talked about it. We thought, "We really need to go to Daytona and show our face." It was discussed, but we were pushed for time. I talked to Morgan Shepherd about driving the car. We came real close to just going on down there on our own. I could get a one-race deal, but there were only two or three weeks before the race.

Then there was this guy who had invented a lubricant called Rescue. He had won an SAE (Society of Automotive Engineers) award out in California for being the first person to make molybdenum disulfide, which is moly in suspension in oil. He had it so fine it would run through the oil line. Moly lubricants are made for metal to metal contact. We've had moly-coated rings forever. There's moly lubricant on the chain of a motorcycle. Nobody could ever get it to do right in oil, though. He finally got it to do right. He was trying to market this oil additive and the stuff really did work — a little. It turned the oil dead black. We tested it on the dyno and sure enough, it helped some. So we did an infomercial during this time. They spent three quarters of a million dollars with this New York outfit to do a half-hour infomercial with me and Harry Gant. They take about 30 minutes to put the make up on you and everything. Man, my nerves are about shot. They got a big name racing announcer. They had this marketing crew come down to the shop. I'm sitting there running a motor on the dyno. I had to figure out how to run the motor where it showed an improvement. They had people watching and I couldn't cheat it. Sure enough, it showed about five horsepower gained, which I kinda had to make sure it did.

We got a race car painted up, and it looked pretty good. We went down to Darlington and ran a test. We took the oil belt off a car and ran three laps with that Rescue additive in it. It didn't blow up! The guy had this machine made up like the ones they had at Ford that check friction like a camshaft rubbing against something rough. You could pour a drop or two of this stuff in there and the oil temperature would go down. It would slicken it up. I figured it was getting around the rings, and it did help it a little bit. There isn't any such thing as a miracle, but this stuff was totally different. Oil additives are the biggest snake oil deal in the world, but this one seemed to do something — or at least it wasn't as big a snake oil as STP. That's just a viscosity modifier. But even STP has its place. It helps with older motors. We had all that synthetic lubricant figured out with the Motorcraft stuff. So we marketed this Rescue additive.

Dave Robinson was going to buy the team over time, and it was to be Robinson-Moore Motorsports. I loved that guy to death. We were going to be right there with him. He wanted me to run it. Daryl was going to do whatever he wanted to, and that suited him. We never did like the idea of selling anything. The whole idea was for us to continue.

The date was August 16, 1998, at Irish Hills, Michigan, when Robinson-Moore Motorsports' black number 15 Rescue Ford Taurus qualified with Ted Musgrave in the saddle for the Pepsi 400 presented by DeVilbiss. Not since November 10, 1996, had Greg and the boys been on the grid of a Winston Cup race. It felt good, the car looked great, and they were back in business with veteran crew chief Joey Knuckles calling the shots. Joey chiefed a couple of wins with Davey Allison at Robert Yates Racing in 1987 and had worked infrequently in Cup since. The team was on the track, a partnership had formed, and the Rescue infomercial hit the airwaves.

We got to Michigan and made the race. We'd hired a crew and had a lot of things going. We started thirty-second and something broke in the motor after 136 laps. I guess that Rescue wasn't so hot after all. Really, it had nothing to do with that stuff. We were back, but it was really nothing too special. We wound up going to Daytona and testing pretty well. We decided we were going to put Blaise Alexander in the car. They already had some marketing going with that Rescue stuff and him in a Busch car. He ended up having a lot of bad luck, too, hitting the wall up there at Charlotte in an ARCA race and dying.

But now it gets interesting. Tim Steele felt better. He recovered from his crash and finally went on to win an ARCA race. So Daddy, Dave Robinson, and I flew up there to Michigan to see him. We asked if he still wanted to drive the car.

"Oh man, yeah," he said. "I didn't think y'all were going to forget about me."

I said, "No, we weren't. We want you to drive the car."

So we got to thinking, "If Tim Steele is OK, well, we've seen how fast he can run. Let's take another look at him." That's when we went to Indy on a test.

Tim had already torn two of Bobby Allison's cars up going into turn one trying to make the race back in '94. Same spot both times. So we went back up there, and he ran pretty well off the truck. We came in and made an adjustment on the car because it was pushing real bad. The car was much, much better then, and felt real good. He went down the backstretch, came back by and went down into one and lost it, exactly where he lost two of Bobby Allison's cars. He wrecked the hell out of that good car. So we took the backup car off the truck.

Dave Robinson was headed up that way to see the test. His wife and he had just gotten ready to get on his airplane. I called him on the phone. "I kind of have bad news."

"What?"

"We tore up a car."

"Oh Lord. Steele wrecked it? Are we going to have anything to run by the time I get there? I would like to see it run a lap." He was laughing. So Dave came up there, and we used the backup car and it ran OK.

In the meantime, they started playing the infomercial. It was really a good infomercial. I liked it, especially since I was in it a lot. It had me and Harry Gant sitting there, with Harry doing some of the commentary. I ran the dyno and it was going, "*rrrrrRRRR!*" It showed the light flashing. It was over 700 horsepower! Then Harry poured the Rescue in it right next to me and we ran it again. Oh, it was funnier than hell.

They ran this infomercial for about four days all over the place — Indianapolis, Los Angeles, Atlanta — but they sold the airtime at around two o'clock in the morning. Late night stuff, pretty lousy airtime. Then I got the telephone call from Dave. "Gregory, I need to ask you something. How many quart bottles of that shit do you think that we sold?"

I said, "Well, I hope it was a bunch." They had projected all these big sales numbers.

He said, "We ran it for four days. We sold 242 quart bottles." I said, "*Do what?*"

He said, "Let me read you some of the doggone things." He started reading the figures. "In LA it sold a hundred and something bottles." It was pretty expensive. He's kind of laughing as he reads it. He said, "This is the one that really got me. Indianapolis: One quart!" When he said that, I started laughing. I said, "You can't be serious." He said, "I am. We got to think about this deal a little bit."

So Robinson got on an airplane and flew to Spartanburg. I mean, he had met France and put a ton of money in the team, and Daddy had put in about a half a million dollars. We'd spent three quarters of a million dollars making this infomercial and sold almost 250 bottles. I think he gave up on it a little too quickly, but I can't blame him a bit. Dave Robinson and I got to be real good friends. He just passed away a few years ago and I had to hear it through the grapevine. He had some nice people who worked for him. Once again because of financial reasons and no sponsorship ... the man had spent probably $2,000,000 and hadn't even started to buy the team yet. And if this stuff wasn't going to sell, I believe I would have put the brakes on, too.

One of the biggest reasons for the failure of Rescue was the synthetics had already come out. The only one that does anything now is Lucas and that isn't anything. I've got stuff better than that in my bedroom. So help me, I've tested it. Only I haven't got a million dollars to try to sell it. Lucas has got a good product. Z-Max? That kit costs $30 for something to pour in your fuel. For the cost of the kit you can get your oil changed twice. That was the reason I interviewed Dennis Groh on our radio show, *Droppin' the Hammer*. He exploded the whole thing. I told him I fooled with a little oil additive myself. It reduced the temperature in a Briggs and Stratton lawnmower by eight or nine degrees.

We were the first ones to run all synthetics through the race car. We had been doing that since Ricky Rudd. We pioneered all that stuff. We had Conoco make our Motorcraft synthetic oil for us. It had "Bud Moore Engineering" on it, and I had 100 five gallon buckets they made for nothing. We always ran our own oil. There wasn't anybody that had that stuff.

But anyway, Dave Robinson had spent a bunch of money. Bud Moore Engineering had spent a bunch of money. This is where we're getting into that million six we spent. Two or three hundred thousand here, two or three hundred thousand there, and we're still paying the bills. But these other people are pumping in the money, too. I think Daddy, Daryl, and I could have really lived with the Dave Robinson deal.

On September 4, 1950, Bud Moore and two extremely brave men named Joe Eubanks and Harold Kite endured days of qualifying and preliminaries to run in the Inaugural Southern 500 at the brand new Darlington International Raceway. Bud Moore won the race in 1957 in the first 500 mile stock car race to be run at an average of 100 miles per hour. He also won in 1960 with Buck Baker crawling under the checkers with the left rear rim showering sparks. Then there was Labor Day 1966 when Darel Dieringer won in the little Mercury Comet number 16 and carried nine-year-old Gregory into Victory Lane with him. Throw in a couple of wins in the spring race by Weatherly and Earnhardt, and it is evident that nowhere do stock car history and Bud Moore mesh any better than at Darlington. On September 6, 1998, only 48 years and two days after he raced in the first Southern 500, Bud Moore ran there for the last time. His wife Betty, Greg and his girlfriend Roberta, and a gritty, gutsy crew were there with him.

The Southern 500 at Darlington in 1998 is the last race that we made that was truly our stuff. Dave Robinson was gone. That was the last race that was all Bud Moore, Greg Moore, Daryl Moore, Brent Moore, Betty Moore ... this was the last deal and I'm proud of it. We'd already tested, and Ted Musgrave ran well. I said, "Hell, let's just go on down to Darlington. It's the Southern 500!"

We get out there practicing and he's running. The car looked great. It was black with those yellow 15s on it trimmed in red, with a yellow stripe with red trim along the rocker panel. It still had "Rescue" in yellow and red on it. Maybe we'd sell a bottle! It was the first race Roberta ever got to go to. I told her, "When he gets ready to run, there's where he's going to pass them." I'm pointing over to the old turns three and four. "That's the way

Bud Moore (left) and David Robinson stand beside the Rescue Engine Formula Ford Taurus at 400 North Fairview Avenue. Although Ted Musgrave had some sizzling laps in the Southern 500 at Darlington on September 6, 1998, it was parked for dead last with engine trouble in the final purely Bud Moore Engineering effort (courtesy Bud Moore Engineering Archives).

Daddy sets the car up down here." Well, I'll be damned. We went to qualify and it bottomed out and he qualified lousy in thirty-second. We also didn't have much of a pit crew, and that would have been the Achilles' Heel. But we had a driver in Ted Musgrave and a Bud Moore car that could handle.

So we started at the back and Ted got all the way up to fourteenth and was outrunning the leaders, so help me. That could have been one of the best runs we ever had. Jeff Gordon was leading the race, and we couldn't believe our watches. We were running three to four tenths quicker than Jeff, and he was clear of traffic. Musgrave went by Ricky Rudd in that doggone Tide car so quick — that's just how fast he was coming. He was sifting through there, and then here he came.

Well, after about 80 laps, a plug wire hopped off it and the car started missing. We were not running for points, so we parked it. As far as I'm concerned, that's when the Moore family parked it, too. It would have been a fantastic Cinderella story if we could have finished in the top five or won the race. Musgrave ran well, and we had the car really hooked up. We walked out of there with our heads up because people saw how well we ran. People knew our sponsorship had pulled out and we didn't have time to change the car. It was funded on Daddy's nickel and cost us $74,000 to pull it off. But that was it. We finished dead last. Forty-first. That was it.

Records state that in some capacity, Bud Moore ran four more races in 1999 and one in 2000. It is not true. Whether the Moores ran any of those races is not a matter of interpretation. Maybe Bud was there for some, but Greg was not, and neither man was in at Talladega in 2000 when Musgrave crashed the Buddy Baker–like white and blue number 15.

Seventeen • Looking for a Savior

Bud Moore was an active racer in five decades at NASCAR's top level of racing. Greg confirmed that they finished last in the last race for Bud Moore Engineering at the 1998 Southern 500. Nothing much happened to change Bud Moore's career statistics after 1996 anyway. Yet for the 1998 Southern 500, the team had battled their way back on the track after 21 agonizing months and thousands of dollars trying to figure out how. The focus changed after 1998. A "For Sale" sign was staked in front of the historic brick building at 400 North Fairview Avenue. Getting out was serious business.

CHAPTER EIGHTEEN

Going Once, Going Twice, *Sold*

The Golden Anniversary of Bud Moore Engineering in 1999 found them still totally capable of fielding a top notch Winston Cup effort. The reality was that behind the smoke and mirrors they were hanging on by a thread. It might take spending a little savings to get back into the race, but Greg could look around at the skeleton crew trying to look busy around the unpainted race cars and hear the words of Bill France, Jr., echoing through the quiet confines of the shop: "We want y'all to get a sponsor. If you don't have a sponsor, don't bring any primered race car to the race track. Don't spend all your daddy's money to do this. That isn't going to be real smart. We need Bud Moore, we don't need you. We like you, but don't spend your daddy's retirement trying to run a race car. If you do, we aren't going to like it at all." The task was crystal clear: Find a sponsor or sell it outright. Welcome to the Golden Anniversary season.

I told Daddy I had a deal down at Daytona for $50,000, but we had to make the race. Knuckles was helping us and we still had all our old guys. I told Daddy that this was going to be a best case-study and I was going to figure it to the penny. We always talked about rising costs and such. Now I didn't have the $100,000 deal from Universal Studios to be on the white car with Larry Pearson, which missed by one spot. But I had $50,000 from of all people, Moon Pie! I got to meet the guy and he'd been on the Food Channel. Once again, I had decals ready. We were going to put it on a black car: Moon Pie, from Chattanooga Bakeries. We went down to Daytona with a black car and yellow numbers and no sponsor so I could have some room for Moon Pie.

I contacted Jeff Green, who was a pissed off son-of-a-bitch because he'd been let go from Felix Sabates' Money Store Chevrolet number 46. He was in between rides, and I told him we'd pay all of his expenses and we had to make the race. I had another deal offered to me, but it wasn't as much money. Mac Tools or somebody was to give me $25,000. The $50,000 wasn't nearly going to cover it like the Universal Studios thing would have. That was all that the man had.

Jeff got along great with the crew and was tickled to death to get to drive a Bud Moore car. He couldn't believe how well it drove. He had very good communication skills. It could have been another Cinderella story like Dallenbach. But we didn't have a very good qualifying time because we had put the wrong shocks on. You could see the cars qualifying and the front ends were lifting real badly. Ours was ridiculous.

They took all that stuff off and we got in race trim. What happened next was funny. There was a group of about ten or twelve hot dogs who went out there to draft, and Jeff was about eighth in line. We waited to see if this thing was going to do its usual deal and pull up and draft with those long trailing arms. They got up to speed, and Jeff had no problem at all hanging on. The first group of six or eight cars got a jump on Jeff and on Dale Jarrett in the 88. Well, you knew Jarrett was in a missile. Jeff and Dale got 50 yards behind, Jeff in our black car and Jarrett in the Quality Care car. In that lead bunch were Rusty and all the hot dogs. We were looking at the stopwatch, and Jeff and Jarrett were catching them and catching them good. They got to the pack and started sifting through them. They got to Rusty and Jeff Gordon, who were high and low, and Jeff Green and Dale Jarrett went right through the middle of them coming through the tri-oval and just went on for a lap or two. Then Happy Hour ended. I'll never forget it. I overheard somebody off of one of the other crews say, "Now, isn't that some shit? That 88 couldn't do a damn thing with that 15, could he? Bud and Greg's down here without a damn nickel." Every time he went out and drafted, that's the way he ran. This was our own deal. If anything came good of this and Moon Pie found some money from somewhere else, we would have taken Jeff Green and been back in business. I had B & B Studios make the decals for different positions on the car with the Moon Pie and possibly something else on it.

As Greg said: "RC Cola and a Moon Pie!" Bud Moore went to Daytona Speedweeks in 1974 with George Follmer and RC Cola, and now Bud and Greg had returned nearly a quarter of a century later with the other half of that southern tradition, Moon Pie — if they can make the race. Bad shocks in time trials put the number 15 Taurus twenty-third of 30 on the grid in the first qualifier. But Jeff was a drafting beast! How could they fail? Right?

Roberta was down there with Momma and our friends from Atlanta, the Holbrooks, in the Goodyear tower getting treated royally. I told Momma and Berta, "If something doesn't happen, we can make this race and run well." We were feeling really, really good. "And there was the green flag." Dallenbach went down to the apron to try to pass somebody, caused a wreck, and we were torn all to hell. Jeff Green said, "I never even had a chance to get out of third gear." You talk about being sick! We had easily a top five or ten car and never got a chance. France Jr. up in the tower told Mike Helton, "Are you believing Bud and them guys' luck?" France Jr. was sick over it. France can only fix things so much. Daddy turned around to me and couldn't believe what had happened. Roberta cried and said, "It just doesn't seem fair." I said, "Baby, that's the way this sport works."

Three reporters came over to me — Deb Williams, Steve Waid, and another guy. They cornered me about 20 minutes after the wreck had happened. They said, "We just want to ask you one question. How much more can you guys take?"

I said, "Well, in this business, you get up and dust your knees off and go forward. That's all I can tell you."

Deb Williams said, "We don't see how you guys can take anymore. Sponsors and buyers that didn't go through — how much more can you take?"

I said, "Whatever it takes."

I walked back over there to the pit box, and Daddy was still kind of sitting there with his mouth hanging open. I said, "Daddy, France said he couldn't believe how bad our luck was."

Daddy said, "Baby, what do you think this all means?"

"Daddy, I can only interpret it as this: The Good Lord wants us to go home and stop this. Go to the house."

Momma agreed. "Yeah, I want it stopped right now before it destroys all of us."

And that's when we were down in Daytona in '99 with Jeff Green.

Confident that Jeff Green would race the car into the Daytona 500, from left to right are Margie "Duck" Holbrook, Betty Moore, and Roberta Albus before the 1999 qualifying race (courtesy Bud Moore Engineering Archives).

Greg was drilled back into a huge personal disappointment, but quickly recovered. He was able to put a price tag on his previously best-case study as he said he could. It was high for them.

Being as this was on our own nickel and I had a good driver lined up, I wanted to figure this thing because I had always done the budgets. I wanted to figure everything to the penny. We didn't get all of our tires free, but we got enough of them free that we didn't have to pay for any. We got four free sets, but we didn't run long enough to use them. That was what was so sickening. It was like running a 9.5 hundred yard dash and you're running against some guys running 9.9. Then your ankle breaks on your second step out of the blocks. No fault of ours.

The costs included motel rooms, labor as far as paying the guys from the first week until he wrecked, the fuel in the truck, overtime for the people, everything. Decals that we never got to use. The whole thing cost us $127,885. That was how expensive racing had become.

But when we got back to Spartanburg, I was not going to throw in the towel. I was still pumped up about this Moon Pie thing.

Bud Moore Engineering was like a former heavyweight champion of the world after his prime. He still knew the game and how to comport himself. The old warrior still exuded class and confidence in and out of the ring. The fight and fire remained in his gut as he searched for one more bout to land a knockout punch that he knew he still had. Greg and Bud had had some great preliminary rounds and flashes of brilliance. They had also taken some shots and staggered away bloodied and dazed, but never knocked out. Inside the walls at 400 North Fairview, Greg continued to prep the team for the next round he knew would come.

I said that we had to keep trying to dig. I spent some money and had decals made. I changed the numbers around and put some pink on it. I thought a black car would look good because a Moon Pie was black. I sent a marketing package to the guy at Chattanooga Bakeries. I had Tommy White from B & B Studios come to the rescue, and we took all these real neat pictures. We got up on ladders and took different angles of the cars with different decals and really made a nice photographic presentation to send to Moon Pie. I utilized the yellow and put some striping on the bottom. We made a pretty nice-looking Moon Pie car. They just didn't have the budget. If we had made the race and put Moon Pie on the car and had a decent finish, it would have gotten the higher-ups there more interested and they could have drawn some money out of other budgets or partnered with somebody else. Can you say "RC Cola?"

So 1999 drifted on by, and there was interest from Auto Nation and some others. The best one was in June. I had received a call from a guy I knew who ran Pi Computers. They had put the data acquisition systems on the race cars. He was working with a Winston West team at an open test in Indianapolis, and they wanted to run Indy. He said, "Are you and Bud willing to sell that thing?"

I said, "If they've got the money."

He said, "These people have the money and they are dead serious. They have a west coast car, and they don't know what they're doing." They had Jeff Davis, who had finished fourth in the west points to Butch Gilliland driving the car. "They want to go Cup racing and they want to buy a race team." They wanted to get out of California. They were tired of the traffic, the crime, and wanted to move out east. They wanted to have some fun.

I said, "If they're interested, get them down here." He told me then that they were going to be in the area in late July and August visiting some teams in Charlotte. He let me know immediately that this wasn't any payment deal or pending on a sponsor. This was going to be cash on the barrelhead.

Then a big fish took the bait and it was an all-out assault by Greg and Bud. This one was the cannot-miss match they were waiting for.

I met this guy by the name of Pat McKnight who had worked with the Moose Lodge. He had been working on this thing for 14 months with AMVETS. They needed to boost their membership, and they had enough money. They had the money in foundations and all kinds of things. It was a war thing, just about like with Remington; guns, Bud Moore, World War Two. All this stuff fit. We were still plugging kind of a Tim Steele possibility, but this was going to be all us. It was going to be Bud Moore Engineering, no investor or anything, and some other good driver.

Daddy and I made two trips to Washington, D.C. We even had the head marketing guy from Winston to go up there with us and speak to the people as to how motorsports had helped them. When we left D. C. after the second trip, we thought we had an agreement. We were all sitting around this big table and thought it had been agreed that they were going to give two million dollars to run the last five races of the season, then get ready for the next year with a three-year deal for something like five and a half, six, and six and a half million. Those people were pumped up. We thought it was a done deal. But they had to have one other guy's approval.

I was so confident when we got back on Thursday that Berta and I went up to a music camp where everybody was camping out and partying. I was the happiest son-of-a-gun. I said, "We got them." I was so doggone happy. This was on a Friday night, and we were going to know something Monday. I was thinking, "We're going racing. We got us a deal now."

Well, we didn't hear from them Monday morning. They had a big meeting on it. That thing had gotten some publicity and some other people had talked to them, too. We thought it was a done deal. Right there at the last minute on Monday at three o' clock, the phone rang. We never understood how they could have done this. They had sort of verbally committed. But one guy who wasn't in the meeting, even though he had also liked the thing, just flat didn't understand racing or something and said, "We just don't need to do this." No deal. We couldn't believe it.

Greg and the Moores were stunned then and cannot accept it easily all these years later. It seemed like a perfect fit. There was Bud Moore with a war record beyond compare, and there were the American Veterans of Foreign Wars needing some attention. A combination made in marketing heaven. Weekly national exposure with the right guy behind the wheel leading the charge would have been arranged. Do you think the AMVETS might have increased their membership? Would the often neglected American veterans have been able to better their plight and have a rallying point every Sunday afternoon? Different branches of the service, different battle groups, and their gallant warriors could have been honored on real rolling thunder. Medal of Honor winners and heroic acts and individuals since the American Revolution could have been recognized on the sheet metal of a streaking Ford Taurus. (And do you think they might have sold a Ford or two?) Another better idea goes by the wayside. The guy who nixed this deal was poorly advised. Greg and Bud were regaining their focus, however, and straightaway opportunity knocked at the door again.

Two weeks later, in August of '99, we had pushed our own spending up to a million five. Three weeks after the AMVETs shot us down after 14 months of work, we had a phone call saying that the Fenleys wanted to come and see the shop. They were from out in California, and Randy and Robert Fenley's daddy was a Winston West inspector. Daddy and I remembered him from when we went to Riverside. It was in their blood. Robert's wife, Sue, was with them, and her father owned a well-known national company. The money was coming from Sue Fenley, and her daddy was loaded.

Eighteen • Going Once, Going Twice, Sold

They had brought about six people with them from the west coast and had been to four or five shops up in Charlotte. Only two were interested in selling; one might have been what was left of Bobby Allison's shop. They looked around our shop and saw we had all new cars ready to go, some in primer and some painted. They liked being in Spartanburg away from Charlotte, and they liked Daddy and us. They weren't in there ten minutes on a Thursday evening and Sue Fenley turned around to Daddy and said, "This is what I want." We went inside the office and talked about the price and didn't even dicker on that. Whatever Bud wanted for it, that was what they were ready to pay.

They drew the paperwork up and *bingo*, on Friday they wired a half a million dollar deposit into our bank account. The actual sale number has always been confidential, but it was a hell of a lot more than I thought we'd ever get for it. It was to be paid within a full month, and it was. They fulfilled their financial obligation to Daddy, Daryl, and me and bought the shop, land, everything, lock, stock, and barrel—and I mean good money. We don't have anything bad to say about them. They had some people who were pretty computer literate and asked a lot of questions. Randy Fenley told me time and time again, "I want you to show me how to be a good team manager." I told him, "Randy, that came with the package. That's what I'll do." They were paying us the whole time we were there. Everything from then on was working with the Fenleys and their driver, Derrike Cope. They were good people; they just didn't get a sponsor. Once again, they were running through money. Randy, Robert, and Sue weren't very experienced. They had run a Winston West car. They wanted us to stay there and help them, and we were interested. They were nothing but nice to us.

With the sale of the team to the Fenleys came another aspect of the deal that perhaps was not totally expected. It was the numbers game—which was actually nothing new at all for NASCAR, and which highlighted that 15 was not just another pair of digits. It brought to mind some other famous numbers in NASCAR history and the safety innovations they inspired.

Andy Petree or somebody wanted the number 15, and we kept renewing our car owner license to hold the number. There's only so many numbers, and 15 isn't the worst looking one. When the Fenleys came around, we were about ready to give it up if we didn't start running some. So Daddy and I went to Bristol, and I had called Kevin Triplett, who was something like third in command at NASCAR. He said, "When y'all get there, let's talk about this number situation because we have people that want it." NASCAR said that under the circumstances, they would let the Fenleys have it, but only if there was a strong association with Bud Moore, with the Moores attached to it. That's when they came up with "Fenley-Moore Motorsports" to keep the number. I told Daddy that I didn't think we needed to go to bat for them about that because it wasn't our stuff anymore. If they had to get another number, it would disassociate them from us if they screwed up—which they did. They were good people and just didn't get a sponsor. They upheld their end of the deal with us.

I felt like this: When you sell somebody your business, you let them move in, and you move out. If you can leave some technology there and some people who are willing to work for the new owners, that's fine. But they weren't in a position to keep the Bud Moore legacy going—and yet there would still be a 15 sitting on the side of the car. NASCAR looked at it that way. But Daddy and I actually went to bat for them to keep the 15 because they thought it would help them get sponsorship and stuff. I was in total disagreement with it. As it turned out, they made so many mistakes and ran through so much money and had so much of a misunderstanding about the way the thing works that they were literally doomed six months after they bought the team.

We left after 2000, and Earnhardt wanted all of his family's old numbers like 8 and 15 for DEI (Dale Earnhardt Incorporated). Somebody else wanted 15, too, like Andy Petree after Leo Jackson turned that team over to him. There was some interest by some pretty powerful teams to get the number 15. So after the Fenleys didn't do anything with it, NASCAR called Randy Fenley and told him that the number was gone. Randy said they couldn't take his number, and they told Randy it wasn't his number. NASCAR owns all numbers. That number was on loan. They didn't need it anyway, and it went to DEI. That made me feel real good, that the number 15 meant enough to Earnhardt that he went to NASCAR and told them that if Bud wasn't going to use it, he wanted it. Also, NASCAR thought enough of Bud Moore and the number 15 that they wanted it on a competitive car. I agreed with them 100 percent. But then, in the first race, Michael Waltrip won the Daytona 500 with the 15 on it and Dale Earnhardt got killed.

Car numbers are special to teams and to NASCAR, especially if a race driver gets killed. The 3 on Earnhardt's car is not Childress' number; it's NASCAR's number. Used to be, in Indy car racing, the number 1 went to the champion, and that's essentially what Daddy did in 1964 with Wade. Wade took over for Weatherly, and Daddy put number 1 on the car because we had won the previous championship. In fact, we had won the previous two championships. When we lost Weatherly it was years before anybody used number 8, and it was Ed Negre. They did give it some time. We thought the 8 was supposed to be permanently retired. Then they came back and said they were only going to retire it for five years. Two more people got killed with number 22 after Fireball Roberts did. Billy Foster died at Riverside in 1967, and Grant Adcox was killed at Atlanta in 1989.

Daryl said he was looking right at Billy Foster. That was before they put a dogleg at the end of the backstretch at Riverside going into turn nine, a fast right-hander. Before then it was a fast straightaway into nine like it was when Foyt about got killed in '65. Daryl said Foster was hauling ass in that Charger going into nine and that brake drum exploded. He was going much faster than Weatherly, and it was at a different part of the track. After Billy Foster's death they made the window net rule. Weatherly's wreck aftermath was when they made everybody start using shoulder harnesses. And Earnhardt's death brought about mandatory use of the HANS device and soft walls.

The first time we ever used a window net was in a test at Riverside. Daddy and Buck Sewell were running a road course tire test with Andretti. Mario remembered it when we interviewed him on *Droppin' the Hammer*. What we used instead of a net was a piece of screen, like the kind in a screen door, that was pulled tight. It was the car Tiny had been driving. Instead of using the seat belt clip to secure it, they had a rod that went down in there, held by a cotter pin. By the way, Andretti demolished the car and we brought it back in a basket. But the crashes that really got the window net made mandatory were Billy Foster at Riverside in 1967 and Richard Petty at Darlington 1970.

Unfortunately, the circumstances for which desirable race car numbers become available are often connected to death. That was the case with Joe Weatherly's number 8 and Billy Wade's acquiring the number 1. Dale Earnhardt obtained number 15 from Bud Moore for a DEI car that went immediately to the Victory Lane in the Daytona 500, but Dale missed seeing it by a matter of minutes.

The first race the Fenleys tried was at Indianapolis with number 62 and Big Daddy's

BBQ Sauce adorning the sides. First Jeff Davis, then Lance Hooper tried to get the car in the field and failed. Greg was not there, and Bud was little more than an interested bystander. It was the Fenleys' deal.

On October 11, 1999, the car officially listed to Fenley-Moore Motorsports qualified for the 1999 UAW-GM Quality 500 at Lowe's Motor Speedway. Derrike Cope was now at the controls of number 15 and time-trialed twenty-fourth in a difficult field to make. Those who missed the show were Darrell Waltrip, Buckshot Jones, Dave Marcis, and Hut Stricklin. Cope out-timed Matt Kenseth, Jeff Burton, Bill Elliott, Elliott Sadler, Joe Nemechek, Ken Schrader, and Sterling Marlin, to name a few. Greg and Bud had sold the Fenleys top-notch equipment, but did not come along for the ride.

Derrike Cope qualified a nice twenty-fourth at Charlotte, and that was pretty tough then. But once again, that was the Fenleys fooling with that. He finished the race in thirty-fifth, six laps behind. Then 2000 rolled around and they went down to Daytona with Cope, and Knuckles was the crew chief. They actually paid him some good up-front money. Daddy went to assist them. I was invited to go, but I didn't want to. They made the Daytona 500 and we felt like we got them going pretty well. They started twelfth, using all our people and everything, and were doing fair. We kept trying to throttle them back on the money until they got a sponsor. "Oh, we'll get a sponsor here and a sponsor there." They were pumped up and had one deal they came fairly close on that fell through. They came close on Harrah's. They didn't do everything exactly right, but they were learning. They liked Spartanburg, and they were good to us. I think Robert even stayed up at our lake house until he got his built. They went through so much money so quickly, but they had already bought the shop and fulfilled their financial obligation with Daddy and me. Then when they didn't get a sponsor, they got a little nervous. They ran a few more races and ran through a ton of money — not only for the shop, but a ton of money playing.

The Fenleys' daddy finally came down to the shop and looked at the books, and he said, "Until you find a sponsor, don't you spend another nickel on this race team." He said the numbers weren't adding up. "It's a very foolish investment without a very lucrative sponsor."

Sue Fenley said, "We're working on it." And he answered, "I'm going to tell you again. I don't want to see another bill come across my desk." Basically what she had done was unload a ton of their company's stock to buy the shop. But when they got the word to put on the brakes, they put on the brakes. By that time, we had every nickel they owed us and were gone. They hung around for a year or two. Robert and Sue went on home, and Randy tried to run an ARCA car a little bit. They actually got into a lawsuit. I had told them that Cope was available if they wanted to sign him to a deal, and they did, but to one without a run-off clause. You can have a performance clause or a morality cause. They all have those. But it's a rule of thumb that you've got to have some fine print in there where if you absolutely have to, you can let the son-of-a-gun go. Well, they didn't have one in there. That's the reason Cope wound up getting all the contents out of the shop.

After all the hours and days and weeks and months that Greg and Bud spent trying to lure first a sponsor, then a partner, and finally a buyer for Bud Moore Engineering, the deal that succeeded required the least effort. A phone call, a visit, a meeting, and a deposit spanned a few hours during a couple of summer days, and it was done. For the Moores' whole family, a lifetime of racing was over. Oh, there was a phone call in early 2000 from Toyota asking if Bud Moore Engineering would be interested in the possibility of fielding a Craftsman Truck Series team, but that was practically laughed off. Greg, Daryl, and their father never, ever entertained entering any circuit other than the top tier of NASCAR stock car racing. When you have conquered the tallest mountain as often as the Moores did, a lower division is out of the question.

Now there was no more worrying about all the problems that had kept Greg up at night, staring into the dark, studying on a plan to keep the fire lit. No more frustrating negotiations, back stabbing, and broken promises. No more disappointment, heartbreak, and tragedy. But also gone were the satisfaction and unbridled joy of that most important of all by-products of auto racing: winning! Gone was the exhilaration of race day with the smells, the sounds, the explosion of colors, and the skin-crawling, heart-pounding feel at the green flag. Gone were the camaraderie and friendships cultivated over more than a half a century in the shop and garage. Never again would Mr. Flow take a hunk of metal and a bunch of glue to fabricate a piece of art that made a powerful engine stronger. No more partying with the stars during down time. No more figuring the gas mileage exactly right or taking two instead of four, resulting in checkers and trophies. Never again would Greg be chauffeured to Victory Lane in the winning car or dash there on foot in a transport of joy. The Golden Anniversary of Bud Moore Engineering was over. The Fenleys came, they saw, they bought, and the Moores went away. Always be careful what you wish for because you just might get it.

Chapter Nineteen

Moving On

At long last, Gregory Clyde Moore would get the chance to live like the rest of us on a permanent basis, more or less. He had experienced life as most everyone else could only dream of it. Now he could spend time with Roberta, be a hand on Bud and Betty's cattle ranch, and do some serious barstool racing. The proceeds from the sale of the race team were split up, and Greg would not have to file for unemployment any time soon. When Speedweeks 2001 rolled around, he followed it like most of us did: in the papers and on TV. On February 18, Greg watched the Daytona 500 with his father as his mom moved in and out of the room. It remains one of those indelible dates in history, and all racers remember where they were.

I watched the race out at the farm with Daddy. It was kind of weird watching it on TV after having been down there all those years. I didn't even watch all the races anymore, and not usually with Daddy. But this time I did.

Earnhardt's wreck didn't look all that bad to me. Of course he probably wouldn't have wrecked at all if he hadn't been blocking to help his cars win. Then, when he came to a stop and Schrader ran over and looked in at him and walked away so quick, Daddy and I had an idea something was terribly wrong. Darrell had said on TV that he hoped Dale was OK, and they were showing Michael in Victory Lane when the phone rang. Daddy answered and it was Pearson. He wasn't at the track; he was at his spread across town. He told Daddy that his sources had just told him that Earnhardt was dead. Daddy and I really couldn't believe it at first, but Pearson wouldn't kid about that. And we didn't think he was kidding. It was just a natural reaction to the news. I mean, nothing could kill Earnhardt—except Earnhardt.

We called Daryl and told him what Pearson had told us. By then the TV was showing the ambulance leaving the track real slow. We believed Pearson, of course, but this made it a sure thing, even though nobody on TV had said a thing about it yet.

A little while later, Brenty called and said, "Can you believe it? Our old driver Dale Earnhardt got killed, the winner had our old number 15, and Dale Jr. was second in a red and black number 8 just like Weatherly had." When he said that, we were amazed, maybe because we hadn't thought of it first. It was so obvious—but leave it to Brenty to come up with the numbers. Steve Park was also in the race, driving Earnhardt's third car with Billy Wade's old number 1. The whole thing seemed like a dream. Just an incredible nightmare.

Greg expounds on stock racing today, safety, and his friend Dale Earnhardt.

I don't like a lot of the stuff that's going on now. NASCAR doesn't like it. But it still beats the crap out of a bunch of $20-million-a-year people who play some of the other sports. It's still a pretty good show. I'm glad that it's safer. We lost Weatherly and Wade, but safety is about fixed. That's what we always wanted. A race driver is supposed to be a daredevil. There's not a damn thing that they've come up with that wasn't already discussed, like raising the halo and moving the driver over towards the center of the car. I argued for moving the driver over four inches in the '70s. What I wanted to do was put a radiator-type device to absorb inertia in the driver's door area. We could have done all that years ago. But they didn't react on a thing until Earnhardt got killed.

I'm not going to cuss them or fuss at them or whatever, but Dale Earnhardt was killed by a seatbelt that broke. He was blocking — something he's never done in his life as far as I know. All he'd ever done was run over somebody or knock them out of the way. He blocked, he hit the wall, and he took a lick. But it wasn't that bad. I've watched it time and time again. He went down, he went up, he hit, and the left side lap belt broke. In a five-point system, if the lap belt one side or the other comes loose, the rest of it's useless. Think about it. You bust that left side lap belt and it turns the whole system loose, and he went forward. If the belt had not broken, he would still be here.

The loss of his old pal Dale Earnhardt and the sale of the race team to the Fenleys really made a clean break for Greg and racing as he had known it. Starting what amounted to a second life, Greg turned his attention to other endeavors, some racing-related, some not. Greg profited handsomely from the sale of the team and as it turned out, he needed it all. He was busy; it was not always fun, and often quite expensive. Truth be told, Greg was wearing himself out all over again, using his expertise acquired running a race team, meeting everybody in the sport, and knowing the ropes.

I wasn't extremely wealthy, but I had a good amount of money in the bank. I didn't have any kind of big house payment or anything. Roberta was there. She had seen the bitter end, and I'm glad that she did. I've got a relationship where I'm not living by myself and I've got somebody I can look after. We haven't been acting foolish, just trying to stay healthy. We took a lot of cruises, which were lots of fun, and tried to enjoy life a little bit. There were a few health problems we had to battle, and mine got pretty serious for a while. I think I'm in the clear now and going to be fine, as will Roberta. It was expensive, though.

I started hanging out at Basil's because

Greg and Roberta enjoy time away from racing on a Caribbean cruise (Moore Family Collection).

they serve booze. Actually, it was close by and it was a classy neighborhood bar. On top of that, they were going to let me promote Cotton Owens Day and, later on, Daddy's book. We were going to do a David Pearson tribute in '99, a Bud Moore celebration in '01, and a Cotton Owens Day to help raise money for the Hall of Fame to be built in Spartanburg.

They did Pearson's around the plaza at the Denny's building downtown. It was a real exclusive thing. I helped at the tail end of that deal with Jerri Green, a woman realtor here in town. They wanted to do one on Daddy and he said, "Let Gregory handle it if you want to do one on me. He can get a hold of anybody." That was about a year-long project. I had an office to work out of downtown through Jerri. I was going down there to the office and staying about a half a day. The rest of the day I'd go by Basil's and talk to people, because I knew word of mouth was important. The Bud Moore Day turned out well. There wasn't an empty seat in the auditorium.

Then the Hall of Fame came along. I helped with the one they were going to build here in Spartanburg. I helped with a legends race they had at the Fairgrounds in 2002.

Greg (right) and Perry Allen Wood were reunited, after decades apart, at the legends charity race held at the Piedmont Interstate Fairgrounds in Spartanburg, South Carolina, in October of 2001 (Perry Wood Racing Collection).

Doug Smith was heading that up. I sat in on some meetings in Washington to get federal funds for that. Then I helped Dr. John Craft write Daddy's book, and that took a long time. It's called *Bud Moore: Man and Machine*. We also all went out to Monterey for Ford's 100th anniversary. I was staying pretty busy. I was involved in racing without racing. I had all this stuff I was involved with, but my health wasn't worth a damn. Momma's was going down, and I was depressed being out of racing.

Back in Greg's racing heyday, television was just figuring out that America loved stock car racing and money could be made showing it live rather than in syndication or on ABC's Wide World of Sports a week later. You could count on the announcers in the booth throwing it down to the reporter in the pits for a word with Bud, or very often, Greg. With his long, lean good looks and trademark black beard and mustache, Greg was quite the dashing figure as he explained the car's gas mileage to millions. Now in retirement, Greg first started appearing on local radio every Saturday morning, and he sounded as easy and at home as he does on a bar stool. Greg is a natural on air, and his start came easily.

I was up at Basil's, and Tina the bartender and I got to know each other really well. Her husband was struggling with cancer as Momma was. She let me put brochures about Daddy's book in there. I've known these people for years. Well, a guy named Dale Wilkerson had this local radio show called *Droppin' the Hammer* going on right up the hill at the radio station, WSPG AM. The show was about local racing, and came on from 8 to 8:30 on Saturday mornings. A great time slot—*not!*

I bumped into Flotacia Clark at Basil's, and she was getting paid a few dollars to plug the tapes in at the station in the early morning. She just had to get up early, walk a few steps over from her house to the radio station, unlock the door, and plug in the tape. She still does it. I got to be friends with her and she was in Basil's one day and Dale Wilkerson was, too. He's a super-nice guy. Flotacia told him, "I've got a friend who I bet could get some really big names to talk on your show if you want him to." Dale said, "Who you got?" She said, "Greg Moore."

"You mean Bud Moore's son Greg?"

"Yeah, he's here now and drinks beer all the time with these people."

Well, Dale called me over there. Now, if I had been Dale, I wouldn't have wanted somebody moving in on my turf. I said, "Dale, this is your show, but if you

Bud Moore: Man and Machine by Dr. John A. Craft was published by Carbon Press in 2009. Greg assisted in the writing of that book, which his mom Betty Moore, wanted to see completed in her lifetime (Perry Wood Racing Collection).

A remote charity broadcast of *Droppin' the Hammer* during the 2011 Christmas holidays with co-host Greg Moore on the left, host and show creator Dale Wilkerson in the center, and Perry Allen Wood on the right. Not pictured is co-host and engineer Ronnie Black (Perry Wood Racing Collection).

want me to, I'll make a few phone calls." Immediately, as soon as I got involved, I became the co-host, and it went to a new time slot: 11 am to 12 noon. They added a half hour and moved it to prime time when people are going to lunch. It just took off. Ronnie Black was the engineer and became the third co-host. Ronnie and Dale had been there for a while doing football. I said then that this thing had a chance. Dale gave me a segment called the Legends Spotlight. Then we started getting guests like Cotton Owens, Bobby Allison, everybody that ever drove for Daddy and more. Mike Helton, Edsel Ford, Don Hawk—you name him, he's been on the show.

That's when I told them, "Look, I got a good friend who might be the greatest NASCAR historian in the world. He could have had Buz McKim's job at the Hall of Fame, but he's actually already got a real job. Would y'all be interested? He knows this stuff better than I do. He's written a book on old speedways. You've got to get Perry Wood involved in this thing." I called Perry during the week and invited him over. He came straight from the soccer fields with his family when we were doing a remote from the Cellar. Daddy was the guest, and my family was there, and Perry won the trivia contest! That was pretty close to a rigged deal, with us being friends and Perry knowing all the answers.

From a little racing show that was a thirty-minute filler, *Droppin' the Hammer* has turned into a monster. I was well received and told Dale, "This is your racing show. I'm here to help. This will always be known as *Dale Wilkerson's Droppin' the Hammer.* I don't know how to do commercials. I can't use computers well. I've got to learn and y'all have to bear with me." I've learned very little about computers since! But one thing led to another, they got some sponsors and a great website, and the thing really started growing.

The basis for the show is to talk about local racing and the legends. We've got a balanced show. I think we get so much response to it because of the people on it. I lived it, Perry lived it as a fan and historian, and Dale was a fan and drove a go-kart a little bit. Perry has published two books about racing history, and he does segments from the books on the show. We've added another hour, so now we're on from 11 A.M. to 1 P.M. each Saturday. I have to give a ton of credit to the station manager then, Mark Hauser. That guy wears a lot of hats! He does his own show every day from 3 to 6 P.M. with Matt Smith and the Hawk. Hauser's also the voice of the Wofford Terriers and is on the road all the time with them. Dale and the show gets the green light on all these remotes we do from Darlington, Rockingham, the NASCAR Hall of Fame, Memory Lane Museum in Mooresville, and all over the Spartanburg area. Mark Hauser has been great and deserves all the credit we can give him for being such a gambler, and putting us on the air. Now Matt Smith is station manager and it's better than ever.

Greg (right) enjoys an evening with two very special people to him, his mentor Leonard Wood and wife Roberta (Moore Family Collection).

Gregory Clyde Moore is a battler. He comes by it naturally. He fought to keep up with the big kids in Fernwood when he was "Baby," often coming home bloody. He proved to be a hard-nosed competitor on the gridiron on both sides of the ball. As Mr. Flow he tackled complex technical issues to corral a handful of horses and eventually find more speed. Greg dueled with egocentric millionaire personalities behind the wheel and in the boardroom, holding his own and winning more times than he lost. Since his retirement, he's still racing around the country, promoting the sport he so dearly loves. A few health scares got in the way for Roberta and him, but those are being handled. Our story has the white flag: one more chapter to go.

CHAPTER TWENTY

Closure

Greg Moore went on racing without racing. In 2003, plans were made, ground was broken, and an eyesore of an old cotton mill within the city limits of Spartanburg was going to be transformed into a stock car hall of fame or racing museum. Events were held, money was raised, and Greg, Bud, Cotton, and David were all seriously in on it.

The idea for the NASCAR Hall of Fame came up from the Spartanburg situation when they realized that we had raised some money. Daddy and Pearson and Cotton made the suggestion to not go through NASCAR and try to do it on their own. Then we'd get support from them after we'd gotten it going. I went to some meetings in Washington to get funds, and we fell short about two million dollars that we needed to raise from other entities to get the federal government to put in funds. We did the fundraising deals and the legends races at the Fairgrounds to raise money. I was tickled to death that people like Jimmy Gibbs contributed to it. He put the air conditioning units into the old Beaumont Mill they were renovating for it. It was right next to Bud Moore Engineering.

Maybe it would have worked. I don't know. We got state money, but couldn't get to the real good federal money. We fell short, and NASCAR waited until our deal faltered. Then it got stagnant for a while. That's when we learned that NASCAR was going to build the Hall of Fame. When they learned we had raised X number of million dollars, they figured this was something pretty worthwhile. Initially, Daddy, Cotton, and I felt like the idea was stolen, but the more we got to thinking about it, maybe Spartanburg wasn't big enough to support the thing. But I think the area where they were going to put it was very good, right on North Pine Street, which turns into a big connector, I-585, to Interstate 85.

When NASCAR first started talk about the Hall of Fame, Bill France, Jr., was already sick. He said, "I think it's a great idea, but I'm not spending any money on a Hall of Fame because we have them in Daytona, Talladega, all over." France said he was behind it. Now they needed to get a city behind it. NASCAR put out all this publicity about Kansas City, Atlanta, and Richmond, but the Charlotte Visitation Authority put on a 2 percent bed tax or whatever it was to help finance it, and that financing won the day. I would have loved to have seen Spartanburg get it, but they put it in the perfect place. Although I was disappointed it wasn't going to be in Spartanburg, I was thrilled it was going to happen. I told Daddy and Cotton at lunch one day that I'm sorry all we did went for naught, but in a way it didn't. We did all those things that raised awareness that something needed to be done on a big scale, and NASCAR did it on a big scale. We made several trips up there with hard hats walking through the construction and were in on the bottom floor of the whole thing. We were invited to the ground breaking, but Daddy didn't want to go. So the NASCAR

Hall of Fame got built in Charlotte, it's only 75 miles up the road, it's got more traffic, there are more race teams up there. I think that Spartanburg still needs a smaller regional museum called the South Carolina Museum and Auto Racing Hall of Fame, but I also think the NASCAR hall in Charlotte is a beautiful place to honor the sport and its people.

> There was going to be a NASCAR Hall of Fame someday, somewhere, one way or the other. Greg makes a very convincing argument that Spartanburg's own effort was the spark that ignited the NASCAR project. The old Beaumont Mill is about a nine-iron across the main rail lines running into the Hub City across from the now historic former site of Bud Moore Engineering at 400 North Fairview Avenue. Recently, the shop housed the Converse College School of Dance. The only tenant the beautifully renovated mill ever got was the NCAA's Southern Conference Headquarters. The shop and the mill could have been tied together somehow with a bridge or a tunnel and Bud's place turned into a wing of the museum, housing—what else?—a race car shop exhibit. The South Carolina Museum and Auto Racing Hall of Fame is a great idea.
>
> The NASCAR Hall of Fame opened at 400 E. Martin Luther King, Jr., Boulevard in Charlotte, North Carolina, on May 11, 2011. Greg has been up there with his father on dozens of occasions. On October 14, 2009, the selection committee chose the inaugural five inductees, and Greg was not far away.

Once they got the thing built, Daddy, Cotton, Ned Jarrett, Richard Petty, Ricky Rudd, and a good mixture of people were put on the voting committee. They got promoters, previous car owners, drivers, and others. It's very diverse. There are people with NASCAR connections and people who have no affiliation with NASCAR anymore. I think that because Daddy and Cotton had so much to do with the Spartanburg effort, they were put on the voting committee. It's public record who's on the voting committee, and it isn't fixed. They've got some sort of professional company that tallies the voting the way it is done for Academy Awards, to make it fair so that nobody can question it."

The strange thing was, after they had the first vote, a lot of people got mad because they didn't go in the first round. They got into a fuss about the Frances. The Frances had to be in. Buz McKim and Winston Kelley, who run the NASCAR Hall of Fame, got into a big discussion about that, and they thought the Frances should have been automatic, which would have left two of the five spots open. But it was said that if they didn't get voted on, the Hall of Fame would have caught hell. So it was decided that the Frances had to be voted on like everybody else. They got voted in, and it was over with. What that did, though, was kick Pearson out of the first class, which was a tremendous screw-up.

So they're sitting in there, and everybody's going through the voting. I was up there, but I could not sit in the actual voting room. I was with Daddy every time he went up there. What they do, they get up in there and promote different people and say different things. It takes about half a day. Richard Petty said from the get-go that you had to do it chronologically. He said, "You've got to put Daddy in before you put me in." He was promoting Dale Inman and his daddy. Winston said, "Well, we kind of understand that, but we got to sell tickets. How can we open up a museum without having Richard Petty and Dale Earnhardt?" Lee Petty was fantastic. Just like Jack Smith, Buck Baker, Herb Thomas—*Herb Thomas!* Daddy and Cotton are sitting there arguing for Herb Thomas. Daddy might have gotten up and talked. Richard argued to the very end that to some degree the inductees should go in historical order. And there were even nominees in there saying, "I don't want to go in right now! You got to put this guy in." Barney Hall got up there and talked about

Pearson, talked about Daddy a little bit, and really talked about Junior Johnson. He lives up there near Junior. Different ones had arguments for different people. There was never an argument against somebody. There was always an argument *for* somebody. It wasn't like, "Well you can't put that son-of-a-bitch in there."

I'm not going to say that Daddy and Cotton didn't vote for themselves. But that's just one vote! You had a lot of the voters arguing for the older guys. You also had to think about the impact guys. Richard Petty's the King. You look at Earnhardt and both Frances. Those two should have been in automatically anyway, but you got to vote them in. The Frances should have been bronze statues standing out front. Now, who else do you put in?

The last guy to go in was the big question mark. When they made the big announcement and did not say, "David Pearson," but, "Junior Johnson," the room went quiet. It was unreal. Now don't get me wrong. Junior Johnson brought R. J. Reynolds in, won 50 races as a driver and six Winston Cup Championships, all this stuff. But everybody was waiting as they went down the list, and they did it in the order of the number of votes: France Sr. first. France Jr. second. You got the King third. You got Dale Earnhardt fourth. Now who's going to be the fifth guy? I figured it was about a 100 to 1 shot it was going to be Daddy or Glen Wood. Everybody thought that David Pearson had to be the fifth guy. Brian France hesitated for a second before he said the name, and when he said, "Junior Johnson," you could have heard a pin drop in the room. I hate to say that, because Junior Johnson definitely deserved to go in one of the first couple of rounds. I love Junior Johnson to death. He's a friend of mine. He helped NASCAR a lot. What flipped everybody out was the greatest race driver in the world didn't go in. I was not surprised that Daddy did not go in the first round. Not at all.

> *The controversy that swirled around the selection of the first five inductees still goes on to this day. But the next five inductees, announced on October 13, 2010, were rock solid selections and are known forever as the Class of 2011. Actually, that class was not entirely without controversy either. But for the Moore family, hearing one inductee's name was truly a dream come true.*

The next year we went through the second round of voting. We promoted the hell out of the Hall of Fame on *Droppin' the Hammer*, trying to get people to go up there. We gave NASCAR total access to the show to promote it. As good friends as Buz, Winston, and I are — and we talk to them all the time — nobody knows who's going in. Pearson and I were standing outside the door where they were voting. We weren't in on the deal. That stuff is top secret.

I still talk to the Wood Brothers a lot, and I talked to Len Wood, Glen's son, who is a year older than me and grew up in the sport, too. We looked at it from a realistic standpoint about who we thought would go in, at what point in time, and the whole thing. Maybe I was being too humble, but I felt like Glen Wood would be twelfth and Bud Moore would be sixteenth. That was my honest-to-God prediction. I picked Glen Wood in the second class and Bud Moore in the third or fourth class.

We were all up there in our seats, and Brian France started announcing the names of the second five inductees. I think it was the same day as the vote. Immediately, the Silver Fox, David Pearson, goes in. Immediately! Pearson was actually smiling instead of frowning, and everybody was tickled to death. They showed a film clip — they had film clips ready on all 25 nominees. Then they announced Bobby Allison, Lee Petty, and Ned Jarrett. Look at what Ned has done: 50 wins, two championships, took that Dale Carnegie course and learned to talk.

Then Brian France got ready to announce the fifth guy. Somebody brought out the envelope—it was sealed—and France said, "We're proud to announce the next inductee into the NASCAR Hall of Fame of 2011 ... Bud Moore."

The people went nuts! I did, too. They really got happy. I nearly messed up my britches. Daddy almost—he didn't, but almost—started crying. The Wood Brothers were sitting behind me and were tickled to death, too. Of course they wanted Glen to go in, and, being dead honest, I thought Glen was going to be twelfth and Bud sixteenth. I was very glad I was wrong. I had no idea Daddy was going to be voted in that quickly. I'm glad he went in while he was still alive so he could appreciate it. I felt like he deserved to be in the top 15 or 20, or better. Daddy went in fifth of the second class and tenth overall in the history of NASCAR.

I'm a little partial, but I think they got it right. He was the first non-driver car owner. You look at the others, and France Jr. is the only one who never raced or owned a race car. France Sr. drove; both Pettys, Earnhardt, Allison, Pearson, and Johnson drove and owned; and Jarrett just drove. Daddy was the first who just owned.

I guess it was a little controversial that Darrel Waltrip didn't go in. Waltrip was a hell of a race driver, and he had to fight a lot of different things. He paved the way for Earnhardt. He paved the way for the modern-day driver. Darrell Waltrip and I are very good friends now. Daddy and he are good friends now. Darrell and Stevie are wonderful people.

We had reporters interviewing us, and we felt like we were on top of the world. The only thing I can compare it to—and it's hard because I was 53 years old when Daddy was elected—is being a nine-year-old riding into Victory Lane with Darel Dieringer at Darlington, or being 21 years old when we won the Daytona 500. Of course, it will never take away losing those two drivers. Nothing could ever do that. We've got that with us forever.

The actual Bud Moore Engineering 1966 Mercury Comet that Darel Dieringer drove to victory in the Southern 500 that year was unloaded behind the Peach Blossom Diner in Spartanburg. Bud (left), Darel, and Greg were proudly there to see it on its way to the NASCAR Hall of Fame in Charlotte from Phoenix, where it was found and restored (courtesy Bud Moore Engineering Archives).

We spent that night in Charlotte at some high-dollar hotel, and when we got in the car the next morning I remember saying, "We did it! We got them!" I wasn't happy because we got in before Herb Thomas or Cotton or Buck Baker. I was happy we got in before they stuck a new guy in there, like a Hendrick or a Roush. I remember the Charlotte paper said, "A Perfect Class," four drivers and one owner. It made every bad thing that ever happened to me or the family seem worth it because he went in the top ten. Daddy's always been my hero and still is. He's my best friend.

The Walter "Bud" Moore exhibit at the NASCAR Hall of Fame is a proud display of information and actual artifacts from his fabulous career. The centerpiece is an amazing discovery, and nothing could be closer to Greg's heart and soul.

Daddy's exhibit in the Hall of Fame was built around the actual 1966 Mercury Comet that Darel Dieringer drove to victory at Asheville-Weaverville and two weeks later in the Southern 500. It didn't just carry Dieringer to Victory Lane at Darlington; it carried me, too. I couldn't believe they found it, but they did. It's got all the paperwork including the proof in the pudding, the correct VIN of the real Comet. Daddy, Daryl and I got our picture made with it, and it was such a proud moment for all of us. It's one of the most famous, if not, *the* most famous car in Bud Moore Engineering history. It was perfect to represent him in the museum display.

Greg tells of a surprise phone call he received and shares some thoughts on the Hall of Fame selection, future nominations, and inductees.

Darrell Waltrip just called me out of the blue one evening. I had talked to him about a week earlier about being on *Droppin' the Hammer*. Roberta answered the phone. She said, "Yeah, Darrell, he's right here," and handed me the phone. I thought it was my brother! I thought, "Now what in the world is Daryl doing, calling me at seven o'clock at night?" It was Waltrip!

He commenced to talk about our past problems. "I feel bad that there was bad blood between Bud and me over that rookie thing, but that car did run. You had to run just a little bit different line because that big motor had just a little bit more torque. We didn't know that we were running against 454s and illegal restrictor plate stuff." We were. That's what Bobby Allison exposed up there at Charlotte, and it didn't fall too favorably with NASCAR that he did that. Daddy and Waltrip are good friends now. Daddy was the first guy to hug Darrell when he came off the stage after getting announced into the Hall of Fame at his ceremony. Kyle Petty said that back in the day there were only two cuss words you couldn't say at their shop: "Darrell" and "Waltrip."

About us getting in the Hall, Daddy made the statement, "Probably one of the reasons we went in in the top ten was because there's almost nothing that we didn't come up with first. We even came up with the Minor's Release so a kid could get in the pits." Daddy, Daryl, and France Sr. handled that. Now Cotton, from what I understand, was the next one vote-wise in the Class of 2012 behind Waltrip, Dale Inman, and — thank goodness — Glen Wood. That one really made all the Moores happy. We've always been close with the Woods. So when my mentor Leonard Wood was elected to the Class of 2013, I was ecstatic. And Cotton Owen was elected with him and has been our friend forever. It was even better with Buck Baker who won a championship and Southern 500 with Daddy. Now we need to get Smokey Yunick, Raymond Parks and Wendell Scott in.

In July of 2012, Greg Moore stands at 400 North Fairview Avenue, where he lived his dreams from boyhood until today and saw them come true for nearly 50 years (courtesy Bud Moore Engineering Archives).

As Greg reflected on his career in stock car racing since the Hall of Fame announcement, he could not help recalling some of the good times he had, the people he met, and how it has all changed so very much. These days there probably are not that many late night card games back at the motel either. One in particular will haunt Greg forever and ever.

We were down in a hotel at Talladega in 1983, and we used to play three-card gut. They deal you three cards and the best hand you can get is three of a kind, which happens about once every 50 years. You get to draw no cards. You get three cards and you bet. If you've got a high pair, you have a pretty good shot at taking the pot. But if you hang in there and bet and go along with it and you lose, you have to match the pot. Now, you can also fold over. If you get a king and a six and a deuce, you don't want to hang around. You just turn your cards over.

I'd already got about four or five hundred dollars in my pocket. It was Harold Stott, Steve Eden with Crane Cams, Earl Parker with Champion Spark Plugs, Earnhardt, and me. You had to have about four people playing. We're drinking my beer; Earnhardt went and got some liquor. I was up real good because I'd been dealt a pair of tens a couple of times, a pair of queens a couple of times, some good hands.

Well, it was eight or nine o' clock at night and Junior's crew was coming in. They stuck their heads in the door and saw what was going on. Henry Benfield came in, and so did Jeff Hammond. Jeff's a good guy and I like him. He's the pretty boy on Fox TV's race coverage now. Steve Eden left the game to go get something to eat, and Jeff said, " I'll play a hand."

I have never gotten over what happened next. The cards were dealt out. There was about $400 in the pot. I got dealt two aces and a queen. There isn't anything going to beat that. Best hand anybody's had all night, and I'm red hot. Can't lose. People drop out. Hammond said, "Yeah, I'm staying." I talk to myself: "*I got this.*" I said, "I got two aces and a queen." He turned over three sevens. In one hand he gets $400. That's what pissed me off. One hand! It wound up costing me $100 or something in the long run, but in one hand he got dealt three sevens. And I'd been playing right, laying low, playing cards right. I was really getting ready to hit me a doggone lick because the game was about to get over with anyway. I'll never get over the three sevens Jeff Hammond turned over on me at Talladega in 1983. But ... we won that race, too.

Remember that Greg said, "What happens on the road stays on the road." He never wavered from that, not even off the record. Greg is loyal to his friends, and probably his enemies, and just would not talk about some things. As for the antics of today's NASCAR members on and off the track, Greg's father is part of a diverse group on the Appeals Committee. He hears the explanations and alibis of alleged wrong-doers and has the power to overturn a NASCAR ruling. Greg is most reluctant to discuss this and gave just one brief example.

Daddy is on the Appeals Committee. He's been doing that up in Charlotte all the time. It is fair. They have a NASCAR rep and two other people who do the voting who are promoters, past car owners, and not a whole lot of people. It is a fair system. You can beat an accusation. NASCAR is a little bit more of a democracy than people think. Of course I liked it better when it was a dictatorship because we were friends with the dictator. That helps!

Michael Waltrip gave the finger out the doggone window on TV on the in-car camera. But he just barely did it. Somebody had wrecked him or got in his way. The TV cameras caught it, he got fined, and he appealed it. John Darby said, "Well, he intended to do it." Daddy said, "I don't know if he intended to do it or not." Somebody else said, "He didn't do it. All he did was hang his hand out the window and he really sort of didn't. He did, but he didn't." Those are borderline calls, and that's one time they overruled it. Michael said, "Yeah, I really appreciate it."

Greg and his family had never drifted far from religion, in spite of the world in which they spent the racing years. Remember, if not for Bobby Allison coming over in 1978, it might have been the Rev. Gregory C. Moore.

Bethlehem Baptist Church over there in Roebuck is where Daddy's momma went. His brother Ralph's a deacon, and a lot of the Moore family goes. It's only been around since 1800 and is a lot older that Spartanburg itself. Not all of the family goes, but a lot of them do, and I go with Daddy sometime. The preacher would come out to the house when Momma was sick, and the guy's super-nice. Daddy had a gap there that he didn't go — like about 50 years. He has time to go now. He always was a Christian, but how do you race and go to church? It's tough. But you can make sure your kids go, and I'm glad that he did. Betty Smith, Jack's wife, goes there, and I've been meaning to go back more often than I do.

The Hall of Fame induction for Bud Moore was truly the stuff dreams are made of. In fact, a lot of dreams came true for Greg and his family, especially for the woman who spent 64 years as the matriarch. Betty Moore was a pillar of strength and support for all that time. She and Greg discussed what she wanted to see come to pass.

Momma told me after we all knew she was sick, "I want a book written on your daddy and in my hands." We made it by four months when she was still in pretty good shape. She got to look at it and be proud of it. She also knew how hard Daddy and Cotton and Pearson and I worked on getting a museum in Spartanburg and holding Cotton Owens Day and Bud Moore Day. She also knew the museum got built in Charlotte instead of Spartanburg. She said, "I want your daddy in that Hall of Fame." I think she knew in her heart and her mind that Daddy would go in, but I don't think she thought he would go in so quickly.

There was one other thing that bothered her. Darrell Waltrip had starting doing the announcing thing, and he and Daddy didn't get along real well. Momma heard Waltrip say something sarcastic during a race on TV after she'd already gotten sick. One day I was taking her to the radiation treatment and she told me that somebody had said something about Daddy and Waltrip had said, "Oh yeah, Bud Moore," in kind of a sarcastic tone. That really got away with Momma — more so than it did with me. I heard it, too, and thought, "Big deal." I told Momma, "It'll get handled." And it did. After seeing Darrell Waltrip almost cry on TV for not getting to go into the Hall of Fame when Daddy did, I figured it was even. It was handled.

Momma died in November of 2009. We had time to prepare for it. I don't know of her having any enemies. Betty France loved her, everybody loved her, and she supported Daddy through everything. She was old school, behind him and us kids 100 percent. I do remember that when I was sick one time, I wasn't quite sure I was going to get through everything, and we knew she wasn't going to get through everything. She and I talked about it over the phone when nobody was listening. She said, "Baby, at least the bad stuff's happening to you and me, because you and me couldn't have handled it happening to somebody else in the family." I said, "Momma, that's exactly right."

What beautiful words from a wonderful lady. In helping and watching his mom's last wishes come true, Greg added his own personal goals. There is also another byproduct of getting into the Hall of Fame.

I achieved three objectives. We got the book *Bud Moore: Man and Machine* written and in Momma's hands in time. I think Dr. John Craft did a wonderful job. Daddy got in the Hall of Fame. And Bud Moore and Darrell Waltrip hugged and made up. Those three things needed to happen, and I'm thankful that they did. Also, Daddy's getting into the Hall of Fame has kept his health up, though he was in great health anyway. I don't think the timing of it had an effect on the voting. It's helped heal a lot of wounds. I'll be quite honest: I feel pretty good. I don't worry about stuff as much. I get more tickled about doing things like the radio show, writing this book, and going up to the racing festivals in Hillsborough and Mooresville. I got a big kick out of those. I'm flattered.

With seven months to savor the experience and aftermath of the Hall of Fame selection, the big day finally arrived. On May 23, 2011, the Class of 2011 was presented to the world on national TV. Greg and the Moore family were seated in the audience right behind the tenth inductee.

They had a photographer who took a picture of the whole family. Then they broke it up and had Daddy with each of his kids and their families. They had Daddy, Roberta, Roberta's son Jason, who is my stepson, and me. I've never been treated so well by the NASCAR community and never felt so proud in my entire life. It was terribly emotional. As I said when I did the eulogy for our pilot Bill Carr, 'When Daddy went in, it was a group of us that went in.' I felt like it was a victory not only for Daddy, but a big victory for Spartanburg through all the people that supported him, like the friends we've had. I personally think that in the last 25 years we raced, he didn't want to do it without me, and I know that I didn't want to race without him. I made a statement in 1990, when we were leading the points and there was a press conference. I told them then, "My interest in racing goes no further than Bud Moore. When Bud Moore quits racing, I'll stop racing." Maybe it was the right thing to say and maybe it was the wrong thing to say. But I said it and I meant it. And I did it.

There was a lot of stuff Daddy did before me and a lot of stuff that happened that I was involved in. And now what we do is have fun. We enjoy our kids, our grandkids, and our friends. We talk on radio shows, write books, and do TV. We have a good time, and everything is fine now.

Greg stood at his father's side, his right hand man, and maneuvered Bud Moore Engineering through the good times and the bad. He had perhaps the greatest mentor in the sport to guide him. Greg was blessed with an incredibly strong and supportive mother to advise him and be the voice of reason when confusion obscured his path. Finally, Greg had two brilliant brothers whose ideas and confidence in him contributed immensely to the team's success. That success was manifested in scores of checkered flags and a Hall of Fame career not just for one, but for all the Moore family. There were wins and losses, happiness and despair, life and death, and an overwhelming feeling of satisfaction in the end. They went into the Hall of Fame together, did the Moores, because they pulled as one with Greg as a leader. A leader with a heart and a legend's right hand man.

Basically, by fulfilling the things that Momma wanted and the family wanted, I felt like I contributed to whatever success we enjoyed. Obviously I didn't fill Daddy's shoes. They cannot be filled. But I feel better about myself. I can look at my face in the mirror and say, "Maybe I did OK. Maybe everything's all right." The Hall of Fame just fixed a lot of things. I made mistakes — like the Rick Hendrick thing in Japan — but I can still fix that, too. I'm feeling a lot better. The radio show has helped a lot. Writing this book is helping a ton. It has enabled me to rethink my whole life and feel good about it.

I have no desire to run a race car or anything, but I do have a desire to preserve the history and integrity of the sport. I want to help it grow today. That's what we do on *Droppin' the Hammer*, and we get so much response from it. We want to get people in the stands.

Pick yourself a hero! If you like Tony Stewart, that's good. There isn't any Fireball Roberts any more. There isn't a Joe Weatherly. Richard Petty and David Pearson have retired. Hell, pick Danica Patrick! Keep it going, because if we don't, we'll lose a great thing, which is the continuation of a fabulous southern idea and a huge piece of our heritage.

Overall, I think the thing I'm most happy about is years of fooling with an internal combustion motor, and having famous heroes like Daddy, Leonard Wood, and Smokey Yunick. I got to live that dream and be somewhat successful with it. I met all these wonderful people and feel very blessed.

Greg Moore (right) and Perry Allen Wood in a recording session for this book. There were 17 such sessions, with a 90 minute audio tape created on each occasion. The site of each session was Wood's residence office (Perry Wood Racing Collection).

Two of these very wonderful and blessed people very close to my family remind that life is always changing. On April 10, 2012, probably one of our oldest friends passed away after a long illness. That was Dorothy Owens, Cotton's wife. It would take another book to tell how well we were all treated by Dot Owens and how much we loved her. She was at Cotton's side through all his hundreds of wins as the driver known as "the King of the Modifieds" and in 1966 as the Grand National Championship car owner. Dot was there for the bad times as Cotton took some tough licks in terrible crashes as a driver over the years. Dot was there for all of it. When Dot passed away, Cotton Owens was right behind her. He apparently had no desire to continue without her. Cotton Owens turned 88 years old on Monday, May 21, and on Wednesday, May 23 was voted into NASCAR Hall of Fame as he so richly deserved. His achievements are as book-worthy as anybody's in the sport. Daddy and his best friend and daily companion since before World War Two were both alive in the Hall of Fame. Even though Cotton was slipping fast, he knew he had made the Hall and was outwardly pleased. But Cotton wanted more to be with Dot than to carry on in this place, and on June 6, 2012, he joined her again. If you don't think losing those two so close together doesn't leave a hole in your life, then nothing will. That era is over — Dot and Cotton gone within weeks of each other. But it is very fitting that three of Cotton's toughest competitors made it in the same NASCAR Hall of Fame class as he did: Herb

Thomas for whom Cotton and Daddy fought so hard, hoping to see him in the Hall; Buck Baker, who drove Daddy's first Grand National Championship car in 1957 and won a Southern 500 with in 1960, and the unbeatable Tim Flock. With these inductees, and with Wendell Scott becoming one of the eligible 25, I think the voters really got it right for 2013.

I have a wife and stepson, and I'm happier now than I've been. My health is better, Daddy went in the NASCAR Hall of Fame, and we've healed from losing Momma, because those things happen and she passed away at ease. I'm not rich, but money can't buy pride. I've got more pride than I've ever had in my life. I've got more to be happy about and feel good about, than I have to be sad about. When I look in the mirror, I'm not too pretty, but I'm OK with it. After all is said and done, I can live with myself. It's called "closure."

The Baby, Gregory Clyde Moore, fought and won in one of the toughest arenas in sports and life. His work was his passion, and we should all be so lucky. What an achievement, to travel the world with other famous people we love and admire, for a quarter of a century, doing our job, and, then end up in the NASCAR Hall of Fame. Bud Moore said the family all went in together, and it is absolutely true. The fellow Greg sees in the mirror every day is truly a Hall of Fame right hand man.

Bibliography

Craft, John A. *Bud Moore: Man and Machine*. Holly Hill, Florida: Carbon Press, 2009.
Ganahl, Pat. "Talking Heads." *Hot Rod*, Vol. 39, no. 2 (February 1986).
Gerald, Dick. "Southern 500." *Stock Car Racing*, Vol. 2, no. 1 (January 1967).
McCredie, Gary. "Racing Won Out in the End." *Grand National Scene*, Vol. 2, no. 4 (July 1983).
Myers, Bob. "The Daytona 500." *Stock Car Racing*, Vol. 13, no. 5 (May 1978).
The Spartanburg Herald-Journal, August 26, 1964.
Wood, Perry Allen. *Silent Speedways of the Carolinas: The Grand National Histories of 29 Former Tracks*. Jefferson, North Carolina: McFarland, 2007.

Websites

www.budmoore.us
www.google.com
www.merriam-webster.com
www.militarytimes.com/valor/army-sgt-stephen-c-high
www.racingone.com
www.racing-reference.com
www.youtube.com

Index

Page numbers in **_bold italics_** indicate illustrations.

AAA *see* Automobile Association of America
Abbeville, SC 39
ABC (Sports/TV/ *Wide World of Sports*) 4, 34, 73–74, 90, 204
Adcox, Grant 60, 198
Afghanistan 42
Alabama 66, 74
Alabama Gang 76
Alabama International Speedway (Talladega) 4, 49, 53–54, 58, 60–**_64_**, 65, **_67_**, 68, **_69_**, 79, 96, **_101_**, 105–107, 116, 144, 148, 152, 155, 157, 159, 172–173, 175, 190
Alexander, Blaise 188
Allen, Donnie 25, 46
Allison, Bobby 6, 44, 51, 53–55, 58, 63, 71–**_75_**, 76–**_81_**, 82–83, 85, 90, 93, 97–98, 109, 135, 145, 152, 161, 188, 197, 205, 209–211, 213
Allison, Bonnie 75, 81
Allison, Clifford 81
Allison, Davey 50, 81, 142, 152, 154–155, 187
Allison, Donnie 48, 54–55, 67, 77–79, 81, **_90_**
Allison, Judy 75
Allison, Pop 75, 81
AMC Matador 60, 71, 81, 97
American Revolution 196
American Speed Association (ASA) 168
American Veterans of Foreign Wars (AMVETS) 196
Amway 59
Anderson, M. C. 69, 73, 90
Anderson, Sterling 37–39
Andretti, Mario 6, 198
ARCA *see* Auto Racing Club of America
Ard, Sam 116

Arizona: Phoenix 132, 210; Yuma 16
Army 42, 63
Arnie, Dave 151
ASA *see* American Speed Association
Asheville-Weaverville, NC 37, 44, 211
Atlanta 4, 6, 44, 46, 172, 176–177, 186, 193, 207
Atlanta 500 8, 60, 79, **_113_**, 130
Atlanta International Raceway (Atlanta/Atlanta Motor Speedway) 4, 24, 55, 57, 63–64, 76, 80, 82, 85, 90, 92–93, 114, 122–123, 127, 130, 132–133, 148, 156, 163, 173, 184, 198
Atlanta Motel 4, **_24_**, 47
Atlantic Ocean 7, 157
Auten, Buster 112, 182
Auto Racing Club of America (ARCA) 65, 184, 188, 199
Autolite Spark Plugs 152
Automobile Association of America (AAA) 7
AutoNation Car Dealers 195

B and B Studios (SC) 193, 195
Babbitt Bearings 92
Bachman, Jim 171
Bahamas 160
Baker, Buck 3, 8–9, 25, 52, 62–63, 92, 147, 186, 189, 208, 211, 217
Baker, Buddy 25, 31, 43, 46, 60–**_64_**, 65–**_67_**, 68, **_69_**, 71, 74–75, 78–80, 88, 97, 116, 120, 122, 161, 179, 190
Baker, Gary 12, 14
Ball, David 18
Ball, Dr. 36, 71
Balmer, Earl 32, 34
Barber, Miller 18

Barr, Buddy 55
Basil's (SC) 202–204
Beadle, Raymond 100
Beam, Alex 92
Beam, Herman "The Turtle" 34
Bean, Joe 179–180
Bearfinder 76
Beaty, Dick 27, 97, 111–112, **_119_**, 128
Beaumont Mill, SC 207–208
Bell, Buster 16, 61–62
Bell Dry Cleaners 61
Benfield, Henry 134, 213
Benson, Johnny 179
Bernstein, Kenny 109, 114, 117, 123, 125
Bethlehem Baptist Church (SC) 213
Bettenhausen, Gary 60
Big Daddy's Barbeque Sauce 198–199
Bilstein Shock Absorbers 167
Black, Ronnie 6, **_205_**
Black Cat Fireworks 134
Blackburn, Bunkie 46
Blocker, Dan "Hoss" 19
Blue Ridge Mountains 70
Bluebell Clothes 86
Bob Bondurant's Driving School 168
Bodine, Brett 116–**_119_**, 120–126, 132, 135, 139, 145, 147, 168, 183
Bodine, Geoff 8, 96, 99, 108–109, 131–133, 136–140, 142, 144–**_147_**, 148–**_149_**, 150–152, 154–157, 172–173, 175
Bodine, Kathy 150
Bodine family 94
Bonanza 19
Bonner, Dr. 31, 61, 112
Bonnett, David 152
Bonnett, Neil 79, 92, 96–97, 108, 120, 152

Boone, Kirby 116
Bouchard, Ron 100, 104, 109
Boy/Cub Scouts 36
Bradberry, Gary 181
Bradshaw, Charlie 34
Brainerd, MN 51–53
Brewer, Tim 135, 139, 142
Brickyard 400 (IN) 125, 154, 160
Bridgehampton, NY 26
Briggs and Stratton Motors 189
Bristol, TN 149–150
Bristol International Speedway 1, 22, 62, 90, 92, 105, 112, 149, 153–154, 156–157, 168, 161, 197
Bristol Lincoln-Mercury 22, 33
Brockman, Bunny 16
Broderick, Bill 52
Brooks, Bob 149
Brooks, Dick 8, 54–55, 76
Brown, Cleve 18, 33–34
Buckley, Charles 49
Bucknam, Ronnie 53
Bud Moore Engineering (Team) 5, 22, 24–27, 31, 33, 37, 44, 48–49, 51, 53–54, 56–57, 62–64, 68, 70–72, 75, 79, 82–83, 89, 92, 101, 107, 109–110, 117, 120, 127, 135, 138–140, 142, 145, 151–155, 157, **158**, 163, 165, 167–169, 171, 173, 176–177, 180–183, 185–186, 189–**190**, 191–192, 195–196, 199–200, 207–208, **210**, 211, 215
Bud Moore: Man and Machine **204**, 214
Bud Moore's Garage (SC) 12–13, 15, 17, 41, 70
Budweiser Beer 100, 102, 137, 163, 175, 178
Buick 76, 79, 109, 114, 117
Bull's Eye Barbeque Sauce 117
Burgess, Billy 66
Burrell, Bill 110, 122
Burrell, Larry 42–43
Burton, Jeff 199
Busch Beer 35
The Busch Clash 80, 84, 88, 96–97, 108–109, 128, 140, 142, 145, 148, 152, 173, 185
Busch Series 81, 84, 107, 116, 125, 134, 152, 167, 173, 181, 186, 188
Bush, George H. W. **146**
Byron, Red 8

Cadillac 173
California 19, 21, 131, 187, 195–196; Caravan Inn 20; Champion Bridge 19; Disneyland 19; Hodgdon Industries 76; Hollywood 19; Los Angeles 188; Monterrey 48, 204; Norris Industries 63–64, 69, 71–72, 76; Ontario Motor Speedway (Ontario) 64, 76; Paramount 19; Riverside 102, 110; Riverside International Raceway 19–22, 36, 44, 79, 85, 101, 111, 147, 196, 198; Sears Point/Sonoma 8, 131–132, 152–153, 155, 167–168, 174–175; Wine Country 131; Winston Western 500 101
Camaro 45–46, 48, 53
Canada: Edmonton, Alberta 51; St. Jovite, Quebec 49
Capri Lounge (SC) 67
Car of Tomorrow 125
Caravan Inn 20
Carelli, Rick 179
Carnegie, Dale 209
Carnegie, Tom 160
Carolina 500 (NC) 89
Carolina Spartan 7
Carr, Bill 137, 149, 215
Carroll, Lenny 14
Carter, Travis 143–145, 147–148, 151, 171, 179
Castaway Motel (FL) 4, 16, 23, 34–35
CBS TV 4, 87–88, 97, 108, 148–**149**, 166
The Cellar (SC) 5, 205
Champion Bridge 19
Champion Spark Plugs 212
Charger 60, 198
Charleston, SC 7, 176–177
Charlotte, NC 120, 150, 178–179, 183, 197, 208, **210**, 211, 213
Charlotte Fairgrounds (NC) 8
Charlotte Motor Speedway (Lowes' Motor Speedway) 6, 8, 23–24, 27, 46, 55, 57–58, 69, 76, 118, 122–123, 130, 132, 154, 163–**164**, 168, 182–184, 188, 199
Charlotte Observer 178
Charlotte Visitation Authority 207
Chattanooga Bakeries 192, 195
Chemung, NY 139
Cherokee County, SC 39
Chesapeake, VA 105
Chester, SC 39
Chevrolet en}8, 48, 54, 56, 69, 76, 79–80, 82–84, 93, 98–100, 139, 169, 186, 192; Camaro 45–46, 48, 53
Chicago 5, 148, 177
Chicago Bears 38
Chihuahua 110

Childress, Richard 86, 99–100, 105, 153, 169, 198
Christian, Frank 8
Christie, Diane 176, 177
Chrysler 29, 73
Cincinnati, OH 7
Cinderella 72, 121, 190, 192
Citgo Gasoline 171
Clark, Clyde 11
Clark, Ethel Gregory 11, 70
Clark, Flotacia 204
Clark Street garage (Chicago) 148
Clements, Crawford 3
Clements, Louis 3, 8
Clements family 61
Clemson University 38, 40, 70, 132
Cleveland Hotel (SC) 7
Clinton, SC 71
Coca-Cola/World 600 (NC) 23, 46, 57, 118, 120, 123, 182
Coconut Grove, FL 149
Cody, Morris 61–62, 65
Coke 16
Columbia, SC 8, 16, 46
Colvin, Bob 34–35, 37; daughter 35
Comet/Cyclone/Marauder/Montego 3, 14, 18, 19, 21–22, 24, 29–**30**, 31, 33, 37–**38**, 44–47, 51, 58, 71, 75–76, 79–80, 82, 85, 189, **210**, 211
Community Cash (SC) 13
Concord, NC 20, 46
Conoco Motor Oil 189
Conover, NC 138
Conseco Insurance 186
Converse College (School of Dance) 7, 42, 208
Cooper, L. Gordon 49
Coors Beer 114
Cope, Derrick 130, 197, 199
Coppertone 63
The Corners Apartments (SC) 137, 180
Cougar 44–46, 48–49, 80–**81**, 82, 85
Cowpens, SC 6, 22
Craft, Dr. John **204**, 214
Craftsman Truck Series 200
Crane Cams 212
CRC Chemicals Rebel 300/500 (SC) 14, **90**, **91**, **92**
Crisco 116–**119**, 120, 122–123
Crown Plastic Mastic 50
Cuba 60

Dahlonega, GA 130
Dale Earnhardt Incorporated (DEI) 198

Dallenbach, Wally 171–*174*, 175–176, 178–181, 192–193
Darby, John 213
Darlington International Raceway (SC) 1, 4–6, 34, 37, 44, 52–53, 55, 57–58, 79, 90, 92, 105, 111–112, 114, 126, 148, 156, 160, 166, 168, 173, 187, 189–*190*, 198, 206, 210
Daughtry, Dan 60
David and Goliath 176
Davis, Bill 162, 171
Davis, Earl "Strawberry" 126, 144, 177
Davis, Jeff 195, 199
Daytona, FL 1, 4, 8, *12*, 34, 63, 71–72, 76–77, 94, 121, 156, 165, 172, 180, 207
Daytona 500 1, 24, 29, 45–46, 53–54, 59, 62, 64–65, 68–70, 74–77, 79–80, 83, 88–89, 93, 98, 105, 108, 117, 130, 142–144, 148, *149*, 156, 166, 172–173, 176, 181–182, 198–199, 201
Daytona International Speedway 8, 14–16, 22, 26, 28–31, 34, 44–46, 48–49, 51, 58, 71, 73, 79, *81*, 82, 88, 90, 96, 99, 105, 110, 117, 123, 125, 128, 138–139, 142, 144–*146*, 148, 152, 157, 161, 163, 167, 172–173, 181–182, 185–188, 192–193, 199
Daytona USA 182, 184
Dearborn, MI 84, 113, 122, 167
"The Declarations of Stock Car Independents" 6
Delaney, Bill 37
Delaney, Jim 29
Delaware: Dover 93; Dover Downs 60, 76, 82, 98, 114, 117, 121–122, 131–132, 134, 147, 154, 175, 179; Iron Gate 93
DeLoach, Jim 15
Deluxe Diner (SC) 43
Denny's (SC) 202
Depression 121
Despain, Dave 121
DeWitt, Ray 151, 154
Dickerson, Bill 18, 33
Dickerson, George 71
Dieringer, Darel 26–27, 29–30, 32, 34, 37–*38*, 51–53, 68, 75, 92, 155, 189, *210*, 211
Digard 59, 66, 82
Dinner Bell Foods 124
Disneyland (CA) 19
Dixie 400 (GA) 24–*25*, 44
Dixon, Donna 183
Doberman Pinscher 110
Dodge 8, 60; Charger 60, 198
Dodge City 167

Dolan, Mose 85
Donahue, Mark 48, 51–52
Donleavy, Junie 54, 73, 76, 114
Donnybrooke International Speedway (MN) 53
Dorton, Kieth 144
Dorton, Randy 144
Dover, DE 93
Dover Downs (DE) 60, 76, 82, 98, 114, 117, 121–122, 131–132, 134, 147, 154, 175, 179
Drake, Bill 5
Drayton, SC 14
Droppin' the Hammer (DTH-radio show) 5–6, 168, 189, 198, 204, *205*, 209, 211, 215
Duke Power 70
Duncan Park (SC) 7
Dunes Motel (FL) 12
Dusenberg 8

Eargle, Eugene "Pop" 15–16, 27
Earnhardt, Dale 53, 79, 81, 85–86, 88–*90*, *92*, 93–*95*, 96–104, 108–110, 114, 123, 130–131, 140, 142, 145, 148–*149*, 151, 153, 156, 161, 165–166, 169, 171–173, 175, 179, 186, 189, 198, 201–202, 208–210, 212; *see also* Dale Earnhardt Incorporated
Earnhardt, Dale, Jr. 201
Earnhardt, Teresa 103
Eastern Air Lines 20
Economacki, Chris 4
Edelbrock 55, 145
Eden, Steve 212–213
Edmonton, Alberta 51
Edsel 6, 85, 110, 150, 205
Elder, "Suitcase" Jake 58–59, 72, 82–83, 146
Ellington, Hoss 77, 117
Elliott, Bill 106, 110, 114, 128, 132, 136–137, 142, 199
Elliott, Ernie 99, 130, 137, 145
Elliott family 98, 132
Emery, Dan 172
England/English 66, 139, 145
Erp, John 166
ESPN 4, 87, 149
ESPNU 97, 145, 147, 168
Eubanks, Cotton 7
Eubanks, Joe 8, 189
Evans Junior High School (SC) 4, 39
Everette, Bert 53
Evernham, Ray 122
Exide Batteries 154

Family Channel 151
Farmer, Red 152

Favre, Brett 183, 185–186
Fenley, Randy 196–199
Fenley, Robert 196–197, 199
Fenley, Sue 196–197, 199, 202
Fenley-Moore Motorsports 197, 199
Fernwood, SC 3, 11–*13*, 14, 18, 29, 31, 33–43, 62, 71, 110
Firecracker 250/400 4, 8, 16, 26, 35, 45–46, *81*, 132, 144–*146*, 157, 173
Firestone 29, 48–49, 52
First Baptist Church (SC) 43
First Union Bank 175
Fisher, Carl 159
Flock, Bob 8
Flock, Fonty 8
Flock, Tim 217
Florida Power and Light 70
Florida 51, 117, 123, 183; The Busch Clash 80, 84, 88, 96–97, 108–109, 128, 140, 142, 145, 148, 152, 173, 185; Castaway Motel 4, 16, 23, 34–35; Coconut Grove 149; Daytona 1, 4, 8, *12*, 34, 63, 71–72, 76–77, 94, 121, 156, 165, 172, 180, 207; Daytona 500 1, 24, 29, 45–46, 53–54, 59, 62, 64–65, 68–70, 74–77, 79–80, 83, 88–89, 93, 98, 105, 108, 117, 130, 142–144, 148, *149*, 156, 166, 172–173, 176, 181–182, 198–199, 201; Daytona International Speedway 8, 14–16, 22, 26, 28–31, 34, 44–46, 48–49, 51, 58, 71, 73, 79, *81*, 82, 88, 90, 96, 99, 105, 110, 117, 123, 125, 128, 138–139, 142, 144–*146*, 148, 152, 157, 161, 163, 167, 172–173, 181–182, 185–188, 192–193, 199; Daytona USA 182, 184; Dunes Motel 12; Firecracker 250/400 4, 8, 16, 26, 35, 45–46, *81*, 132, 144–*146*, 157, 173; Florida Power and Light 70; Howard Johnson's 94; Lake Lloyd 77; Miami 149; 125 mile qualifying race 59, 73–74, 84, 88, 98, 117, 128, 142, 148, 156, 166, 172, 181; The Party Room 34–35; Paul Revere 250 45, 48; S and S Jacobs Construction 51; Speedweeks 22, 34–35, 63, 73, 79–80, 84, 88, 96, 107, 117, 123, 128, 139–140, 165, 172, 181, 187, 193, 201; Streamline Hotel 8; 24 Hours of Daytona 49; Universal Studios 31, 181, 192

Folger's Coffee 115
Follmer, George 43, 49, 52, 59–60, 122, 168, 193
Food Channel 192
Ford (Fairmont/Taurus/Torino) 9, 22, 24–26, 46, 51, 53, 59, 61, 63–64, *67*, *69*, 71–72, 93–94, 110, 170, 182, 187, *190*, 193, 196
Ford, Henry II 162
Ford Motor Company 22, 45, 48–51, 53–55, 57, 76, 79–81, 84–85, 87, 96, 99, 101, 106–107, 110, 113–115, 124–125, 127–128, 132–133, 137, 142–145, 147, 150–151, 153–156, 159, 161–165–166, 168–171, 184, 187, 204; Edsel 6, 85, 110, 150, 205; Ford (Fairmont/Taurus/Torino) 9, 22, 24–26, 46, 51, 53, 59, 61, 63–64, *67*, *69*, 71–72, 93–94, 110, 170, 182, 187, *190*, 193, 196; 429 ci 54; 427 ci engine 22, 51, 85, 139; 426 ci engine 53; Motorcraft 110–116, 122–124, 131, 135, *136*, 139, *146*, 148–*149*, 151, 155–156, 168, 187, 189; Mustang 45–46, 48–49, 51, 53–54, 59, 162; SVO (Special Vehicle Operations) 80, 171; 351 ci (Cleveland) engine 53–55, 57, 101, 182; 366 ci engine 51, 53–54; 302 ci engine 54; 305 ci engine 51, 54; Thunderbird (T-Bird/Diamond Jubilee) 8, 71–72, 74–*75*, 76–77, 80, 84–85, 89, *91*, 92, *95*–96, 101, 104, 118–*119*, 120, 122–123, 127, *131*, 135, 144, *149*, 152, 156, 163, 165, 169, *173*; Quality Care 133, 151, 154, 159, 165, 193
Formula One 52–53, 178
Forry, Sam 18, 25, 33
Foster, Billy 198
Foster, Jim 45
400 North Fairview Avenue, Spartanburg, SC 5, 9, 17, 22, 29, 44, 50–51, 55, 59, 64, 66, 68, 72–73, 76, 79, 81, 87–88, 98, 101, 104, 107, 112, 114–115, 122, 125, 127, 130, *131*, 135, 138–139, 147, 150, 152, 156, 165, 167–168, 170, *173*, 176, 180, 182–183, 186, *190*, 191, 195, *212*
426 ci engine 53
427 ci engine 22, 51, 85, 139
429 ci engine 54
Fowler, Daniel (engine builder) 145, 177

Fowler, Danny (jack man) 4–5, *92*, 135
Fox (TV) 213
Fox, Ray 22
Foyt, A. J. 4, 34, *35*, 36, 48, 62, 75, 77, 98–99, 142, 186, 198
France: Normandy 177
France, Betty 214
France, Bill, Jr. 97, 180, 182, 192–193, 207, 209–210
France, Bill, Sr. "Big Bill" 8, 14, 23, 29, 32, 45, 51–52, 72, 209–211
France, Brian 209–210
France family 121, 176, 208–209
Franklin Hotel (SC) 43
Frasson, Joe 6
Frehely, Ace 43
Froude, William 66
Fueling, Jim 50
Fukuyama, Hideo 179
Fuller, Steve 14, 38–39, 42

Gale, Tommy 55
Gant, Harry 99, 120, 143, 187, 188
Gardner-Webb, NC 38
Gardte (aircraft engines) 149
Gasoline Alley 154, 160
Gates, Bill 172
Gatorade 53
Gazaway, Bill 50, 54, 78, 97–98
Gemini 5 49
General Motors 29, 73, 79, 156; Mr. Goodwrench 156
General Tire 34
George, Tony 160
Georgia: Atlanta 4, 6, 44, 46, 172, 176–177, 186, 193, 207; Atlanta 500 8, 60, 79, *113*, 130; Atlanta International Raceway 4, 24, 55, 57, 63–64, 76, 80, 82, 85, 90, 92–93, 114, 122–123, 127, 130, 132–133, 148, 156, 163, 173, 184, 198; Atlanta Motel 4, *24*, 47; Dahlonega 130; Dixie 400 24–*25*, 44; Highway 41/19 4, 24; Lakewood Speedway 6; Lockheed Wind Tunnel 105–106; Marietta 105; Nippon Shipping 176–177; Road Atlanta 175
Gerhardt's Restaurant (SC) 175
Germany 42
Gibbs, Jimmy 207
Gibbs, Joe 138, 142, 162
Gibson, Charles 135
Gibson L6S Guitar 43
Gilliland, Butch 179–180, 195
Glotzbach, Charlie 59

Glover, Tony 118
Golden Gloves 78
Goldsmith, Paul 46–47
Goodyear 29, 30–31, 34, 122, 176, 178, 193
Gordon, Jeff 122, 125, 148, 165, 175, 179, 181, 190
Gordon, Robby 179
Grand National Division 7–8, 18–20, 25–26, 44–46, 49, 57, 63, 116, 179, 186, 216–217
Grand Touring (GT) Division 45, 47, 49
Green, Jeff 192–194
Green, Jerri 203
Green Street Baptist Church (SC) 14
Greenville-Pickens, SC 8, 12
Greenville-Spartanburg International Airport 19
Gregg, Peter 51–53
Grim Reaper 63
Grissom, Steve 173
Groh, Dennis 189
GTO 63
Guild, Peter 145
Gurney, Dan 6, 44–45, 52–53
Guy, Charlie 16

H. S. Die 183, 185
Hagan, Billy 153
Hall, Barney 208
Hall of Fame 1, 3, 6, 9, 27, 103, 107, 178, 205–206, 208–*210*, 211–212, 214–215, 216–217
Hammond, Jeff 213
HANS Device 198
Hardee's 34
Hardwick, Dr. 61
Hardy, Billy 34
Harrah's Casino 199
Harris, Ray 118, 130, 135, 177
Hauser, Mark 6, 206
Hawk, Don 168–169, 205
Hawkins, Alvin 8
Hayes, Dennis 172, 175, 180
Hayes, Wormy 177, 180
Hayes Modems 172–*173*, 176, 180
Helton, Mike 6, 193, 205
Hemi 22
Henderson, Elmo 3, 6, 9
Hendrick, Rick 100, 109, 113–114, 116, 121, 125, 137, 139, 150, 152–153, 175, 177–178, 211, 215; Rainbow Warriors (crew) 178
Hernandez, Fran 44–45, 53
Hershey, PA 113–114
Heveron, NJ 50
Hickock, "Wild Bill" 86
Higgins, Tom 125

High, Phil 42, 43
High, Stephen 42
Highway 115 (PA) 94
Highway 41/19 (GA) 4, 24
Hillbrook, SC 14, 40, 42
Hillcrest Shopping Center (SC) 12
Hillin, Bobby 107, 130, 179
Hillsborough, NC 19, 148
Hobbs, David 88
Hobby, Gene 6
Hodgdon, Warner 76, 96
Hodgdon Industries 76
Holbrook, Margie "Duck" 194
Holbrook family 193
Holiday Inn (company) 63
Holiday Inn (TN) 149
Holley Carburetor 54
Holly Farms, NC 177
Hollywood, CA 19
Holman-Moody 8, 18, 24–25, 54
Home Depot 183
Honda (50/90/Prelude) 3, 5, 14, 33–34
Hooley's Underground (SC) 43
Hooper, Lance 199
Hoosier Tires 120, 154, 156
Hooters Restaurants 149, 162, 186
Hornaday, Ron 179, 186
Houston, TX 22
Houston and Dorsey 16
Houston Elementary School (SC) 14, 31
Howard Johnson's (FL) 94
The Hub City 7–8, 208
Hueytown, AL 80
Huggins, Ross 46
Hughes Helicopters 152
Hulman, Mary 160
Hurst-Airheart Brakes 64
Hutcherson, Ron 76
Hwech, Horst 53
Hyde, Harry 60
Hylton, James 3, 6, 8
Hylton, Tweety 48

Iaccoca, Lee 162
Ifft, David 59
Igloo Coolers 167
Illinois: Chicago 5, 148, 177; Chicago Bears 38; Clark Street garage (Chicago) 148
Indiana: Brickyard 400 125, 154, 160; Gasoline Alley 154, 160; Indianapolis 160, 188; Indianapolis 500 7, 57, 160, 174; Indianapolis Motor Speedway 24, 27, 53, 115, 125, 154, 160–161, 167, 195, 198
Indianapolis 160, 188
Indianapolis 500 7, 57, 160, 174

Indianapolis Motor Speedway 24, 27, 53, 115, 125, 154, 160–161, 167, 195, 198
Inman, Dale 25, 208, 211
Interstate 85 (I-85) 70, 207
Interstate 585 (I-585) 207
Interstate Batteries 162
Irish Hills, MI 187
Irmo, SC 39
Iron Gate (DE) 93
Irvin, Ernie 140, 142, 152, 157, 162, 172, 179
Irwin, Tommy 3, 77
Isaac, Bobby 57–58
Islip, NY 26

J. B. Weld 50
Jackson, Leo 198
Jantzen Swimwear 86
Japan (Japanese) 14, 45, 178–179, 181, 215; Nagoya 177; Suzuka Circuitland 176, Suzuka City (Suzuka) 176, 178, 180; Suzuka Thunder Special 177
Jarrett, Dale 24–25, 137, 124, 142, 148–**149**, 162–163, 172, 179, 193
Jarrett, Glenn 24–25
Jarrett, Ned 4, 6, 23–28, 46, 148–**149**, 208–210
Jarrett boys 4, 24–25
Jarrett family 23
Jesse Boyd Elementary School (SC) 14
JoAnne "Short Track" (Weatherly's finacée) 19–21
Johncock, Gordon 44
Johnny Reb 37
Johns, Bobby 8, 25
Johnson, Flossie 23
Johnson, Junior 23, 66, **75**, 76–78, 99–101, 112, 127, 131, 135, 137, 142–143, 148, 163, 183, 209–210, 212
Jones, Buckshot 198
Jones, Parnelli 19, 44–45, 48–49, 51–53
Judge, Judy 22

K and K Insurance 60
Kansas City, Missouri 207
Keesler, Kent 60
Keller's Styling Salon (SC) 15, 17
Kellogg's Cereal 153
Kelly, Winston 208–209
Kenseth, Matt 199
Kent, WA 45
Keselowski, Brad 8
Kiekhaefer, Carl 12
Kile, Harold 189

King Air (aircraft) 149
Kiss 43
Knuckles, Joey 187, 192, 199
Kodak Film 115, 124
Kodiak Tobacco 113
Kranefuss, Michael 85, 114, 171
Kreb, Art 128
Kulwicki, Alan 115, 121, 130–131, 149–151, 154–155

Labonte, Bobby 162
Labonte, Terry 85, 153, 155, 179
LaJoie, Randy 165
Lake Keowee, SC 70
Lake Lloyd, FL 77
Lake Santee, SC 45
Lakewood Speedway (GA) 6
Lanford, Hugh 8
Langley, Elmo 179
Lanier, Hugh 40
Lanier family 41
Lan-Yair Country Club (SC) 40–41
Laughlin, Mike 127
Lawson's Fork Creek (SC) 3
Le Mans 63
Leslie, Ed 48
Levi Garrett Tobacco 137
Lewis, Jerry 19
Lincoln-Mercury 18–19, 22–23, 27, 44; Comet/Cyclone/Marauder/Montego 3, 14, 18, 19, 21–22, 24, 29–**30**, 31, 33, 37–**38**, 44–47, 51, 58, 71, 75–76, 79–80, 82, 85, 189, **210**, 211; Cougar 44–46, 48–49, 80–**81**, 82, 85
Lindbergh, Colonel Charles H. 7
Link, Terry 63
Littlejohn, Joe, Sr. 8, 16, 26–28, 32, 34, 41, 61
Locke, John, and Mrs. 34
Lockheed Wind Tunnel (GA) 105–106
Long, Bondy 23
Lorenzen, Fred 24
Los Angeles, CA 188
Louisiana: New Orleans 7
Lucas Motor Oil 189
Lunar Lander 110
Lund, DeWayne "Tiny" 45–49, 63–64, 198
Lynyrd Skynyrd 43

Mack Tools 192
MacKenzie, Doc 7
Maggiacomo, Jocko 63
Mahaffey, George 37–39, 52
Mahaffey boys 14, 36
Manufacturer's Championship 144, 176, 151

Marcis, Dave 67–68, 75–76, 90, 120, 198
Marietta, GA 105
Marlin, Coo Coo 58
Marlin, Sterling 142, 167, 173, 179–180
Marshall Tucker Band 42–43
Martin, Mark 117, 134, 140, 142, 148, 175, 199
Martinsville International Raceway 23, 57, 105, 144–*147*, 148, 152, 155, 173, 175
Mason, Jerry 66–67
Material Safety Data (MSD) 176
Mattel Varoom bicycle 33
Matthews, Banjo 55, 58, 71, 80, 84, 108, 121, 126–127
Mayne, Roy 63
Mayo Clinic 186
McCann, Dick 19
McClure, Larry 152
McDonald, Dave 24
McDonald's 70, 148
McGarahan, Mike 34
McGriff, Herschel 179
McKay, Jim 4
McKim, Buz 6, 205, 208–209
McKnight, Pat 196
McQuagg, Sam 44
Means, Jimmy "Smut" 171, 181
Medal of Honor 196
Melling, Harry 83–84, 86–87, 110, 122
Melton, Ray 37, 160
Members Only Jackets 151–152
Memory Lane Museum (NC) 6, 92, 206
Mercury 7 49
Merlin (aircraft) 149
Miami, FL 149
Miccosukee Indian Gaming 8
Michigan 184; Dearborn 84, 113, 122, 167; Irish Hills 187; Michigan International Speedway 51, 154, 162, 166, 169, 188; Pepsi 400 presented by DeVilbiss 187
Michigan International Speedway 51, 154, 162, 166, 169, 188
Mieneke Mufflers 152
Miller 8
Miller, Don 60
Miller, Preston 131–132, 157, 173
Miller, Roy 39
Minnesota 52; Brainerd 51–53; Donnybrooke International Speedway 53; Mayo Clinic 186
Miss Southern 500 37
Miss Teen America 14, *15*, 28
Mississippi 156
Mr. Big Voice 6

Mr. Goodwrench 156
Moncks Corner, SC 45
Money Store Chevrolet (Number 46) 192
Monroe Shock Absorbers 35
Monterrey, CA 48, 204
Montgomery, Captain John H. 7
Moon Pie 192–193, 195
Moon's Tavern 16
Moonshine Country (NC) 147
Moore, Albus, Roberta 6, 175, 189, 193–194, 196, 201–202, 206, 215
Moore, Betty Clark 11, 13, 19–20, 23–*24*, 27–28, 31, 34–38, 40, 42, 47–48, 51, 110, *113*, 120–121, 133, 160, 177, 182, 189, 193–194, 201, 204, 214–215, 217
Moore, Brent "Brenty" 3–4, 6, 11, 13–14, 18, 24–*25*, 33–*35*, 36, 38, 40–42, 45, 47–48, 63, 65–66, 70, 73, *86*, *91*, *92*, *131*, *136*, *146*, 172, 177, 180, 189, 201
Moore, Candy 79
Moore, Carol 78–79, 98, 120–121
Moore, Cecil 46
Moore, Daryl 1, 4–6, 11–*12*, 13–*15*, 16, 22, 24, 27–29, 31, 33, 35–36, 39–40, 42, 45–46, 48, 54, 57, 65–67, 70, 73, 78–79, 90, 98–99, 107, 115, 120–121, 126, 128, 140–141, 144, 157, *158*, 161, 163, 167, 169, 177, 183, 189, 197–198, 200–201, *210*, 211, 214
Moore, Dick 22, 42
Moore, Jason 215
Moore, Missy 79
Moore, Ralph 213
Moore boys 4, 24, 27
Moore family 24, 32, 63, 73, 75, 91, 115, 120–121, 128, 131, 182, 186, 190, 196–197, 199–200, 209, 211, 213, 215
Mooresville, NC 6, 145
Moose Lodge 195
Mopar 26
Morgan-McClure Motorsports 114, 124
Morgan Square 7
Morris, Sid 88, 116
Morse, Lee 50, 55, 80, 85, 96, 123, 154, 156
Motor Trend Magazine 162
Motorcraft 8, 110–116, 122–124, 131, 135, *136*, 139, *146*, 148–*149*, 151, 155–156, 168, 187, 189

Motorsport Design 133
Mountain Dew 500 (PA) *95*
Mulhern, Mike 125, 151
Murr, Bob 12
Murr, David 12, 14
Musgrave, Ted 151, 153, 162, *190*
Mustang 45–46, 48–49, 51, 53–54, 59, 162
Myler, Ken 45, 126

Nagoya 177
NASA 49
NASCAR 7, 11, 26–27, 31, 45, 49–51, 53, 56, 59–60, 63–65, 76, 78, 83, 85, 88, 95–98, 121, 128, 133, 165, 169, 172, 175–178, 181–182, 186, 191, 197–198, 200–201, 205, 207–209, 213, 215; Appeals Committee 213; Busch Series 81, 84, 107, 116, 125, 134, 152, 167, 173, 181, 186, 188; Car of Tomorrow 125; Craftsman Truck Series 200; Grand National Division 7–8, 18–20, 25–26, 44–46, 49, 57, 63, 116, 179, 186, 216–217; Grand Touring (GT) Division 45, 47, 49; Hall of Fame 1, 3, 6, 9, 27, 103, 107, 178, 205–206, 208–*210*, 211–212, 214–215, 216–217; Manufacturer's Championship 144, 176, 151; Sprint Cup 8, 125; Strictly Stock Division 8; Winners' Circle Plan 74; Winston Cup 51, 53, 58, 71–72, 76, 79, 83, 86, 103–104, 107, 132, 139, 152–153, 160, 168, 171, 176–177, 183, 186–187, 192, 195, 209; Winston West 176, 180, 196
NASCAR Appeals Committee 213
Nash, Bill "Fat Willie" 16
Nashville 420 53
Nashville International Raceway 57, 60, *86*, 99
National Guard Armory 43
National Speed Sport News 46
Navy 42, 48, 70
NCAA's Southern Conference Headquarters 208
Negre, Ed 198
Nelson, Gary 182
Nemechek, Joe 199
New Jersey: Heveron 50; Old Bridge 26
New Orleans, LA 7
New York 94; Bridgehampton 26; Chemung 139; Islip 26; New York City 7, 133, 161–

162, 177; Waldorf Astoria Hotel (Waldorf) 133, 162, 171; Watkins Glen 26, 51, 128, 154, 161, 167, 171, 174
New York, NY 7, 133, 161–162, 177
Newman, "Ducky" 57, 66, 126
Nichels, Ray 22, 63
Nicholson, "Dyno" Don 85
Nike 185–186
Nippon Shipping (GA) 176–177
Nodine, Ronnie 7
Nolan, Mose 55
Normandy, France 177
Norris Industries 63–64, 69, 71–72, 76
North Carolina 124, 147, 195; Asheville-Weaverville 37, 44, 211; Blue Ridge Mountains 70; Carolina 500 89; Charlotte 120, 150, 178–179, 183, 197, 208, *210*, 211, 213; Charlotte Fairgrounds 8; Charlotte Motor Speedway (Charlotte/Lowes' Motor Speedway) 6, 8, 23–24, 27, 46, 55, 57–58, 69, 76, 118, 122–123, 130, 132, 154, 163–*164*, 168, 182–184, 188, 199; *Charlotte Observer* 178; Charlotte Visitation Authority 207; Coca-Cola/World 600 23, 46, 57, 118, 120, 123, 182; Concord 20, 46; Conover 138; Gardner-Webb 38; Hillsborough 19, 148; Holly Farms 177; Memory Lane Museum 6, 92, 206; Moonshine Country 147; Mooresville 6, 145; North Wilkesboro (Wilkesboro) 79, 82, 109, 112, 125, 133, 147–148, 152, 157, 162; Rockingham Speedway (Rockingham/The Rock) 4, 6, 44, 46, 55, 62, *75*, 79, 81, 85, 89, 135, 142, 148, 173, 175, 206; Sandhills 85, 124; Shelby 8; Silver Bucket 85; Textilc 250 47; The Torch Club 43; Tryon 43; UAW-GM Quality 500 199; Winston Open 118; *Winston-Salem Journal* 178
North Wilkesboro, NC 79, 82, 109, 112, 125, 133, 147–148, 152, 157, 162
Nu-Way (Spartanburg, SC) 4
Nuber, Larry 4

Oconee Nuclear Station 70
O'Dear, Bob 86, 102, 104–105
Ohio: Cincinnati 7

Old Bridge, NJ 26
Old Milwaukee Beer 100
Oldsmobile (Olds) 8, 69, 71–*75*, 76–77, 79–80, 115–116, 156
One Hour Martinizing 61
125 mile qualifying race (FL) 59, 73–74, 84, 88, 98, 117, 128, 142, 148, 156, 166, 172, 181
Ontario Motor Speedway (Ontario) 64, 76
Ortieg Prize 7
Osterland, Rod 75, 111
Overland Drive (SC) 3, 33–34
Owens, Cotton "King of the Modifieds" 3, 8, 22, 25, 28, 107, 121, 132, 150, 203, 205, 207–209, 211, 216–217
Owens, Donnie 28
Owens, Dorothy "Dot" 216
Owens, Randy 62

Panasonic Beta VCR 4
Paramount, CA 19
Pardue, Jimmy 27–28
Paris, France 7
Park, Steve 186, 201
Parker, Earl 212
Parks, Raymond 211
Parsons, Benny 53, 72–73, 76, 83–*86*, 87–88, 90, 92–93, 113, 122, 140, 143, 147
The Party Room (FL) 34–35
Paschal, Jim 24
Passino, Jacques 46, 53
Patrick, Danica 215
Paul Revere 250 (FL) 45, 48
Peach Blossom Diner (SC) *210*
Pearson, David 3, 6, 8–9, 22, 25–28, 44–45, 52, 54–55, 58–60, 62, 69, 74, 81, 90, 103, 111, 164–165, 181–182, 201, 203, 207, 209–210, 215
Pearson, Larry 31, 173, 181, 192
Pennsylvania 114; Hershey 113–114; Highway 115 94; Mountain Dew 500 *95*; Pocono 94, 113; Pocono International Raceway (Pocono) 60, 63, *95*, 167
Pennzoil Motor Oil 167, 186
Penske, Roger 48, 53, 60, 97; shock absorbers 167
Pepsi-Cola 52, 187
Pepsi 400 presented by DeVilbiss (MI) 187
Petree, Andy 197–198
Pettit, Dr. 71
Petty, Kyle 119, 145, 180, 211
Petty, Lee 25, 208, 210, 68
Petty, Lynda 62
Petty, Maurice 28, 211

Petty, Richard 22, 24–27, 30, 37, 57, 62, 67–68, 70, 74, 79, 99, 108, 110–111, 117, 142, 171, 198, 208–209, 215
Petty family 24, 130, 96, 149
Phifer, Peggy 12
Phoenix, AZ 132, 210
Phoenix Racing 8
Pi Computer 195
Piedmont Air Lines 105
Piedmont Interstate Fairgrounds (SC) 6–7, 25–26, 41, 203, 207
Pierce Acres, SC 14
Pierce Motor Company 72
Pine Street Drive In (SC) 42
Pineville Road (Spartanburg, SC) 3, 33
Pistone, Tom 49
Player, Gary 18
Plymouth 8
Pocono, PA 94, 113
Pocono International Raceway (PA) 60, 63, *95*, 167
Pond, Lenny 58–59, 68, 85
Pontiac (Bonneville) 8, 17, 19, 20, 46, 79, 100, 107, 154; GTO 63; Le Mans 63
Poole, Perry 12
Poole, Randy 12
Poole, Steve 12
Porsche 53
Posey, Sam 49
Powell, Floyd 9
Pratt, Billy 33, 38
Presbyterian College (PC) 71–72
Pressley, Robert 166
Price, Baxter 58
Pro Motor Engineering 1545
Proctor, Clem 20
Procter and Gamble 116, 122
Prout, Warren 27, 46
Pruitt, Scott 115
Punch, Dr. Jerry 6
Purple Heart 121
Pyle, Artimus 43

Quaker State Motor Oil 109, 114–115, 117, 124–125
Quincy's Steak House 115
QVC Shopping Network 154, 157

Rahilly, Bob 124, 128; Raymoc 172
Rainbow Warriors 178
Rainey, Bill 33
Ranier, Harry 80, 82, 86
Rawls, Betsy 18
Red Line 7000 36
Remington Fire Arms 171–172, 196

Rescue Oil Additives 187–*190*
Revson, Peter 52–53
Rich, Mike 132
Richardson, Jerry 34
Richmond, Tim 85, 92, *95*, 99–101, 104, 107, 111, 116
Richmond, VA 109
Richmond International Raceway 57–58, 79, 82, 90, 92, 98, 107, 109, 118, 122, 142, 148, 173, 207
Rickenbacker Guitar 43
Rider, Chuck 167
Ridley, Jody 85, 108–109
Riley, Bob 106
Riverside, CA 102, 110
Riverside International Raceway (Riverside) 19–22, 36, 44, 79, 85, 101, 111, 147, 196, 198
R. J. Reynolds Tobacco Co. 76, 209
Road Atlanta (GA) 175
Robert Yates Racing 152, 154, 157, 162–163, 165, 169, 187
Roberts, "Fireball" 14, 17, 22–24, 27–28, 215; Doris (wife) 22
Roberts, Pernell "Adam Cartwright" 19
Robinson, Dave 183, 186–*190*
Robinson-Moore Racing Team 183, 187
Rockingham Speedway (The Rock, NC) 4, 6, 44, 46, 55, 62, *75*, 79, 81, 85, 89, 135, 142, 148, 173, 175, 206
Rockingham World Championship Pit Crew Competition 135, 176
Rodriquez, Ricardo 49
Roebuck, SC 213
Rogers, Edmund 41
The Rolling Stones 35, 43
Rooster Rule 121
Rossi, Mario 3, 8, 31, 139
Roush, Jack 134, 151, 154, 177, 211
Royal Crown Cola (RC) 59–60, 193, 195
Ruby, Lloyd 48, 57
Rudd, Linda 109–110, *113*
Rudd, Ricky (Rooster) 53, 82, 105–*113*, 114–115, 117, 121–123, 125, 132, 142, 147, 151–153, 155, 161, 168, 185, 189–190, 208
Rudd family 115
Rutherford, Johnny 22–24
Ruttman, Joe 85–86, 88, 115

S and S Jacobs Construction (FL) 51

Sabates, Felix 171, 175–176, 192
Sachs, Eddie 24
Sacks, Greg 182, 184
Sadler, Elliott 198
Sadler, Hermie 165
Said, Boris 168
St. John Street (SC) 4, 11–12, 14–15, 17, 107
St. Jovite, Quebec 49
Sall, Bob 7
Salvation Army 38
Sandhills, NC 85, 124
Sanitone 61–62
Santana, Carlos 43
Satisfaction 35
Satterfield, David 37–39
Satterfield, Randy 38
Sauter, Joe 85
Savage, Swede 52
SCCA *see* Sports Car Club of America
Scenic Drive In 42
Schessler, Jo 23
Schlitz Beer 65, 67
Schrader, Ken 114, 116, 142, 199, 201
Scott, Sam 133, 137, 143, 151
Scott, Wendell 6, 25, 211, 217
Sears, John 48
Sears Point/Sonoma, CA 8, 131–132, 152–153, 155, 167–168, 174–175
Seay, Lloyd 8
Sewell, Buck 52, 198
Sharp, Bill 135
Shelby, Carroll 45, 48–49, 53
Shelby, NC 8
Shepherd, Morgan 124–128, 130–*131*, 132–135, 137–138, 142, 154, 162, 171–173, 187
Sherman Chiropractic College 12
Shoney's 63
Shoolbred, Bill 3, 14, 18, *33*–34, 61
Silent Speedways of America 6
Silent Speedways of the Carolinas 5
Silver Bucket (NC) 85
Simmons, Gene 43
Six Flags 177
Six Pack 104
Skinner, Mike 153, 179
Smith, Betty 213
Smith, Doug 203–204
Smith, Jack 3, 8–9, 12, 147, 208, 213
Smith, Larry 58
Smith, Matt 206
Smith-Outz Drugs 13
Smokin' Joe's Racing Team 171, 179
Snead, Sam 18

Snyder Field (SC) 39
Society of Automotive Engineers (SAE) 187
Sony Electronics 185–186
Sosebee, Gober 8
Sound and Light Lounge (SC) 43
South Carolina *91*; Abbeville 39; B and B Studios 193, 195; Basil's 202–204; Beacon 42; Beaumont Mill 207–208; Bethlehem Baptist Church 213; Bud Moore Engineering (Team) 5, 22, 24–27, 31, 33, 37, 44, 48–49, 51, 53–54, 56–57, 62–64, 68, 70–72, 75, 79, 82–83, 89, 92, 101, 107, 109–110, 117, 120, 127, 135, 138–140, 142, 145, 151–155, 157, *158*, 163, 165, 167–169, 171, 173, 176–177, 180–183, 185–186, 189–*190*, 191–192, 195–196, 199–200, 207–208, *210*, 211, 215; Bud Moore's Garage 12–13, 15, 17, 41, 70; Capri Lounge 67; *Carolina Spartan* 7; The Cellar 5, 205; Charleston 7, 176–177; Cherokee County 39; Chester 39; Clemson University 38, 40, 70, 132; Cleveland Hotel 7; Clinton 71; Columbia 8, 16, 46; Community Cash 13; Converse College (School of Dance) 7, 42, 208; The Corners Apartments 137, 180; Cowpens 6, 22; CRC Chemicals Rebel 300/500 14, *90*, *91*, *92*; Darlington International Raceway (Darlington) 1, 4–6, 34, 37, 44, 52–53, 55, 57–58, 79, 90, 92, 105, 111–112, 114, 126, 148, 156, 160, 166, 168, 173, 187, 189–*190*, 198, 206, 210; Deluxe Diner 43; Denny's 202; Drayton 14; Duncan Park 7; Dupre Drive 12; East Main Street 3; Emory Road 43; Evans Junior High School 4, 39; Fernwood 3, 11–*13*, 14, 18, 29, 31, 33–43, 62, 71, 110; First Baptist Church 43; 400 North Fairview Avenue 5, 9, 17, 22, 29, 44, 50–51, 55, 59, 64, 66, 68, 72–73, 76, 79, 81, 87–88, 98, 101, 104, 107, 112, 114–115, 122, 125, 127, 130, *131*, 135, 138–139, 147, 150, 152, 156, 165, 167–168, 170, *173*, 176, 180, 182–183, 186, *190*, 191, 195, *212*; Franklin Hotel 43; Gerhardt's Restaurant 175;

Greengate Lane 33; Green Street Baptist Church 14; Greenville-Pickens 8, 12; Greenville-Spartanburg International Airport 19; Hillbrook 14, 40, 42; Hillcrest Shopping Center 12; Hooley's Underground 43; Houston Elementary School 14, 31; The Hub City 7–8, 208; I-585 207; Interstate 85 (I-85) 70, 207; Irmo 39; Jesse Boyd Elementary School 14; Johnson Street 11; Keller's Styling Salon 15, 17; Lake Keowee 70; Lake Santee 45; Lan-Yair Country Club 40–41; Lawson's Fork Creek 3; Moncks Corner 45; Morgan Square 7; National Guard Armory 43; NCAA's Southern Conference Headquarters 208; The Nu-Way 4; Oconee Nuclear Station 70; Overland Drive 3, 33–34; Peach Blossom Diner *210*; Piedmont Interstate Fairgrounds 6–7, 25–26, 41, 203, 207; Pierce Acres 14; Pierce Motor Company 72; Pine Street 70, 107; Pine Street Drive In 42; Pineville Road 3, 33; Presbyterian College (PC) 71–72; Roebuck 213; St. John Street 4, 11–12, 14–15, 17, 107; Scenic Drive In 42; Sherman Chiropractic College 12; Smith-Outz Drugs 13; Snyder Field 39; Sound and Light Lounge 43; South Carolina Museum and Auto Racing Hall of Fame 208; Southern 500 8, 37, 53, 55, 58, 92, 186, 189–*190*, 191, *210*, 217; Spartan Mill 7, 11, 14; Spartanburg 3, 5, 7–8, 16–17, 22, 24–26, 39, 42, 71–72, 76, 80, 96, 121, 130, 133, 143, 145, 147, 163, 168, 172, 175, 177, 179, 183, 188, 195, 197, 199, 206–208, *210*, 211, 213, 215; Spartanburg City Police 3, 14; Spartanburg Country Club 40; Spartanburg Hall of Fame 203, 207; *Spartanburg Herald-Journal,* 16; Spartanburg (Spartan) High School 12, 27, 31, 34, 38–40, 62, 70, 172; University of South Carolina 4; University of South Carolina-Spartanburg (Branch/Upstate) 43, 70, 72; Wagon Wheel Fish Camp 22; Wakefield Buick 16;

Westminster Presbyterian Church 71; Wofford College (Terriers) 6, 39, 206
South Carolina Museum and Auto Racing Hall of Fame 208
Southern Baptist 71
Southern 500 (SC) 8, 37, 53, 55, 58, 92, 186, 189–***190***, 191, ***210***, 217
Spartan Mill 7, 11, 14
Spartanburg, SC 3, 5, 7–8, 16–17, 22, 24–26, 39, 42, 71–72, 76, 80, 96, 121, 130, 133, 143, 145, 147, 163, 168, 172, 175, 177, 179, 183, 188, 195, 197, 199, 206–208, ***210***, 211, 213, 215
Spartanburg City Police 3, 14
Spartanburg Country Club 40
Spartanburg Hall of Fame 203, 207
Spartanburg Herald-Journal 16
Spartanburg (Spartan) High School 12, 27, 31, 34, 38–40, 62, 70, 172
Special Vehicle Operations (SVO) 80, 171
Speed, Lake 154–157, 159–***164***, 168, 173–174
Speed, Rice 156
Speedweeks (FL) 22, 34–35, 63, 73, 79–80, 84, 88, 96, 107, 117, 123, 128, 139–140, 165, 172, 181, 187, 193, 201
Spencer, G. C. 3
Spencer, Jimmy 152, 155, 171, 175
Spirit of St. Louis 7
Sports Car Club of America (SCCA): Can Am Division 59; Trans Am Series 40, 44–45, 48–49, 51–54, 57, 59, 70, 101, 106
Sports Illustrated 74
Sprint Cup 8, 125
Spurlock, K. C. 183
Sta-Power Engine Conditioners 57–59
Stacy, J. D. 85–86, 88, 90, 95
Stairway 42
Stanley, Paul 43
Steele, Harry 184–185
Steele, Tim 183–186, 188, 195
Steele family 186–187
Stewart, Jackie 4
Stewart, Len 42–43
Stewart, Tony 215
Stock Car Racing Magazine 68, 75
Stott, Harold 94, 120, 135, 149, 161
STP 57, 187

Streamline Hotel (FL) 8
Stricklin, Hut 148, 198
Strictly Stock Division 8
Strope, Willie 180
Stroppe, Bill 19–20, 26, 180
Stuart, VA 1
Sunny King Ford 63–***64***
Super Bowl 38
Suzuka Circuitland 176
Suzuka City 176, 178, 180
Suzuka Thunder Special 177
Suzuki, Seichi 45
SVO *see* Special Vehicle Operations

Talladega 207, 212
Taylor, E. W. 12
Tennessee: Bristol 149–150; Bristol International Speedway (Bristol) 1, 22, 62, 90, 92, 105, 112, 149, 153–154, 156–157, 168, 161, 197; Chattanooga Bakeries 192, 195; Holiday Inn 149; Moon Pie 192–193, 195; Nashville 420 53; Nashville International Raceway 57, 60, ***86***, 99
Terminal Transport 58
Terry, Bill 183
Texaco Havoline Motor Oil 152
Texas 23, 31; Houston 22; Texas Bloodsucker 16–17; Texas World Speedway 85, 93
Texas Bloodsucker 16–17
Texas World Speedway 85, 93
Textile 250 (NC) 47
Tezak, Bob 105
Thomas, Herb 208, 211
Thomas, Phil 135, 177
Thompson, Speedy 92, 186
302 cu. in. engine 54, 101
305 cu. in. engine 51, 54
351 cu. in. engine 53–55, 57, 101, 182
366 cu. in. engine 51, 53–54
Thunderbird (T-Bird/Diamond Jubilee) 8, 71–72, 74–***75***, 76–77, 80, 84–85, 89, ***91***, 92, ***95***–96, 101, 104, 118–***119***, 120, 122–123, 127, ***131***, 135, 144, ***149***, 152, 156, 163, 165, 169, ***173***
Tide Detergent 152–153, 190
Tina the Bartender 204
Tire testing 27, 29–30, 155
Titus, Jerry 48
The Torch Club 43
Torrence, Wayne 122
Toyota Celica 4
Trent, Buck ***86***
Trickle, Dick 65, 148, 161, 165–168, 171, 173–174

Triplett, Kevin 197
Tryon, NC 43
Turner, Curtis 44
24 Hours of Daytona 49

UAW-GM Quality 500 (NC) 199
Uncle Walt's Band 42
Union 76 52; Rockingham World Championship Pit Crew Competition 135, 176
United Gunite 63
United States 16, 180; President of *146*; United States Secret Service 5
United States Auto Club (USAC) 35
United States Secret Service 5
Universal Studios (FL) 31, 181, 192
University of South Carolina 4
University of South Carolina–Spartanburg (Branch/Upstate) 43, 70, 72
UNO 105
USAC *see* United States Auto Club
Utah: Salt Lake City 171

Valvoline Motor Oil 124
Venturini, Bill 48
Vermont, Dolph 17, 121
Vick, Glenn 38–39
Virginia 21; Bristol Lincoln-Mercury 22, 33; Chesapeake 105; Martinsville International Raceway 23, 57, 105, 144–*147*, 148, 152, 155, 173, 175; Richmond 109; Richmond International Raceway 57–58, 79, 82, 90, 92, 98, 107, 109, 118, 122, 142, 148, 173, 207; Stuart 1
V. O. Whiskey 67

Wade, Billy 3, 8, 14, 21–23, 26–31, 33, 62, 147, 155, 165, 175, 186, 198, 201–201; wrecked car *30*
Wade, Stella 27, 29–31, 33
Wagon Wheel Fish Camp (SC) 22
Waid, Steve 125, 193
Wakefield Buick 16
Waldorf Astoria Hotel (NY) 133, 162, 171
Wallace, Kenny 181–182
Wallace, Rusty 106–107, 113, 120, 132, 140, 142, 145, 148, 163, 176, 179

Walther, Salt 68
Waltrip, Darrell 58–59, 74, 76–77, 79, 83–84, 88, 90, 99, 109–111, 120, 123, 142, 150, 198, 201, 211
Waltrip, Michael 167, 171–172, 178–179, 198, 201, 210–211, 214
Waltrip, Stevie 59, 210
Wand, Don 106
Ward, Larry 162–163
Washington: Kent 45
Washington, DC 196, 204, 207; American Veterans of Foreign Wars (AMVETS) 196
Watkins Glen, NY 26, 51, 128, 154, 161, 167, 171, 174
Watson, Dave 79
Wayne, John 42
Weatherly, Joe "The Clown Prince of Racing" 12, 14–17, 19–20, 23–24, 27–28, 31, 46–47, 75–76, 92–93, 147–148, 155, 165, 186, 189, 198, 201–202, 215; wrecked car *21*
Welch, Jack 38
Welsh Corgi 18
Westminster Presbyterian Church 71
White, Rex 8, 24, 26
White, Tommy 195
Wilkerson, Dale 5–6, 204–*205*, 206
Williams, Deb 151, 193
Williams, Doug 94, 120–12, 126
Williams, Raymond "Captain America" 6, 85
Wilson, John 12, 14, 18, 33, 38
Wilson, Rick 120, 124–125
Wilson, Waddell 82, 128
Wine Country (CA) 131
Wingo, Donnie 126–127, 130, 132, 136, 143–144, 149, 161, 167, 171, 179
Winn, Billy 7
Winners' Circle Plan 74
Winston Cigarettes 76
Winston Cup 51, 53, 58, 71–72, 76, 79, 83, 86, 103–104, 107, 132, 139, 152–153, 160, 168, 171, 176–177, 183, 186–187, 192, 195, 209
Winston 500 *67*
Winston Open (NC) 118
Winston-Salem Journal 178
Winston West 176, 180, 196
Winston Western 500 (CA) 101
Wisconsin 168
Wofford College 6, 39, 206

Woo, Denny 50
Wood, Anne 6, 42
Wood, Eddie 119–120, 138, 164, 169, 171, 177
Wood, Glen 209–211
Wood, Hannah 5
Wood, Jake 5
Wood, Jesse L., Jr. "Little Smoke/"Smoke" 6, 11, 24–*25*, 27, *35*, 42
Wood, Jesse L., Sr. "Big Smoke"/Lt./"Smoky" 3, 5, 14, 16, *24*, *35*, 53, 121
Wood, Len 209
Wood, Leonard 1, 42, 114, 211, 215
Wood, Naomi 13, 18, *24*
Wood, Perry Allen 11, 13–16, 18, 24–*25*, *33*, 34, *35*, *131*, *140*, 203, 205–206, *216*
Wood, Yaneth 5
Wood family 1, 18, 24, 25, 33, 35, 55, 60, 93, 96–97, 108, 119, 127, 130, 133, 137–138, 154, 209–211; Duke 18
Woodpecker Trail 71
World War II 8, 31, 53, 121, 196
Wrangler Jeans Team 85–*90*, *91*, *92*, *95*, 100–*101*, 102, 104–105, 107, 109, 169
WSPG-AM/FM (ESPN Spartanburg) 5, 168, 204–*205*; Black, Ronnie (station engineer) 6, *205*; *Droppin' the Hammer* (DTH-radio show) 5–6, 168, 189, 198, 204–*205*, 209, 211, 215; Hauser, Mark 6, 206; Mr. Big Voice 6; Smith, Matt 206; Wilkerson, Dale 5–6, 204–*205*, 206
Wyatt, George 42
Wynn's/K-Mart 156

Xerox Antifeeeze 115

Yamaha Motorcycles 40
Yarborough, Cale 5, 25, 48, 60–61, *75*, 76–79, 83, *90*, 92, *95*, 108–109, 117, 120, 143, 149
Yarbrough, LeeRoy 25, 44, 54
You Tube 175
Yuma, AZ 16
Yunick, Smokey 14, 42, 46, 150, 154, 211, 215
Yunick, Trish 22
Yunick family: Carbon Press *204*

Z-Max Oil Additive 189

 www.ingramcontent.com/pod-product-compliance
Ingram Content Group UK Ltd.
Pitfield, Milton Keynes, MK11 3LW, UK
UKHW050531150426
5217IPUK00026B/1889